Network Architect's Handbook

An expert-led journey to building a successful career
as a network architect

Alim H. Ali

(CCIE 2x: #36988, CISSP, GCP/AWS Professional Architect and Security)

Network Architect's Handbook

Group Product Manager: Pavan Ramchandani
Publishing Product Manager: Prachi Sawant
Senior Editor: Sayali Pingale
Technical Editor: Arjun Varma
Copy Editor: Safis Editing
Project Manager: Neil Dmello
Proofreader: Safis Editing
Indexer: Subalakshmi Govindhan
Production Designer: Ponraj Dhandapani
Marketing Coordinator: Dhruvil Dudakiya

First published: February 2024

Production reference: 1120124

Published by Packt Publishing Ltd.
Grosvenor House
11 St Paul's Square
Birmingham
B3 1RB, UK

ISBN 978-1-83763-783-6

www.packtpub.com

To my beloved daughter, Alisha,

As I pen these words, I reflect on the journey of writing my first book—this journey was far more challenging and rewarding than I ever anticipated. This achievement, my dear Alisha, would have remained an unfulfilled dream without your presence in my life.

Your light, my child, has been the guiding star in my darkest nights and the warm sunshine in my brightest days. It is your spirit that has given me the strength to move forward, and your unwavering belief in me that has driven me to pursue my dreams. All of which I do for you.

From the moment you entered this world, you have been my greatest source of inspiration. Your existence has pushed me to be better than I ever thought possible. My every effort, my every accomplishment, is a testament to my desire to show you that dreams can be achieved through hard work and determination.

I am beyond grateful and consider myself blessed to have you, Alisha, as my daughter. Your kindness, intelligence, and love enrich my life in ways words can scarcely capture.

This book is as much a part of you as it is of me. It stands as a symbol of our shared journey, of the endless possibilities that lie ahead, and of the enduring love that binds us together.

With all my heart - I love you, Alisha!

– Alim H. Ali

Foreword

Network Architect's Handbook is a testament to the relentless pursuit of expertise, innovation, and vision in the world of networking. As someone who has had the privilege of knowing Alim both professionally and personally for over two decades, I can attest to the unwavering dedication and ability that he brings to the ever-evolving landscape of technology. At one time, Alim was a student of mine, and I've had the pleasure of seeing him consistently achieve new heights in his career. This book is not just a roadmap to becoming a network architect but a profound testament to Alim's journey—a journey marked by passion, expertise, and an unyielding commitment to excellence.

Within these pages lies an abundance of knowledge gained from Alim's extensive experience navigating the intricate world of network architecture. From the foundational principles of network protocols to the advanced strategies that define this field, you will find yourself guided by Alim's expertise, which goes beyond technical mastery. Each chapter is a testament to his practical insights, hard-earned lessons, and the innovative spirit that has propelled him through countless challenges in the pursuit of becoming the network architect he is today.

Alim's journey from apprentice to expert resonates profoundly throughout this book. It's a narrative that not only imparts technical knowledge but also encapsulates the mindset, resilience, and passion required to excel in this dynamic domain. For those setting foot on this path or seeking to deepen their understanding, *Network Architect's Handbook* stands as an invaluable companion—an ode to perseverance, innovation, and the relentless pursuit of excellence in the world of networking.

Steven Parker

CISSP, Chief Information Security Officer

TBC Corporation

In the constantly evolving and perhaps overly complicated world of enterprise technology, it's truly a unique opportunity to encounter someone with both deep expertise and an undeniable passion for innovation. I was fortunate enough to experience this when I crossed paths with Alim H. Ali during our respective careers at **Hewlett Packard Enterprise (HPE)**.

This book is a narrative of Alim's own journey and his profound grasp of enterprise networking. It captures his technical expertise and, more importantly, his visionary approach to leveraging technology for business growth. You will discover a collection of knowledge and insights, all stemming from his real-life experiences. These insights are shared with the kind of clear and compelling voice that I've always admired in him.

Alim skillfully explains the evolving role of the network architect in today's increasingly intricate and sophisticated IT landscape. Drawing from his substantial experience, he guides you through the expansive "network fabric" that has developed over the decades. The book probes into the network architect's role across different organizational scales, detailing the vital tasks from the planning and designing to the maintenance of network infrastructures.

Furthermore, Alim highlights the essential roles, from entry level to senior level, offering a useful framework for understanding and traversing the route to becoming a network architect. The book goes beyond technical insights. It underscores the strategic operational significance of network architects who are key in shaping IT business units and, eventually, aiding in the success of contemporary enterprises.

In closing, I am confident that this book will serve as a valuable resource, illuminating the path for navigating through the complex landscape of enterprise technology. It is with great pleasure and immense pride that I introduce Alim and his remarkable work.

Russell Ware

CEO and founder, Cloud33and3

Former Solutions Architect Director, Hewlett Packard Enterprise

Contributors

About the author

Alim H. Ali (CCIE 2x #36988, CISSP #34527, CCSI #32568) has a career spanning over 28 years at the forefront of technological innovation. He is a distinguished figure in the IT industry. As a 2xCCIE and CISSP, Alim combines deep technical expertise with visionary leadership, and he currently serves as the CEO of Asancha Corp.

Alim's academic journey laid the foundation for an illustrious career, starting with a BS in bioengineering from the New York Institute of Technology and an MS in management of technology from New York University. His pursuit of knowledge is ongoing, as he is currently working toward an MBA and a PhD in IT.

Throughout his career, Alim has been a dynamic force across various industry verticals, including oil and gas, global telecoms, financial services, finance, and healthcare. His tenure at Fortune 100 giants such as HP/HPE, VMware, Accenture, and Verizon has identified him as a thought leader, innovator, and visionary in the field.

As an industry technologist at heart, Alim is known for his groundbreaking work in IT networking, cloud and data infrastructure, edge computing, high-performance computing, application modernization, and security adaptation. His visionary approach and relentless pursuit of next-generation IT solutions have positioned him as a key influencer and strategic thinker in the field.

Furthermore, Alim aspires to share his insights and expertise on global platforms such as CNBC, Bloomberg, Fox News, and MSN as a sought-after analyst. His goal is to contribute to broader conversations about technology and business, providing valuable perspectives on emerging trends and innovations.

Above all, Alim is celebrated for his ability to demystify complex technical concepts into strategic business solutions, driving industry progress and shaping the future of technology.

About the reviewer

Ashish Kumar serves as a senior enterprise architect, specializing in AI/ML within the AWS Professional Services organization. His role involves providing support to organizations in conceptualizing and implementing generative AI initiatives, turning visions into reality. Before joining AWS, Ashish was part of the AI team at Change Healthcare, where he contributed to the development of ML models for medical imaging. His extensive experience in the healthcare industry includes several years in various leadership roles. Ashish holds a master's in data science from the University of Illinois Urbana-Champaign. In his spare time, he likes to unravel the mysteries of the universe, watch sci-fi movies, and get cozy with a good book.

Table of Contents

3

Roadmap to Becoming a Network Architect   49

Part 2 – Crafting the Architectural Mind: Attributes and Mindset of a Network Architect

4

Attributes of a Network Architect   73

5

Part 3 – Constructing the Core: Building Blocks of a Network Architect

7

The Foundation of Network Architecture, Part Two – Network Services 171

8

Foundations of Network Automation 221

9

Paradigm Shift to Cloud Computing   251

Part 4 – Mastering the Craft: Advancing Your Journey as a Network Architect

10

Preparing for Certifications and Cracking the Job Interview   289

11

The Skills to Become a Better Network Architect and Overcome Daily Challenges   315

12

Additional Information and Recommended Books   343

Preface

In the expansive realm of integrated technology, a multitude of "architects" shape the digital landscapes of organizations. Among these pivotal roles, the network architect stands as a cornerstone, intricately weaving the fabric of an organization's IT system. The essence of this role, as the title suggests, is deeply intertwined with the network – the vital backbone that supports and interconnects the various facets of an IT system within an organization.

A network architect is not just a technician but also a visionary, tasked with designing and implementing network architectures that not only cater to the immediate needs but also anticipate the future demands of various business units (BUs) within an organization or a client. This role transcends the mere functionality of networks; it is about creating a system that is resilient, reliable, agile, and flexible, yet simultaneously efficient, cost-effective, and secure.

As you embark on this book's journey, you will delve into the multifaceted world of IT architects, gaining insights into their different roles and how they collaboratively contribute to the broader IT strategy. We will then zoom into the fundamental characteristics that define a network architect. You will explore the depth of their roles and responsibilities, understanding what it takes to excel in this dynamic and crucial position.

Through the chapters of this book, we will unravel the layers of knowledge and skills essential for a network architect. You will gain a comprehensive understanding of the technological, strategic, and interpersonal competencies required to thrive in this role. The book will guide you through the nuances of network design, the subtleties of balancing technical requirements with business objectives, and the art of envisioning a network that not only supports but also elevates an organization's goals.

By the end of this book, you will have embarked on a complete journey through the landscape of network architecture. You will possess a thorough understanding of what it takes to build a career as a network architect, equipped with the knowledge and insights to navigate the challenges and seize the opportunities that come with this vital role in the ever-evolving world of IT.

Embrace this journey as we chart the course to becoming a network architect, a role that is not just about connecting devices and data but also about connecting aspirations, strategies, and ultimately, people.

Who this book is for

This book is meticulously crafted for network engineers and network technicians who stand at a pivotal point in their careers, aspiring to ascend to the role of a network architect. If you find yourself with 7 to 10 years of experience in the dynamic realm of IT and technology and are seeking a path to elevate your career, this book is your compass.

The journey to becoming a network architect is both challenging and rewarding, demanding a unique blend of skills, knowledge, and visionary thinking. This book is tailored for professionals who have honed their technical abilities and are now ready to delve into the strategic and design aspects of network architecture.

The expert-led narrative will guide you through the intricate landscape of design concepts, architectural requirements, and the nuanced skills that set a network architect apart. We focus on the pivotal elements that form the backbone of this role:

- **Design concepts**: Understanding the principles of designing robust, scalable, and efficient network systems

- **Architectural requirements**: Grasping the intricacies of network infrastructure and how to align it with business goals

- **Relevant experience**: Leveraging your years of experience in IT to make informed, strategic decisions in network design and implementation

- **Certifications and advanced education**: Identifying the certifications and educational paths that will enrich your expertise and recognition in the field

- **Expansion to cloud best practices**: Navigating the cloud-centric landscape, where cloud computing and network architecture intersect, creating new opportunities and challenges

However, it is essential to recognize that this book is only a starting point on your journey. It is not intended to be a deep dive into any one particular facet of IT, such as network infrastructure, compute, databases, cloud computing, programming, or similar areas. Instead, this book serves as a guide to aid in translating business and strategic initiatives into technical requirements and solutions, and vice versa. It aims to bridge the gap between the technical and strategic aspects of IT, providing a foundational understanding to help you navigate the complex landscape of network architecture.

Whether you are a seasoned network professional aiming to transition into a more strategic role or a technician ready to take a significant leap forward, this book is designed to be your roadmap. It will not only enhance your understanding of what it takes to be a successful network architect but will also equip you with the knowledge to make that transformation.

Embark on this journey with me as we unravel the essence of network architecture, preparing you to not just meet but exceed the expectations of this pivotal role in the modern IT landscape.

What this book covers

Chapter 1, Understanding the Network Architect's Role, explains how the network architect has many facets, from understanding network concepts to communication up to, and including, CXO. Network architects are responsible for designing and managing data communication, networks for organizations and/or clients. They must also be forward thinkers to ensure these systems are in line with business outcomes and goals. The network architect is one of many under the IT architect umbrella.

Chapter 2, Network Architect in an Organization, focuses on the roles and responsibilities that come with being a network architect.

Chapter 3, Roadmap to Becoming a Network Architect, introduces you to the roadmap toward becoming a network architect, from being a technician to a senior network engineer. Each role possesses key skills required, as well as responsibilities to move toward a career as a network architect. We will also look at the challenges that are faced in becoming a network architect.

Chapter 4, Attributes of a Network Architect, describes some of the qualities a network architect should obtain and possess. Though network architects are one of many "architects" and professionals in an organization, overlapping skill sets can and do occur with respect to the business. This chapter will introduce those overlapping skill sets.

Chapter 5, The Mindset of the Network Architect – the Principles of Design, goes into the mindset a network architect should have in order to be successful. It starts with the principles of network architecting, reading IT blogs and whitepapers, and reading the WSJ to listen to a company's earnings report. Attributes are one part, but bringing it all together is the mindset.

Chapter 6, Foundations of Network Architecture – Part 1: Route/Switch, begins with the foundational knowledge and skills necessary to advance into a network architect role and looks at the physical infrastructure (cabling, routers, and switches). Routing and switching are vital for any network to be sustainable. These are the building blocks upon which databases, compute and storage, and applications rely. Having a complete understanding of what is used to build a network is key to any network architect's success. This chapter is not intended to go into a deep dive on any one topic.

Chapter 7, Foundations of Network Architecture – Part 2: Network Services, describes the network services used to build the extensive network infrastructure companies rely on to support their business endeavors. ACLs, firewall rules, load balancing, and more play a critical role in supporting these endeavors.

Chapter 8, Foundations of Network Automation, discusses how, in the evolving landscape of network architecture, the shift toward automation is not just a trend but a fundamental transformation. Network automation stands at the forefront of this change, offering unprecedented efficiency, agility, and reliability. This chapter delves into the essential building blocks of network automation, laying a solid foundation for those seeking to harness its full potential.

Chapter 9, Paradigm Shift to Cloud Computing, introduces you to a paradigm shift to cloud and cloud technologies that can further aid a network architect's growth to next-generation IT infrastructure and services. You will learn about the different "as a Service" models, the key cloud providers, and their services, as well as understand private cloud, hybrid cloud, and multi-cloud.

Chapter 10, Preparing for Certifications and Cracking the Job Interview, describes IT certifications that a person who is looking to move into a network architect's role/position should obtain and how to prepare for those interview questions. There is no silver bullet on this topic. It takes hard work, commitment, and practice, practice, practice.

Chapter 11, The Skills to Become a Better Network Architect and Overcome Daily Challenges, covers how, in the journey to becoming a proficient network architect, technical skills are just one part of the equation. Equally vital are the interpersonal skills that enable you to navigate the complexities of a collaborative work environment. This chapter delves into the essential interpersonal competencies that will not only enhance your role as a network architect but also help you overcome daily challenges effectively.

Chapter 12, Additional Information and Recommended Books, shows how, while this book provides a comprehensive guide to becoming a network architect, the journey of learning and professional development is an ongoing one. To aid you in this continuous pursuit, we have compiled a selection of recommended books and other resources. These materials have been carefully chosen to complement the topics covered in this book and to provide deeper insights into specific areas of network architecture and related fields.

To get the most out of this book

As you embark on the enriching journey outlined in this book to become a network architect, it's important to approach it with the right mindset and background. This book is crafted for network professionals who bring at least five years of experience in IT, particularly in networking. It's tailored to readers who already understand networking concepts and technologies and are familiar with the fundamentals of networking solutions as they apply to IT infrastructure. Here are key strategies to help you get the most out of this book, provided that it aligns with your existing knowledge and experience:

- **Prerequisites for starting**: *Before delving into the chapters, recognize that this book is intended for those already midway through their IT career journey. It is not designed for individuals just beginning in IT. As a reader, you should have a robust understanding of network protocols, topologies, and a general grasp of IT systems.*

- **Set your learning objectives**: *Clearly define what you wish to achieve with this book. Whether it's deepening your knowledge of advanced network architecture, refining specific technical skills, or developing leadership qualities within a network team, having specific goals will focus and enhance your learning process.*

- **Actively engage with the material**: *While reading, actively engage with the content. This could involve applying theories to your current work scenarios, participating in discussions with peers, or experimenting with concepts in a lab setting. Active engagement not only reinforces learning but also enhances understanding.*

- **Practical application**: *Try to implement the strategies and techniques discussed in your current role or simulated environments. Applying these concepts in real-world scenarios will solidify your understanding and provide valuable insights into practical challenges and their solutions.*

- **Explore additional resources**: *Utilize the supplementary resources recommended throughout the book. These resources are selected to complement the main content and offer a deeper exploration into specific areas of network architecture.*

- **Continuous review and reflection**: *Regularly reflect on and review the material you've covered. This not only ensures a comprehensive understanding of the content but also helps in connecting various concepts together.*

- **Maintain a learning mindset**: *The field of network architecture is dynamic and ever-evolving. Stay open and curious about new technologies, methodologies, and ideas that go beyond this book. Continuous learning is key in the IT field.*

By following these steps and keeping in mind the intended audience and prerequisite knowledge, you will be well-equipped to not only grasp the concepts in this book but also to apply them effectively in your career. This book is a step in your ongoing journey of professional development in the field of network architecture.

Conventions used

There are a number of text conventions used throughout this book.

Bold: Indicates a new term, an important word, or words that you see onscreen. For instance, words in menus or dialog boxes appear in **bold**. Here is an example: "Select **System info** from the **Administration** panel."

> **Tips or important notes**
> Appear like this.

Get in touch

Feedback from our readers is always welcome.

General feedback: If you have questions about any aspect of this book, email us at customercare@ packtpub.com and mention the book title in the subject of your message.

Errata: Although we have taken every care to ensure the accuracy of our content, mistakes do happen. If you have found a mistake in this book, we would be grateful if you would report this to us. Please visit www.packtpub.com/support/errata and fill in the form.

Piracy: If you come across any illegal copies of our works in any form on the internet, we would be grateful if you would provide us with the location address or website name. Please contact us at copyright@packt.com with a link to the material.

If you are interested in becoming an author: If there is a topic that you have expertise in and you are interested in either writing or contributing to a book, please visit authors.packtpub.com.

Share Your Thoughts

Once you've read *Network Architect's Handbook*, we'd love to hear your thoughts! Scan the QR code below to go straight to the Amazon review page for this book and share your feedback.

https://packt.link/r/1837637830

Your review is important to us and the tech community and will help us make sure we're delivering excellent quality content.

Download a free PDF copy of this book

Thanks for purchasing this book!

Do you like to read on the go but are unable to carry your print books everywhere?

Is your eBook purchase not compatible with the device of your choice?

Don't worry, now with every Packt book you get a DRM-free PDF version of that book at no cost.

Read anywhere, any place, on any device. Search, copy, and paste code from your favorite technical books directly into your application.

The perks don't stop there, you can get exclusive access to discounts, newsletters, and great free content in your inbox daily

Follow these simple steps to get the benefits:

1.   Scan the QR code or visit the link below

https://packt.link/free-ebook/9781837637836

2.   Submit your proof of purchase

3.   That's it! We'll send your free PDF and other benefits to your email directly

Part 1 –
Navigating the Architectural
Blueprint of Networking

In the ever-evolving world of technology, the role of a network architect has become increasingly pivotal. As we delve into the intricate world of network design and management, it is essential to understand the multifaceted nature of a network architect's role, its place within an organization, and the path you must undertake to embody this key position. This section serves as the cornerstone to understanding the full scope of responsibilities, skills, and pathways associated with becoming a successful network architect.

This section has the following chapters:

- *Chapter 1, Understanding the Network Architect's Role*
- *Chapter 2, Network Architect in an Organization*
- *Chapter 3, Roadmap to Becoming a Network Architect*

1
Understanding the Network Architect's Role

Today, the network infrastructure (or *fabric* as I like to call it) is vast compared to how it was just 23 years ago, and even more sophisticated than when networks were around in the early 1970s. The infrastructure has evolved, and so has the people required to take care of and maintain them. But even in doing so, the role and responsibility have also evolved to be more. Before, the responsibility could have seen one or two people doing everything, such as racking and stacking, cabling, router configurations (as there were no switches at the time), installing hubs, and storage consolidation. Now, there are many roles in an organization that specialize in these varied tasks.

So much emphasis is put on the various roles within an organization when it comes to the IT business unit versus the IT department. Let's not confuse the two – the IT department is your desktop/laptop support team who can grant you access to various services, while your IT business unit is responsible for making sure that your various lines of business are functional and sustainable to generate revenue for your organization. The latter encompasses the network architect.

In this chapter, we're going to cover the following main topics:

- What is a network architect?
- The function of a network architect
- Understanding network architecture

Let's get started!

What is a network architect?

The network architect is vital to an organization's sustainability within their industry's vertical. A network architect is one of many architects that an organization has.

Here's my twist on the definition of the network architect:

> *"The expertise and skills necessary to design an end-to-end system to meet the criteria*
> *set forth, by encompassing best practices, principles, capabilities, and components a*
> *well defined network architecture should have, to meet and exceed the expectation of*
> *key stakeholders while taking account concerns, constraints, and cost."*

Before diving into what a network architect does in an organization, a brief articulation of other architects that you'll find in an organization will help to discern the difference from that of a network architect. Each has unique technical skills to address business needs, goals, and complexity. Moreover, there will be some overlap in tasks, deliverables to an organization, responsibilities, and maybe even KPIs.

KPIs

Key Performance Indicators (**KPIs**) are used to evaluate the success of an organization/team or a particular activity they are engaged in.

Solutions architects

Solution architects evaluate the requirements from the **line of business** (**LoB**) and determine what solution(s), whether it be products or services, can be used to meet or fulfill those requirements.

They design, describe, and manage the solution. This includes the networking (fabric) aspects, the storage aspect, database systems, security, and the overall scheme that will be deployed. In some ways, the **solutions architect** (**SA**) bridges a business problem and the technology solution. Additionally, the SA outlines each of the desideratum and the phases to make that solution work, after which they must confer with the other architects in the organization to validate the design feasibility.

To some degree, SAs create the overall technical vision for a specific solution to a (specific) business problem. I say *to some degree* because an organization's overall IT/technical vision comes from the **Chief Technical Officer** (**CTO**).

Storage architects

A storage architect builds central database systems; one such system is a **Configuration Management Database** (**CMDB**), which holds the most crucial business information for an organization. Some crucial information includes (but is not limited to) finance, compliance, accounting, and human resources.

They typically design based on the SA's findings, install new data storage systems using different software and various hardware, liaise with IT experts, and identify storage requirements to meet the needs of business units.

Examples of storage architects' designs include the following:

- FC zoning
- SAN and vSAN
- NAS, NFS, and SMB shares

Some routine operations can include analyzing data, potential issues, frequency of updates, maintenance, and hardware/software **Service Level Agreements (SLAs)**. Storage architects also need to communicate critical information to clients (internal or external) or an organization's management team.

The role of a storage architect can vary, depending on the organization itself and what they're looking for in the architect, but the storage architect's main task is to design a stable, reliable, and resilient storage architecture.

Database architects

A **database architect's (DBA's)** function is to understand an organization's main needs for data and its current data infrastructure. DBAs in some respects work closely with storage architects.

After taking the needs of an organization and conversing with the SA (and other stakeholders), the DBA analyzes the organization's priorities and goals, assesses whether the current data infrastructure is design-feasible, and then determines where changes should and must be made.

They must design the database's infrastructure to ensure that it's scalable, secure, reliable, and, like other designs, cost-effective.

Depending on a country's boundaries and compliances, DBAs must also ensure that a database meets any regulations and standards, especially when dealing with sensitive data.

Enterprise architects

An **enterprise architect (EA)** is somewhat similar to an SA. While the SA is charged with defining the correct services/infrastructure to meet the BU's needs, the **EA** is responsible for the upkeep and maintenance of those services/infrastructure.

They're also responsible for improving and upgrading enterprise services (e.g., CRMs, HRMs, and PoS systems), software, and hardware.

Like the SA, EAs must have a wide view and scope (vision) of what's happening within an organization, as well as being abreast of new trends and technologies, and any software services or hardware that might improve business processes.

Cloud architects

As you may have guessed, a cloud architect is involved with cloud computing. Their function is to oversee an organization's cloud adoption strategy. Cloud architects oversee application architecture and deployment in cloud environments, including the public cloud, private cloud, and hybrid cloud. Additionally, they act as consultants to their organization and also need to stay abreast of the latest trends and issues (`https://www.techtarget.com/searchcloudcomputing/definition/cloud-architect`).

Cloud architects must understand application owners' and application developers' needs and requirements. Then, they must survey *how* to closely replicate it, if possible, in a cloud-centric environment based on what's already allocated and consumed on-premises. The premises can be an organization's leased space, owned property, or IT setup, solely owned by that organization, which would then be migrated.

In all cases, the cloud architect has to determine whether the application (workload) fits into one of Gartner's five Rs of migrating applications into the cloud (*Migrating Applications to the Cloud: Rehost, Refactor, Revise, Rebuild, or Replace?, available at* `https://www.gartner.com/en/documents/1485116`)

The following diagram is a cloud migration strategy currently used by AWS, based on Gartner's original five Rs:

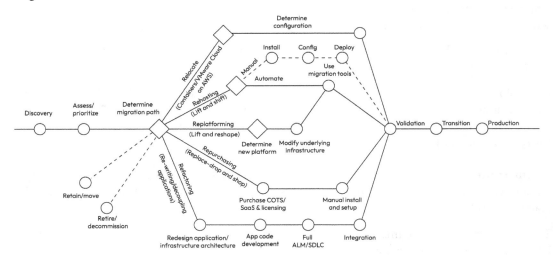

Figure 1.1 – AWS's version of Gartner's five Rs of cloud migration strategies
(source: https://aws.amazon.com/blogs/enterprise-strategy/new-possibilities-
seven-strategies-to-accelerate-your-application-migration-to-aws/)

Technical architects

While other architects may be broad(er) in scope, **technical architects** (**TAs**) are more specific. They take the most hands-on approach during the execution of IT projects and focus mainly on a single implementation for a specific domain that they're, technically, inclined for. An example would be a TA who is extremely familiar with SAP, MongoDB, Python, or even Cisco.

Because of this, TAs produce best practice strategies utilized by an organization, which, in most cases, are used by other IT architects during their development and strategy sessions for their own solutions.

Out of all the IT architects, TAs are the closest to an organization's end user. Thus, they have to ensure that the technology is not only delivered on time but is fully functional for the end user (`https://rb.gy/uw31fb`).

Chief architects

Depending on the organization, the **chief architect** (**CA**) may oversee and coordinate the efforts of other technology-specific architects, including the chief security architect, the chief data architect, the chief mobile architect, and the chief cloud architect.

A CA is primarily a leader and communicator. They need to understand and influence the business strategy and lead the development of an architecture strategy that supports and enables that strategy (`https://www.redhat.com/architect/what-is-chief-architect`). A CA can also be referred to as an EA, as defined previously.

In addition, there are other architect roles, such as the following:

- Application
- Migration
- Security
- Automation
- **Site Reliability Engineer** (**SRE**)
- Software

The role of every architect in IT is directly related to the added complexities of information technology, and the need for a strategic top-down approach to the management of shared data and processes.

There can be varying degrees of overlap with some or all of these IT architects in an organization. Many are structured differently when it comes to who owns what, who's in charge, or who has the last say and signs things off.

Relatively speaking from my experience, this is what I came across from a hierarchy perspective:

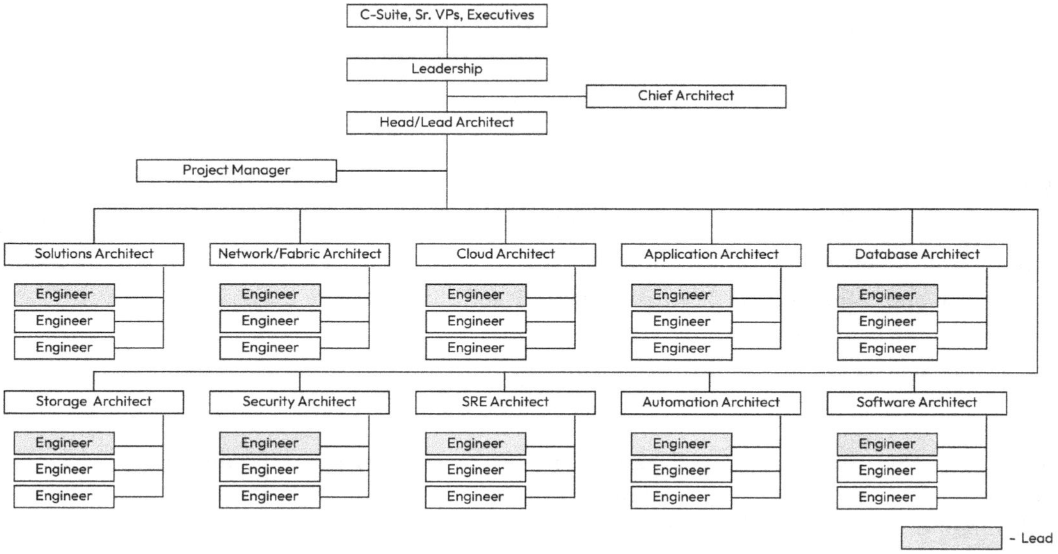

Figure 1.2 – The IT architect hierarchy in an organization

As I said before, there are not only overlaps in job function and responsibility but also overlaps when it comes to the roles within an organization, including business-centric, operations-centric, or even vendor and application-centric roles.

In general, the role of an IT architect is to ensure that an organization's IT systems are aligned with its business objectives and able to support its operations effectively.

Network architects

A network architect is mainly responsible for designing, managing, and implementing an organization's data communication networks, including the computer networks that support their IT systems, storage networks, and the internet edge. This means the network architect is responsible for the following:

- Designing **local area networks (LANs)**, **wide area networks (WANs)**, and intranets for organizations
- Designing the data and **storage area networks (SANs)**
- Both the hardware and software components of a network
- The policies and procedures that govern its use

While other IT architects may have a more general focus and be responsible for designing and implementing the *overall* IT infrastructure of an organization, a network architect must be fully embedded and have the required knowledge of many different network technologies (platforms) related to network routing and switching, networking protocols, network hardware and software, and the latest trends.

The network architect does overlap with the other architects mentioned. They also need to fully understand a business's operations and its operating model, which is discussed in *Chapter 4*. It's prudent to say network architects do not operate in siloes and should be a part of any meeting that requires a change, addition/removal, request, or ideation for an organization's network (fabric) infrastructure.

Now that we have a general overview of the various architects in an IT organization, let's talk more in depth about the topic this book is dedicated to, the network architect.

The function of a network architect

The function of a network architect is characterized by their responsibilities, which can vary, depending on the specific organization and the size and complexity of their network. However, some common functions/responsibilities of a network architect might include the following:

- Designing and planning the overall architecture of an organization's network, including its physical and logical layout
- Selecting and configuring the hardware and software components that make up the network, such as switches, routers, protocols, and firewall appliances
- Implementing and maintaining network security measures to protect against external threats and unauthorized access
- Ensuring the network is scalable, agile, flexible, and able to handle growing demands from business units
- Monitoring the performance of the network and identifying and troubleshooting any issues that arise
- Developing and implementing policies and procedures for the use of the network
- Collaborating with other IT professionals, such as system administrators and application developers, to support the overall IT infrastructure of the organization, and other architects to express opinions about design concerns, constraints, and success
- Articulating business needs to the leadership
- Managing vendor relationships and working with external contractors or service providers as needed
- Staying up to date with the latest technologies and trends in networking and evaluating their potential impact on the organization's network

A network architect may also be responsible for designing and implementing specific subsystems within a network, such as the data center, the campus network, the metro network, and other private network systems.

In most cases, these responsibilities are completed standalone, meaning without validation or approval from other IT architects. Generally speaking, activities, concerns, or anything similar are brought up during a stand-up or regularly scheduled IT meeting.

In summary, a network architect is responsible for the overall design, implementation, and maintenance of an organization's computer networks. They play a key role in ensuring that a network is reliable, secure, and able to support the needs of an organization.

Understanding network architecture

Network architecture refers to the overall design of a computer network, along with other auxiliary networks. It includes the hardware, software, and protocols that make up the network, as well as the physical and logical layout of the network and the relationships between the various components.

Network architecture should be designed to support the needs and goals of an organization, taking into account factors such as the size of the network, the types of devices and applications that will be traversed across, the number of end users (consumers), the level of security required, and the availability and performance requirements.

The architecture must be able to support the current organizational needs (from the various lines of businesses, stakeholders, leadership, and end users), be flexible for future growth, meet multiple degrees of SLx (such as SLAs and SLOs), and be agile to support shifts in the market, all the while maintaining a cost balance between CapEx and OpEx.

There are many different approaches to designing network architecture, and the most appropriate one will depend on the specific needs and constraints of an organization. Some common types of network architectures include the following:

- **Client-server architecture**, in which one or more central servers provide services to multiple clients
- **Peer-to-peer architecture**, in which all devices on a network are able to communicate directly with each other
- **Hierarchical architecture**, in which a network is divided into multiple layers, each with a specific function
- **Hybrid architecture**, in which multiple different architectures are combined in order to meet the needs of an organization
- **Spine-leaf architecture**, to take advantage of high-speed throughput for east–west traffic and a higher level of redundancy

Let's take a closer look at these architectures.

Client/server architecture

The client/server architecture is a computing model in which the server hosts, delivers, and manages most of the resources and services requested by the client.

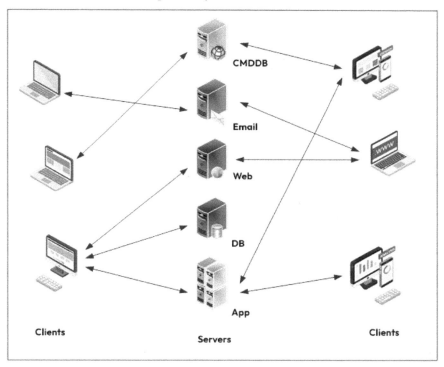

Figure 1.3 – An example of a client/server architecture

It's also known as a *networking computing model* or *client/server network*, as all requests and services are delivered over a network. Client/server architecture is a common way to design and implement computer systems. It is used in a wide variety of applications, including web applications, email systems, and database management systems.

These systems can be HR, CMDB, network (fabric) monitoring and logging, or storage systems.

Multiple clients' requests are made to and from a central server. The server is responsible for handling requests, processing data, and providing a client with the requested information. The client, on the other hand, initiates the request and displays the received data to the user. This architecture is commonly used in *distributed computing*, where a centralized server manages and distributes data to multiple clients over a network.

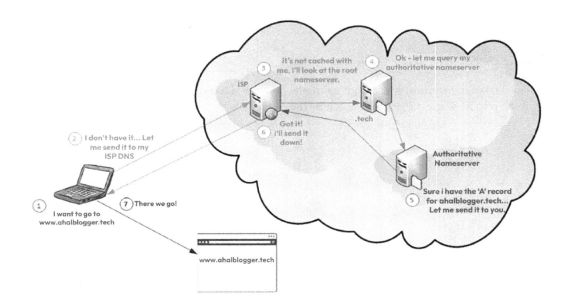

Figure 1.4 – A DNS request flow to ahaliblogger.tech

In the diagram, a *client* makes a request to reach `ahaliblogger.tech`. As the request flows through several DNS servers, an authoritative *server* responds to the client with the proper information.

Client/server architecture has several advantages over other computing models. One advantage is that it is scalable. The systems can be easily expanded to accommodate more users. Another advantage is that it is reliable. Client/server systems are less likely to fail than other networking computing models.

However, client/server architectures also have some disadvantages. One disadvantage is that it can be complex to design and implement. Another disadvantage is that it can be expensive to maintain.

Peer-to-peer architecture

A **peer-to-peer** (**P2P**) network architecture is a type of network in which each computer or device (known as a *peer*) is able to act as both the client and the server. This means that each peer is able to both request and provide a response to other peers on the network, without the need for a central server or authority to manage the network.

Peer-to-peer networks are often decentralized and self-organizing and can be used for a wide range of applications, including file sharing, online gaming, and distributed computing.

An example of a peer-to-peer network architecture is a BitTorrent file-sharing network.

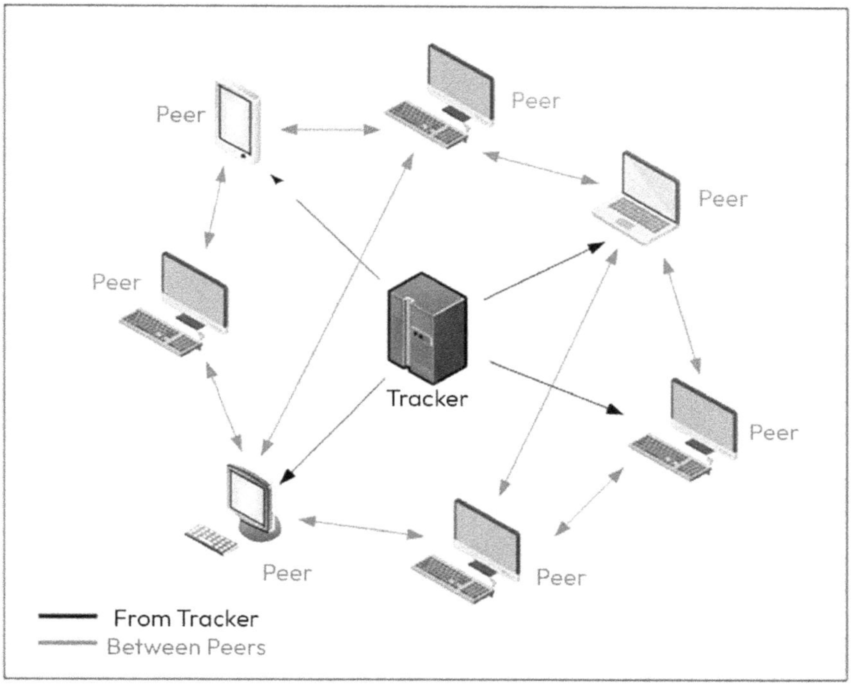

Figure 1.5 – How BitTorrent works

In this network, clients (peers) share files with each another by breaking the files into small pieces and distributing them across the network. The (BitTorrent) client contacts a "tracker" specified in the `.torrent` file (`https://www.howtogeek.com/141257/htg-explains-how-does-bittorrent-work/`).

Each client is able to download pieces of the file from multiple other peers and can also upload pieces of the file to other peers. This allows the efficient distribution of large files, as the load is distributed among many users rather than relying on a central server.

Hierarchical architecture

Hierarchical network architecture is a type of network design that uses a multi-layered approach to organize and manage network resources. It separates a network into distinct layers, where each layer has a defined function that, in turn, defines its role in the network. These layers are the access layer, the distribution layer, and the core layer.

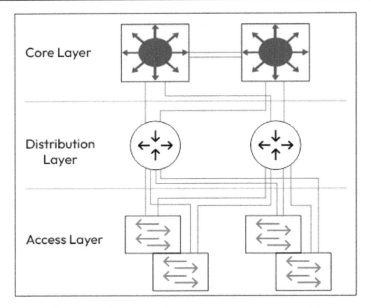

Figure 1.6 – The three-tier network architecture model

The preceding diagram illustrates each layer in the hierarchical architecture model.

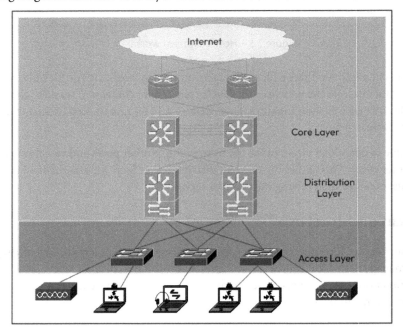

Figure 1.7 – The access layer of the three-tier hierarchical architecture model

The **access layer** is the point of entry into a network, and it is where end user devices such as computers, servers, printers, VOIP phones, and other IP devices connect. The access layer is responsible for providing basic (and, at times, more complex) connectivity and controlling access to the network.

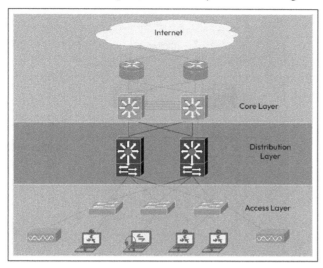

Figure 1.8 – The distribution layer of the three-tier hierarchical architecture model

The **distribution layer** is where a network is divided into different segments or VLANs, and it acts as a bridge between the access and core layers. This layer is responsible for routing and filtering traffic, and providing security and **Quality of Service (QoS)** features.

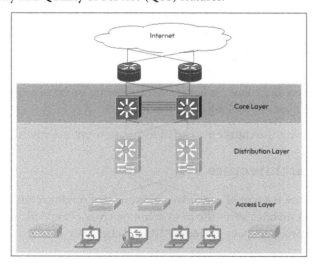

Figure 1.9 – The core layer of the three-tier hierarchical architecture model

The **core layer** is the backbone of a network, and it is responsible for the high-speed switching and routing of traffic between different segments of the network. This layer is designed to be highly available and redundant, providing a fast and efficient data transfer throughout the network.

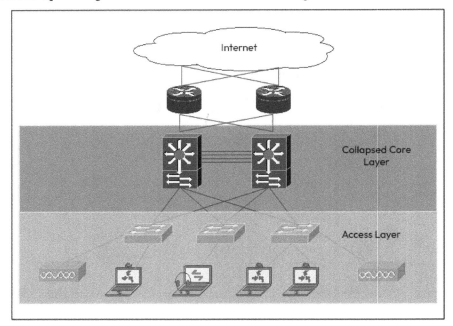

Figure 1.10 – The collapsed core model

The preceding diagram shows a variation of the hierarchical architecture, where the distribution and core layers are combined into what is known as a **collapsed layer**. In this design, the core and distribution functions are performed within one device (or a pair of devices).

The hierarchical design allows for better scalability, security, and manageability. Separating the different functions into specific layers also allows for better troubleshooting, as the network administrators can easily identify the problem area by looking at the specific layer.

The most common hierarchical architecture used in today's network is spine/leaf.

Hybrid network architecture

Hybrid network architecture is a type of network architecture that combines elements of two or more different types of network architectures. The most common types of network architectures that are combined in a hybrid network are **peer-to-peer** (**P2P**) and **client-server** (**C/S**) architectures.

In a hybrid P2P/C/S network, a network is made up of both clients and servers, but the clients also have the ability to act as servers. This allows for network resources to be used more efficiently and can provide a better user experience, as data can be shared and distributed more easily.

For example, a hybrid P2P/C/S network might be used in a file-sharing application, where users can upload and download files from a central server but also share files directly with one another.

Another example would be combining the use of both wired and wireless connections. This allows a more flexible and reliable network – for example, a wireless connection can be used for mobile devices, while a wired connection can be used for more demanding applications such as video conferencing.

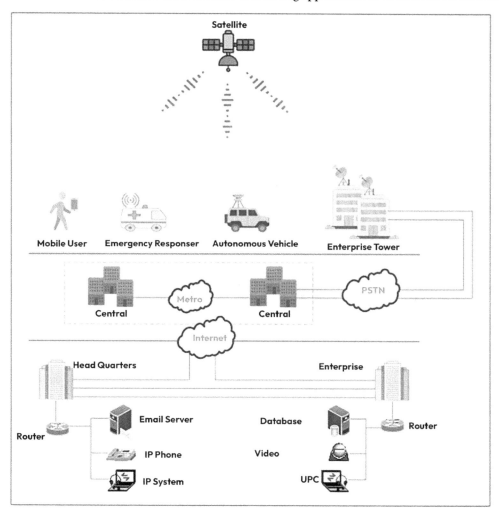

Figure 1.11 – An example of hybrid architecture – wireless and wired

A more common approach to hybrid network architecture is distributed computing systems, where a combination of cloud computing and edge computing is used. This allows data processing to take place at the edge of the network, close to the source of the data, while still giving you the ability to offload to the cloud for more processing power and storage.

An example is Tesla's self-driving car. The car's sensor constantly monitors certain regions around it, detecting an obstacle or pedestrian in its way, and then the car must be stopped or move around without hitting anything (https://www.geeksforgeeks.org/difference-between-edge-computing-and-fog-computing/). The vehicle must process the data quickly to determine what needs to be done next and also send it to backend systems (cloud or on-premises), where it is put in a data store (i.e., Hadoop clusters or cloud buckets). At this point, the data can be processed for further analysis, such as ETL processing or AI/ML pipelines.

The following diagram illustrates the use of edge devices in hybrid network architecture.

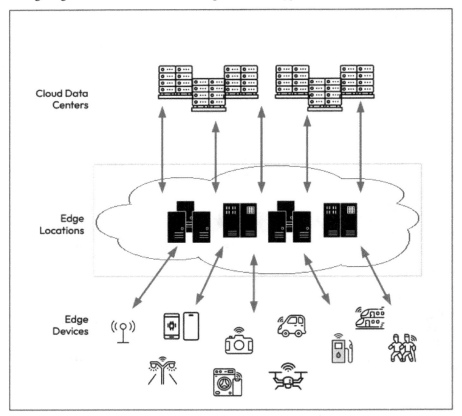

Figure 1.12 – Hybrid architecture – edge computing to cloud computing

Hybrid network architectures can provide the best of both worlds, the flexibility of P2P and the central control of C/S, and it can also allow for more efficient use of resources, better security and scalability, and a better user experience.

Spine-leaf architecture

A spine-leaf network architecture is a type of data center network architecture in which all devices are connected to leaf switches, which, in turn, are connected to spine switches.

The leaf switches provide end devices with access to a network, while the spine switches provide high-speed interconnections between the leaf switches. This architecture creates a flat, non-blocking network that allows efficient communication between devices and provides high redundancy.

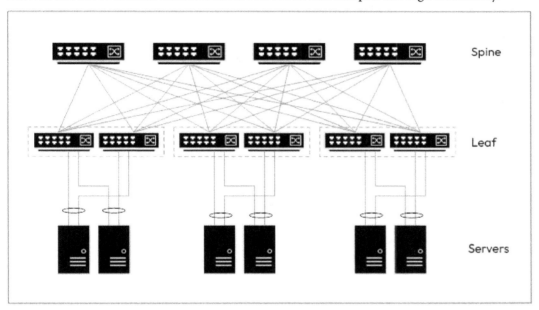

Figure 1.13 – Spine-leaf architecture

The architecture can also be easily scaled to support a large number of devices and high throughput. The purpose of this architecture is to provide a cost-effective, scalable, and high-performance solution for modern data centers.

Summary

A network architect falls under the umbrella of the many architects that an organization may have, and it is vital to any organization's success. The role and function of the network architect are more specific than that of a CA or SA but just as important when understanding the needs and requirements of stakeholders, end users, and leadership within an organization.

The network architecture is just as vital, as it's the backbone of the entire organization. The design determines its flexibility, capacity to change, ability to introduce newer technologies and decommission older systems, and whether it is agile enough to support market changes in an organization, while simultaneously supporting end user requests for resources and services.

In the next chapter, we'll dive deeper into the network architect in an organization.

Further reading

- *Why Networks Are Evolving Toward Leaf-Spine Architectures*: https://www.networkcomputing.com/networking/why-networks-are-evolving-toward-leaf-spine-architectures/

- *Multitier architecture*: https://en.wikipedia.org/wiki/Multitier_architecture

- *Cisco Networking Academy Connecting Networks Companion Guide: Hierarchical Network Design*: https://www.ciscopress.com/articles/article.asp?p=2202410&seqNum=4

2
Network Architect in an Organization

This chapter will dive deeper into the function of a network architect in an organization. The position of a network architect within an organization can vary depending on the size and structure of the company. In general, the network architect is often found in the IT department and may report to a manager or director of IT.

In larger organizations, the network architect may be part of a dedicated network architecture team that is responsible for designing, planning, and maintaining the organization's network infrastructure. In smaller organizations, the network architect position may be standalone or combined with other IT roles.

In some cases, the network architect may also be part of a larger technical architecture team that is responsible for the overall technical direction of the organization. This team may include other types of architects responsible for other areas, such as security, data centers, or software development.

Additionally, network architects may also report to a CTO or CIO who is responsible for the overall technology strategy of the organization.

In this chapter, we're going to cover the following main topics:

- Planning, designing, installing, upgrading, and maintaining network projects
- Making recommendations to move the network to an advanced level and reduce operating costs
- Documenting the network process for future uses

Let's get started!

Planning, designing, installing, upgrading, and maintaining network projects

The purpose of a network architect's role in planning, designing, installing, and upgrading network projects is to ensure that the organization's network infrastructure is reliable, efficient, and secure and that it supports the organization's business needs.

Some projects may be completed within a few weeks, while others may take well over two years just to witness and reap the benefits of cost savings identified from the start. It's not an easy endeavor to undertake, as a tremendous amount of effort goes into these events. A network architect must be involved from beginning to end and materially participate, to some extent, at all levels.

Let's break down each event:

- **Planning**: The network architect plans the project by gathering requirements, identifying objectives, and defining the project scope. This helps to ensure that the project is aligned with the organization's business needs and that all stakeholders are aligned on the project goals.

- **Designing**: The network architect designs the new network infrastructure, creating detailed logical and physical diagrams, and specifying the hardware and software that will be used. This helps to ensure that the new network will be efficient, reliable, agile, and secure, to support the organization's business needs and current requirements.

- **Installing**: The network architect oversees the installation of the new network, including the installation and configuration of hardware and software. This helps to ensure that the new network is installed correctly and that it is ready to be used by the organization.

- **Upgrading**: The network architect is also responsible for upgrading the network infrastructure as needed, which is essential to keep the network up to date with the latest technologies and security standards and to meet the growth needs of the organization.

- **Maintaining**: The network architect maintains the network infrastructure and ensures that it's running smoothly and efficiently and that it's able to support the organization's business needs. This may involve troubleshooting, resolving network issues, compliance checks, auditing, and making changes to the network as needed.

Regardless of which of these events are being performed, questions a network architect should ask are *"What is the organization trying to accomplish with this project?"* and *"What is the intended goal/ outcome of this project?"*

Let's take a closer look at these steps.

Planning

A network architect begins the planning process by following these steps:

1. **Defining the project scope**: The first step is to define the scope of the project, including the objectives, requirements, and constraints of the project. This involves working with stakeholders to understand their needs and requirements and gathering information about the current network infrastructure. Additional information may come from industry reports, such as Gartner, to provide insight into what other organizations are looking to do.

   Example: A high-frequency trading platform has a requirement for low latency to serve its customers with the most accurate financial data possible.

2. **Conducting a network assessment**: A network assessment is vital in an IT project because it provides a comprehensive understanding of the current state of the network. It establishes a baseline for activities moving forward from that point in time. The network architect will conduct an assessment of the current network infrastructure, determining network readiness and compliance with industry standards, identifying any issues or bottlenecks that need to be addressed, as well as opportunities for improvement.

   Example: Because of the **high-frequency trading (HFT)** platform's requirement for low latency, an assessment was done illustrating that the current switching fabric is past its usefulness and cannot support the requirement. A new switching fabric will be needed to support the platform.

3. **Developing a project plan**: Based on the information gathered during the project scope definition and network assessment, the network architect will develop a detailed project plan. It provides a roadmap for the project and helps to ensure that the project is completed on time, within budget, and to the desired quality level. A project plan outlines the objectives, scope, deliverables, timeline, budget, and resources required for a project.

   This plan will outline milestones, timelines, resource requirements, and any other relevant information to complete the project successfully. The project plan will be used to determine how much funding will be allocated for the project. A well-defined project plan can increase the chances of project success and minimize the impact of unexpected events on the project.

   Example: Based on the information gathered about the HFT platform, the project will take about 4 months:

   * Month 1 – procure new switches

   * Month 2 – install, configure, and test new switches

   * Month 3 – place new switches into production, cutover, and test

   * Month 4 – decommission old switching fabric

4. **Identifying risks and constraints**: In addition and inclusive in the project plan are identifying the potential risks and constraints that can impede progress, impact current operations, or cause potential outages for an extended period of time. It helps to ensure that the project is completed on time, within budget, and to the desired quality level.

   By identifying potential risks and constraints, contingency plans can be developed to minimize the impact of these risks and constraints on the project. The network architect will identify and evaluate any potential risks or constraints that may impact the project and create a mitigation plan.

   Example: Two potential risks have been identified of not moving to an HFT switching platform to support trading:

   • Higher than normal latency due to network congestion

   • Revenue lost from trades not occurring within a specific time frame because of latency

5. **Allocating resources**: Resources are another essential component. It's important to allocate resources effectively to ensure that the project is completed on time, within budget, and to the desired quality level.

   Resources include human, financial (budget), technical (hardware and software), and in some cases, office space, too. The network architect must consider the availability, cost, and suitability of each type of resource when making decisions about resource allocation, such as using internal teams versus outsourcing, which manufacturer to use, and the necessary lead times.

   They must also consider the dependencies between different types of resources and ensure that the right resources are available at the right time to ensure the success of the project.

   Example: Based on the project plan timelines, the project needs a technical lead, one architect, four engineers, and two technicians. The cost will be about $550K plus hardware, licensing, and support.

6. **Reviewing and approving**: The project plan will be reviewed and approved by the relevant stakeholders and IT management before implementation. This ensures that all stakeholders agree on the project scope, timeline, allocation of resources, and budget. Any vagueness or ambiguity in the project plan is identified and reviewed for clarity and completeness. Any concerns are addressed before moving forward.

   Reviewing and approving the project plan helps to ensure that all stakeholders understand and agree on what is expected of the project.

   Example: The project plan for the new HFT switching platform was reviewed and acknowledged by all teams on the leadership call. Signatures will be ascertained a week from today.

7. **Communicating the plan**: Effective communication is crucial and can impact the success of the project. The network architect will communicate the project plan to all relevant stakeholders, including IT staff, management, and external vendors. It helps ensure all stakeholders understand the project goals, objectives, timeline, budget, and expectations.

Communicating the project plan increases buy-in and support for the project, as stakeholders are more likely to support a project that they understand and feel involved in.

Example: After the project plan was reviewed and approved, the leadership, along with the network architect and team, held a town hall meeting to communicate and present the plan for a new HFT platform to support next-generation trading applications and a focus on global reach. Once the project commences, leadership will hold monthly town hall meetings to give an update on the project.

8. **Monitoring and controlling**: It's important to monitor and control a project's progress. The metrics were defined as part of the initial scope and more so in the project plan. The network architect will monitor and control the project metrics (i.e., budget and timelines) and report regularly on progress (weekly or bi-weekly), milestones achieved, tasks completed, and any concerns or issues that come about.

   Risk management helps ensure that any impact on a project is mitigated appropriately. This might involve conducting risk assessments, developing contingency plans, and monitoring risk levels throughout the project.

   By defining project metrics, conducting regular progress reporting, tracking performance, managing issues and changes, and managing risks, the network architect can help to ensure that the project is completed on time, within budget, and to a high quality standard.

   Example: Because of a delay with procurement, the timeline will be pushed out by 3 weeks. From a budget perspective, we're still within our target of 28%. There is minimal risk to the project. The forecast is within the target timeframe to date.

Design

Once the project scope and plan have been defined, a network architect begins the design process for a network project by following these steps:

1. **Identifying the requirements**: A review of the requirements gathered during the project scope definition phase aids in aligning with business needs, defining performance criteria, creating a technical roadmap, avoiding rework, and minimizing risks. This help to ensure that the project scope is still accurate and relevant.

   More importantly, from an IT infrastructure perspective, the requirements must support the infrastructure's scalability, reliability, and performance, interoperate with current infrastructure, meet compliance regulations (if any), and be secure, flexible, and cost-effective.

   The network architect must work with stakeholders and other members of the IT team to identify and prioritize the requirements for the IT infrastructure and to ensure that the infrastructure is designed to meet these requirements.

2. **Creating logical and physical diagrams**: Creating logical and physical diagrams is an essential step in the design of an IT infrastructure, as it helps the network architect (and network

engineers) to visualize and understand the relationships between different components of the network, as well as the connections between the network and its end users. In addition, these diagrams help clarify the scope and objectives of a project and provide a clear understanding of the overall architecture of the network.

Logical diagrams provide a high-level overview of the network infrastructure, showing how the different components interact and how data flows between them. This can include diagrams showing the network topology, IP scheme, routing and switching infrastructure, and the security and access controls in place.

Physical diagrams, on the other hand, provide a more detailed view of the physical components of the network, including the servers, storage devices, switches, routers, and other equipment (i.e., electric layout). These diagrams help to ensure that the network infrastructure is properly installed and configured and that the components are correctly cabled and connected.

By creating both logical and physical diagrams, the network architect can ensure that the network is designed correctly, installed accordingly, and configured to meet the needs of the organization and identify potential issues, if any.

> **Note**
> There are many IT architect tools on the market such as Visio or Lucidchart. It's best to standardize a tool or tools across all teams to minimize any disruption when viewing diagrams.

3.   **Specifying hardware and software**: This is an important step in the design process, as it helps the network architect to ensure that the network is configured correctly and optimized for performance, security, and reliability. This may include routers, switches, firewalls, load balancers, other network devices, and network management software.

When specifying hardware, the network architect must consider factors such as the capacity and performance requirements of the network, the availability of spare components for redundancy and failover, and the power and cooling requirements of the equipment. The network architect must also consider the compatibility of the hardware components with other devices and systems currently in use on the network (fabric) and choose components capable of supporting the desired features and functionalities of the network.

Similarly, when specifying software, the network architect must consider factors such as the compatibility of the software with the hardware components, the support and maintenance needs of the software, and the security and performance requirements of the network. The network architect must also choose software that is capable of supporting the desired features and functionalities of the network and must ensure that the software is configured correctly and optimized for performance and reliability to support the network.

Specifying the hardware and software components of the network infrastructure supports the network design to meet the organization's needs, and ensures that the components are correctly configured and optimized for performance, security, and reliability. It ensures that the network infrastructure is efficient, effective, and capable of supporting the desired applications and services, and helps to ensure the success of the IT project.

4. **Designing for security**: The network infrastructure must be protected from threats and vulnerabilities, such as unauthorized access, malware, and data breaches.

Inclusive of the design are security best practices, such as implementing firewalls, intrusion detection and prevention systems, and encryption to protect the network infrastructure. In addition, regular security assessments must be conducted to ensure that the security measures in place are effective and to identify any new threats or vulnerabilities that may have emerged throughout the life cycle of the infrastructure.

Access controls must be implemented to ensure that only authorized users can access the network infrastructure and its resources. This helps to prevent unauthorized access and potential security breaches. If a security incident does occur, the network should be designed with redundancy and failover, so the network continues to operate even in the event of a failure or security breach.

Monitoring and logging capabilities are needed to keep track of network activity, detect potential security threats and vulnerabilities, and respond to security incidents in a timely manner.

As a network architect designing for security, you're able to safeguard the confidentiality, integrity, and availability of the network and its resources, and it helps to ensure not only the success of the project but also the organization's sustainability and future growth.

> **Note**
>
> At the time of writing, many principles exist related to security and securing network infrastructure. The concept of *shift-left security* is one that has been adopted as of late.

5. **Designing for scalability, agility, and availability**: Scalability refers to the ability of the network infrastructure to grow and accommodate increased demand. Agility refers to the network fabric's flexibility and adaptability to changing requirements and ability to accommodate new services and applications quickly and efficiently, while availability refers to the ability of the network to continue to operate and provide services even in the event of failures or disruptions. All of this requires a combination of thoughtful planning and implementation of various technologies and best practices.

The network topology plays a vital role in a network fabric's scalability, agility, and availability. This may involve using redundant links and paths and designing the network to minimize the impact of failures (i.e., considering load balancing to distribute network traffic across multiple devices, such as routers, switches, or servers, to ensure that no single device becomes a bottleneck).

Also, consider the size and complexity of the network, the types of services and applications being offered/utilized, the security requirements, and the budget when designing a network infrastructure for these aspects.

6. **Review and validation**: This is an important step in the design process. It helps to ensure that the design meets the requirements and expectations of the stakeholders and that it will be effective in meeting the goals of the project and its scope.

    The network design will be reviewed and validated by relevant stakeholders, IT management, and technical experts to ensure that it meets the organization's needs and standards. Any potential problems or limitations with the design can be identified during this process and changes made as necessary.

    Feedback from stakeholders and other members of the team is crucial to improve the design or catch errors/omissions early in the design process, which can save time and resources in the long run.

    By validating the design, the network architect can ensure that the design is aligned with industry best practices and standards, meets organizational objectives, and that it complies with any relevant regulations or security requirements. This can help to increase the overall security and reliability of the network infrastructure and reduce the risk of unexpected problems or issues in the future.

7. **Documenting the design**: A well-documented design can help communicate the intended architecture to stakeholders, such as management, other IT personnel, and customers. It provides clear, concise, and accurate information about the design, its components, and how they interact with each other. This ensures that everyone involved in the project has a shared understanding of the network architecture.

    The network architect will document the design, including the logical and physical diagrams that show the overall architecture of the network (and the relationships between different components), hardware and software specifications (and their detailed configurations for installation), and any other relevant information.

    This documentation will be used as a reference during the implementation and maintenance of the network. So, it is important to keep the documentation up to date as the network infrastructure evolves over time to ensure that it remains accurate and relevant.

8. **Communicating the design**: The purpose of communicating the network design of the network infrastructure is to ensure that all stakeholders have a clear understanding of the design and the expected outcome of the project. This includes the technical details of the network infrastructure (documenting the design), how it will meet the organization's needs, and how it will support the goals and objectives of the organization.

    Communicating the design is not only relevant to the stakeholders but also to the IT staff, management, external vendors, project managers, and developers – all of which have a stake in the outcome of the project.

Effectively communicating the design is critical for the success of the project, and it helps to ensure that the network infrastructure meets the organization's needs and provides value to the organization. This will ensure that everyone understands the design of the network and what is expected of them in the implementation phase.

Installing

After designing the network architecture, a network architect goes about installing the network in the following steps:

1. **Preparing for installation**: As part of preparing for installation, a network architect must ensure that all necessary hardware and software components are available and ready to be installed as part of the project plan. This includes ordering the necessary hardware and software, having the team available to perform the installation, and scheduling the installation with relevant stakeholders and IT staff.

   The network architect must also create detailed installation and configuration procedures, which should be reviewed and tested before being used in a live environment.

   > **Note**
   >
   > A **proof of concept (PoC)** is required to make sure that the configurations, setup, design, and failover can support the hardware/software/application/service/technology being instantiated.

   When scheduling the installation, the network architect will need to coordinate with other IT teams and stakeholders to ensure that the installation and configuration of the network infrastructure are done in a manner that minimizes downtime and disruption.

   This includes an initial sign-off and approvals from various departments or stakeholders, including security teams, to ensure that the installation complies with any relevant policies and regulations and to commence with the installation. This is done through a change control program management meeting.

2. **Connecting devices**: Connecting devices as part of a network infrastructure IT project is important because it establishes the physical connectivity between different network components, such as servers, switches, routers, firewalls, IDS/IPS systems, and end user devices. The network team will connect the devices according to the physical diagram and test them to ensure they are properly connected.

   These connected devices help to ensure that all components of the network infrastructure can communicate with each other, facilitate the transfer of data between different parts of the network, support the day-to-day operations of a business, and minimize the potential for network outages and downtime – all of which is essential for the network to function effectively.

3. **Configuring the hardware**: The process of configuring the hardware involves setting up the physical components of the network infrastructure, cabling them in accordance with the physical diagram, and testing the connectivity, such as routers, switches, and firewalls, to meet the specific requirements of the project. This includes specifying the required ports, routing switching configurations, interfaces and IP addressing/subnets, ACLs, services, and other protocols that the hardware must support, as well as setting up any necessary security measures.

The network architect will work with engineers and stakeholders to verify that the configuration of the hardware is in line with the project scope, project plan, detailed network design document, and the solution(s) being articulated by the organization.

Proper configuration of the hardware is critical to ensuring the stability, security, and performance of the network infrastructure. If the hardware is not configured correctly, it can cause network outages, security vulnerabilities, and performance issues, which can have a negative impact on the success of the IT project.

4. **Installing software**: This involves setting up or modifying the software components of the network, such as the operating system, network management software, security software, monitoring and visibility software, and application software, to meet the requirements and specifications of the network design and for the network to function correctly.

    The purpose of configuring the software is to ensure that the network infrastructure is functioning properly and efficiently. The software configuration must be consistent with the network design so that the hardware components and the software components are working together seamlessly. The software configuration must also be secure, reliable, and scalable to meet the needs of the organization and its users over time.

    Configuring the software helps to ensure that the network infrastructure is scalable and flexible so that it can adapt to changing requirements as the project progresses and as the needs of the business change.

5. **Testing the network**: Testing the network ensures that the network functions as intended and meets the requirements of the IT project. The testing should be conducted through a test plan called the **user acceptance test plan** (**UATP**). This plan can include verifying that devices are communicating correctly, the network is secure, the performance is acceptable, the desired capabilities are functioning, and the network is available under load testing or duress. If any issues are identified during testing, the network architect can make any necessary adjustments before the network is put into production. It ensures that the system works as expected from a user's perspective and that it is ready for deployment into production.

    By conducting thorough network testing, a network architect can gain confidence in the network design and implementation and make any necessary modifications to improve performance and reliability.

6. **Deployment**: Once testing of the network infrastructure is complete, the deployment into production will commence. This entails a detailed go-live plan outlining the steps to transition to the new network infrastructure. This plan should include details such as the timeline, roles and responsibilities, and any contingencies that need to be put in place in case of any issues.

    The network architect should plan the switchover (or cutover) carefully to minimize any disruptions to network services. This may involve a phased approach to cutting over to the new infrastructure.

As the cutover is in progress, monitoring this activity becomes critical to the overall success of the project, making sure everything is running smoothly. This may involve monitoring network performance, availability, and security, as well as tracking any issues that arise and resolving them as quickly as possible.

Overall, the goal of the deployment process is to ensure that the network infrastructure is operational and performing as expected while minimizing any disruptions to network services.

7. **Validation and sign-off**: The network architecture must be validated to ensure that it meets the project requirements, including performance, security, scalability, availability, and end user acceptance. The UATP is used to verify that what was tested is actually what was placed into production with the desired results achieved.

   All documentation related to the network infrastructure, at this point, must be completed and updated, including configuration, hardware and software specifications, and network diagrams. The network infrastructure must be reviewed and approved by relevant stakeholders, including IT management, business stakeholders, and any external partners.

   Once the network infrastructure verification and validation are completed and approved, the network infrastructure can be put into production and made available for use.

8. **Monitoring and maintenance**: After a network infrastructure has been deployed, monitoring and maintenance are conducted to ensure that the network continues to perform optimally and to detect and resolve any issues.

   Monitoring involves constantly monitoring the performance and availability of the network, as well as its components, such as routers, switches, firewalls, and servers. This helps to detect potential problems early and resolve them before they become serious. Various tools are used to monitor the network, such as network management software, performance monitoring tools, and syslog servers.

   Maintenance activities can include software and firmware upgrades, hardware replacements, and performance tuning. Regular maintenance helps to prevent equipment failures and to ensure that the network continues to meet the needs of the organization. Maintenance schedules are typically established and documented in the network design and planning process.

   It's important for a network architect to be involved in the monitoring and maintenance activities, as they have the expertise to assess the impact of changes to the network and to make recommendations to ensure that the network continues to meet the needs of the organization for business continuity.

Overall, the network architect will play a vital role in the installation process, overseeing all aspects of it. The network architect will work closely with the project team, workstream leads, and other stakeholders to ensure that the project is delivered on time, within budget, and to the desired quality standards, and ensure that it is done correctly and that the network infrastructure is ready to support the organization's business needs.

Upgrading

A network architect will determine when a network design needs to be upgraded based on a variety of factors, such as the following:

- **Business growth and expansion**: As an organization grows and expands, its network requirements will change, and the network infrastructure may need to be upgraded to support the increased traffic and new applications.

  The network architect considers the current and future business requirements, assesses the current network capabilities, and identifies any bottlenecks or limitations that might affect the network's ability to accommodate business growth and expansion.

- **Changes in technology**: With advancements in technology, there may be new or improved products and services available that can enhance the functionality, performance, and security of a network infrastructure.

  As technologies become available, the network architect will evaluate whether they can be used to improve the network's performance, security, or scalability, as well as considering how they may impact the current network infrastructure.

  For example, new hardware components or software solutions may significantly improve network performance or provide better security. There may also be new networking protocols or standards that can improve network scalability and interoperability.

  The landscape of technologies changes rapidly as products and solutions evolve. But with new entries into the market, a network architect must be able to navigate, formalize, and assess the impact on the current network infrastructure and determine whether upgrades are necessary to maintain the network's functionality and meet the changing needs of the business.

- **Security threats**: As new technologies are introduced into the marketplace and new IT trends take shape, the threat landscape also evolves. New security threats are created that can affect a network infrastructure.

  For example, with the rise of cloud computing, virtualization, and the **Internet of Things (IoT)**, attackers have more ways to access sensitive information and compromise networks. In addition, new types of malware and hacking techniques are continually being developed, and these can pose a threat to network infrastructure.

  To address these security threats, a network architect must continually assess the security posture of the network infrastructure and implement security upgrades as necessary. This can include implementing (or reconfiguring) firewalls, intrusion detection and prevention systems, encryption, and other security technologies, and staying up to date with the latest security best practices and guidelines.

  Additionally, the network architect must collaborate with other stakeholders, such as security teams and compliance officers, to ensure that security is integrated into the design and implementation of the network infrastructure, if possible, to better protect against new threats.

- **Compliance requirements**: As hardware and software are upgraded, along with addressing security threats, meeting compliance regulations/requirements is equally important when upgrading the network infrastructure. Meeting these requirements starts with a thorough understanding of the regulations and standards that apply to the organization. This might include data privacy and security regulations such as the **General Data Protection Regulation (GDPR), Health Insurance Portability and Accountability Act (HIPPA), Payment Card Industry Data Security Standard (PCI DSS)**, and others.

  When upgrading the network infrastructure, the network architect must ensure that the new infrastructure meets all relevant compliance regulations. This may involve reviewing the regulations, conducting a risk assessment, implementing security controls, and testing the new infrastructure to verify that it complies with the regulations. The network architect should also keep up to date with changes to the regulations and ensure that the infrastructure continues to meet the regulations over time. Finally, as the industry regulations change, the network architect will evaluate whether the network needs to be upgraded to meet the new requirements.

  It may also be necessary to engage with external auditors or security consultants to perform independent assessments and verify that the upgrade plan meets all necessary compliance requirements. This can help to provide additional assurance, certify, and validate with confidence in the security of the network infrastructure and minimize the risk of non-compliance or data breaches.

- **Performance issues**: As an organization grows and expands, the amount of data being transmitted across the network can increase dramatically, and the network infrastructure must be able to keep up with this increased demand. If the network is experiencing performance issues, such as slow speeds, high latency, and frequent downtime, an upgrade is needed to address these issues.

  To address performance issues, a network architect must carefully evaluate the current infrastructure, identify bottlenecks and areas for improvement, and plan and execute the upgrade in a way that addresses the underlying performance issues. This may involve upgrading hardware components, fine-tuning software configurations, or implementing new technologies and solutions that are designed to improve network performance.

  By upgrading the network infrastructure, organizations can improve the reliability and stability of their network to meet the evolving needs of the business while providing a fast, reliable, and secure experience to meet the demands of their users and customers.

- **Age of equipment**: The age of the network equipment can play a factor in the upgrade process of the network infrastructure. As network equipment ages, it may become obsolete and no longer capable of supporting the needs of the network, such as reliability, the latest technologies (hardware and software), and performance, which can limit the ability to take advantage of new features and capabilities. In addition, regulatory compliance requirements may dictate that certain equipment be updated or replaced.

  Additionally, older equipment may no longer receive security updates, which can make it vulnerable to attacks, leaving the organization exposed to additional threats and possible loss of reputation. It may also become more expensive to repair and maintain, leading to higher operational costs over time.

Upgrading the network infrastructure to more recent and advanced equipment can help ensure that the network can meet the needs of the organization and provide adequate performance, security, and compliance.

- **Network usage**: As network usage increases, the existing network infrastructure may become overwhelmed, leading to bottlenecks, slowdowns, and other performance issues. If a network infrastructure is not designed to handle current and future network usage, it may need to be upgraded to meet the demands of the users and the business.

  Upgrading the network infrastructure can involve adding more bandwidth, upgrading switches and routers, and adding new hardware and software to meet the needs of the network. If the network usage has increased dramatically, the network architect will assess whether the existing infrastructure can support the increased traffic or whether an upgrade is necessary.

It's worth noting that a network upgrade is not always necessary, but regular assessments and evaluations are important to ensure that the network infrastructure is meeting the organization's current and future needs. The network architect will need to balance the cost of any upgrade, any impact on the existing network, and any potential risks and constraints with the potential benefits and make a decision accordingly.

It's important for the network architect to communicate the upgrade plan to all stakeholders, including the IT team and business users, to ensure that everyone understands the changes and is prepared for any disruptions that might occur during the upgrade process.

In addition, communicating the upgrade plan helps to build trust and confidence in the network architect and the upgrade process. This can be particularly important in cases where the upgrade involves significant changes to the network infrastructure and may require the organization to change how it operates.

Maintenance

A network architect is responsible for maintaining and performing maintenance on a network infrastructure to ensure that it continues to function properly and meet the organization's needs. Here are a few ways a network architect can do that:

- **Developing a maintenance plan**: A maintenance plan is important because it provides a structured approach for ensuring (taking into account the organization's critical systems and data) the stability, reliability, and availability of the network. The maintenance plan should outline the tasks that need to be performed regularly, such as software updates, hardware replacement, and performance monitoring. The plan should also include guidelines for dealing with potential issues, such as security threats or system failures.

By having a comprehensive maintenance plan in place, network architects (and teams) can proactively address issues and prevent problems from becoming major disruptions to network operations.

Optimizing network performance, improving system efficiency, and extending the lifespan of network equipment should all be a part of the maintenance plan. It also provides a clear understanding of the resources required for maintenance and helps ensure that maintenance tasks are completed in a timely and cost-effective manner.

It can aid **business intelligence** (**BI**) tools to predict when a major maintenance activity is likely to occur, what the expected budget should be, and how much of an impact it may have on the organization.

A well-designed maintenance plan should consider any regulatory or compliance requirements that need to be met. Regular monitoring and updates to the maintenance plan can help organizations stay ahead of potential issues and minimize disruptions to their IT systems and services.

- **Monitoring the network**: Regular monitoring of the network architecture allows the IT team to keep track of the performance and availability of the network, its usage (e.g., peak versus off-peak), traffic density, and resource utilization, and to proactively address any potential issues before they become major problems. Monitoring the network is defined as part of an organization's maintenance plan.

  By monitoring the network architecture, the IT team can identify trends and patterns in network usage and performance and can use this information to make informed decisions about network upgrades, capacity planning, and security measures. Regular monitoring of the network architecture also helps to ensure that the network infrastructure is operating optimally and is able to meet the needs of the organization.

  Additionally, the network architect will use this opportunity to evaluate the current networking monitoring tools used and make recommendations, if any, for the support of additional tools (or deprecation of others) based on trends identified by the IT teams monitoring the network.

- **Performing regular maintenance**: Regular maintenance helps to ensure that the network infrastructure remains stable and performs at optimal levels, reducing the likelihood of downtime and data loss. It allows the IT team to detect and fix problems before they become critical. This can prevent significant network outages and minimize the impact of network downtime.

  Another benefit includes security threat management. Maintenance ensures security software and devices are up to date and functioning properly. This helps protect against the latest security threats and vulnerabilities, which is essential for maintaining the security and confidentiality of sensitive information.

  As technology evolves, regular maintenance ensures that the network infrastructure remains up to date and compatible with the latest devices and technologies. This ensures that the organization is using the most current and practical solutions, which can help improve overall efficiency and effectiveness.

Depending on the industry, regular maintenance may be required by industry regulations or standards, such as the PCI DSS for organizations that process credit card transactions or the HIPPA for organizations maintaining patient health records, or even the GDPR for data collection and privacy in the EU.

Regular maintenance can help reduce the cost of repairs and/or replacements by identifying and resolving issues before they become significant problems. Additionally, by optimizing the performance of the network, regular maintenance can help reduce energy costs and improve resource utilization.

- **Managing capacity**: As an organization expands or curtails, shifts its strategy, and invokes newer technologies while deprecating others, network capacity must be managed in a way that ensures that the network can support the growing demands of the organization and its applications and services. As organization grows and its use of technology increases, the network infrastructure may become congested, leading to performance issues, slowdowns, and even outages.

By monitoring network capacity and proactively managing it, a network architect can help prevent these issues and ensure that the network infrastructure is able to support the organization's needs. This can include tasks such as adding additional bandwidth, upgrading hardware, and reconfiguring network traffic to ensure that critical applications and services have the resources they need to perform optimally.

For example, if network bandwidth saturation is above 80% for an extended period of time, then it's an indication to add additional fiber to handle the load. If the switching fabric has many dropped packets or queuing buffers are constantly high, this may be an indication that the switching needs more backplane throughput and an upgrade is required.

Ensuring that the network infrastructure has enough capacity to handle the current and future needs of the organization is critical for maintaining good performance and preventing issues such as bottlenecks or slowdowns.

- **Managing security**: As the network infrastructure evolves, so do the risks. Network security threats are constantly evolving, so it's important to stay up to date on the latest vulnerabilities and potential threats. This helps to prevent unauthorized access, data breaches, and other security incidents that could compromise the confidentiality, integrity, and availability of the network and its data (assets).

In addition, regulatory requirements may mandate that certain security measures be in place and that regular security audits are conducted. Keeping the network secure and compliant with these regulations helps to avoid penalties and other legal consequences. If security is not well maintained, security breaches can have serious consequences for an organization, including financial losses, loss of reputation, and even legal liabilities. Also important is the trust of users and customers, who expect that their personal and confidential information will be protected when they use the network.

Regularly managing security as part of the network architecture infrastructure maintenance helps to ensure these expectations are met.

- **Disaster recovery and business continuity**: Disaster recovery ensures that the network infrastructure is resistant to catastrophic events because it helps ensure the availability of critical network resources in the event of a disaster, such as a natural disaster, cyber-attack, power outage, or hardware failure. The goal of disaster recovery is to minimize the impact of a disaster on the network and its users and to restore network operations as quickly as possible.

  To achieve this goal, it is important to have a well-designed and tested disaster recovery plan in place. This plan should include procedures for backing up critical data, restoring network operations, and ensuring that all network components are functioning properly, along with developing and documenting procedures for quickly restoring the network infrastructure and services to full functionality in the event of a disruption. Regular maintenance of the network infrastructure should also include monitoring of disaster recovery procedures and regular testing of the disaster recovery plan to ensure that it remains effective and relevant.

  By planning and testing for disaster recovery, a network architect can help ensure that their organizations are prepared to quickly resume normal operations in the event of an interruption to the network. This helps to minimize downtime, reduce the risk of data loss, and minimize the impact on the organization's reputation and bottom line. Additionally, having a solid disaster recovery plan can help organizations comply with various regulations, such as those related to data privacy and security.

- **Communication**: Communicating the regular maintenance of a network architecture infrastructure is typically accomplished through a combination of written and verbal communication. Written communication can include things such as maintenance schedules, status reports, and progress updates that are shared with stakeholders and other relevant parties. Verbal communication can include meetings, conference calls, and different types of interactions that allow for real-time updates and discussions about the status of the maintenance work.

  Regular communication about the maintenance activities provides transparency to stakeholders. It ensures that everyone is informed about what is being done to maintain the network infrastructure and helps avoid any confusion or misunderstandings.

  It is important to communicate the regular maintenance of a network architecture infrastructure to ensure that stakeholders and other relevant parties are aware of any disruptions that may occur during the maintenance process, as well as to provide them with information about when the maintenance work is expected to be completed and what impact it may have on the network's performance and availability.

  This type of communication helps build trust and confidence in the network architecture, and can also help identify and resolve any issues that may arise during the maintenance process.

Overall, a network architect will play a key role in maintaining and performing maintenance on a network infrastructure, overseeing all aspects of it, from the development of a maintenance plan to effectively communicating maintenance activities and ensuring that the network continues to function correctly and meet the organization's needs.

Next, we'll dive into making recommendations in order to move the network to an advanced level and reduce operating costs.

Making recommendations to improve the network infrastructure and reduce operational costs

Network infrastructures are not static entities. It changes on a daily basis. As a network architect, you're tasked with making sure that the infrastructure itself continues to meet the needs and demands of all your stakeholders (end users, customers/clients, and business units). This means finding ways to improve on what you've already implemented and, based on those desired improvements, making recommendations.

In order to make recommendations and improvements, the network architect must first assess the current network infrastructure landscape. This assessment should include identifying the network's strengths and weaknesses, analyzing its performance, identifying any security issues, and identifying areas for improvement.

The following figure shows examples of some items that came up as a result of assessing the network infrastructure and speaking to the network team, stakeholders, and end users:

Stakeholder	Issues Identified	Assessment
IT Infrastructure Manager	• Switchport capacity is about 16% available in key data centers • Switchports are oversubscribed	• Switching environment does not have capacity to support growth • Switching has reached EoL. 80% of hardware requires replacement • Doesn't support newer technology to overcome challenges
Operation lead	• Network infrastructure running at 78% - 82% for 75% of the quarter • High latency weekly	• Monitoring has become labor intensive • Infrastructure not able to support changes to revenue generating streams • Increase in end users, development BUs has direct correlation to latency concerns
App Business Lead	• Apps require a more agile deployment model	• 60% of environment is virtualized. Other are bare metal or proprietary hardware • Legacy hardware not supported by vendor • Application source code is unknown on these servers
Security Operation Center Engineer	• Increase in security patching • Appliance(s) have been EoL for 2 years	• Increase in frequency of alerts over the last three months • Security patching is not sustainable • Current security infrastructure is unable to scale
Chief Technology Officer	• Need a new strategy for East-West traffic to minimize disruption • Need to modernize infrastructure	• Current network infrastructure cannot support the needs of the business • Issues are arising from inflexibility of the current design • Multiple points of failure have been identified • Higher-density switching, higher bandwidth throughput is required

Figure 2.1 – Example of network assessment

From there, conduct a thorough analysis of the current network architecture and its capabilities, considering the organization's goals, objectives, and requirements. Based on this analysis (with the aid of the monitoring and performance tools mentioned in the previous section), the network architect can make recommendations on improving the network infrastructure to meet the organization's needs and support future growth.

The following is an example of what was discovered after conducting an analysis of the current infrastructure:

Analysis: Network Infrastructure

In reviewing the network infrastructure and assessing the current state of its capabilities, the following was discovered:

- Network hardware
    - Around 80% of the switching in organization-owned data center are end-of-life or reaching end-of-life
        - 436 out of 545 network devices
- Power
    - 22.45% increase in power consumption due to hardware inefficiencies
- Heating, Ventilation, & Air Conditioning (HVAC)
    - 28.7% increase in year-over-year (YoY) to maintain data centers
- Servers
    - Only 60% virtualized. Other are mixed legacy hardware or propriety
        - Of those virtualized, 45% are at capacity limits
- Security
    - Appliances have reached end-of-life (EoL)
    - Patching updates will be deprecated in 18 months by vendor

Figure 2.2 – Example of network analysis

Note

The network architect provides guidance and direction to help organizations improve their network infrastructure and make recommendations that align with the organization's business goals and objectives.

Some steps in making recommendations to improve the network infrastructure involve the following:

- Cost-benefit analysis
- Researching new technologies and solutions
- Developing a roadmap

Let's look at them in detail.

Cost-benefit analysis

This involves analyzing the costs of implementing different upgrades and comparing them with the benefits that the upgrades would provide. This helps to identify the most effective upgrades that would provide the greatest value for the organization.

Some items to consider when performing the **cost-benefit analysis (CBA)** are as follows:

- The current operating cost established in the environment
- Estimating the **capital expenditure (CAPEX)** as well as the **operational expenditure (OPEX)** of instantiating new hardware, software, and services
- How to spread the financial impact over the estimated lifespan of the network upgrades
- The cost difference (delta) between the current environment and the proposed one
- Estimated **return on investment (ROI)**
- Costs due to any potential risks and uncertainties

> **Note**
>
> Intangible costs should be included in the CBA. These are the costs that are difficult to measure in monetary terms but can have a significant impact on an organization's business operations, productivity, and revenue.
>
> Examples of intangible costs include lost productivity due to system downtime, lost business opportunities due to inefficient systems, or the cost of lost customer confidence due to data breaches or security incidents.

Researching new technologies and solutions

From the analysis, assessment, and data collected on the current network infrastructure and having an idea of the current goals, a network architect should begin the research process. This research should include identifying potential hardware and software solutions, evaluating their performance and capabilities, and determining their cost-effectiveness, all of which are inputs for the CBA.

A network architect must be up to date with the latest technologies and solutions available. This could involve reading industry publications, attending conferences and trade shows, and consulting with vendors, colleagues, and industry experts.

> **Note**
>
> At the time of writing, several industry trade shows are very important from my perspective. They are Cisco Live, VMWare Explore, Google Next, Dell Tech World, HPE Discover, CES Conference, AWS re:Invent, KubeCon, OpenInfra Summit, and Red Hat Summit.

By researching and testing new technologies, the network architect can identify solutions that can improve the network infrastructure, performance, reliability, and security.

Some questions a network architect should consider are as follows:

- Does the hardware/software meet and exceed the expectations of the stakeholders?
- Can the current infrastructure support this upgrade/add-on/complementary component?
- Is a redesign required? If so, how much of a redesign?
- Is the capability worth implementing now? Or can it be held off?
- How much of the current budget will be required to undertake the new technology?
- Does the organization have the skill set required to use this technology or implement it? Will training be required? How much time is required to upskill?

The question list could be endless, but these are some of the critical ones to take into consideration.

After researching the available options, the network architect must evaluate and compare them based on the defined requirements and intended goals. This may involve contacting the vendors and solutions providers via a **request for proposal** (**RFP**).

Vendors and solutions providers who receive the RFP will respond by submitting proposals that outline how they would meet the organization's requirements. The proposals will typically include a detailed description of the vendor's proposed solution, including its technical specifications and capabilities, and a cost estimate.

> **Note**
> The RFP may include a PoC environment established to test features before finalizing the short list of vendors.

The organization will evaluate the proposals received and determine which vendor best suits their requirements. The evaluation may consider factors such as the vendor's technical capabilities, experience, pricing, customer support, and overall fit with the organization's needs. All of these are necessary when developing a roadmap strategy for the organization. The network architect helps ensure that the vendor's proposed solution meets the technical requirements and aligns with the organization's IT strategy and long-term goals.

Developing a roadmap

A roadmap is just as important as a CBA and researching new technologies. It is a plan for the upgrades to be implemented over time. It helps to prioritize the upgrades and ensures that they are implemented systematically and efficiently. The roadmap will outline the specific steps and activities required to achieve the desired state of the network infrastructure.

The roadmap for network infrastructure upgrades, whether it's part of ongoing maintenance activities or a new IT project, could include several phases. These phases are as follows:

- Assessment phase
- Planning phase
- Procuring phase
- Implementation phase
- Testing and validation phase
- Deployment phase
- Maintenance and monitoring phase

Let's briefly discuss each.

Assessment phase

In this phase, the network architect will evaluate the current state of the network infrastructure and identify any gaps or areas for improvement. This may include a review of network performance, security, compliance, capacity, strengths, weaknesses, opportunities for improvement, and potential risks. As I said before, this is part of routine monitoring operations. And that data is relevant to the assessment phase for developing the roadmap.

The information gathered during the assessment phase will provide the network architect with the necessary data to develop a roadmap that is tailored to the specific needs of the organization. Without a comprehensive assessment, it is difficult to develop a roadmap that is both effective and realistic.

Planning phase

The planning phase of developing a roadmap involves determining the goals and objectives for an organization's technology strategy and using the assessment phase results to define the projects, initiatives, and investments required to achieve those goals.

During this phase, the network architect will work closely with other stakeholders, such as business leaders, IT staff, and vendors, to ensure the plan aligns with the organization's overall goals and objectives.

The plan will include, but not be limited to, the following:

- Scope
- Budget
- Cost (not the same as budget)
- Resource allocation
- Personnel

- Solution design
- Timeline required

Procurement phase

The procurement phase is an important part of developing a roadmap for a network infrastructure project because it involves identifying and selecting the specific technologies, products, and vendors that will be used to implement the project. This phase involves developing a detailed list of requirements and specifications for the equipment and software needed to meet the project's goals and then evaluating different vendors and solutions to determine the best fit. This phase is quite similar to *Researching new technologies and solutions* mentioned previously; however, it's more refined on the specifics of what the organization is looking for with intended use.

The network architect will work with the project team to develop a more comprehensive RFP or **request for quotation** (**RFQ**) document that outlines the project requirements, including the specific solution (hardware and software) needed. The RFP/RFQ will then be distributed to the short list of potential vendors, who will respond with proposals outlining how they can meet the project's needs. A pilot will be conducted to finalize the selection of the vendor(s) to procure the hardware/software/ services that meets or exceeds the expectations of the design required.

> **Note**
> A pilot is similar to a PoC; however, a pilot is larger in scale and involves having a subset of users to test the system's overall functionality.

The procurement phase is critical to the project's success because it ensures that the selected vendors and solutions are the right fit for the project's needs and goals. Making the wrong choices at this stage can lead to increased costs, delays, and compatibility issues.

Implementation phase

The implementation phase is when the plan is put into action. During this phase, the network architect oversees the installation and configuration of the new equipment, software, and processes identified and selected during the planning and procurement phases.

This phase consists of the following:

- **Change control management**: Change control helps to manage and control changes to the network infrastructure. All procedures for assessing the impact of changes and identifying potential risks should be properly documented and communicated to relevant stakeholders. The *go* or *no-go* decision is made on continuing with the implementation.
- **Preparing the environment**: This includes tasks such as installing cabling and other infrastructure to support the new network components. Network components such as routers, switches, and other devices are installed and powered on. This is commonly referred to as the *burn-in* period.

- **Configuring hardware and software**: This involves installing and configuring the hardware and software that was selected during the planning and procurement phases.

Throughout the implementation phase, the network architect works closely with the rest of the project team to ensure that the rollout is proceeding according to plan, and to make any necessary adjustments. The network architect and their team may also be responsible for training staff on the new equipment and processes to ensure they can be used effectively.

Testing and validation phase

The testing and validation phase typically involves verifying that the new infrastructure is operating correctly and meets the performance, security, and other requirements specified in the planning phase aspect of the solution design roadmap. This may involve testing individual components of the infrastructure and testing the system as a whole to ensure that it is integrated and working as expected.

It's important to have a testing plan that outlines the tests to be performed, the criteria for success, and the steps to be taken if any issues are identified. This test plan is commonly called a UATP. The testing plan should be developed during the planning phase of the IT roadmap, and it should be reviewed and updated throughout the implementation phase.

The validation phase is conducted simultaneously with the testing phase. Those involved are typically key stakeholders designated to sign off on the UATP. These stakeholders may include the network architect, IT project leads, IT directors, third-party auditors, consultants whose job is to make sure the UATP is followed accordingly, and other personnel.

Once the testing is complete, the results should be reviewed to ensure that the new infrastructure is ready for production use. If any issues are identified, they should be addressed and retested as necessary. Once the testing is successful and any issues are resolved, the new infrastructure is ready for deployment.

Deployment phase

After the new network infrastructure has been tested and validated, any issues have been resolved, and the required sign-off is completed, it can be deployed to the production environment. Again, this typically involves a phased rollout to minimize disruption to the organization.

During the deployment phase, a second *burn-in* period is conducted to ensure all systems (hardware and software) are operating within the parameters outlined in the solution design (as well as outlined in the documentation provided by the vendors), but more important is the end user's experience.

Some deployment phases can last about two to three weeks before ownership is handed over to the operations team. From then on, the operations teams manage, monitor, and maintain the network infrastructure.

It is important to approach this phase with a high degree of care and attention to detail to ensure that everything goes as smoothly as possible. Any missteps during this phase can have significant consequences, including delays, downtime, and other disruptions that can impact business operations.

Maintenance and monitoring phase

The maintenance and monitoring phase is important because it ensures that the network infrastructure continues to function as intended and that any issues or potential problems are identified and resolved promptly. This phase concludes the development of a roadmap instituted by the network architect.

The deployment phase and the maintenance and monitoring phase overlap one another; as the deployment phase attenuates, the maintenance and monitoring phase ramps up. This phase will become *business-as-usual activities* for the operations teams of an organization when the migration monitoring timeframe is completed.

This phase typically includes ongoing activities such as regular software updates, performance monitoring, and system backups, as well as periodic assessments to ensure that the infrastructure remains aligned with the organization's goals and objectives.

By implementing a proactive maintenance and monitoring strategy, a network architect can help ensure that the network infrastructure continues to meet the needs of the organization and can help prevent downtime and other disruptions that can negatively impact the end user experience.

This phase is critical because it provides an opportunity to identify areas for improvement, such as the need for additional capacity or new technologies that can help improve network performance and reliability. By regularly monitoring the network infrastructure and analyzing performance data, a network architect can develop actionable insight (future roadmaps) that can inform future upgrades or enhancements to the network.

Roadmapping a network infrastructure project can be, in most cases, an arduous task. Therefore, having a detailed roadmap of your project will benefit everyone involved.

Let's discuss the documentation of the network process next.

Documenting the network process for future use

Documentation of the network is extremely important to an organization's IT infrastructure, the network process, and any other activities that are going on. It provides the paper trail and a history of events that have occurred – whether it be a new implementation of next-generation switching, moving from a bare-metal environment to a virtual one, applying the DevOps process to life cycle management, or changing to a different routing protocol. It's a single source of truth of the organization's infrastructure.

Network documentation allows team members to share knowledge and communicate effectively about a project or adjustments to the current design. In addition, it enables team members to understand how the network is structured, its architecture, and its components, which is crucial for effective troubleshooting, maintenance, and upgrading.

An example would be: *You discovered that ISIS was being used on a remote network. The entire infrastructure was migrated from RIP to OSPF about 10 years ago; however, not this one. Several architects who joined before you are no longer there, and you're curious as to why it was left. Aside from trying to reach out to those who might know why it was done, the best idea is to go through the archive documents related to the infrastructure and some of its implementations. After some research, the previous architects were experimenting with the benefits of ISIS over OSPF and were looking to evolve it into a service provider offering...*

Documentation helps to reduce risk by identifying potential issues, risks, and dependencies in advance, allowing the team to plan and prepare accordingly. This reduces the chances of unexpected network outages or failures, which could lead to downtime, data loss, or security breaches. It is essential for regulatory compliance, auditing, and reporting purposes. Many organizations are required to comply with industry-specific regulations or standards, such as HIPAA or PCI DSS, which mandate that they have adequate documentation of their network infrastructure and security controls.

> **Note**
> Documentation comes in various formats such as PDFs, Word documents, PPT, Excel spreadsheets, Visio, Lucidchart, Corel Paint, and more. What's important to recognize is that these documents should be held with strict confidentiality as they may contain information that, if leaked, could cause damage to the organization, and must be stored in a repository for only those individuals who require access to them.

As a network architect, reviewing an organization's network documents is essential for several reasons, such as the following:

- Making sure the documents are consistent with what is currently in production
- The current documents accurately describe the processes you and your team developed
- Routinely making updates to reflect changes that were made to network
- Brainstorming new ways to enhance the current design
- Finding ways of improving the network without incurring major downtime in funding
- Used as training and knowledge transfer material to bring new members up to speed
- Fostering a sense of innovation in the organization

An organization's network documents are a reference point for future changes, upgrades, or maintenance. By having a clear understanding of the existing network infrastructure and how it was implemented, it is easier to make informed decisions about future endeavors.

Summary

In this chapter, we explored two key aspects or functions of a network architect in an organization. We focused on the network architect's role in planning, designing, installing, and upgrading network projects, along with a phased approach for an IT roadmap, what each phase comprises, and how the network architect plays a key role in each.

This chapter is very important for success as a network architect. If you recall, the network architect may also be part of a larger technical architecture team, which is responsible for the overall technical direction of the organization.

In the next chapter, we'll continue the topic of a network architect in an organization.

3

Roadmap to Becoming a Network Architect

The road to becoming a network architect can be exciting and rewarding. Simultaneously, it can be challenging. It all depends on your level of enthusiasm, how much passion you have for the role and IT, as well as your level of commitment to achieving this goal.

Ultimately, you have to ask yourself these questions:

"Is this the career path I want to take? If so, what do I need to achieve this goal?"

"Is this worth my time and effort?"

"Where am I now?... I want more..."

"What can help me propel my IT career?"

These are some of the questions I asked myself several years ago in my pursuit of becoming a network architect. In your mind, you must ask these same questions, as well as go into depth about the outcome. It's not an easy task. It may take you several days, weeks, or years to make a decision. There are other factors/drivers worth considering as you contemplate pursuing a role as a network architect, such as family, lifestyle, current position, economics, job market, and more, all of which are beyond the scope of this book.

In this chapter, we'll look into the roadmap of a network architect by exploring the following topics:

- Roles and responsibilities – entry level
- Roles and responsibilities – mid level
- Roles and responsibilities – senior level
- The career path to becoming a network architect

Let's get started!

Roles and responsibilities – entry level

An entry-level position in IT typically refers to a job that requires little to no professional work experience in the field. It is designed to give those who graduated with a degree in IT or individuals with basic skills the opportunity to gain experience and begin a career in IT.

Some common entry-level network IT positions on the current job market radar are as follows:

- **Network support technician**: This role involves providing technical support for computer networks, including troubleshooting connectivity problems and configuration issues, and maintaining network hardware and software
- **Network technician**: This job involves setting up and maintaining computer networks, including hardware and software
- **Network operations center (NOC) technician**: This position involves monitoring and maintaining network systems and responding to issues as they arise

Let's consider each and look into their roles and responsibilities.

Network support technician

A network support technician provides technical support for computer networks, including troubleshooting issues and maintaining network hardware and software. Their main responsibility is to ensure that the network is running efficiently and effectively. They may work in a variety of industries, including healthcare, finance, and education.

Although their main responsibility is ensuring network efficacy, the tasks that are assigned to them are determined by senior personnel such as a network manager or a network architect.

> **Note**
> A network support technician may, at times, be referred to as a network help desk technician.

In this role, a basic understanding of networks is needed. They must know the answers to the following questions:

- What is CAT5, CAT5e, CAT6, CAT7, and CAT8 cabling? What's the difference between them, as well as their limitations and usage?
- When should you use fiber single mode versus multimode?
- What is a switch? What is a router?
- What is LAN versus MAN versus WAN?

All of this, and more, can be learned in an entry-level book, but also with hands-on experience in this role.

Some of the specific job duties of a network support technician are as follows:

- **Installing and configuring network hardware and software**: This involves setting up routers, switches, firewalls, and other network equipment, as well as installing and performing basic configuration of network operating systems and applications

- **Troubleshooting network connectivity issues**: This involves identifying the root cause of the problem, opening/closing support tickets, and implementing solutions from network technicians

- **Monitoring network performance**: This involves regularly monitoring network performance metrics to identify areas for improvement and ensure that the network is running efficiently

- **Maintaining network security and implementing security protocols**: This is responsible for implementing and maintaining network security protocols to protect against cyber threats

- **Performing regular network backups**: This involves creating backup copies of network data and ensuring that disaster recovery procedures are in place in case of a network outage or other disaster

- **Providing technical support to end users for network-related issues**: Here, support is provided to end users for network-related issues, including connectivity problems and configuration issues

- **Collaborating with network administrators and engineers**: Work closely with network administrators and engineers to identify and resolve complex network issues

These duties shouldn't be taken too lightly as continued practice will create confidence in not only yourself but also confidence in your manager to trust you with unsupervised tasks and greater responsibility.

Regarding these duties, a network support technician needs to have strong problem-solving skills, be able to pay attention to detail, and have or begin to develop communication skills. They should also have or begin to develop a deep understanding of network protocols, hardware, and software, as well as the ability to work in a fast-paced environment. More importantly, you must begin preparing for industry-level certifications such as CompTIA Network+ or Cisco CCNA. We'll cover certifications in more detail in *Chapter 10*.

In general, someone should spend at least a year or two as a network support technician before considering a career advancement. This will give them enough time to develop a strong foundation of technical skills and gain experience troubleshooting network issues. However, if they are ready to take on more responsibility and have a clear career goal in mind, they may be able to advance their career sooner. Ultimately, the decision to advance their career is a personal one and should be based on individual goals and circumstances.

> **Note**
> 1 or 2 years spent as a network support technician is an industry average. This time will vary based on several factors, such as career goals, skills, experience, and certifications.

Network technician

A network technician should have a good understanding of computer networking concepts, protocols, and hardware. They should be familiar with various network operating systems, such as Windows Server, Linux, and Unix, and have experience working with network troubleshooting tools and techniques. They are considered a level above a network support technician. They should have at least 1 to 3 years of basic IT and compute experience working with network infrastructure and supporting end users.

While the network support technician performs basic activities, a network technician is more advanced and should be familiar with and be able to answer the following questions:

- What is the OSI model? How does it relate to a network fabric?
- How does it differ from the TCP/IP model or stack?
- What is the administrative distance of a routing protocol?
- What are the pros and cons of link state versus distance vector protocols?
- What are the steps in a packet walk?

A network technician should know about the following:

- Networking concepts such as the OSI model, TCP/IP, DNS, DHCP, and routing protocols
- Network hardware, such as routers, switches, firewalls, wireless, and network facilities (that is, racks, cabling termination boxes, and more)
- Compute and network operating systems, such as Windows Server, Linux, and Unix
- Network troubleshooting tools, such as PING, Tracert, and Wireshark
- Network security concepts, such as firewall rules and tags, VPNs, and access control lists
- Basic scripting and programming skills in programs such as Python and Ansible
- Familiarity with cloud computing technologies and virtualization

Similar to a network support technician, the network technician is hands-on and is the *eyes and ears* of a network manager and/or network architect. They can provide valuable insight into what's happening on the network, what's occurring with the users, and what's taking place on the data center's floor.

> **Note**
> The responsibility of a network architect is to mentor junior talent, such as network technicians and support technicians. Such talents are eager to learn and put in the effort to make a network architect's job a bit easier.

Some of the key core responsibilities of a network technician are as follows:

- **Install and configure network hardware**: They are responsible for installing and configuring network hardware, such as routers, switches, firewalls, and other network devices such as wireless access points and other networking peripherals.

- **Monitor network performance**: They are responsible for monitoring network performance, adjusting threshold levels, and identifying issues that may affect network performance using various network monitoring tools to track bandwidth usage, network traffic, and other metrics.

- **Troubleshoot network issues**: When issues arise, network technicians must identify the source of the problem and troubleshoot the issue (network triage). They must be able to use various network troubleshooting tools to identify the cause of the issue and recommend solutions to a network manager or have a support technician investigate.

- **Maintain network security**: They are responsible for maintaining network security, ensuring that the network is protected against external and internal threats. They configure firewalls, VPNs, and other security measures to protect the network based on approved organizational configurations vetted by the security team.

- **Provide end user support**: They must provide deeper end user support, helping employees troubleshoot network-related issues, configuring devices to connect to the network, and educating users on network best practices.

- **Perform routine maintenance**: They are responsible for performing routine maintenance tasks, such as upgrading firmware, replacing hardware, and installing patches.

- **Document network configurations and procedures**: Network technicians should document network configurations and procedures, ensuring that this information is up to date and easily accessible to other IT staff.

In general, a network technician should have a good understanding of the network topology, protocols, and network operating systems, and should be familiar with network troubleshooting tools and techniques. They work closely with network administrators to ensure that network systems are reliable, secure, and functioning optimally. In doing so, the network technician provides valuable information that can be used by a network architect to make informed (senior) decisions on how the network should be designed, upgraded, advanced, and secured to support future users' needs and requirements.

It's recommended for a network technician to spend 2 to 5 years in their role before they consider advancing to a higher-level position, such as a network administrator or network engineer. However, this timeline is not set in stone, and some network technicians may be able to advance more quickly if they demonstrate strong technical skills, take on additional responsibilities, and pursue relevant certifications and education.

Here are some certifications worth pursuing for a network technician:

- CompTIA A+, Security+, Network+, and Linux+
- **Cisco Certified Entry Networking Technician (CCENT)**
- **Cisco Certified Network Associate (CCNA)**
- **Microsoft Certified Solutions Associate (MCSA)**

In addition to technical skills, a network technician should also have good communication skills and should be able to work well in a team environment. They should be able to explain technical concepts to non-technical users and be able to document network configurations and procedures effectively.

NOC technician

A NOC technician, also known as a NOC engineer or network operations technician, is responsible for monitoring and maintaining the operational efficiency and stability of the infrastructure network. Their role is to ensure *continuous availability* and *performance* of the network systems and address any network-related issues. These technicians typically report to a NOC manager, who oversees all the daily operations within the operation center environment.

NOC technicians should have a similar tool set and skills as network technicians. However, their focus is on the overall health of the network infrastructure and utilizing network monitoring hardware and software tools. Some of their key responsibilities are as follows:

- **Network monitoring**: NOC technicians continuously monitor the network infrastructure, including routers, switches, servers, firewalls, and other network devices. They use network monitoring tools to track network health, performance, and security, and promptly identify any anomalies or issues that occur because of inconsistencies outside of baseline parameters.

- **Incident management**: They handle network incidents and outages reported or detected through network monitoring tools. NOC technicians respond to incidents (trouble tickets), triage them based on severity, and initiate troubleshooting and resolution processes to restore network services.

- **Troubleshooting and resolution**: NOC technicians perform troubleshooting procedures to diagnose network issues and work toward resolving them. They follow established procedures, document their actions, and coordinate with other teams or vendors if needed to address complex issues.

- **Security monitoring**: Though mainly a **security operation center** (**SOC**) duty, NOC technicians monitor network security systems and alerts, such as **intrusion detection systems** (**IDSs**) or firewalls, to detect and respond to potential security threats. NOC technicians may take appropriate actions or escalate security incidents to the relevant teams for further investigation and mitigation.

- **Network configuration and maintenance**: They assist in configuring network devices and implementing network changes as per established procedures and from the network architect. This may involve adding or modifying network devices, updating firmware or software, and ensuring proper network configurations are in place.

- **Network documentation**: NOC technicians maintain accurate and up-to-date documentation of network configurations, procedures, and troubleshooting guides. This documentation helps in troubleshooting, knowledge sharing, and ensuring consistency in network operations. Here are some examples of such documents:

  - As-built diagrams (that is, networks, floor plans, HVAC, electrical)
  - **Method of procedure** (**MoP**) documents
  - **Standards and protocols** (**S&P**) documents
  - **Best practice** (**BP**) documents

- **Network performance optimization**: They work to optimize network performance and ensure efficient utilization of network resources. This may involve analyzing network traffic patterns, identifying bottlenecks, and recommending improvements to enhance network performance.

- **Incident reporting and communication**: NOC technicians prepare incident reports, documenting the details of network incidents, their impact, and the actions taken for resolution. They also communicate with stakeholders, such as network administrators/engineers, architects, or end users, to provide updates on network incidents and their resolution status.

- **Proactive maintenance and upgrades**: They assist in performing routine maintenance tasks, including applying software updates, patches, and security fixes to network devices. NOC technicians also participate in network capacity planning and may recommend infrastructure upgrades or changes to support future network requirements.

- **Collaboration and escalation**: They collaborate with other teams, such as network administrators, architects, or service providers, to address complex network issues. NOC technicians escalate critical incidents or issues to higher-level support teams or management when necessary.

- **Adherence to policies and procedures**: NOC technicians follow established network policies, procedures, and best practices to ensure compliance with security standards, operational guidelines, and regulatory requirements.

> **Note**
> NOC personnel live and breathe runbooks and SOP documentation. Robust documentation aids NOC technicians in excelling at their jobs.

Along with several attributes of a network technician, a NOC technician should possess a solid knowledge base in various areas of networking and be able to answer questions related to network monitoring, troubleshooting, and incident management. Some key questions a NOC technician should be able to address are as follows:

- What metrics should be monitored to assess network performance?
- How do you identify and troubleshoot network connectivity issues?
- How do you generate reports and alerts based on monitoring data?
- How do you handle and prioritize incidents in a NOC environment?
- What steps are involved in incident triage and escalation?
- How do you effectively communicate with stakeholders during an incident?
- What documentation is important when managing incidents?

The number of years of experience a NOC technician should possess can vary depending on several factors, including the specific job requirements, the complexity of the network environment, the level of responsibility within the NOC center, and individual goals, experience, and opportunities. It's recommended to have about 2 to 3 years of experience before attempting to transition into another role such as network technician for a different set of responsibilities. An additional 2 years or more is recommended to move into an advanced role.

Here are some certifications or training worth pursuing for a NOC technician:

- CompTIA A+, Security+, Network+, and Linux+
- CCENT
- CCNA
- MCSA
- Network tools (Solar Winds, Cacti, DataDog, Nagios. Wireshark, Nmap)
- Vulnerability tools (Qualys, Nessus, OpenVAS)
- Security tools (Snort, Nikto, Burp Suite, Splunk, ELK Stack)

Overall, the role of a NOC technician is to proactively monitor, maintain, and troubleshoot network systems, ensuring their availability, performance, and security. They play a crucial role in incident management, network stability, and the smooth functioning of the network infrastructure.

> **Note**
> All these entry-level roles have some degree of overlap concerning responsibilities and certification pursuant. Generally speaking, entry-level networking positions must have a fundamental understanding of networking principles, protocols, and technologies.

Roles and responsibilities – mid level

A mid-level network IT position typically refers to a job that requires a moderate level of experience and expertise in the field of information technology and networking. This would require 3 to 5 years of IT-related experience in networking and networking technologies. These positions generally require more experience and knowledge than entry-level positions, but less than senior-level or managerial positions.

Middle-level network IT positions often involve responsibilities such as designing and configuring network infrastructure, troubleshooting issues with network hardware and software, and managing network security. They may also involve managing servers, databases, and other IT systems, as well as providing technical support to end users.

Some mid-level network IT positions are as follows:

- **Network administrator**: They are responsible for maintaining the network infrastructure, including installing, configuring, and troubleshooting network hardware and software.

- **Network security engineer**: Their focus is on ensuring the security of an organization's network infrastructure. They design and implement security measures, such as firewalls, intrusion detection systems, and VPNs.

- **Network engineer**: They are responsible for aspects of designing and implementing network infrastructure, including LAN, WAN, and wireless networks, as well as cloud-based networks. They are responsible for analyzing network performance and implementing changes to improve efficiency, capacity, and reliability.

Let's briefly discuss these positions.

Network administrator

Network administrators are responsible for ensuring that an organization's computer network is operating efficiently and effectively. Similar to a network support technician, network administrators need to have a strong understanding of network protocols, hardware, and software. However, network administrators are responsible for designing, implementing, and maintaining an organization's computer networks.

A network administrator should have a little more *depth* than a network support technician. They should be able to answer the following questions:

- What's the difference between distance vector and link state routing protocols?

- What are blocking and non-blocking switching?

- What is a broadcast domain?

- What are class A, B, C, and D IP addresses? How are they used?

The following duties are aligned with network administrators:

- **Designing and implementing network infrastructure**: Network administrators implement the network infrastructure, including hardware, software, and protocols. They determine the network's layout, bandwidth requirements, and security protocols.

- **Installing and configuring network hardware and software**: They are responsible for installing and configuring routers, switches, firewalls, and other network hardware and software.

- **Monitoring network performance**: They use network monitoring tools to track network performance metrics and identify areas for improvement.

- **Ensuring network security**: They manage user accounts and permissions, monitor network access, and configure firewalls and other security tools.

- **Performing network maintenance**: They perform regular network maintenance, including backups, updates, and disaster recovery procedures.

- **Collaborating with other IT professionals**: They also work closely with other IT professionals, such as network engineers and network support technicians.

A network administrator must be able to solve user-related problems and issues, such as user account credentials or permission access to applications and systems. They must also be able to handle more complex tasks. Here are some examples:

- They may need 17 subnets to support a minimum of 32 users each and have those IPs available in the IPAM services for a particular region or campus

- They may need to align with a network architect on an approach to configure another routing protocol and provide higher bandwidth to the already existing infrastructure without impacting the current design

For most IT professionals, spending between 3 to 5 years in a network administrator role before advancing to a higher-level position is typically recommended. During this time, a network administrator can gain the necessary experience and knowledge to take on more complex projects and responsibilities. It's also important to invest in professional development during this time. Obtaining Cisco's CCNA, Microsoft's MCSE, and CompTIA's Network+ and Security+ are essential. However, obtaining advanced certifications is recommended, such as the **Cisco Certified Network Professional (CCNP)** or the **Certified Information Systems Security Professional (CISSP)**.

> **Note**
>
> Although you might find similarities between network support technicians and network administrators, network administrators will have a higher level of experience, decision-making, and network access.

Network engineer

A network engineer is an IT professional who is responsible for implementing and maintaining networks for organizations. They work to ensure that the network infrastructure meets the organization's needs for connectivity, performance, and security. They also work closely with network architects to ensure their design is deployed and provisioned accordingly.

> **Note**
>
> This might sound redundant from the previous positions, but the technical acumen is advanced and has increased responsibilities.

Here are some of the key responsibilities of a network engineer:

- **Network design**: They design aspects of the architecture of the network infrastructure, including the physical and logical layout of the network, the selection of hardware and software components, and the integration of new technologies.

- **Advanced network implementation**: A network engineer creates and implements advanced configurations for network hardware and software components. They will lead **point of view (PoV)** and **proof of concept (PoC)** activities and may oversee the deployment of new network applications and services.

- **Network maintenance**: A network engineer maintains the health and stability of the network infrastructure, including monitoring network performance, troubleshooting network issues, and performing regular maintenance tasks such as software upgrades and security patches.

- **Network security**: A network engineer implements security measures to protect the network from unauthorized access, viruses, and other security threats. They work closely with the security team to align and develop disaster recovery plans and perform regular backups of network data.

- **Network documentation**: A network engineer creates and maintains documentation of the network infrastructure, including as-built diagrams, network diagrams, system configurations, and troubleshooting guides.

A network engineer should be able to address a wide range of questions related to designing, implementing, and maintaining computer networks for organizations. Some examples are as follows:

- How does the network infrastructure meet the organization's needs for connectivity, performance, and security?

- How can we design the network infrastructure to meet the organization's needs for scalability and flexibility?

- What network protocols and technologies should be used to support the flow of data between different parts of the network, and how can they be optimized for performance and reliability?

- How can we ensure that the network infrastructure is highly available and can recover quickly in the event of an outage or other disruption?

- How can we ensure that the network infrastructure is compliant with relevant industry standards and regulations?

A network engineer is not only hands-on dealing with more complex tasks such as configuring routing/switching for an enterprise network or implementing a SAN environment for **Fibre Channel over IP (FCIP)** traffic; they must be able to begin having business-related discussions with stakeholders in the organization to aid a senior network engineer or a network architect to make informed decisions on how the network is upgraded, implemented, and advanced.

To become a network engineer, an individual typically needs a strong foundation in networking concepts and technologies, as well as a degree in computer science or a related field (this isn't necessary but it's nice to have). They should obtain professional certifications such as the CCNA or the **Juniper Networks Certified Internet Associate (JNCIA)** or an advanced certification such as CCNP. Network engineers need to be analytical problem solvers, effective communicators, and have a keen attention to detail.

> **Note**
> Once a network engineer obtains a professional level certification(s), they should look toward starting an expert-level certification such as Cisco's CCIE to commensurate with their current and continued level of experience thus far.

Network security engineer

A network security engineer is a *specialist* as it relates to the network infrastructure. In other words, their focus is on securing the network and data. Their primary focus is on protecting the network from potential threats, vulnerabilities, and unauthorized access.

A network security engineer must be able to answer the following questions:

- What is false positive versus false negative?

- What is a host-based IDS versus a network-based IDS?

- What is a stateful versus stateless firewall rule?

- What is the role of firewalls, IDS, and IPS in network security?

- How do you assess and mitigate network vulnerabilities?

- What are the best practices for securing network infrastructure?

The network security engineer must be able to understand the network infrastructure just as a network engineer does but should be well versed on hardware and software solutions to mitigate any risk of data exfiltration by unauthorized users or systems, limit the exposure of data to authorized end users and applications, and remediate any anomalies and vulnerabilities that may exist in the hardware and software.

Here are some of the key responsibilities of a network security engineer:

- **Network security architecture**: Network security engineers design and implement network security architecture with input from network and security architects to safeguard the organization's network infrastructure. They develop and enforce security policies, standards, and procedures. This includes defining access controls and implementing firewalls, IDS/IPS, and other security measures.

- **Vulnerability assessment and penetration testing**: They conduct regular vulnerability assessments and penetration tests to identify weaknesses and potential security risks within the network. They analyze the results and provide recommendations for patching vulnerabilities and strengthening security controls.

- **Incident response and threat management**: Network security engineers respond to security incidents, such as network breaches, malware infections, or unauthorized access attempts. They investigate security breaches, contain and mitigate the impact, and implement measures to prevent future incidents. They also stay updated on emerging threats and proactively manage potential risks.

- **Network monitoring and security event management**: Along with NOC and SOC technicians, a network security engineer may lead a team to monitor network traffic, logs, and security events to identify suspicious activities and potential security breaches. Network security engineers use **security information and event management** (SIEM) tools to collect, analyze, and respond to security alerts. They ensure timely detection, response, and resolution of security incidents.

- **Security auditing and compliance**: A core responsibility, the network security engineers perform security audits and assessments to ensure compliance with industry regulations and internal security policies. They collaborate with internal and external auditors to address security gaps, conduct risk assessments, and implement necessary security controls.

- **Security infrastructure management**: They manage and maintain security infrastructure, including firewalls, VPNs, authentication systems, and encryption technologies. Network security engineers configure, monitor, and update security devices and technologies to ensure optimal performance and protection.

Note

In some organizations, network security engineers perform security awareness programs to educate staff and employees about best practices, security policies, and potential threats.

Network security engineers should have 3 to 5 years, or more, of experience before looking to advance their careers. During this time frame, network security engineers should look to obtain vendor-specific certifications from organizations, such as the following:

- Palo Alto, and Fortinet

- F5 and CheckPoint

- Cisco

- Zscalar

- Cloud security (GCP, AWS, and Azure)

They should also look to obtain industry security certifications such as the following:

- **Certified Information Systems Security Professional (CISSP)**

- **Systems Security Certified Practitioner (SSCP)**

- **Certified Ethical Hacker (CEH)**

Like network engineers, network security engineers are hands-on and deal with more complex tasks and items (that is, setting up security appliances, determining firewall and allowability matrices, compliance reporting, and audit signoffs). With such tasks comes more responsibility. With more responsibilities comes more accountability.

> **Note**
> The reality is that network security engineers (and SOC) are the first line of defense for an organization.

Roles and responsibilities – senior level

A senior-level network IT position is typically a role that requires a higher level (and wide range) of professional experience, expertise, and responsibility compared to lower-level positions in the same field. This could range from 8 to 10 years or more, depending on the organization and industry. Most importantly, they must possess a deep understanding of network technologies, protocols, and best practices. They must also have in-depth and advanced knowledge of the following topics:

- Networking concepts such as routing and switching

- Network security

- Virtualization

- Network architecture

The landscape of a senior-level networking position has breadth and depth due to the complexity and diverse nature of the responsibilities involved. Though you can specialize to some degree, an individual must be well-versed across all solutions and technologies of a network infrastructure.

At this level, an individual is expected to have a high level of responsibility within the organization. It's not only learning or knowing the technology (stack) aspect for an organization. At the senior level, you're making decisions as it relates to the business of an organization. Such decisions can be headcount, budget allocation, outlook/forecast, revenue, leading teams, team growth/training, vendors, and more.

Senior-level positions are typically at the *architectural level*, where the knowledge base, as mentioned previously, must be broad and deep. Here are some key senior-level networking roles:

- **Senior network architect**: This is a general senior-level role where the individual is responsible for designing and implementing network architectures, creating technical roadmaps, and providing strategic guidance for the organization's network infrastructure.

- **Data center network architect**: This role focuses on designing and optimizing network architectures specifically for data centers. It involves planning and implementing network solutions that support high availability, scalability, and efficient data center operations.

- **Cloud network architect**: In this role, the network architect designs and implements network architectures that integrate with cloud services and platforms. They ensure secure connectivity, optimal performance, and reliable communication between on-premises infrastructure and cloud environments.

- **Network security architect**: This role combines network architecture expertise with a focus on security. The architect designs and implements secure network architectures, integrating firewalls, IPS, secure access controls, and other security measures to protect the organization's network infrastructure and data.

> **Note**
>
> There are other architect roles, such as wireless, enterprise, virtualization, storage, and transformational. All of these are specialized versions of a network architect and are outside the scope of this book.
>
> *Chapter 2, Network Architect in an Organization*, covers the role of a network architect in more detail.

The architect-level (senior) positions listed previously all share the following common areas of responsibilities:

- **Network architecture and design**: These senior professionals are responsible for designing network architectures that meet or exceed the organization's requirements and consider factors such as scalability, security, performance, and reliability. They develop network designs that align with business goals to ensure optimal functionality, efficiency, and solution efficacy.

- **Technical leadership and guidance**: They provide technical leadership and guidance to network engineers and administrators. They serve as subject matter experts and assist in solving complex networking issues, troubleshooting problems, and making critical decisions related to network design, deployment, and optimization. They may also lead teams in delivering projects on critical applications and systems.

- **Network implementation and configuration**: Senior networking professionals are often involved in implementing network solutions. They verify and test configurations through PoC and pilots before any deployment takes place. Once completed, they disseminate the actual configurations (that is, runbooks) to network engineers to configure network devices and ensure proper integration of networking technologies. They oversee the deployment process, ensure adherence to best practices, and validate that network configurations align with the designed architecture.

- **Network performance and optimization**: They offer guidelines, policies, and procedures for monitoring and analyzing network performance, identifying bottlenecks, optimizing network resources, and ensuring efficient data transmission. The strategies to improve network performance, reduce latency, and enhance overall network efficiency are carried out through NOC teams.

- **Network security and compliance**: Senior networking professionals are responsible for implementing and maintaining network security measures to protect against unauthorized access, data breaches, and other network security threats. They ensure compliance with industry regulations and standards, implement security protocols, and establish secure access controls.

- **Vendor management and collaboration**: They work closely with network equipment vendors, service providers, and other technology partners to evaluate and select the most suitable networking solutions. They manage vendor relationships, negotiate contracts, and ensure smooth collaboration with external parties.

- **Project management**: Senior networking professionals often lead network-related projects, overseeing the planning, execution, and completion of network initiatives. They coordinate with cross-functional teams, manage project timelines, allocate resources, and ensure project objectives are achieved.

- **Documentation and standards**: They establish network documentation practices and standards to maintain accurate records of network configurations, designs, and changes. They ensure the availability of up-to-date network documentation, including network diagrams, inventory, and operational procedures.

- **Technology evaluation and roadmapping**: Senior networking professionals stay abreast of emerging networking technologies, assess their potential impact on the organization, and make recommendations for technology adoption or upgrades. They develop technology roadmaps aligned with business strategies and industry trends.

  They are forward thinkers who determine the next generation's outlook for an organization's infrastructure evolution.

> **Note**
>
> Not all businesses have the capability to do or have every desired solution now. Typical **service-level agreements (SLAs)** (hardware and software) are often 3 to 5 years. During this time, it's best to have quarterly discussions with vendors, OEMs, and solution providers to determine the next steps and actionable solutions.

- **Continuous learning and professional development**: Networking professionals at the senior level are expected to continuously update their knowledge and skills to keep up with the evolving networking landscape. They actively pursue professional certifications, attend industry conferences, and engage in self-directed learning to stay current with the latest networking technologies and best practices.

In the next section, we'll discuss a career path to becoming a network architect.

The career path to becoming a network architect

The career path to becoming a network architect typically involves progressive growth in knowledge, skills, and experience in the field of networking. The journey itself may need several years to ascertain. A typical path may take between 7 to 10 years.

> **Note**
>
> My journey started with taking an MSCE in 1999 while working for a telephone company as an outside plant engineer. It took me 8 years of working in different areas of IT (such as a LAN admin, IT instructor, and part-time network engineer) to become a network architect.

While individual paths may vary, a generalized career progression that can lead to a network architect role is shown in the following diagram:

Network Architect RoadMap

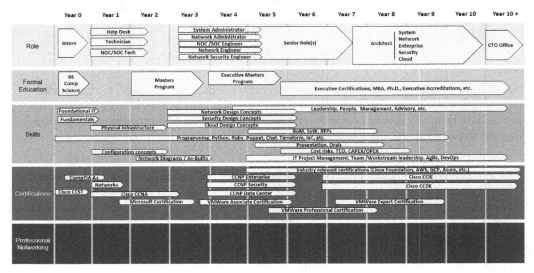

Figure 3.1 – Network architect career roadmap

This roadmap shows the suggested role, formal education, skills, and certifications that must be taken over 10 years to become a network architect. The roadmap encompasses such items as the following:

- **Obtain a strong foundation in networking concepts**: Start by gaining a solid understanding of networking fundamentals, including TCP/IP, subnetting, routing, switching, and network protocols. You can do this by pursuing a relevant degree in computer science, information technology, or a networking-specific program or course.

- **Gain practical experience**: Alongside your education, it's crucial to gain hands-on experience with networking technologies. Look for opportunities to work on real-world projects, such as internships, part-time jobs, or volunteering with organizations that require networking support. This experience will help you apply theoretical knowledge and develop practical skills.

- **Earn industry certifications**: Certifications validate your expertise and can significantly enhance your professional credentials. Some important certifications for network architects include CompTIAA+ &Network+, CCNA, CCNP, CCIE, and CISSP.

  These certifications demonstrate your proficiency in specific networking technologies and protocols, which is highly valued in the industry. We'll cover these in more depth in *Chapter 10*.

- **Develop a strong understanding of network design**: As a network architect, you'll be responsible for designing complex network architectures that meet the organization's requirements. Focus on learning about network design principles, such as scalability, redundancy, security, and performance optimization. Familiarize yourself with different network topologies, architectural frameworks, and best practices.

  Tools such as Visio and Lucid Charts will help you design different network topologies and ideas to articulate to upper management and colleagues.

- **Master network security**: Security is a critical aspect of modern networks. Network architects need a deep understanding of security protocols, encryption, firewalls, **intrusion detection and prevention systems** (**IDPSs**), **virtual private networks** (**VPNs**), and other security mechanisms. Staying up to date with the latest security trends and technologies will be an asset in designing stable network environments.

- **Learn about cloud and virtualization technologies**: With the increasing adoption of cloud computing and virtualization, network architects need to understand how networks integrate with these technologies. Familiarize yourself with virtualization platforms such as VMware, OpenStack, or Hyper-V, and understand how networking is implemented in cloud environments, such as **Amazon Web Services** (**AWS**), Microsoft Azure, or **Google Cloud Platform** (**GCP**).

- **Continuously learn and stay up to date**: Networking technologies evolve rapidly, so it's essential to stay up to date with the latest trends, protocols, and innovations. Engage in continuous learning through professional development courses, attending industry conferences, participating in online forums, and reading books and articles.

- **Gain experience with network automation and programmability**: Network automation and **software-defined networking** (**SDN**) are transforming the industry. Acquire skills in network automation frameworks such as Ansible, Python programming, network APIs, and SDN controllers such as OpenDaylight or Cisco ACI. This knowledge will make you a well-rounded network architect and help you design and manage programmable networks.

- **Build a professional network**: Networking with other professionals in the field can provide valuable insights, career opportunities, and mentorship. Attend industry events, join professional organizations such as the **Association for Computing Machinery** (**ACM**) or the **Institute of Electrical and Electronics Engineers** (**IEEE**), and connect with peers through online platforms such as LinkedIn.

> Note
>
> Keep in mind that this is a suggested roadmap or a general guideline. It's up to the individual to determine the path they want to take and their career objective.

Figure 3.2 shows the progression an individual can take to become a network architect, and beyond. Here, we can see the year of experience concerning the knowledge base someone must have to be a good fit for the role. As their years of experience increases, so should their knowledge base:

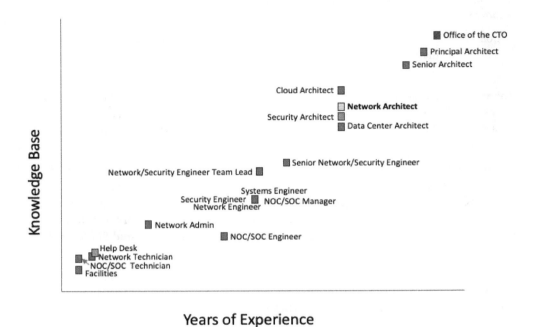

Figure 3.2 – Networking roles related to years of experience and knowledge base

Figure 3.3 shows the responsibility level related to scope. As you move forward outward, the level of responsibility increases, as does the scope breadth. The *more* responsibility someone undertakes, the *wider* the scope of those responsibilities are:

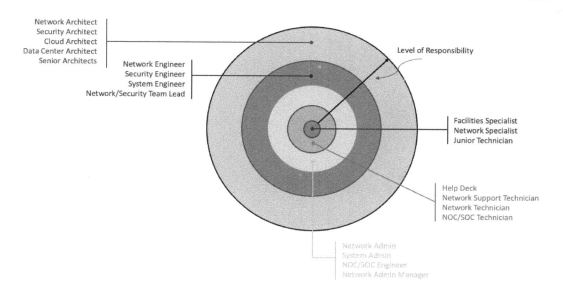

Figure 3.3 – Responsibility and scope related to networking roles

The career path to becoming a network architect typically involves progressive growth in knowledge, skills, and experience in the field of networking. The journey itself may need several years to ascertain.

Summary

In this chapter, we looked at the roles and responsibilities of several entry-level, mid-level, and senior-level positions you might come across in the IT industry and within organizations. Each role has its responsibilities characterized by the required level of networking acumen.

As an individual progresses throughout their career to become a network architect, not only does their knowledge base related to networking increase, but the level of responsibility and scope, their visibility in the organization, their knowledge of different technologies, decision making, and *business sense* also increase.

In the next chapter, we'll discuss the attributes of a network architect.

Part 2 – Crafting the Architectural Mind: Attributes and Mindset of a Network Architect

In the intricate dance of technology and business, the network architect stands out as a pivotal figure, orchestrating the seamless flow of data and communication. But what lies beneath the surface of this critical role? What are the attributes that distinguish a good network architect from a great one, and how does their mindset contribute to their success and that of their organization? In this section, we explore the inherent qualities and the intellectual framework that a network architect must cultivate to excel in this complex and ever-evolving field.

This section has the following chapters:

- *Chapter 4, Attributes of a Network Architect*
- *Chapter 5, The Mindset of the Network Architect – the Principles of Design*

4

Attributes of a Network Architect

In the previous two chapters, we touched on network architects, their placement within the organization, and the roadmap to becoming one. Now, we want to dive into the attributes of a network architect. As mentioned in *Chapter 1*, network architects are one of many "architects" in an organization, with overlapping skill sets with other architects. This chapter will introduce those overlapping skill sets.

I'm quite sure in your experiences and job roles thus far (the same for me, too), you've worn different hats when a co-worker or a manager was out of the office. We've had to update reports, present business roadmaps, or be an SME on a project – all of which were outside our day-to-day activities. Being a network architect encompasses everything I mentioned and more.

In this chapter, we'll be discussing the attributes a network architect, or someone who is pursuing this profession, should have, along with the following topics:

- The network architect's role in the business
- Business logistics – the structure
- Business financials
- **Cross-functional teams** (**CFTs**)
- Managing business relationships

The network architect's role in the business

The role of a network architect is critical to the success of any organization. Without a well-designed and implemented network, businesses would not be able to communicate effectively, share information, or access critical data. Network architects play a vital role in ensuring that businesses and **business units** (**BUs**) can operate smoothly and efficiently and that their infrastructure (network) is secure, reliable, performant, and scalable.

In essence, the network architect's role in the business is to design and build the network infrastructure that supports the business's operations.

A network architect is essential to an organization in the following areas:

- Network infrastructure design
- Network security
- Network management
- Network procurement
- Technical leadership

Let's go further in depth on each of these.

Network infrastructure design

The network architect designs the *network infrastructure*, which is the foundation of the organization's IT systems. A well-designed network infrastructure can improve the efficiency, productivity, and security of the organization's IT systems:

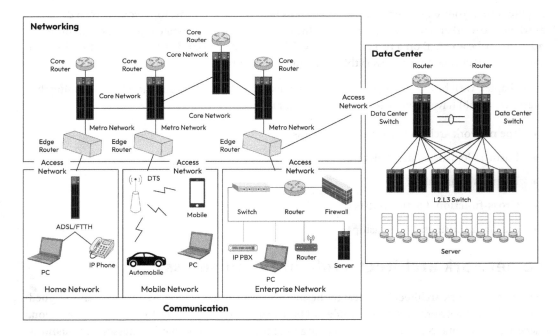

Figure 4.1 – Designing a secure network infrastructure

The design, or topology, must be cohesively integrated with other designs and/or IT systems that are present within an organization.

A well-designed infrastructure's touchpoints will include the following:

- **WAN edge**: Refers to the network infrastructure and devices that are deployed at the edge of a **wide area network** (**WAN**) that are responsible for connecting an organization's local networks, such as branch offices, data centers, or cloud resources, to the WAN.

- **Storage area network** (**SAN**) **farm**: This is a collection of storage devices and infrastructure that are interconnected and managed as a unified storage system. It provides high-performance, scalable, and shared storage resources that can be accessed by multiple servers or applications.

- **Wireless**: This encompasses the **wireless access points** (**APs**), wireless controllers, and associated components that enable wireless communication and provide connectivity to wireless devices such as laptops, smartphones, tablets, **Internet of Things** (**IoT**) devices, and other wireless endpoints.

- **Private backbone**: Dedicated and privately owned network fabric that connects multiple locations or data centers within an organization. It provides a high-performance, secure, and reliable network backbone for internal communications, data transfer, and resource sharing.

- **Edge devices** (**IoT systems, mobile, laptops, VoIP, printers, sensors, HVAC, and so on**): Devices that are located at the edge of a network or the periphery of a computing infrastructure. These devices facilitate the collection, processing, and transmission of data at or near the point of origin, often in real time or with minimal latency.

- **Security information and event management** (**SIEM**) **systems**: A system that collects and analyzes security event data from various sources within an organization's IT infrastructure to provide real-time monitoring, threat detection, and **incident response** (**IR**) capabilities.

- **Security systems**: These encompass a wide range of technologies, solutions, tools, and practices designed to protect information technology infrastructure, data, and systems from unauthorized access, cyber threats, and potential vulnerabilities.

Each of these will require their own parameters to function optimally and, in all cases, will require a network architect to provide guidance. Network architects understand different types of networks and how to design them to meet the specific needs of an organization. They also understand the latest technologies to ensure integration is done as seamlessly as possible.

Network security

Network architects are responsible for designing network architectures that are secure and can protect against unauthorized/unauthenticated access, data breaches, malware, and other security threats. A well-designed network security infrastructure can prevent data breaches, protect sensitive data, and ensure regulatory compliance. Network architects need to consider various security best practices, such as implementing proper network segmentation, designing secure authentication and authorization mechanisms, and implementing encryption protocols, among others.

Network security is a complex and ever-changing field; as such, the network architect must also need to stay up to date with the latest security threats/technologies and incorporate appropriate security measures into their network designs.

Architectural design considerations will include the following:

- **Network access control lists (NACLs)**
- Authenticated routing peers, such as **Border Gateway Protocol (BGP)/Open Shortest Path First (OSPF)/Enhanced Interior Gateway Routing Protocol Message Digest 5 (EIGRP MD5)** authentication
- **Virtual routing and forwarding (VRF)** implementation
- **Virtual local area networks (VLANs)** and **Virtual Extensible LAN (VXLAN)**
- **Virtual private networks (VPNs)**
- **Authentication, authorization, and accounting (AAA)** mechanisms
- Hardware encryption appliances
- Certificate servers
- Identity management services (that is, Active Directory, the **Lightweight Directory Access Protocol (LDAP)**, and third-party solutions)

Ultimately, the complete security infrastructure framework doesn't fall on the shoulders of *only* the network architect. A security architect plays a significant role in the overall security framework.

Note

A network architect is not the same as a security architect. A security architect designs the overall security perimeter of an organization, which includes identifying **intrusion protection systems (IPSs)/intrusion detection systems (IDSs)**, firewall appliances, a secure WAN edge, and more.

Network management

The network architect is responsible for managing the organization's computer network, which includes monitoring network performance, identifying and resolving network issues, being available for consultation on the day-to-day operation of a network, and ensuring that the network meets **service-level agreements (SLAs)**. A well-managed network infrastructure can improve the reliability and availability of the organization's IT systems.

Network management involves planning for future network capacity needs. Network architects need to be able to anticipate future growth and plan for it by designing network architectures that are scalable and can accommodate future capacity requirements. They may need to adjust the network design or configurations to ensure that the network infrastructure can handle increased capacity demands.

Some key responsibilities of network management are as follows:

- Monitoring the network for performance and security issues

- Troubleshooting problems and making changes to the network as needed

- Developing and implementing network management policies and procedures

- Working with other IT professionals to ensure that the network is properly managed

- Staying up to date on the latest technologies and best practices

> **Note**
>
> Network management is a team effort. Network architects must work with other IT professionals, such as system administrators and security engineers, to effectively manage a network.

Network management is a critical part of the overall IT strategy of an organization. Network architects must understand the business needs of the organization and how the network can be used to support those needs.

Network procurement

Network architects play a key role in the process of acquiring network hardware, software, and services for an organization's network infrastructure. Network architects can be involved in network procurement in several ways:

- **Specifying network equipment and services**: Network architects play a key role in specifying the network equipment and services needed for the organization's network infrastructure. They work closely with other stakeholders, such as IT managers, procurement teams, and vendors, to identify the requirements for the network infrastructure.

  Some key responsibilities include the following:

  - Identifying switches, routers, servers, and firewalls

  - Recommending network management solutions

  - Proposing ancillary network components

  Network architects need to consider factors such as performance, scalability, interoperability, and security requirements when specifying network equipment and services to meet the organization's needs.

- **Evaluating vendor proposals**: Network architects should be involved in evaluating vendor proposals for network equipment and services during any procurement engagement. They review and analyze vendor proposals, technical specifications, pricing, and other relevant information to assess the suitability of the proposed solutions for the organization's network infrastructure. They may work closely with procurement teams to evaluate vendors based on technical and business criteria and provide input on the selection of network equipment and services that best meet the organization's requirements.

- **Contract negotiations**: Network architects also participate in contract negotiations with vendors during network procurement engagements. They can provide technical expertise and insights to ensure that contracts and SLAs are aligned with the organization's network architecture, requirements, and best practices. They may work with procurement teams and legal teams to negotiate pricing, terms and conditions, warranties, and other contractual aspects related to network equipment and services.

- **Vendor relationship management**: Network architects are responsible for managing relationships with vendors before, during, and after network equipment and services are procured. This includes monitoring vendor performance, managing SLAs, and ensuring that vendors deliver as per contractual agreements. Network architects may work closely with vendors to troubleshoot technical issues, manage upgrades and patches, and maintain a positive working relationship to ensure smooth and efficient network operations.

Network architects can be involved in network procurement by specifying network equipment and services, evaluating vendor proposals, participating in contract negotiations, and managing vendor relationships. Their technical expertise and understanding of the organization's network architecture and requirements are valuable in ensuring that the network procurement process is aligned with the organization's needs and objectives.

Technical leadership

A network architect provides technical leadership to the organization, ensuring that the network infrastructure is aligned with the organization's strategic goals and objectives and that it is able to support the organization's business processes and applications. This can help the organization to innovate and stay ahead of the competition.

Network architects are highly skilled and experienced technical experts in the field of computer networking. As such, they are often called upon to provide that technical leadership within their organizations. They may be responsible for leading teams of network engineers or other technical staff (that is, the **network operations center** (**NOC**) or **security operations center** (**SOC**)) and for providing guidance and direction on technical issues related to the network infrastructure.

> **Note**
> As there are several IT architects within an organization, collectively all the architects form the brain trust of technical advisors to the organization's leadership teams.

Aside from the points previously mentioned, a network architect brings two key elements to technical leadership:

- **Technical guidance and expertise**: Network architects provide technical guidance and expertise to other IT teams, such as network engineers, system administrators, and security teams. They serve as **subject-matter experts (SMEs)** and provide mentorship to junior team members. They help with technical troubleshooting and problem resolution and provide guidance on best practices for network configuration, deployment, and management. They also stay updated with emerging technologies and industry trends and provide strategic recommendations on how the organization can leverage new technologies to improve its network infrastructure.

- **Technology innovation and strategy**: Network architects contribute to the organization's technology innovation and strategy by staying updated on emerging networking technologies, industry trends, and best practices. They provide strategic recommendations on how the organization can leverage new technologies to improve its network infrastructure, enhance network performance, increase security, and drive innovation. They work closely with other IT teams, BUs, and stakeholders to align the organization's network strategy with its overall IT strategy and business goals and ensure that the network infrastructure supports the organization's current and future needs.

> **Note**
> Network architects are evangelists within the IT community. Whether it be blogging, podcasts, or whitepapers, they propel and propose new ideas that can be used for future solutions in the industry.

In summary, as a technical leader, a network architect brings expertise in network design, technology evaluation and selection, technical guidance, network performance optimization, network security and compliance, and technology innovation and strategy to an organization. These contributions help ensure that the organization's network infrastructure is designed, implemented, and managed efficiently, securely, and in alignment with the organization's overall IT strategy and business objectives

Business logistics – the structure

The corporate structure for a network architect in an organization may vary depending on the size, industry, and organizational culture of the company. However, typically, a network architect may fall under the IT department, which is responsible for managing the organization's technology infrastructure and systems.

In *Chapter 1*, I showed a hierarchical perspective of where the architects are in an organization.

Let's now look closer at where a network architect is typically present in relationship to the BUs, where they have influence, responsibilities, and oversight, make decisions, and manage subordinates/staff:

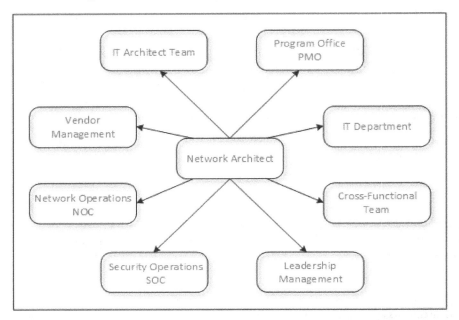

Figure 4.2 – Network architect influence on other business units

These eight BUs, or functional branches, of an organization represent common points of interest where a network architect plays an important role. Let's touch on each one:

- **IT department**: The network architect may report to the IT department, which is usually headed by a **chief information officer** (**CIO**) or an IT director. The IT department is responsible for overseeing all technology-related functions in the organization, including network architecture, infrastructure, applications, security, and support.

  A network architect has a great deal of influence on the design and key architectural aspects of an organization's entire IT infrastructure and IT system design.

  As part of the IT department, the network architect has a duty to assist in upskilling engineers. Some related activities can include the following:

  - Having weekly or bi-weekly meetings to understand what the team is doing
  - Having **knowledge transfer** (**KT**) sessions on projects
  - Setting up training sessions and programs
  - Staffing the team for projects

> **Note**
>
> The IT department is not only staffed with network architect(s) or network engineers. It will also consist of security professionals, database and storage engineers, applications engineers, and architects related to these disciplines.

- **IT architecture team**: The network architect is a member of the IT architecture team, which is responsible for designing, planning, and implementing the organization's technology architecture, including the network infrastructure. The team may include other roles such as enterprise architects, solution architects, and data architects, who work collectively to ensure that the organization's technology landscape is aligned with business goals and requirements.

  The IT architecture team are trusted advisors to the CIO or **chief technology officer** (**CTO**) as they are the *forward thinkers* to make some or all the objectives the CIO/CTO has come to fruition. The team may or may not report to the CIO/CTO directly.

  This team is usually considered the brain trust when it comes to an organization's technology advancement landscape.

  In some organizations, this team is often referred to as **field CTOs**.

- **Network operations team** (NOC): The network architect may collaborate with the network operations team, which is responsible for the day-to-day operations and management of the organization's network infrastructure. This team is responsible for monitoring network performance, troubleshooting network issues, implementing network changes, and ensuring network availability and security.

  The network architect in some organizations may also partake in daily activities and is consulted when major disruptions occur or when a significant change is required.

  Between the IT department and the NOC, the network architect *can* have direct reporting staff.

> **Note**
>
> The **security operations team** (**SOC**) works closely with the NOC, and there can be shared responsibilities for the network architect between both teams.

- **Project management office** (**PMO**): The network architect works closely with the PMO, which is responsible for managing and overseeing all projects within the organization, including network-related projects.

  The PMO may provide project management frameworks, methodologies, and tools, and work with the network architect to ensure that network projects are executed according to established project management standards.

  Just as important, the PMO provides support for the network architect when having to consult with other leadership teams.

> **Note**
>
> *Program management office* and *project management office* are used interchangeably. In some organizations, particularly with **system integrators (SIs)**, the PMO (program) is the leadership team that provides governance on how a project is supported. The network architect is a vital member of the PMO.

- **CFTs**: The network architect collaborates with CFTs within the organization, such as security, operations, applications, and BUs, because the network infrastructure is a critical component of the overall IT ecosystem and business operations.

  These teams may work together on various initiatives that require network architecture expertise. Such initiatives are security projects, application deployments, change management, and business process improvements.

  Collaborating with CFTs ensures that the network architecture aligns with the needs and requirements of different departments and functions within the organization. The network architect ensures all processes, designs, and systems are in accordance with the policies, procedures, and standards set up by the IT department.

> **Note**
>
> Be aware that not all teams in an organization have the same objectives. Each team may have its own set of policies, procedures, and standards to comply with. Teams will require exceptions to have their initiatives passed.

- **Vendor management**: The network architect plays an integral role in vendor management within an organization to ensure that it is getting the best possible value for its network investment. The network architect liaisons between procurement, the CTO, the IT department, and the vendors.

  Vendors of interest should include the following:

  - Networking hardware (that is, Cisco, Arista, or Juniper)
  - Networking software (that is, Auvik, ScienceLogic, or Dynatrace)
  - Security appliances (that is Fortinet, Palo Alto, or Check Point)
  - Load balancer appliances (that is, F5, A10 Networks, or Citrix)
  - DNS (that is, Infoblox or BlueCat)
  - **Software-defined WAN (SD-WAN)**/WAN edge (that is, Silver Peak, Versa, or VeloCloud)
  - Telco/**communication service provider (CSP)** (that is, Verizon, AT&T, or Comcast)
  - Fiber (that is, Google, Cox, or Frontier)
  - Wireless (that is, Aruba, Meraki, Extreme, or Ruckus)

Key and critical aspects of vendor management are as follows:

- **Identifying and evaluating potential vendors**: Identify potential vendors who can provide the organization with the network equipment and services it needs. The network architect and team will then evaluate each vendor's capabilities, pricing, and terms and conditions to determine which solution(s) fit the project goals.

  It will be necessary to execute a **request for information** (**RFI**) to shortlist vendors who can provide and exceed expectations of a desired solution. From there, the network architect should conduct a **proof of concept** (**PoC**) to further reduce vendors and proceed accordingly.

- **Managing vendor relationships**: The network architect will be responsible for managing the relationship with the vendor. This includes things such as communicating with the vendor, resolving any issues that arise, and ensuring that the vendor is meeting the terms of the contract.

- **Building relationships with vendors**: From a leadership perspective, it's important to build relationships with vendors as they are more likely to be responsive to your needs. The relationship should be symbiotic in nature. An example is providing or co-developing a whitepaper based on a use case.

> **Note**
>
> Managing vendor relationships and building relationships with vendors may sound the same thing but are actually quite different. The former is contractual obligations, SLAs, and any of the like, while the latter is business development.

- **Monitoring vendor performance**: The network architect will also be responsible for monitoring the vendor's performance. This ensures that the vendor delivers products or services that meet the organization's expectations and requirements. This includes things such as tracking the vendor's service levels, resolving any issues that arise, and making changes to the contract as needed. Just as important is to track their progress holistically with respect to their market presence in the industry (that is, Wall Street).

  Keeping track of your vendor across industries, in the news, and at trade shows can help the network architect maintain a certain level of confidence with their current vendor selection. Simultaneously, it can be a turning point for the network architect to determine if it's time to change vendors.

- **Negotiating contracts**: A network architect can play a significant role in facilitating contract negotiations with vendors by leveraging their technical expertise, knowledge of the organization's network requirements, and understanding of the vendor landscape.

  Network architects manage vendor contracts, including reviewing and understanding contractual terms and conditions, monitoring contract expiration dates, and coordinating contract renewals or terminations.

Network architects will also work with legal and procurement teams to ensure that contracts are compliant with the organization's policies and regulations and that appropriate contractual protections are in place.

- **Leadership and management**: Depending on the organization's structure, the network architect may also be in a leadership or management role, overseeing a team of network engineers, administrators, or other related roles. In such cases, the network architect will have responsibilities related to team management, performance evaluations, mentoring, and talent development.

As mentioned before, the network architect is one of many architects that form an organization's brain trust. In itself, this brain trust is a leadership role that can dictate the direction an organization will take with current and future endeavors.

Other leadership activities can include the following:

- Strategic planning
- Budgeting/finance management
- Stakeholder management
- Partner management and development
- Sales forecasting (depending on the industry)
- Consultancy
- Mentoring and mentorship

> **Note**
> These are some of the activities I've come across throughout my career thus far in positions and roles I've held. This list can vary, again, depending on the organization.

- **Reporting lines**: The reporting structure for network architects can vary depending on the size and structure of the organization. In some cases, network architects may report to the CIO, CTO, director of IT infrastructure, or director of network services.

More experienced network architects may have more autonomy and may report directly to the CIO or CTO. Less experienced network architects may report to a senior network manager.

It's important to understand that the corporate structure for a network architect may vary in different organizations. Smaller organizations may have a flatter structure with fewer layers, while larger organizations may have a more complex structure with multiple teams and reporting lines.

Other **lines of business (LOBs)** a network architect may be a part of are as follows:

- Human resources/resource management
- Procurement

- **Product line management (PLM)**/product team
- Advisory board
- Office of the CTO

Building trust and effective relationships, both internally and with external entities such as vendors and regulatory agencies, is crucial to the success of a network architect in optimizing an organization's network infrastructure and ensuring its alignment with business goals.

In the next section, we'll look at the financial aspects of IT – **return on investment (ROI)**, forecasting, participation in budget planning, and more.

Business financials

Understanding the financials of a business is important for a network architect because it allows them to make informed decisions about the network infrastructure that align with the organization's financial goals and budget allocation for IT services. The frequency of budget allocation for IT may vary depending on the organization and its budgeting process. In general, budget allocation for IT is typically done on an annual basis, as part of the organization's overall budgeting process.

However, some organizations may allocate budgets for IT on a more frequent basis, such as quarterly or semi-annually, particularly if the organization is undergoing significant changes or growth that require additional IT resources.

The IT budget may be revised or adjusted throughout the year as needed, particularly if there are unexpected changes or events that have an impact on an organization's financial situation or IT needs.

Several key terms are important to understand. They are as follows:

- **Capital Expenditure (CapEx)**: Money spent on acquiring assets that have a useful life between 1 and 3 years. It relates to the cost incurred in acquiring or upgrading network infrastructure assets, such as racks, fiber termination equipment, switches, routers, security appliances, servers, and storage devices. These expenditures are typically associated with one-time or infrequent investments that have a long-term impact on the organization's network infrastructure.

  Examples of CapEx for a network architect may include purchasing new hardware, upgrading existing network infrastructure, or investing in new technologies that can improve network performance, security, or scalability. CapEx expenses are typically amortized over the useful life of the asset and depreciated over time.

- **Operational Expenditure (OpEx)**: Costs incurred in the day-to-day management and maintenance of the network infrastructure. These expenses are typically recurring and necessary to ensure the smooth and reliable operation of the network.

  Examples of OpEx for a network architect may include ongoing expenses related to network monitoring and management tools, software licenses, network maintenance contracts, third-party services (that is, cloud or SaaS), and salaries for network operations staff. OpEx expenses are typically charged to the organization's operating budget and are considered a regular cost of doing business.

> **Note**
>
> While CapEx and OpEx terms cannot be used interchangeably, what they are aligned with can be. In some cases, to maximize the balance between the two, items can be moved based on *how* costs are structured in the contract.

- **ROI**: This is an important financial metric for a network architect, as it can help justify the cost of network infrastructure investments, prioritize investments based on their expected return, and demonstrate the value of the network to the organization.

  It measures the profitability of that network infrastructure investment. ROI is calculated as the net profit or cost savings resulting from the investment, divided by the cost of the investment, expressed as a percentage or ratio:

$$ROI = \frac{(Gross\ profit - Expenditures)}{Expenditures} \ x\ 100\%$$

  For a network architect, ROI can be used to evaluate the potential impact of network infrastructure investments on the organization's financial performance. For example, investing in new network hardware or software may improve network performance and reduce downtime, resulting in cost savings and increased productivity.

  By calculating the ROI of such an investment, the network architect can demonstrate the potential value of the investment to senior management and secure funding for the project.

  To calculate ROI, a network architect will need to gather data on the cost of the investment, the expected benefits, and the projected savings or revenue generated over time. This may involve conducting a **cost-benefit analysis (CBA)** (discussed in *Chapter 2*), which compares the expected costs and benefits of the investment to determine its potential ROI.

- **Total cost of ownership (TCO)**: This is the total cost of owning and operating a network infrastructure asset over its entire life cycle. TCO includes not only the initial purchase price of the asset but also ongoing operational costs such as maintenance, upgrades, and support.

  For a network architect, understanding the TCO of network infrastructure investments is important because it can help to inform decision-making about which assets to acquire, how to configure and manage those assets, and how to allocate resources for ongoing maintenance and support.

  Calculating the TCO of a network infrastructure asset requires a thorough analysis of all associated costs over its entire life cycle. This may include the following factors:

  - Acquisition costs, including purchase price, installation, and configuration

  - Operating costs, such as power consumption, maintenance, and upgrades

- Support costs, such as licensing fees, warranties, and technical support

- Disposal or replacement costs at the end of the asset's useful life

TCO is calculated as follows:

$$TCO = (Initial\ Cost + Maintenance) - Remaining\ Value$$

*Here, maintenance includes operational and downtime cost

- **Balance sheet**: This is a financial statement that provides a snapshot of an organization's financial position at a specific point in time. The balance sheet lists the organization's assets, liabilities, and equity, and is used to calculate key financial ratios and metrics that help to evaluate the organization's financial health.

For a network architect, understanding the balance sheet can be important for several reasons. First, it can help to provide a sense of the organization's overall financial strength and stability, which can influence decisions about investing in network infrastructure projects. For example, if the organization has high levels of debt or low levels of equity, it may be more cautious about making large CapEx in network infrastructure.

Second, the balance sheet can be used to calculate financial ratios and metrics that can help to evaluate the effectiveness of the organization's network infrastructure investments. For example, **return on assets** (**ROA**) compares the organization's net income to its total assets, providing a measure of the profitability of its investments. Similarly, the debt-to-equity ratio compares the organization's debt to its equity, providing a measure of its financial leverage and risk.

An example balance sheet would look like this:

ABC Enterprise

02/28/2023

ASSETS			LIABILITIES		
Current Assets			**Current Liabilities**		
Cash & cash equivalents	$	6,000.00	Short-term debts	$	93,000.00
Inventory	$	93,000.00	Wages payable	$	6,000.00
Accounts receivable	$	120,000.00	Dividends payable	$	200,000.00
Prepaid expenses	$	4,500.00	Accounts payable	$	118,000.00
Short-term investments	$	30,000.00	Income taxes payable	$	30,000.00
Total current assets	$	253,500.00	Total current liabilities	$	447,000.00
Fixed Assets			**Long-term Liabilities**		
Long-term investments	$	118,000.00	Long-term debts	$	250,000.00
Property costs	$	200,000.00	Capital lease obligations	$	12,000.00
Equipment costs	$	250,000.00	Notes payable	$	6,000.00
Intangible assets	$	300,000.00	Bonds payable	$	3,000.00
Total fixed assets	$	868,000.00	Total long-term liabilities	$	271,000.00
			Total liabilities	$	718,000.00
Other Assets			OWNER'S EQUITY		
Deferred income tax	$	3,000.00	Owner's investment	$	300,000.00
Bond issue costs	$	2,500.00	Retained earnings	$	1,500.00
Prepaid pension costs	$	12,000.00	Less: Treasury stock	$	120,000.00
Other assets	$	3,000.00	Other equity	$	2,500.00
Total other assets	$	20,500.00	Total owner's equity	$	424,000.00
TOTAL ASSETS	$	1,142,000.00	TOTAL LIABILITIES & OWNER'S EQUITY	$	1,142,000.00

CURRENT RATIO
0.5671

DEBT RATIO
0.6287

DEBT-TO-EQUITY RATIO
1.6934

ASSETS-TO-EQUITY RATIO
2.6934

QUICK RATIO
0.3591

Figure 4.3 – Example of a balance sheet

- **Budget variance:** Refers to the difference between the actual cost of a network infrastructure project or initiative and the planned or budgeted cost. Budget variance can be expressed as a percentage or a dollar amount and can be positive or negative.

  Positive budget variance occurs when the actual cost of a project is less than the budgeted cost. This can be seen as a positive outcome, as it indicates that the project was completed within the planned budget and may allow for additional resources to be allocated to other projects or initiatives.

  Negative budget variance occurs when the actual cost of a project exceeds the budgeted cost. This can be seen as a negative outcome, as it indicates that the project was over budget and may require additional resources or adjustments to meet planned objectives.

> **Note**
> These terms are the standard meanings/definitions. In practical terms, if you have a positive variance of a project outcome, you're implying (financially) that you can do more with less. When it comes time for yearly budget reviews, the financial team will look at the positive variance as an indicator to give you *less funding*.
>
> The opposite is true for negative variance – where you as the network architect can leverage to ask for more funding. It's the act of "*if you don't use it, you'll lose it.*"

For a network architect, monitoring and analyzing budget variance is important for several reasons. First, it can help to identify areas where costs may be higher or lower than expected, allowing for adjustments to be made to the project plan or budget. Second, it can help to inform decision-making about future projects or initiatives, based on a better understanding of the actual costs and resources required for similar projects.

- **Financial forecasting:** Financial forecasting refers to the process of using financial data and trends to project future financial outcomes and performance for the organization's network infrastructure projects or initiatives. Financial forecasting can help a network architect plan for future resource needs, identify potential risks and opportunities, and make informed decisions about network infrastructure investments and projects.

  It's an exercise with leadership on a yearly or bi-annual basis. It typically involves analyzing historical financial data and trends, such as revenue, expenses, and budget variances, to identify patterns and predict future financial outcomes. This can be done using a variety of techniques, such as regression analysis, time-series analysis, and predictive modeling. Moreover, it is an opportunity to prioritize initiatives, showcase new ideas, and create potentially new revenue streams for the organization while taking current needs into consideration.

  Financial forecasting is important for a network architect's success, for several reasons. First, it can help to identify potential gaps or shortfalls in funding or resources for network infrastructure projects, allowing for adjustments to be made to project plans or budgets. Second, it can help to identify opportunities for cost savings or efficiencies in network infrastructure projects, based on a better understanding of factors that contribute to project costs.

Providing financial forecasts and analysis, the network architect can articulate the financial impact of network infrastructure projects to a variety of stakeholders and the value that it brings to the organization.

- **Profit and loss statement (P&L)**: Otherwise known as an income statement, this is a financial statement that shows the revenues, costs, and expenses of an organization over a specific period – typically a month, quarter, or year.

To a network architect, the P&L provides information on the financial performance of the organization and the impact of network infrastructure investments and projects on the organization's bottom line. By analyzing revenues and expenses related to network infrastructure investments and projects, a network architect can determine the ROI for these initiatives and identify areas where cost savings or revenue growth opportunities may exist.

A P&L typically includes line items such as revenue, cost of goods sold, gross profit, operating expenses, and net income or loss. It is an important tool for financial planning and decision-making as it provides a snapshot of the organization's financial health and performance over time.

Understanding the P&L is important to align network infrastructure investments and projects with the organization's financial goals and constraints, as well as providing a basis for financial planning and forecasting. By analyzing the financial impact of network infrastructure initiatives, a network architect can make informed decisions about resource allocation, project prioritization, and overall network strategy.

Here's a sample P&L:

Sample Profit and Loss Statement (Income Statement)			
End of Year December 31, 2017			
Particulars/Items	Amount ($M)	Loss ($M)	Profit ($M)
Sales			
Goods Sold	$1,500,000.00		
Sevices Sold	$500,000.00		
Net Profit			$2,000,000.00
Sales Expense			
Cost of Goods	$600,000.00		
Gross Profit			$1,400,000.00
Operating Expense			
Advertising	$50,000.00		
Payroll taxes	$80,000.00		
Salaries and Wages	$55,000.00		
Rent/Mortage/Lease	$17,800.00		
Other OpEx	$8,000.00		
Total Operating Expenses		$210,800.00	
Operating Income			$1,189,200.00
Non-Operating Income			
Interest Revenue	$25,000.00		
Total Non-Operating Income			$25,000.00
Net Income			$1,214,200.00

Figure 4.4 – Sample P&L (income statement)

- **Net present value (NPV)**: Another financial term that represents the present value of future cash flows, discounted to the present at a given rate of return. In the context of network architecture, NPV is used to evaluate the financial *feasibility* of proposed network infrastructure investments.

When a network architect is considering a new network infrastructure project, they can calculate the NPV to determine whether the project will generate positive or negative value for the organization. If the NPV is positive, the project is considered financially viable, as it will generate more value than the cost of the investment. If the NPV is negative, the project may not be financially viable, as it will generate less value than the cost of the investment.

To calculate the NPV, a network architect will need to estimate future cash flows that the project will generate, and discount them to the present using a rate of return that represents the cost of capital for the organization. The NPV calculation takes into account the time value of money, as money received in the future is worth less than money received today due to inflation and other factors:

$$NPV = \frac{Cash\ Flow}{(1 - i)^t} - Initial\ Investment$$

i = rate of return or discount rate

t = number of periods

Here's an NPV example:

Particulars	Value
Initial Investment ($)	80000
Cash Flow ($)	100000
Time (years)	3
Rate of Return (%)	10.00%
NPV	57174.21

Figure 4.5 – Example of NPV

- **Compound annual growth rate (CAGR)**: This is a major financial concept that measures the annual growth rate of an investment over a specified period of time. As a network architect, understanding the CAGR is important for assessing the *long-term* financial performance of network infrastructure investments.

The CAGR takes into account the effect of compounding, where investment returns are reinvested over time, and provides a more accurate measure of investment growth compared to simple average growth rates. It is calculated as the nth root of the total return, where n is the number of years in the investment period, minus 1:

$$CAGR = \left(\frac{Ending\ Investment\ Value}{Initial\ Investment}\right)^{(\frac{1}{t})} - 1$$

For example, if an investment grew from $10,000 to $15,000 over a 5-year period, the CAGR would be approximately 8.45%:

Particulars	Value
Initial Investment ($)	10000
Final Value ($)	15000
Time (years)	5
CAGR	8.45%

Figure 4.6 – Example of CAGR

By understanding the CAGR, a network architect can evaluate the long-term financial performance of network infrastructure investments and use this information to make informed decisions about future investments. For example, if a particular investment has a low CAGR, the architect may need to consider alternative investments that offer higher growth potential. On the other hand, if an investment has a high CAGR, the architect may decide to continue investing in that area to maximize returns.

> **Note**
> The percentage of CAGR is important to the organization's overall cash flow and profit. How much is a great outlook (1% versus 10%)? It depends on the organization's size, market space, valuation, and other metrics set forth by the organization.

The IT budgeting process typically involves collaboration between the CIO/CTO, the finance department, and other department heads who are responsible for IT-related expenses, which includes the network architect. The network architect may provide input on budget requirements related to network infrastructure, hardware, and software, based on the organization's strategic priorities, goals, and requirements.

As part of the IT budgeting process, the network architect may work with the finance department and senior management to allocate funds for OpEx investments in network infrastructure. This may involve identifying areas where cost savings can be achieved through operational efficiencies, such as automation or outsourcing, or prioritizing investments in critical areas of the network that require ongoing maintenance and support.

The budget allocation process may involve analyzing previous spending and identifying areas where cost savings can be achieved, as well as forecasting future spending requirements based on business growth and technology trends. Once a budget is allocated, the network architect is responsible for managing the network infrastructure budget, monitoring spending, and ensuring that expenses align with the budget and strategic priorities.

As a network architect, though non-technical, one must be able to understand these constraints and be well versed in the *business* aspect of an organization. Typically, a network architect will go through a *budget planning* exercise to determine their needs for the IT infrastructure.

Overall, the responsibility for allocating the IT budget in an organization typically lies with senior management or the executive team, which includes the CIO or CTO. The CIO or CTO is responsible for overseeing the organization's technology strategy and ensuring that IT investments align with the organization's goals and objectives.

Cross Functional Teams (CFTs)

I touched on CFTs when discussing the business logistics – the structure of an organization. A CFT is a group of individuals with diverse backgrounds and skill sets who come together to work on a *specific project* or *goal*. For a particular IT project, this would be one of these teams:

- **Project management:** The project management team brings a structured approach to planning, executing, and monitoring the progress of a project to the CFT. The CFT is typically led by a project manager or team leader and is designed to break down silos and encourage collaboration between departments.

  The project management team performs the following duties:

  - Makes sure IT project(s) are completed on time, within budget, and meet the requirements of the business stakeholders

  - Defines project scope, objectives, timelines, and resource allocation

  - Creates project plans and schedules, identifies and manages risks, and tracks progress against milestones

- **IT operations team:** The IT operations team brings its expertise in day-to-day operations to the CFT. This includes an understanding of the network architecture, hardware and software systems, security protocols, and other IT-related considerations that impact a project's success.

  IT operations team members can help ensure that a project is feasible from a technical standpoint and can provide guidance on how to effectively implement and maintain IT systems to support the project's goals. The network architect may lead or have a senior engineer lead.

- **Security team:** The security team brings expertise in identifying and mitigating potential security risks to a CFT. They can help identify potential vulnerabilities in the IT infrastructure and recommend solutions to address them.

  They also bring an understanding of industry-standard security practices and regulations and can ensure that the project is compliant with relevant standards and regulations. The security team can also help the CFT develop policies and procedures to ensure the security of any sensitive data or information involved in the project.

- **Application development team**: The application team brings its expertise in designing, developing, and maintaining software applications. Typically, they are spoken to first, via questionaries, to identify which applications are the following:

  - Mission critical

  - Business critical

  - Business support applications

  - Non-critical

  The application team works closely with the network architect to ensure that the application can be deployed and run effectively on the network infrastructure. They also collaborate with the IT operations team to ensure that the application can be monitored, managed, and supported in production. They also ensure that the application is scalable, maintainable, and meets required performance and security standards.

- **Business stakeholders**: Business stakeholders bring their perspective and expertise on the business needs, requirements, and goals of a project or initiative to the CFT. They provide insights into the business processes, workflows, and strategies that may impact the project, and help the team ensure that the project aligns with the overall business objectives.

> **Note**
>
> The business stakeholders are the ones who sponsor the IT project for the organization. It's critical to keep them up to date on the progress of any project they are a part of.

  The network architect is one of a few trusted advisors to business stakeholders to assist them in understanding the project and its requirements in order for them to make informed decisions that are necessary for the project's success.

- **Finance team**: You may work with the finance team to understand budget and financial constraints and ensure that network infrastructure investments align with the organization's financial goals.

  Their goal is to provide support in financial planning, budgeting, and forecasting to the CFT. They help to ensure that the project is financially viable and can provide insight into the costs associated with different solutions or approaches.

  The finance team also plays a key role in tracking project costs and providing regular updates on budget variance. They can provide guidance on financial metrics, such as ROI and TCO, to help inform decision-making. Additionally, the finance team can work with the project management team to develop financial projections and ensure that the project stays within budget.

> **Note**
>
> Not all projects stay aligned with the current budget. The majority of projects do exceed the current budget (**firm fixed price**, **FFP**), and funding allocation will need to be revisited and possibly move to a **time and material budget** (**T&M**). Or, a project can be stopped until additional funding is made available as a revision to the current FFP contract.

- **Procurement team**: The procurement team is integral to the CFT. Along with the network architect and other teams, they facilitate sourcing, negotiating, and managing contracts with vendors and suppliers. This includes discount pricing, rebates, and SLAs or terms and conditions being satisfied throughout the lifetime of what's being procured. They also ensure these contracts are properly executed and fulfilled.

  The procurement team works with the finance team to make sure funding is aligned with the project's needs and scope.

> **Note**
>
> It's important for the network architect to work with procurement and provide an accurate **bill of materials** (**BOM**) of what is needed for their project. Remember – the procurement team is only concerned with the **purchase order** (**PO**), not *what is* being purchased, as they are not the technical experts.

To put this all into perspective, here is a diagram of what a CFT organizational chart looks like:

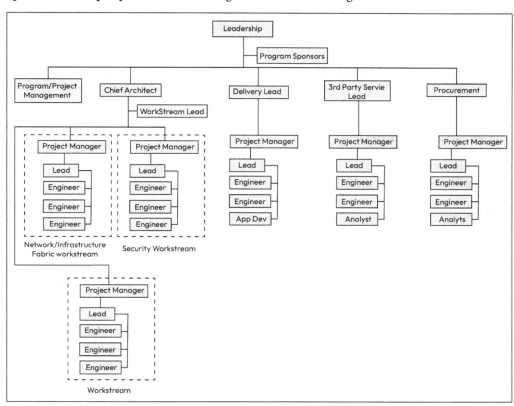

Figure 4.7 – Example of a CFT

In summary, by working in CFTs, IT projects can benefit from enhanced communication, improved problem-solving, and increased efficiency in streamlined decision-making processes. By leveraging the strengths and expertise of team members from different functional areas, IT projects can achieve higher-quality outcomes that are aligned with the broader organizational goals.

Managing business relationships

Have you ever had an irate customer, whether it's a customer who bought a network solution or was internally trying to connect to the network? And once the issue was resolved, you followed up to make sure that the service or solution met their needs? If the answer is "yes," then you're managing a business relationship.

It is important for a network architect to manage business relationships because it helps to establish trust and effective communication between the IT department and other departments or stakeholders within the organization. This enables the network architect to better understand the needs and priorities of the business and to ensure that the network infrastructure is aligned with the goals and objectives of the organization.

There are various types of business relationships that a network architect may need to manage. Let's look at a few important ones.

Vendors and suppliers

A network architect needs to manage relationships with vendors and suppliers who provide technology solutions, hardware, software, and other services to the organization.

The network architect is the liaison between vendors/suppliers and upper management. When new technology comes to the market, the network architect is contacted to see if it's a right fit for any current or upcoming organizational needs. Conversely, all vendors/suppliers, and their solutions, may not be pertinent at the moment, and it's up to the network architect to facilitate and manage communication.

It's important for the network architect to check in with vendors and suppliers, or vice versa, regularly to establish a trusted relationship. This can lead to a more efficient and effective procurement process, as well as a better understanding of the vendor's products and services. Moreover, it can lead to more favorable terms and conditions in contracts and can help to ensure that vendors and suppliers prioritize the network architect's needs and concerns. Additionally, a trusted relationship can help mitigate potential issues or conflicts that may arise in the future, as everyone involved is more likely to work collaboratively to find a mutually beneficial solution.

Internal stakeholders

There are many internal stakeholders, such as finance, operations, security, management, and application owners – each with their own unique needs. The network architect needs to work with these stakeholders to find out what's required of them. Similarly, with vendors and suppliers, a level of trust needs to be established among internal stakeholders, which is important for several reasons:

- It allows the network architect to better understand the needs and requirements of the stakeholders, which can inform the design and implementation of IT solutions that meet those needs.
- It can help to create a more collaborative working environment, where stakeholders feel comfortable sharing their ideas and concerns with the network architect. This can lead to more effective communication and problem-solving, as well as improved project outcomes.
- Building trust can help to establish the network architect as a trusted advisor within the organization, which can lead to increased influence and opportunities to contribute to strategic decision-making.

Overall, building trusted relationships with internal stakeholders is essential for a network architect to effectively serve the needs of the organization and achieve its goals.

Partners and clients

The value of business relationships between a network architect and partners/clients is significant. These relationships can help the network architect to gain a better understanding of the business of their partners, which can aid them in future projects, and their clients, where they can design solutions to fit their needs.

> **Note**
>
> An architect may not have the in-house capabilities to undertake a large transformational project (for a client or internally), for example, and a need arises for specialized skills. By building and managing partner relationships, they can turn to a trusted partner to fulfill the requirement(s).

By building strong relationships with partners/clients, the network architect can establish a reputation for the organization as a *trusted* and *reliable partner*. This can lead to repeat business, referrals, and even partnerships with other organizations. Strong relationships can also help to increase collaboration, communication, and overall satisfaction with the services provided.

Ultimately, the value of business relationships for a network architect lies in the potential for long-term partnerships that can benefit both the organization and its partners/clients.

> **Note**
>
> As you continue to grow the level of trust with partners and clients, begin to think about co-developing solutions and **go-to-market** (**GTM**) strategies. This will not only bring more visibility to you but also increase your brand as an SME/SMA.

Industry groups and associations

A network architect may need to manage relationships with industry groups and associations to keep up with the latest trends and developments in their field.

Examples of such groups are as follows:

- **Cisco Community and User Groups**
- **Juniper Elevate Community**
- **Open Compute Project (OCP)**
- **The Open Networking User Group (ONUG)**
- **Google Cloud Innovators**

- **Cloud Native Computing Foundation (CNCF)**
- **Information Systems Audit and Control Association (ISACA)**

Building and maintaining business relationships with industry groups and associations can bring several benefits to a network architect, such as the following:

- **Knowledge sharing**: Engaging with industry groups and associations provides access to a wealth of knowledge and expertise. Network architects can learn about new trends, best practices, and emerging technologies that can help them improve their skills and stay up to date with the latest industry developments.

- **Networking opportunities**: Industry groups and associations provide networking opportunities where network architects can meet and connect with other professionals in the field. This can lead to new business opportunities, partnerships, and collaborations.

- **Industry recognition**: By participating in industry groups and associations, network architects can establish themselves as thought leaders in the industry. This can help them gain recognition, build credibility, and enhance their professional reputation.

- **Advocacy**: Industry groups and associations often advocate for the interests of their members. By participating in these groups, network architects can help shape industry policy and regulations and promote the interests of their organizations.

Regulatory agencies

A network architect may need to manage relationships with regulatory agencies to ensure that the organization complies with relevant regulations and standards.

Building and maintaining strong business relationships is important for a network architect because these agencies play a key role in shaping the legal and regulatory environment in which the organization operates.

Some legal and regulatory compliances are as follows:

- **Data privacy regulations**: The **General Data Protection Regulation (GDPR)**, the **California Consumer Privacy Act (CCPA)**, the **Health Insurance Portability and Accountability Act (HIPAA)**

- **Cybersecurity regulations**: The **New York Department of Financial Services (NYDFS)**, the **Payment Card Industry Data Security Standard (PCI DSS)**

- **Intellectual property (IP) laws**: Trademarks, patents, and copyrights

- **Anti-spam and email marketing regulations**: The **Controlling the Assault of Non-Solicited Pornography and Marketing (CAN-SPAM)** Act, the EU's *ePrivacy Directive*

- **Accessibility regulations**: **Americans with Disabilities Act (ADA)**

- **Export control regulations**: The **International Traffic in Arms Regulations (ITAR)**, the **Export Administration Regulations (EAR)**

- **Telecommunications regulations**: The **Federal Communications Commission (FCC)**

- **Labor laws**: The **Occupational Safety and Health Act (OSHA)**, the **Fair Labor Standards Act (FLSA)**

By establishing good relationships with regulatory agencies, the network architect can stay informed about changes in regulations, guidelines, and standards and ensure that their organization is compliant. Additionally, these relationships can help the network architect advocate for the organization's needs and goals within the regulatory environment as well as receive guidance and support from these agencies and minimize the risk of regulatory violations and penalties. They can also help to enhance the reputation and credibility of the organization as a responsible and compliant player in its industry.

By effectively handling the management of business relationships within an organization or across many, the network architect can aid in facilitating collaboration and teamwork across departments and can lead to more successful implementation of IT projects and initiatives. Building and maintaining positive business relationships can help to increase the network architect's influence and credibility within the organization, which can be valuable when seeking support and resources for IT initiatives.

> **Note**
> By establishing credibility, the network architect can become a major influence in the organization, which could potentially lead to career advancements internally within the organization or externally.

Summary

In this chapter, we covered some important key elements that a network architect must possess in order to be successful. The network architect must not only be tech savvy but also have the ability to manage and lead teams, whether those teams report to them or not. The network architect must have an understanding of the business and business financials – not to the extent of a CEO or **chief financial officer (CFO)**, but a working knowledge in order to justify funding for projects and initiatives, help customers make an educated decision on how to apply certain technology costs (CapEx or OpEx model), and speak coherently to internal finance teams. They must be able to manage relationships they come across through the life of a project and daily activities. Business relationships help a network architect establish credibility and the reputation of a trusted advisor.

In the next chapter, we'll explore the mindset of a network architect.

5

The Mindset of the Network Architect – the Principles of Design

The mindset of a network architect is developed over time. It starts by having an interest – in this case, networking; from there, reading, learning, listening (actively and passively), attending meetups or conferences, and working with experts in the field. Important enough is to ask questions and *question* the answer, and the process repeats itself. But along the way, you'll begin to develop your own mindset on how you'd approach networking. Is there a correct mindset to have? That can be left for debate.

How I'd Iike to describe this is as follows:

"Taking outside knowledge and combining it with your own... to create new knowledge."

In other words, take the learning you acquired from mentors, books, and work – then take your own ideas/thoughts to create your *own* knowledge that you can articulate to others.

In this chapter, we'll take a look at the mindset of a network architect when it comes to the principles of design. Key topics we'll be discussing are the following:

- Principles of network architecting
- Thinking like a CxO
- What other industries are doing
- Always thinking – innovating and exploring new trends

So, let's get started!

Principles of network architecting

Designing networks differs from one organization to another. Organizations regard their designs to be proprietary, including IP addresses, **virtual LAN (VLAN)** assignments, firewall rules, and the overall naming conventions used, yet the concepts are the same. However, all networks follow the same principles. It's these principles that help ensure these networks are designed in a way that is secure, reliable, and meets the needs of the organization.

> **Note**
> There are pros and cons to each network architecture type. And in my opinion, there is no "one-size-fits-all" approach. Every organization will have an opinion on what they believe they need, and it's up to the network architect to make sure the correct design is in place.

Some of the key principles of network architecting include the following:

- Hierarchical
- Scalability
- Modularity
- Resilience
- Performant

Let's explore each.

Hierarchical

The hierarchical design principle is used in the context of network architecture to refer to a specific design approach that is based on a hierarchical structure. In this approach, the network(s) is(are) divided into multiple layers or tiers, with each layer serving a specific function and providing services to the layers above and below it.

> **Note**
> These layers or tiers can extend outside the boundaries of a data center or enterprise network, as seen in *Figure 5.3*.

Hierarchal design patterns

In *Chapter 1*, we discussed two variants:

- The classical three-tier architecture:

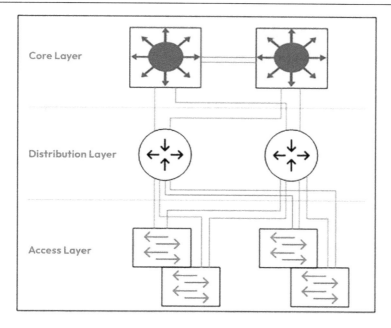

Figure 5.1 – Classical three-tier network architecture

- The modern Clos network architecture:

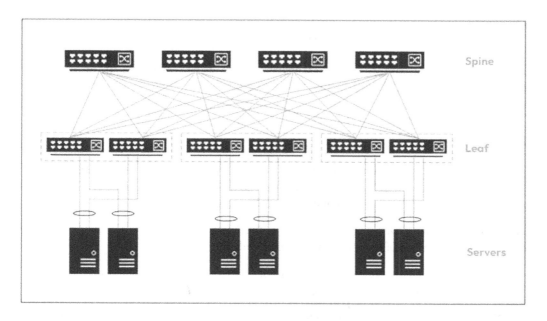

Figure 5.2 – Clos (spine-leaf) network architecture

And here's another design to extend past the boundaries of a typical data center:

- Global cloud network architecture:

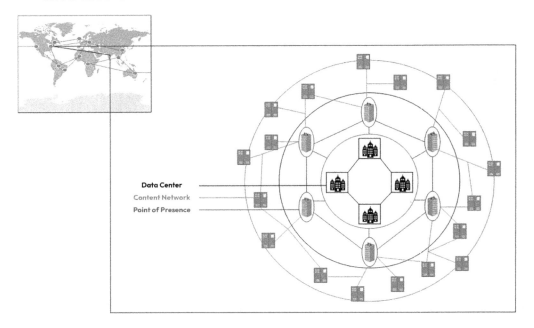

Figure 5.3 – Global cloud network architecture

As you can see in the preceding diagrams, each layer is designed to provide specific functions and services with their own responsibilities and certain capabilities.

Let's discuss each of them.

Three-tier architecture

The three-tier network architecture is one of the most widely used network designs in enterprise networks. It consists of three main layers: the access layer, the distribution layer, and the core layer. Each layer has its own specific functions and responsibilities within the network.

The access layer, as the name suggests, provides access to the network and to end devices and peripherals. However, the main function of the access layer is to provide the following:

- **Network subnet segmentation** with the usage of VLANs to disseminate traffic on the network, accordingly. It functions to create separate broadcast domains as well.

- **Port security** so that only authorized devices are allowed to connect to the network, through MAC address filtering and 802.1x authentication.

- **Quality of service (QoS)**, whereby policies are applied to prioritize critical applications and services so that they have the necessary bandwidth and resources to function properly.

- **Power over Ethernet (PoE)** capabilities, through CAT5/5e/6, to power network devices such as IP phones, **wireless access points (WAPs)**, and security cameras where conventional power options cannot be applied.

> **Note**
>
> With mobile workers, SaaS-based solutions, and work-from-home initiatives, the access layer is more abstract.

The distribution layer is the second layer. This layer provides a consistent path to the core layer and to other access-layer devices. Moreover, it *controls* access to resources at the core. This layer has routers or switches with high port density to accommodate growth, expansion, and aggregated bandwidth (that is, port channeling). Key functions are the following:

- **Aggregation of network traffic**: Network traffic must be aggregated to make sufficient usage of bandwidth as data reaches the core layer to reduce network congestion

- **Distribution of network traffic**: Uses routing protocols (that is, **Open Shortest Path First (OSPF)**, **Enhanced Interior Gateway Routing Protocol (EIGRP)**, **Intermediate System to Intermediate System (ISIS)**) to disseminate network traffic between different VLANs and subnets, allowing for communication between devices on different parts of the network

- **Security enforcement**: On top of port security at the access layers, the distribution layer provides additional security through the usage of **access control lists (ACLs)**

- **QoS**: Additional QoS is performed for traffic shaping and policing in order to make or have bandwidth available for high-priority traffic

- **Service appliances and tooling**: The distribution layer also serves other network appliances, firewalls, load balancers, **intrusion detection systems/intrusion prevention systems (IDS/IPS)**, network monitoring tools (**security information and event management (SIEM)**), and other tools

> **Note**
>
> As mentioned, the distribution layer is designed for network traffic aggregation and filtering. This means that any traffic leaving (egressing) should be "clean" traffic when reaching (ingressing) the core layer as minimal processing is done at this layer.

The core layer is designed to provide fast and reliable transportation of data between the distribution layer switches, without introducing delays or bottlenecks. It's optimized for high-speed data transfer and consists of high-performance switches and routers. In general, network traffic traversing the core should not require any additional filtering as that process was completed at the distribution layer.

The core layer has several essential functions:

- **High-speed data transfer**: The core layer is designed to provide fast and reliable transportation of data between the distribution layer switches to minimize congestion of network traffic

- **Redundancy**: Typically designed with redundancy in mind to ensure that the network remains operational in the event of a failure

- **Minimal processing**: Designed to minimize processing and avoid introducing additional delays in the network

- **Scalability**: The core layer is designed to be highly scalable, allowing for the addition of new switches and routers as the network grows

- **Traffic prioritization**: The core layer supports QoS features, such as traffic prioritization, to ensure that critical applications receive the necessary bandwidth and minimize the impact of less important traffic

> **Note**
> Consider the core layer to be an interstate highway where cars that need to get to another state can reach it (fast) without dealing with traffic lights, stop signs, rerouting, local congestion, and so on.

There are several benefits of using a three-tier network architecture:

- **Scalability**: The architecture is scalable, which allows for the network to easily grow and expand as the organization's needs change. Additional switches or routers can be added at each tier to accommodate increased traffic and user activities.

- **Modular design**: Each tier is independent of the others and is designed as a modular building block that can be easily replaced or upgraded without affecting the rest of the network. This makes it easier to manage and maintain the network over time and reduces the risk of downtime or disruptions.

- **Simplified management**: Because of its modularity, the three-tier network architecture makes it easier to manage the network by separating different functions into distinct tiers, each with its own set of responsibilities and management requirements. This makes it easier to troubleshoot and diagnose issues and allows network architects to focus on specific areas of the network.

- **Improved performance**: By separating different functions into distinct tiers, the three-tier network architecture can improve the performance of the network by reducing bottlenecks and improving traffic flow. This can help ensure that critical applications and services have the necessary bandwidth and resources to function properly.

- **High availability (HA)**: Provides redundancy and load balancing at each tier, which helps ensure the HA and reliability of the network. In case of a failure in one tier, the network can continue to function without significant disruption.

There are also some downsides to the three-tier network architecture that must be taken into consideration when designing. Some factors include the following:

- **Complexity**: The architecture can be complex to design, configure, and maintain, especially for larger networks. It requires careful planning and coordination between the different layers to ensure that the network is optimized for performance, scalability, and reliability. Additionally, highly skilled individuals are required to maintain this level of complexity.

- **Cost**: As complexity increases, so does the cost to procure equipment and maintain the network design. It can be more expensive to implement than other network architectures, such as a flat network architecture. It requires more hardware and cabling, which can increase the cost of deployment.

- **Skill and expertise level**: The three-tier network architecture is complex to deploy, manage, and maintain. If one mishap occurs during an upgrade process or a change to add a new feature, the results could be catastrophic. Therefore, highly skilled and confident individuals are needed to ensure, in the event of an incident, minimal disruptions occur.

- **Limited flexibility**: This can be less flexible than other network architectures, as changes to the network may require changes to the other layers. This can increase the time, cost, and effort required to make changes to the network.

Overall, the three-tier architecture is a proven and widely used design principle in IT networking, providing a scalable, modular, and easy-to-manage network design that can meet the needs of enterprise networks of all sizes.

Clos network (spine-leaf) architecture

The modern Clos network architecture is a popular network design approach used in modern data center environments. It is also known as a spine-leaf or fabric architecture. This network architecture is characterized by the usage of the non-blocking switching fabric of a multistage switching network.

> **Note**
> Non-blocking means that each port on the switch can send and receive traffic at wire speed (the maximum speed of the interface) to and from any other port.

Compared to the traditional three-tier network architecture, the Clos network features only two layers: **leaf** and **spine**.

You may think of a spine-leaf architecture as a collapsed core, but the opposite is true. It's a collapsed distribution ideology.

The spine-leaf architecture provides a simple and scalable network design that can support large-scale data center deployments. The **spine** switches provide high-speed connectivity between the leaf switches, while the **leaf** switches provide connectivity to the end devices. This design eliminates the need for complex protocols such as **Spanning Tree Protocol (STP)** and allows for more efficient use of network resources. Let's look at its components:

- **Spine layer**: The spine layer is the core layer of the spine-leaf architecture, and it is responsible for providing high-speed, non-blocking connectivity between the leaf switches, with high-speed, high-capacity switches that are designed to handle a large volume of traffic with low latency.

  The spine switches are usually interconnected in a full-mesh topology, which provides multiple paths for traffic to flow between the leaf switches. The spine layer is designed to be highly resilient, with redundant links and hardware components, to ensure HA and **fault tolerance (FT)**.

- **Leaf layer**: The leaf layer is the access layer of the spine-leaf architecture, and it is responsible for connecting end devices such as servers, storage systems, and network appliances to the network.

  Leaf switches are typically deployed in a **top-of-rack (ToR)** configuration, where each switch is connected to multiple servers or appliances. The leaf switches are connected to every spine switch, providing high-bandwidth connectivity to all devices in the network. This is designed to be highly scalable, allowing new switches to be added to the network as needed, without disrupting the existing traffic flow.

> **Note**
> Leaf switches are deployed as a pair connected to each spine. All downstream devices are dual-homed to leaf switches, creating a *pod*.

The Clos network architecture offers several benefits:

- **Highly scalable**: The architecture is highly scalable, allowing organizations to easily add more switches and devices as their network needs grow. This makes it easier for organizations to accommodate new applications, services, and users without worrying about network capacity limitations.

- **High bandwidth**: It provides high-bandwidth connectivity between devices, allowing organizations to efficiently handle large amounts of data traffic. This is important for applications such as big data analytics, video streaming, and cloud computing.

- **Low latency**: It provides low-latency connectivity between devices, which is important for applications that require real-time data processing or low-latency communication. This can improve overall network performance and user experience.

- **Redundancy**: Redundant paths between devices increase network availability and reduce the risk of downtime in the event of a device failure.

- **Non-blocking**: Clos networks are designed to be non-blocking, meaning that they can provide full connectivity between any pair of devices in the network without contention or performance degradation. This is crucial in high-performance computing and data center environments where low-latency, high-throughput communication is essential.

- **Equal-cost multi-path (ECMP) routing**: Clos networks are well suited for ECMP, which allows traffic to be load-balanced (from a routing perspective) across multiple equal-cost paths, enhancing network utilization and FT.

- **Cost-effective**: They are typically more cost-effective than traditional three-tier network designs because they require fewer network devices and can operate more efficiently, resulting in lower power and cooling costs.

> **Note**
> Ultimately, the key benefit that encompasses the aforementioned capacities is that no one end device is *no more than one hop away from another end device*.

While the Clos network architecture offers many benefits, there could be some drawbacks:

- **Complexity**: Although there is a clear separation between the core (spine) and access (leaf) layers, the Clos architecture can be more complex to design, deploy, and manage than traditional three-tier network designs. This is because spine/leaf networks require more network devices and more sophisticated network routing and forwarding protocols.

- **Cost**: Although more cost-effective than traditional three-tier designs in some cases, they can also be more expensive in others. This is because Clos networks require specialized network devices that can be more expensive to purchase and operate. Also, operating in a full-mesh capacity increases costs due to additional copper or fiber connections to every switch at each layer.

- **Limited flexibility**: Clos networks are designed for a low latency and line rate bandwidth and may not be as flexible as other network architectures. Compatibility may be a concern with certain legacy applications or networking technologies. For example, adding or removing network devices may require significant reconfiguration of the network fabric.

- **Vendor lock-in**: The leaf-spine architecture typically requires specialized network devices from a single vendor. This can result in vendor lock-in, limiting the organization's flexibility and ability to negotiate pricing and terms with multiple vendors.

Global cloud network architecture

A global cloud network is a complex and extensive system designed to deliver cloud computing services and resources across the world. It consists of numerous interconnected components that work together to provide reliable, scalable, and efficient services.

The network, itself, represents an extensive and sophisticated infrastructure designed to facilitate cloud computing services across the globe, ensuring HA, redundancy, and performance. At its core lies multiple data centers, distributed strategically to minimize latency and maximize efficiency, each packed with an array of servers dedicated to computing, storage, and database management. These facilities are interconnected by a robust backbone network, comprising high-speed internet connections, advanced routers, switches, and security appliances that work in concert to manage and direct the flow of data.

Crucial to this ecosystem are **content delivery networks (CDNs)**, which optimize service delivery to users based on geographic proximity. The network is also fortified with cutting-edge security measures such as encryption and stringent access controls to safeguard data integrity and privacy.

An integral component of this architecture is the suite of cloud services it offers, encompassing IaaS, PaaS, and SaaS, which are maintained, updated, and supported by a continuous cycle of management, automation tools, and technical support teams. This harmonious orchestration ensures that the global cloud network remains resilient, scalable, and primed to meet the ever-expanding demands of the digital world.

Chapter 9, Paradigm Shift to Cloud Computing, goes into the benefits, services, and solutions of cloud computing in depth.

> **Note**
> Global cloud networks foster both Clos architectures (and variants of it) inside the provider's physical data centers and three-tier architectures relating to regions/zones/DC. Additional hierarchical patterns relating to elements such as resources, users/teams, and permissions are distributed (that is, organizations, folders, projects, and resources).

Additional design patterns

Hierarchical design patterns are architectural approaches that organize complex systems or structures into a *hierarchy* of interconnected layers or levels, each with distinct roles and responsibilities. This hierarchical arrangement simplifies system management, scalability, and maintenance by breaking down intricate systems into more manageable and structured components.

These are considered hybrid/variants or extensions, with respect to the design patterns already mentioned. These patterns, in turn, have the advantages and disadvantages of their parent pattern.

Three-tier hub and spoke

The three-tier hub-and-spoke network design pattern is an amalgamation of a hierarchical structure and centralized topology, aimed at optimizing resource allocation and simplifying management.

In this pattern, the core layer functions as the central hub, providing high-speed, redundant connectivity and serving as the backbone for data transportation. The distribution layer acts as an intermediary set of spokes, which aggregates the traffic from the access layer before it is routed through the core. Each spoke in the distribution layer serves a specific set of access-layer switches, segmenting the network into distinct manageable blocks and controlling access to network resources.

The access layer directly connects end-user devices or local peripherals to the network, operating as the entry point to the hierarchical infrastructure.

Super-spine Clos architecture

The super-spine Clos network represents an evolution of the traditional spine-leaf architecture, tailored for modern data centers that demand high throughput and scalability. In this topology, the super-spine layer is introduced as an additional hierarchical level above the spine layer, essentially serving as a backbone for multiple spine switches. The leaf switches connect end devices, such as servers and storage systems, and aggregate traffic upward to the spine switches. The spine switches, in turn, are responsible for internal data center routing and connect the leaf switches to the super spine.

This super-spine layer provides interconnectivity between different spine switches, facilitating efficient east-west traffic flow within the data center. It's designed to support massive data transfer rates and a large number of connections while maintaining low latency.

In summary, the purpose of the hierarchical design is to provide a scalable and flexible framework for adding new devices and systems to the network as the organization grows. The design also simplifies network management by dividing the network into smaller, more tangible segments and providing different levels of access control and security. Overall, a hierarchical design helps to optimize network performance, improve reliability and availability, and enhance security and manageability.

Scalability

The second main principle of network architecting is scalability. The network should be designed with scale in mind. As an organization matures, so does the infrastructure. Its growth is dependent on the needs of the organization and adapts to changes required. This can involve adding more hardware, increasing processing power, or optimizing software to handle more data.

Over the years in my career, I have heard the following questions and statements from business leaders, upper management, and sales teams:

"The business needs to scale!"

"...if we don't scale, we'll miss out..."

"What does it take to scale the infrastructure?"

"The customer is looking to scale their IT network infrastructure..."

"We're actively inquiring about solution x because it can scale..."

"How do we scale?"

Sometimes, my answer is: *"Scale what?"* It may draw some ire, but truthfully, what needs to be scaled must be identified. What are they really asking? Well, they're asking:

"What does it take from a network infrastructure perspective to meet the demands driven by our end users, customers, clientele, and Wall Street?"

And the answer is:

"We need to scale the infrastructure, but it depends on what needs to be done..."

In order to scale a network, several factors must be taken into consideration and require specific steps to ensure the network can handle increased traffic and data flow or to determine whether a redesign or upgrade is necessary. Some of the steps that a network architect may take to scale a network infrastructure include the following:

- **Conducting a thorough assessment** of the existing network infrastructure to identify potential bottlenecks or areas that require optimization
- **Identifying the specific needs of the organization** and determining the appropriate capacity required to handle future growth
- **Choosing the appropriate network topology** and design that can handle increased traffic and data flow
- **Selecting the appropriate hardware and software components or solutions** that can handle the increased workload and provide optimal performance
- **Monitoring network resources** over a period to determine the scaling requirements of the network

> **Note**
>
> In my opinion, if the network infrastructure has a constant saturation level between 75% and 80%, it would be necessary to start looking at scaling and upgrading options.

Scaling a network infrastructure can be performed in several ways. Some common approaches to scaling a network infrastructure include:

- **Vertical scaling**: This involves adding more resources to an existing device, such as adding more RAM, CPU, or storage. This can improve the device's capacity to handle increased traffic and data flow:

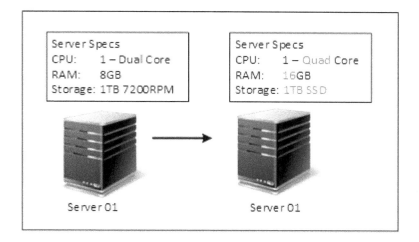

Figure 5.4 – Example of vertical scaling

- **Horizontal scaling**: This involves adding more devices to the network, such as adding more servers or switches. This can distribute the workload across multiple devices, which can improve overall network performance and capacity:

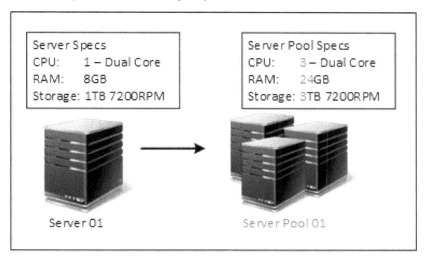

Figure 5.5 – Example of horizontal scaling

- **Load balancing**: This involves distributing traffic across multiple devices or servers, which can help prevent overloading a single device and improve overall network performance and capacity:

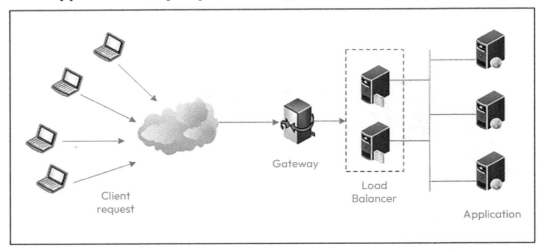

Figure 5.6 – Application load balancing

- **Network segmentation**: This involves dividing the network into smaller, more manageable segments, which can help reduce congestion and improve overall network performance:

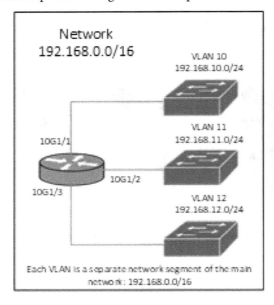

Figure 5.7 – Network segmentation

> **Note**
>
> Cloud computing is another approach to scaling by utilizing software to build, deploy, and manage an organization's IT infrastructure.

Modularity

The third principle is modularity. A modular network infrastructure is designed such that it allows for easy expansion and modification. This is accomplished by dividing the network into smaller, self-contained *units*. Each unit can then be independently configured and managed, which makes it easier to troubleshoot problems and make changes to the network.

Consider the following example:

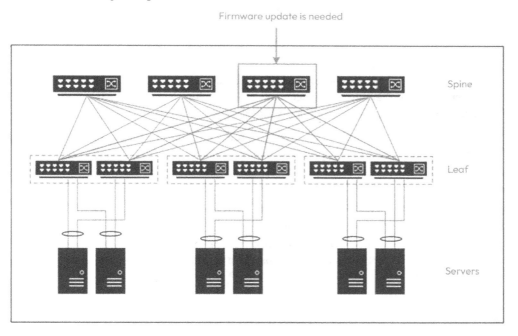

Figure 5.8 – Fault in a spine switch

Let's say a core switch has been rebooting quite often. After investigating a bit further, you find out that a firmware update is needed to rectify the issue. These are the questions to ask:

"*Is the entire spine/leaf fabric affected?*"

"*Must we put the entire fabric into a maintenance window?*"

"*Will end devices lose connectivity to the fabric?*"

The answer is no. Since the spine/leaf fabric incorporated the design principle of *modularity* and all spine switches are independent of each other (with multiple connector paths), the affected switch can be placed in a maintenance window without impeding activity across the fabric.

There are several ways in which a network infrastructure can be designed to be modular:

- **Modular network devices**: Use network devices, such as switches and routers, that offer a modular architecture. This allows for the addition or removal of modules or line cards, enabling scalability and flexibility.

  For example, modular switches have slots where you can add or replace line cards for specific functionalities such as additional ports, specialized interfaces, or security features.

- **Virtualization and software-defined networking (SDN)**: Enable the separation (decoupling) of network control and data planes. This allows for the creation of **virtual network functions (VNFs)** and virtualized network services that can be deployed, modified, or scaled independently. It promotes flexibility and simplifies network management.

- **Network segmentation**: Divides the network into smaller segments or VLANs based on specific requirements or logical boundaries. Each segment can be treated as a modular unit, allowing for independent configuration, management, and scalability. Network segmentation enhances security, performance, and ease of maintenance.

  Examples would be the usage of VLANs or **virtual extensible LANs (VxLANs)** to segment traffic types, and pod design in spine/leaf architecture.

Note

Microservices is another approach to modularity where an application is divided into small, independent services that can be developed, deployed, and scaled independently.

However, this approach applies to software development rather than IT network infrastructure. It's worth noting Arista Networks uses a microservice approach to its EOS operating system on its switching platform.

Modularity offers several key benefits:

- **Flexibility and adaptability**: Modularity allows for the creation of independent modules or components that can be easily modified, replaced, or upgraded without affecting the entire system. This flexibility enables organizations to adapt to changing requirements, technologies, or business needs without undergoing a complete overhaul of the network infrastructure. It promotes agility and reduces the disruption caused by modifications.

  Example: Replacing a 1G 24-port line card in a Cisco Catalyst 6500 with a 10G 24-port line card to support higher bandwidth applications or creating a service pod for IDS tools.

- **Scalability**: Modularity facilitates scalability by allowing for the addition or removal of devices to meet increased or decreased demand. New devices or technology can be seamlessly integrated into the existing infrastructure, reducing the complexity and cost of scaling. This modular approach ensures that the network can expand and accommodate future growth without impacting the overall system performance.

Example: Arista 7500R series switches come in various scalable options of 4, 8, 12, and 16 slots to support a variety of connectivity options:

Figure 5.9 – Arista 7500R universal spine series switches (Source: https://www. arista.com/en/products/7500r-series-network-switch-datasheet)

- **Fault isolation**: Modularity enhances fault isolation, making it easier to identify and troubleshoot issues. When a problem occurs in one layer or tier, it can be isolated and addressed without affecting the functionality of other modules. This helps in reducing downtime and improving the overall reliability and availability of the network.

Example: A faulty line card in a data center chassis switch can be easily removed and replaced without impacting the entire switch's function.

- **Ease of maintenance**: With modularity, maintenance and updates become more streamlined. Each component can be maintained or upgraded independently, minimizing the impact on the rest of the network. This simplifies the management process, reduces the risk of errors, and allows for quicker implementation of updates or patches.

Example: Updating firmware or software on Cisco Nexus supervisor modules in a dual-supervisor, dual-chassis configuration.

In summary, modularity is significant to the principles of network design as it provides flexibility, scalability, fault isolation, ease of maintenance, interoperability, complexity management, and organizational efficiency. It enables the development of adaptable systems that can evolve, scale, and integrate effectively, leading to improved performance, reduced risks, and enhanced productivity.

> **Note**
> Keep in mind that modularity offers the *ability* to scale. But you can scale without modularity.

Resilience

The network design principle of resilience refers to the ability of a network to maintain its functionality, performance, and availability in the face of various challenges, failures, or disruptions. Resilience ensures that the network can continue to operate effectively, deliver services, and recover quickly from any adverse events.

Let's look at the following diagram:

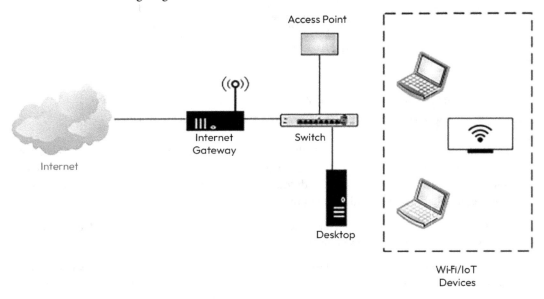

Figure 5.10 – Home internet network

This is what we'll find in our homes when we connect to the internet. Can you determine whether resilience is built into this network? The answer is no. There are multiple **points of failure** (**POFs**) where this network will not be able to maintain its functionality for end users.

If we look back at either the three-tier network diagram or the spine/leaf architecture, we can determine multiple levels of resilience:

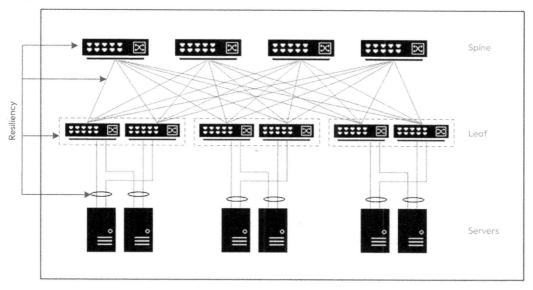

Figure 5.11 – Resiliency in spine-leaf network design

Here are some key aspects and considerations related to network resilience:

- **Redundancy**: Network designs must incorporate redundancy at various levels to mitigate the impact of failures. Redundancy involves the duplication of critical components, links, or systems to provide backup or alternative paths for network traffic.

   Some examples of redundancy are as follows:

   - Backup power supplies

   - Network switches

   - Multiple connections between switches

   - Additional physical connections to **internet service providers** (**ISPs**)

   - Dynamic routing protocols

- **FT**: Resilient networks are designed with FT in mind. Fault-tolerant systems can detect and recover from failures without significant disruption to the overall network. This can involve implementing mechanisms such as the following:

   - Automatic failover

- **First Hop Redundancy Protocol (FHRP)** (that is, **Hot Standby Router Protocol (HSRP)**, **Virtual Router Redundancy Protocol (VRRP)**, **Gateway Load Balancing Protocol (GLBP)**)

- Power redundant options (that is, **uninterruptible power supply (UPS)**, multiple power utility connective)

- Physical cabling (that is, **Link Aggregation Control Protocol (LACP)**, **Port Aggregation Protocol (PAGP)**)

- **Diverse pathways**: Resilient network design considers the use of diverse pathways for network traffic. By leveraging multiple physical routes or logical paths, network resilience is improved. This approach helps to minimize the impact of failures or outages in a single path, ensuring that network traffic can be rerouted to alternative paths without disruption.

- **Rapid recovery and convergence**: Network design should focus on minimizing the time required to recover from failures and restore normal operations. Quick recovery involves mechanisms such as fast network convergence, automated network monitoring, and proactive fault detection. By reducing downtime and the time needed for network recovery, resilience enhances the user experience and minimizes business disruptions.

  Some options are the following:

  - STP (that is, **Rapid Per VLAN Spanning Tree (RPVST)**, **Multiple Spanning Tree (MST)**)

  - Graceful restart

  - **Fast Reroute (FRR)**

  - **Bidirectional Forwarding Detection (BFD)**

- **Security and protection**: Network design should incorporate robust security measures to protect the network from threats and vulnerabilities. This includes implementing firewalls, **intrusion detection and prevention systems (IDPS)**, secure access controls, encryption, and regular security audits. By ensuring the network's security, resilience is enhanced against potential attacks or breaches.

- **Disaster recovery (DR) planning**: A comprehensive **DR plan (DRP)** should be in place to ensure that if the network is compromised, it can recover in a timely manner.

  This involves the following:

  - Creating backup and recovery strategies

  - Off-site data replication

  - Periodic data backups and testing of DR processes

Overall, the principle of network resilience focuses on designing networks that can withstand and recover from failures, disruptions, or attacks. By incorporating redundancy, FT, diverse pathways, rapid recovery mechanisms, security measures, and DR planning, resilient network design helps ensure the continuity, reliability, and availability of network services.

Performant

This principle of network architecting refers to designing a network infrastructure that can deliver optimal speed, throughput, and responsiveness to meet the requirements of the applications and services it supports as expected. A performant network architecture is capable of meeting the demands of the applications, services, and users it supports, without experiencing significant bottlenecks or degradation in performance.

There are several characteristics by which high performance can be achieved:

- **Low latency**: A performant network architecture minimizes the delay in data transmission, ensuring that applications and services can operate with minimal latency. This is particularly important for real-time applications such as video conferencing, online gaming, and financial transactions, where even slight delays can have a significant impact.

  Example: Arista 7130 platform to support ultra-low latency (100ns) for financial services applications.

- **High bandwidth**: A performant network architecture should provide sufficient bandwidth to accommodate the data traffic generated by applications and services. It ensures that the network can handle high volumes of data without experiencing congestion or throughput limitations.

  Example: Replacing 10G network switches with 40G switches.

- **Reliability and availability**: A performant network architecture is designed to be highly reliable and available. It incorporates redundancy and fault-tolerant mechanisms to minimize downtime and ensure continuous operation even in the event of failures or outages.

  Example: Redundant or HA hardware and pathways in case of failure. Load balancing mechanisms to efficiently distribute traffic across backend devices. FT such as multiple connections to server applications in an active/standby or active/active configuration.

- **Efficient traffic management**: Efficient traffic management plays a crucial role in achieving a performant network architecture. It involves optimizing the allocation of network resources, prioritizing critical traffic, and ensuring optimal utilization of bandwidth. This helps ensure that important applications receive the necessary bandwidth and resources to maintain performance.

  Examples: QoS mechanisms, traffic shaping techniques, bandwidth reservation, traffic prioritization, congestion management, and application delivery optimization.

- **Optimal routing and switching**: Network architecture employs efficient routing and switching protocols to ensure that data is transmitted along the most optimal paths. It involves designing efficient paths for data transmission and selecting the best routes for network traffic to minimize unnecessary hops and reduce packet loss, contributing to improved performance.

Example: Effectively using routing protocols (such as OSPF, EIGRP, **Border Gateway Protocol (BGP)**) techniques and features to create an optimal routing and distribution of network and data traffic.

- **Monitoring and optimization**: Monitoring and optimization are essential aspects of maintaining a performant network. It involves actively monitoring the network's performance, analyzing data, and making adjustments to improve its efficiency and responsiveness through the usage of network monitoring and optimization tools.

Some techniques to utilize are the following:

  - Network monitoring

  - Traffic analysis

  - Performance baseline

  - Configuration optimization

  - Performance tuning

By following these principles, network architects can help ensure that their networks are designed in a way that is efficient, reliable, and meets the needs of the organization.

Let's move on to the next section, *Thinking like a CxO*.

Thinking like a CxO

As a network architect, thinking like a CxO (Chief Executive Officer, Chief Financial Officer, and so on) can help you align your network architecture decisions with the strategic goals and objectives of the organization. The mindset is not developed overnight, but more developed as one's career moves forward, and is gained through experience. That experience may come from working on projects, doing research and reading periodicals on CxO roles and responsibilities, attending seminars, or through formal education. Thinking like a CxO requires a combination of mindset, skills, and actions.

To think like a CxO as a network architect, you can follow these necessary steps:

- **Understand the business context**: It's imperative to gain a deep understanding of your organization's business strategy, objectives, and key priorities, not only as it relates to your current role or function, but to the overall viewpoint of the organization and the direction it wants to go in.

Familiarize yourself with the industry landscape, competitive challenges, and market trends. This knowledge will provide the foundation for aligning your network architecture decisions with the organization's strategic goals.

- **Develop a strategic mindset**: Begin to shift your perspective from a *purely* technical focus to a strategic one. Think beyond individual projects and consider the long-term implications of your network architecture decisions. Align your thinking with the organization's strategic direction and evaluate how your work contributes to its success.

Begin to ask questions outside the scope of projects and routine activities. Questions to begin developing are the following:

"What will be the ROI on this initiative? Can we take a look?"

"How does this [project/solution] fit into the long-term strategy we're seeking to achieve?"

"How can I/we achieve better utilization of our current resources without having to spend x amount in the next quarter to maximize discount rates at year-end to save on next year's budget?"

It will get easier as you continue to couple technical questions with business strategy questions.

> **Note**
>
> At first, it will seem overwhelming or frustrating to some (I can attest to this), but gradually, the mindset will begin to be established.

- **Engage with stakeholders**: Actively engage with stakeholders, including business leaders, CxOs, IT teams, and end users. Understand their needs, priorities, and pain points. Collaborate with them to gather insights, address challenges, and align your network architecture decisions with their requirements.

When conversing with stakeholders in meetings, don't hesitate to ask questions to clarify points of interest. This will show the stakeholders you have a vested interest in their needs and wants. Potentially, down the road, the same stakeholders will seek your opinion on a direction that is prudent to undertake.

> **Note**
>
> Today's organizations are transitioning from hierarchal to more of a flat organizational structure where one can directly communicate with the CTO without having to ask their immediate manager for approval.

- **Translate technical concepts into business language**: Develop the ability to effectively communicate technical concepts in business terms. Understand how your network architecture decisions impact the organization's key metrics, such as revenue, cost savings, operational efficiency, and customer satisfaction. Articulate the business value and benefits of your proposed solutions to gain support from CxOs and other stakeholders.

Begin to research business jargon (also covered in *Chapter 10*) and the meaning of financial terms, such as the following:

- **Rate of return (RoR)**
- **Compound annual growth rate (CAGR)**
- **Cost of goods sold (COGS)**
- Gross and net profit
- **Key performance indicators (KPIs)**
- Income statement (**profit and loss (P&L)** statement)
- **Return on equity (ROE)**
- **Earnings before interest, taxes, depreciation, and amortization (EBITDA)**

- **Consider financial implications**: Take a financial perspective when making network architecture decisions. Understand the financial impact of proposals, including costs, **return on investment (ROI)**, and cost savings. Evaluate the **total cost of ownership (TCO)** and consider cost optimization strategies to align your network architecture decisions with the organization's financial goals.

  These implications can make or break a current or future project. Questions such as these may arise:

  "If a project is extremely overspent, how is this going to impact funding for the next phase?"

  "If the project is taking too long to complete, when will the next project commence?"

  It encourages you to make informed choices based on financial analysis, cost-benefit assessments, and long-term financial sustainability.

- **Embrace risk management**: Network architects can contribute to the organization's overall risk management strategy by aligning network architecture decisions with business objectives to assess the potential risks and rewards of those decisions. This includes evaluating the financial impact or ramifications of security breaches, system failures, regulatory compliance, or **business continuity (BC)** disruptions. Such considerations allow the development of robust risk management strategies and prioritizing investments in risk mitigation measures.

- **Focus on BC and resilience**: Ensure that your network architecture decisions promote BC and resilience. Design solutions that provide HA, DR capabilities, and scalability to support the organization's critical business processes. Consider the impact of potential disruptions, from a business perspective, and develop plans to minimize downtime and data loss.

- **Stay abreast of technology trends**: Stay continuously updated with emerging technologies, industry trends, and best practices related to network architecture. Identify opportunities to leverage new technologies and innovations to drive business growth, efficiency, and competitive advantage. Be aware of advancements in cloud computing, hybrid or multi-cloud consumption,

SDN, network virtualization, security solutions, and other relevant areas where the organization can benefit from these advancements.

Newer trends in technology can increase an organization's competitive advantage in its vertical or allow the organization to move into other verticals.

> **Note**
>
> Consider how Netflix went from delivering physical DVDs to providing on-demand streaming services by embracing cloud content delivery systems and solutions.

- **Demonstrate leadership and initiative**: Take a proactive approach and demonstrate leadership within your role as a network architect. Identify opportunities for improvement, propose innovative solutions, and take ownership of driving change. Act as a trusted advisor to CxOs and other stakeholders by providing insights and recommendations that align with their strategic objectives.

An additional point – not every idea is worth developing *right now*. Assessing every idea and recommendation and developing a prioritization matrix will put into perspective what can be completed/remediated/designed now and what can be initiated at a later stage.

> **Note**
>
> I have a philosophy: *There is no such thing as a stupid question... All questions have relevance, and don't be shy to ask for understanding and clarity.*

- **Seek mentorship and role models**: Identify experienced professionals in CxO positions or those with a strategic mindset. Seek their guidance and learn from their experiences. Look for mentors who can provide insights, challenge your thinking, and help you develop the skills necessary for a CxO mindset.

Seek out two to three mentors across different industries to learn their perspectives. Though you may not have the opportunity to see them in person or work with them daily, set time up when it's convenient to discuss topics of interest.

Other avenues for seeking mentorship are the following:

- Searching for leadership through business social media (that is, LinkedIn)
- Joining local meetups to find prospective mentors
- Looking internally in your organization for mentee opportunities
- Researching books by leaders in their industry
- Keeping abreast of news related to leaders in their industry
- Attending networking events

> **Note**
> The easiest way to find mentors is to join forums, communities, meetups, and other meeting events in your local area.

- **Cultivate a continuous learning mindset**: Network technologies and business environments evolve rapidly, so it's crucial to continuously learn and enhance your knowledge. Invest in professional development, attend relevant training programs, obtain certifications, and participate in industry events. Seek feedback and learn from your experiences to refine your thinking and decision-making.

Thinking like a CxO doesn't occur overnight. As time progresses, these concepts will become second nature and help you in your role pursuant to a network architect. By embracing these perspectives, a network architect can elevate their role from a purely technical focus to a strategic partner, contributing to the organization's success by aligning network architecture decisions with broader business objectives.

Remember – thinking like a CxO is a journey that requires ongoing self-reflection, learning, and adaptation. Again, it takes time to develop the necessary skills and mindset, but with dedication and a proactive approach, you can cultivate a CxO mindset and make a significant impact within your organization.

> **Note**
> It's worth mentioning potentially looking into higher education programs, such as executive education programs. These programs are specifically designed to provide a comprehensive understanding of business strategy, leadership, and management.

What other industries are doing

The need to know what other industries are doing when it comes to the network architect's mindset is important because it can help you stay ahead of the curve and ensure that your network is secure and reliable. By understanding the challenges and best practices that other industries are facing, you can make better decisions about how to design and manage your own network.

Consider the following example:

The financial services industry is one of the most heavily regulated industries in the world. This means that financial institutions have to take extra precautions to protect their networks from cyberattacks. As a result, financial institutions have developed some of the most sophisticated network security practices in the world. By learning from the financial services industry, you can improve the security of your own network.

Regardless of which vertical/industry you're currently involved in, having a wider perspective across other industries is important for your success as a network architect as it will broaden your mindset and help you stay informed about emerging trends and best practices.

Remember – as you look across industries and solutions, you're looking from a macro infrastructure perspective, not necessarily at one solution or design. You're looking at the overall strategy, logic, business needs and use cases, and relevancy.

There are several reasons why this is important:

- **Innovation and adaptability**: Technology and network architecture are constantly evolving. By looking beyond your specific industry, you can gain insights into innovative approaches, new technologies, and emerging trends that may not be immediately apparent within your own industry. Understanding what other industries are doing allows you to adapt and apply relevant ideas, techniques, and solutions to your own network architecture strategies.

  For example, an organization transitioned its data center and replaced its older hardware with a **hyper-converged infrastructure** (**HCI**). Two years later, while attending a conference, they realized maybe a move to cloud computing could be the better option.

- **Cross-pollination of ideas**: Different industries face unique challenges and opportunities. By exploring what other industries are doing, you can uncover creative solutions and approaches that may be applicable to your own network architecture. Cross-pollination of ideas enables you to think outside the box, challenge conventional thinking, and find unique ways to address complex problems or optimize network infrastructure.

  For example, edge solutions are designed to optimize use cases for Telco providers/**cloud SPs** (**CSPs**). However, edge solutions can also be used for remote offices to bring applications closer to the end users.

- **Technological convergence**: Many industries are experiencing increased convergence and integration of technologies. For example, the healthcare industry is leveraging **Internet of Things** (**IoT**) devices, the financial sector is adopting blockchain technology, and the manufacturing sector is embracing automation and robotics.

  Keeping abreast of these technological advancements in other industries helps network architects understand the potential impact on their own industry and prepare for future integration requirements.

- **User experience and expectations**: User experience and expectations are shaped by interactions across industries. For example, the seamless and personalized experiences provided by e-commerce platforms or digital streaming services influence user expectations in other sectors.

  By understanding how user expectations are evolving in different industries, network architects can design a network infrastructure that meets or exceeds those expectations, delivering a superior user experience.

> **Note**
> Regular surveys (quarterly or bi-annually) are recommended to get an idea of end users' views on their experience and expectations.

- **Collaboration and partnerships**: Collaboration with vendors, SPs, and technology partners is very important. Understanding what other industries are doing helps in evaluating potential partners, identifying emerging vendors or technologies, and fostering collaborations that can drive innovation and shared learning. It enables network architects to tap into external expertise and leverage industry-specific solutions to enhance their own network architecture.

- **Future-proofing and scalability**: Learning from other industries helps network architects anticipate future needs and scale their network architecture accordingly. By observing trends in scalability, flexibility, and adaptability from different sectors, network architects can design a network infrastructure that is agile and capable of accommodating future growth, technological advancements, and changing business requirements.

- **Competitive advantage**: Being aware of what other industries are doing can provide a competitive advantage. It allows network architects to identify opportunities for differentiation and innovation within their own industry. By staying ahead of the curve and bringing fresh ideas from other industries, network architects can position themselves as strategic leaders, driving digital transformation and delivering business value.

Note

Across my career working on client projects (either at stage 0 or in the midst of a project), many of the executive teams have asked: *"How have others* [in the industry or other industries] *implemented this?"* As part of the leadership team, be prepared with or find a reference use case when required.

Knowing what other industries are doing enables network architects to broaden their perspectives, foster innovation, anticipate future needs, and stay relevant in a rapidly evolving technological landscape. It allows them to apply cross-industry learnings, adapt to changing user expectations, and drive impactful network architecture strategies that align with broader industry trends and business objectives.

Always thinking – innovating, exploring new trends

Have you heard the adage, *If it's not broken, don't fix it...*? While it may work in some instances of life, it may not be applicable to network infrastructure and shouldn't be taken as an absolute rule.

What I'm referring to is if your infrastructure is stable and functioning properly, there is always room for improvement. There may be better ways to increase productivity or to make better efficiencies by utilizing another solution.

The point of all this is that a network architect should always be thinking, and asking themselves the following:

What could have I done better...?

What can be improved next...?

Where do we go from here?

At times, it will not be easy to answer these questions. You may find yourself in a quagmire trying to find an answer to a question that doesn't need to be answered yet. Or, you may find yourself cemented in addressing a desired solution. Through it all, you're opening your mind to exploring newer ways of approaching common tasks or creating new ways to do new things.

A great example would be in a previous position with HPE.

I was tasked to build out a proof of concept (PoC) lab for my team to train, perform demonstrations for customers, and highlight innovation. One key innovation was around SDN & SD-WAN, where I wanted to showcase how their usage would make customers' on-premise environments more efficient, reduce latency, and optimize data traffic. Some challenges I ran into were how to demonstrate the public cloud without having a public cloud available to me, how to provision public IPs without an ISP, how to demonstrate to remote locations (that is, New York, London, Los Angeles), and using WAN edge. All without any funding.

For a week I tried to come up with a solution, but anything I thought of would require funding. One day, I saw a device in my office I received from Aruba's (HPE's acquisition) enterprise team. The device, a plug-and-play device, is used to connect end users back to the corporate network, via VPN services automatically over the internet no matter where the user is located.

The backend controller would register the device, give it an IP address, and allow it on the network based on routing, security policies, and so on. After staring at it for a while, it hit me!

I could use the combination of the VPN device (called an IAP) and the backend controller to perform the following:

- *Use the backend controller to supply public IPs to simulate an ISP*
- *Use the backend controller to simulate a public cloud*
- *Use the IAP device to simulate customer WAN edge locations*
- *Use the IAP device to simulate different regions of the world*

After speaking with leadership, presenting them with the idea and concept, and asking for their sponsorship, I was able to obtain all the required hardware and software and began the infrastructure build – some in the POC lab and some at home.

When the environment was completed, the team was able to demonstrate the value of SDN to customers with great success!

As I was sleeping after the lab environment was completed, I realized I'd just built my very own private/ public cloud with little to no funding out of miscellaneous, yet useful material used for a completely different purpose.

> **Note**
> This goes to show you how thinking *outside of the box* can lead to new, creative ways of making the impossible possible!

Always thinking and exploring new trends is not a new concept. It's a focus and a skill set one must be willing to adapt to when pursuing a network architect's position – or any position in leadership, for that matter.

When you foster the approach of always thinking, there are several advantages:

- **Expanding domain knowledge**: Network architects typically specialize in networking, but the field is interconnected with various other domains. Exploring new trends exposes them to related fields such as cybersecurity, cloud computing, SDN, and IoT. This broader domain knowledge allows network architects to see the bigger picture, understand the interdependencies, and make more informed decisions when designing network architectures.

- **Driving innovation**: Though mentioned frequently in this chapter, network architects who continuously think, innovate, and explore new trends are more likely to drive innovation within their organizations. They can identify opportunities for improvement, propose novel solutions, and challenge traditional approaches. By embracing innovation, network architects can enhance network performance, security, and scalability, leading to improved business outcomes.

- **Addressing emerging challenges**: In recent times, the digital landscape has become more dynamic, and new challenges and threats arise frequently. By actively exploring new trends, network architects can anticipate and address emerging challenges in a proactive manner. They can identify potential risks, vulnerabilities, or inefficiencies and develop strategies to mitigate them. This proactive approach ensures network architectures are robust and adaptable to changing circumstances.

- **Enhancing professional growth**: Continuous learning and exploration of new trends contribute to the professional growth of network architects. It expands their knowledge base, strengthens their skills, and positions them as experts in their field. Their ability to think innovatively and stay current with industry trends enhances their professional reputation and opens doors to new opportunities for career advancement.

- **Influencing organizational strategy**: Network architects who are always thinking, innovating, and exploring new trends become influential stakeholders within their organizations. They can provide valuable insights and recommendations on technology roadmaps, network infrastructure investments, and future-proofing strategies. Their expertise helps shape the overall organizational strategy and ensures network architecture aligns with the long-term vision.

- **Differentiating from competitors**: In a competitive landscape, organizations need to differentiate themselves to stay ahead. Network architects who actively explore new trends can identify unique opportunities or approaches that set their organization apart from competitors.

By being at the forefront of technological advancements, network architects contribute to developing innovative solutions that give their organization a competitive edge.

In summary, always thinking, innovating, and exploring new trends is crucial for a network architect's success as it enables them to stay relevant, drive innovation, address emerging challenges, adapt to business needs, enhance efficiency, contribute to their professional growth, influence organizational strategy, and differentiate their organization from competitors. By embracing this mindset, network architects can position themselves as strategic leaders and an asset (valuable) to their organization.

Summary

This chapter covered some important topics of the mindset of a network architect and the skills they should possess to become successful in their career. Understanding the principles of design and its key elements will fortify any infrastructure fabric being built for any organization. Aside from being savvy technically, a network architect must begin to develop a strategic mindset like those at the CxO level. Bringing these two facets together will make a network architect a valuable asset to any organization.

The only question left is, *Are you willing to take on the challenge?*

In the next chapter, we'll discuss the foundations of network architecture, routing, and switching.

Part 3 – Constructing the Core: Building Blocks of a Network Architect

As the digital landscape continues to expand and evolve, the role of the network architect grows increasingly complex and critical. At the heart of this role lies a deep understanding of the foundational elements that make up the vast and intricate world of network architecture. This section is dedicated to unraveling these building blocks, from the physical infrastructure to the advanced paradigms of cloud computing. As we navigate through these chapters, we aim to provide a comprehensive guide on the essential knowledge and emerging trends that every network architect must master to drive success and innovation in their field.

This section has the following chapters:

- *Chapter 6, Foundations of Network Architecture – Part 1: Route/Switch*
- *Chapter 7, Foundations of Network Architecture – Part 2: Network Services*
- *Chapter 8, Foundations of Network Automation*
- *Chapter 9, Paradigm Shift to Cloud Computing*

6

Foundations of Network Architecture – Part 1: Route/Switch

In the previous chapters, we discussed the role a network architect plays within an organization, the skillset needed to fulfill a network architect's position, along with the concepts and mental framework required to be successful in the role. Now, let's transition to the technical aspects of the network architect's role and dive into the foundation of network architecture.

The foundation of network architecture refers to the underlying principles and design concepts that guide the development and organization of computer networks. It encompasses the fundamental components, protocols, and technologies that are used to create and maintain networks to support the following:

- **Fault tolerance**: The ability of a network to continue operating even when some of its components fail

- **Scalability**: The ability of a network to grow and adapt to changing demands

- **Quality of service (QoS)**: The ability of a network to provide different levels of service to different types of traffic

- **Security**: The ability of a network to protect its data and resources from unauthorized access, use, disclosure, disruption, modification, or destruction

In this first of two chapters dedicated to the foundation of network architecture, we'll explore the following:

- Overview of the **Open Systems Interconnection (OSI)** model

- Physical infrastructure

- Switches and switching concepts

- Routers and routing concepts

- Supporting vendors

Let's get started!

Overview of the OSI model

The OSI model is a framework (conceptual) that standardizes the functions of a telecommunication or computing system into *seven* distinct layers, with each layer representing a specific set of tasks and responsibilities. The model serves as a reference for understanding how different networking protocols and technologies interact with each other.

Before the OSI model, there were various proprietary networking architectures and protocols that lacked interoperability. This made it difficult for different vendors' equipment and software to work together in a cohesive manner, hindering the growth and advancement of computer networking.

The model is devised to serve the purpose of the following:

- **Creating a level of standardization**: The goal is to establish a common and consistent way of outlining network communication functions and interactions. Defining specific layers and their respective responsibilities provides a clear blueprint for networking protocols, making it easier for vendors to create interoperable products (and innovative solutions).

- **Introducing interoperability**: This can ensure that networking systems from different manufacturers can communicate seamlessly and effectively with each other. By adhering to the OSI standards, vendors can develop networking equipment and software that can interoperate with devices from other vendors, fostering a more open and competitive networking market.

- **Promoting a modular and layered approach**: Because of the OSI model's layered structure, it's easier to modify or upgrade individual layers without affecting the others. Modularity is key to the evolution of modern networking technologies.

- **Ease of understanding**: The OSI model's layered structure provides a conceptual framework that is intuitive and easy to understand. Each layer represents a specific set of functions, allowing network technicians, engineers, developers, and architects to focus on specific aspects of the network infrastructure.

The OSI model's seven layers are shown in *Figure 6.1*:

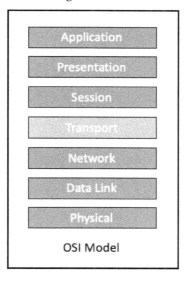

Figure 6.1 – OSI model

Although a network architect *must* be familiar with and well versed in each layer of the OSI model, from a network infrastructure perspective, the majority of design and solutions will focus on layers 4 through 1.

OSI model versus TCP/IP model

Figure 6.2 shows both the OSI model and TCP/IP models. Both are conceptual frameworks – however, the TCP/IP model is more aligned with Internet communication. It was developed to guide the design and implementation of the protocols used on the Internet:

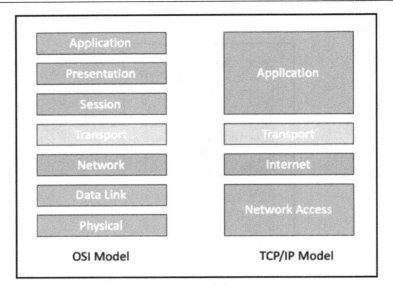

Figure 6.2 – OSI and TCP/IP models

Unlike the seven layers of the OSI model, the TCP/IP model consists of four layers, each responsible for specific aspects of data communication. It's important to note that the TCP/IP model is often compared to the OSI model, as the layers of both models can be loosely mapped to one another.

> **Note**
>
> For all intents and purposes, the TCP/IP model is considered the de facto standard for practical networking implementations as the model is more streamlined and directly reflects the protocols used by/on the Internet and modern networking implementations (that is, the cloud).

Physical infrastructure

In *Chapters 1* and *5*, we looked at the three-tier and the spine/leaf reference architectures with respect to network architecting. However, the diagrams don't tell us or have enough information about the components and logical aspects of the overall network design. They are high-level diagrams showing general concepts and demarcation points.

The physical infrastructure of network architecture refers to tangible components and elements that form the physical foundation of the network. It encompasses hardware devices, cabling, and physical connections that enable communication and data transmission between devices. It's important for a network architect to know the physical infrastructure in depth to make choice decisions in designing/building a safe, secure, stable, and reliable network fabric.

Network cabling

Physical network infrastructure often includes various types of cables that carry data between devices. These cables adhere to specific Ethernet standards defined by the **Institute of Electrical and Electronics Engineers (IEEE)**.

> **Note**
>
> Initially defined by Xerox Corporation's **Palo Alto Research Center (PARC)** in the early 1970s, Ethernet has developed into a widely used networking technology that enables devices to connect and communicate within a **local area network (LAN)**.
>
> Ethernet is known for its reliability, scalability, and versatility, and it has become the de facto standard for wired LAN connections.
>
> More information on Ethernet can be found here: `https://standards.ieee.org/ieee/802.3/7071/`.

The two most often-used forms of network cabling are as follows:

- Twisted pair (copper)
- Fiber optic

Let's review them in detail.

Twisted pair (copper)

It consists of multiple pairs of copper wires twisted together to reduce electromagnetic interference. The variant used for network design is called *Ethernet twisted pairs*.

In Ethernet twisted pairs, four pairs of insulated (color code) copper wires are twisted together in a specific pattern that follows the **Telecommunications Industry Association (TIA)/Electronics Industries Alliance (EIA)** *568-B* standard.

> **Note**
>
> The color code for Ethernet twisted pairs follows a standard known as *TIA/EIA 568-B*, which specifies the color-coding scheme for individual wires within the twisted pairs. This standard is commonly used in the United States.

This standard ensures consistency and proper identification of the wires in Ethernet cables. The color codes are as follows:

- **Pair 1 (White-Orange, Orange)**
  - **Wire 1**: White and Orange
  - **Wire 2**: Orange

- **Pair 2 (White-Green, Green)**

  - **Wire 3**: White and Green

  - **Wire 4**: Green

- **Pair 3 (White-Blue, Blue)**

  - **Wire 5**: White and Blue

  - **Wire 6**: Blue

- **Pair 4 (White-Brown, Brown)**

  - **Wire 7**: White and Brown

  - **Wire 8**: Brown

Ethernet twisted pairs are either a **shielded twisted pair (STP)** or an **unshielded twisted pair (UTP)**.

UTP

UTP is the most common type of cable used for Ethernet connections in many network environments. UTP cables typically contain four pairs of twisted wires. Each pair consists of two insulated copper wires twisted together in a specific configuration. The individual wire pairs within UTP cables have a specific twist ratio.

The twisting helps reduce **electromagnetic interference (EMI)** and crosstalk between adjacent pairs, enhancing the overall signal quality. Because of the lack of shielding, UTP cables rely solely on the twisting of the wire pairs to mitigate EMI and crosstalk. In addition, a UTP cable has the following attributes:

- Supports various Ethernet standards, including **Fast Ethernet (FE)** (10/100 Mbps), **Gigabit Ethernet (GE)** (10/100/1,000 Mbps), and 10 GE (10 Gbps)

- Is the most common type of cable used in many network environments, including homes, offices, and data centers

- Each pair of wires carries a separate data signal, enabling bidirectional communication

- Cost-effective compared to STP cables

Here's an example:

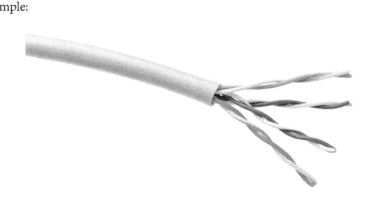

Figure 6.3 – Example of UTP cable

Let's move to the next one.

STP

STP is another type of copper cable used for Ethernet networking. Unlike unshielded UTP cables, STP cables incorporate additional shielding to provide enhanced protection against EMI and crosstalk. STP cables consist of multiple pairs of insulated copper wires twisted together, just like UTP cables. Each pair comprises two individual wires, typically made of *solid* or *stranded* copper. As with UTP, four pairs are commonly used for Ethernet connections.

In addition to the insulation surrounding each pair of wires, STP cables have one or more shielding layers. The shielding is typically made of metallic foil or braided metal, such as aluminum or copper. Because of this, the shielding is typically connected to a grounding wire or metal connector shells at both ends of the cable. This helps maintain the integrity of the shield and enhances the cable's overall performance. In addition, STP cables have the following attributes:

- Less flexible than UTP cables

- More costly than UTP cables ($0.53/ft versus $0.23/ft)

- Less susceptible to EMI and other electromagnetic interferences and provide better noise immunity, making them suitable for environments with high levels of electrical noise

Here's what an STP cable looks like:

Figure 6.4 – Example of STP cable

In the following diagram, you'll see the differences between an STP and a UTP cable:

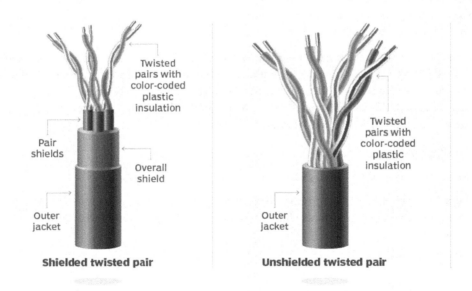

Figure 6.5 – STP versus UTP (courtesy of https://www.techtarget.com/
searchnetworking/definition/shielded-twisted-pair)

The most prevalent types of twisted pair cables used in networking are Cat5e, Cat6 and 6a, Cat 7, and Cat 8.

Table 6.1 shows the various Ethernet twisted pair categories used for the physical infrastructure of a network:

Twisted Pairs	Maximum Data Rate	Maximum Bandwidth	Supported Cable Types	Maximum Supported Distance (m)	Applications/ Usage
Category 5e	1 Gbps	100 MHz	UTP, STP	100	GE – home
Category 6	1 Gbps	250 MHz	UTP, STP	100	GE – commercial use
Category 6a	10 Gbps	500 MHz	UTP	100	GE – commercial use, data centers
Category 7	10 Gbps	600 MHz	STP	100	10 GE – core infrastructure
Category 7a	10 Gbps	1 GHz	STP	100	10 GE – core infrastructure
Category 8	25 Gbps or 40 Gbps	2 GHz	STP	30	25/40 GE – core infrastructure, top-of-rank (ToR) spine/leaf uplinks

Table 6.1 – Twisted pair copper cabling comparison chart

For network design, the variants in twisted pairs are important for a network architect to understand with respect to their capabilities, usage, and limitations:

Figure 6.6 – RJ45 connector and RJ11 connector types (source: https://www.linx-com.com/rj45-connector-what-is-it-and-how-does-it-differ-from-rj11/)

> **Note**
>
> The connector type for Ethernet twisted pairs is an RJ45 connector versus RJ11, which is typically used for **Plain Old Telephone Service (POTS)** lines for wired telephone services.

Straight-through versus crossover Ethernet twisted pairs

Aside from the variants of twisted pairs and categories used for network design, twisted pairs can be wired as straight-through and crossover. Straight-through and crossover are two different wiring configurations for twisted pairs used in Ethernet networking. These configurations determine how the wires within a cable are connected to the pins of the connectors at each end. Let's look at them in a bit more detail:

- **Straight-through cable**: A straight-through cable, also known as a patch cable, is mostly used as a type of Ethernet cable for connecting different types of devices. In a straight-through cable, the wire connections at one end of the cable match the corresponding wire connections at the other end. For both ends of the cable, the wires within each twisted pair are connected to the same pins in a consistent manner.

  The straight-through configuration is used when connecting different types of devices, such as a computer to a switch or a router to a switch.

  In a straight-through cable, the transmitting pins (Tx) at one end are connected to the receiving pins (Rx) at the other end, allowing for proper signal transmission. Straight-through cabling is typically used to connect:

  - Switch to router

  - Switch to PC or server

  - Hub to PC or server

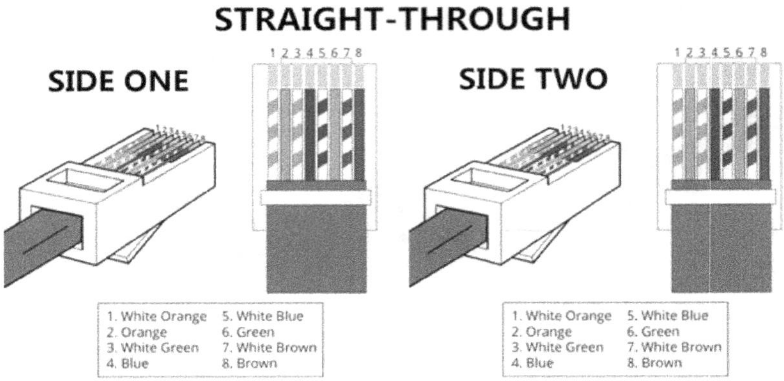

Figure 6.7 – Straight-through Ethernet cable wiring layout TIA/EIS 368B (source: https://www.cables-solutions.com/difference-between-straight-through-and-crossover-cable.html)

- **Crossover cable**: A crossover cable is used for direct connection between two similar types of devices, such as two computers or two switches, without the need for an intermediate device such as a switch or a hub. In a crossover cable, the wire connections at one end of the cable are crossed or swapped with the corresponding wire connections at the other end.

The crossover configuration ensures that the transmitting pins (Tx) at one end are connected to the receiving pins (Rx) at the other end. This allows two similar devices to communicate directly by transmitting and receiving signals correctly without the need for a separate network switch.

The most common use cases for a crossover cable are as follows:

- Switch to switch

- Switch to hub

- Hub to hub

- Router to router

- Router Ethernet port to PC NIC

- PC to PC

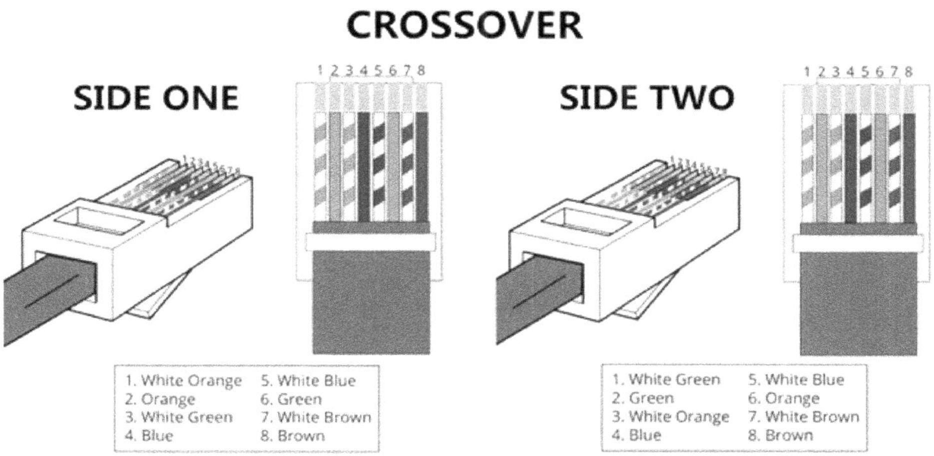

Figure 6.8 – Crossover Ethernet cable wiring layout TIA/EIS 368B (source: https://www.cables-solutions.com/difference-between-straight-through-and-crossover-cable.html)

> **Note**
>
> In modern networking environments, crossover cabling is rarely used as networking devices (that is, routers and switches) can auto-sense connectivity.

Next, we'll move on to another network cabling type: fiber optics.

Fiber optics

Fiber optics is a technology used in the physical infrastructure of a network for transmitting data over long distances at high speeds. Instead of using electrical signals like traditional copper cables, fiber optic cables utilize pulses of light to carry information. Fiber optics offers several advantages in terms of speed, bandwidth, distance, and immunity to electromagnetic interference over the traditional twisted pair.

As with the twisted pair, the network architect must be versed in fiber optics variants to make prudent decisions on when to use certain types of optics when designing the network infrastructure for an organization.

There are primarily two variants of fiber optics commonly used in network infrastructure: **single-mode fiber (SMF)** and **multi-mode fiber (MMF)**. Each one consists of a core, cladding, and buffer:

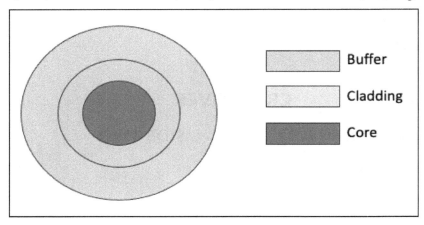

Figure 6.9 – Cross-section of a fiber optic cable

> **Note**
> The core and cladding are always together as one unit.

These variants differ in terms of their core size, the way they transmit light, and their distance capabilities. Each variant has its own characteristics and is suitable for different network applications based on distance requirements and bandwidth needs.

SMF

SMF has a cladding of 125 microns (μm) and a core diameter of 9 μm. It uses a single transmission mode, allowing only one mode of light to propagate through the fiber.

SMF provides longer transmission distances and lower signal loss compared to MMF. It is primarily used for long-haul applications, such as telecommunications networks, internet backbone connections, and high-speed data transmission over vast distances.

SMF can transmit data over tens of kilometers or even hundreds of kilometers without significant signal degradation:

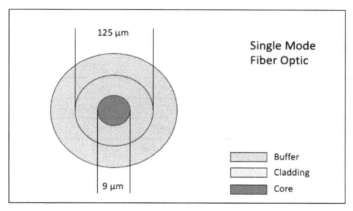

Figure 6.10 – SMF cross-section

MMF

MMF has a larger core diameter, typically ranging from 50 or 62.5 µm. MMF provides higher bandwidth capacity but is limited in terms of maximum transmission distances due to modal dispersion. It is commonly used in short-distance applications, such as LANs, data centers, and campus networks.

MMF is suitable for distances ranging from a few hundred meters up to a few kilometers, depending on the specific fiber type and network requirements:

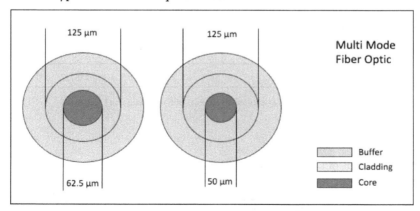

Figure 6.11 – MMF cross-section

There is a variant of MMF called **optical multi-mode** (**OM**), which allows different modes of light to be transmitted on a single fiber. It supports multiple transmission modes, allowing multiple paths for light to propagate through the fiber.

The following table outlines the different operational modes of MMF:

Operational MMF	Fiber Diameter	Jacket Color	Optical Type	Bandwidth MHz*km
OM1	62.5/125 μm	Orange	LED	200
OM2	50/125 μm	Orange	LED	500
OM3	50/125 μm	Aqua	VSCEL	2000
OM4	50/125 μm	Aqua	VSCEL	4700
OM5	50/125 μm	Lime Green	VSCEL	28000

Table 6.2 – MMF OM

The next table shows the maximum supported distance for the various data transmission rates for each optical mode:

Distance in meters (m)					
Support data rates					
Operational MMF	FE	1 GbE	10 GbE	40 GbE	100 GbE
OM1	2000	275	33	--	--
OM2	2000	550	82	--	--
OM3	2000	--	300	150	70
OM4	2000	--	550	150	150
OM5	--	--	550	150	150

Table 6.3 – MMF OM transmission rate maximum support distance

> **Note**
>
> There are other versions of either SMF or MMF for various purposes: plenum fiber, designed for use in plenum spaces, which are areas used for air circulation in buildings, such as drop ceilings or raised floors, and armored fiber, which has an additional protective layer, such as a corrugated metal tube or interlocking metal armor, surrounding the fiber core used for outdoor and industrial purposes.

All fiber connectivity requires specific transceivers called **gigabit interface converters (GBICs)** or **small form-factor pluggables (SFPs)** to support their fiber types, wavelength, and distance needs, as shown in *Figure 6.12* and *Figure 6.13*:

GBIC   SFP

Figure 6.12 – Physical layout (form factor size) of a GBIC and SFP (source: https://www.fiber-optic-transceiver-module.com/when-its-best-to-use-gbic-and-when-to-use-sfp.html)

Multimode SFP   Single-mode SFP

Figure 6.13 – MMF (black clasp) versus SMF (blue clasp) (source: https://www.fiber-optic-solutions.com/single-mode-sfp-vs-multimode-sfp.html)

> **Note**
> The terms *GBICs* and *SFPs* are often used interchangeably to describe the fiber transceiver; however, SFPs have replaced GBICs as the physical transceivers used in IT networking.

A network architect should be well versed on the specifics of networking connectivity options in order to make informed decisions about cabling selection, optimize bandwidth and throughput, accommodate network traffic and applications, mitigate interference, consider cost-effectiveness, and ensure integration and compatibility (that is, legacy systems, retrofitting) within the network environment.

Switches and switching concepts

While the "first" switch was primarily designed as a build-it-yourself kit for hobbyists and computer enthusiasts, the first "actual" switch emerged from the development of Ethernet in the late 1970s and early 1980s. Since then, switches and switching have evolved both in terms of capabilities and features.

In modern network infrastructures, network architects will come across switches (of various types) throughout the enterprise network, WAN Edge, and data center environments. Switches, and *switching fabric*, play a vital role in network infrastructure by facilitating connectivity and efficient communication between devices within the LAN, enterprise network, cloud environments, or even across the **data center interconnection (DCI)**.

Switching concepts

Let's go over a few switching concepts that are necessary for a network architect to know and have a full understanding of.

Spanning Tree Protocol

Spanning Tree Protocol (STP), an IEEE standard, is a protocol that prevents loops from forming on a network. Loops can occur when multiple switches are connected to each other in a way that creates a circular path for traffic. STP prevents loops by electing a root bridge and then blocking certain ports on switches so that traffic does not flow in a loop.

A network architect must make sure to place and designate the root (bridge) switch accordingly within the network and ensure STP features such as **bridge protocol data unit (BPDU)** guard, BPDU filter, root guard, loop guard, and EtherChannel guard are utilized to safeguard the network.

> **Note**
> There are other features such as bridge assurance, storm control, portfast, and others, as well as vendor-specific versions of STP (that is, Rapid PVST+, MST) that a network architect must be familiar with. See the *Further reading* section at the of the chapter for more information.

Broadcast and collision domains

A *broadcast domain* is a group of devices on a network that can receive broadcast frames. Broadcast frames are sent to all devices on a network, so it is important to limit the size of broadcast domains to improve performance and security.

A *collision domain* is a group of devices on a network that can collide with each other. Collisions occur when two devices transmit data at the same time on the same network segment. By default, each port on a switch is its own collision domain.

Virtual LANs

Virtual LANs (**VLANs**) allow you to divide a network into logical segments. More importantly, they are used on switches to create logical network segments within a single physical network infrastructure. VLANs enable the isolation and separation of traffic, allowing different groups of devices to communicate with each other while remaining logically separated from other devices on the network and within the switch. This can be useful for improving security, performance, and scalability. VLANs are implemented on switches as follows:

1. Configuring a physical port on the switch to be assigned to a specific VLAN.

2. Creating and configuring a **switch virtual interface** (**SVI**) and assigning it to a VLAN.

> **Note**
>
> Using VLANs allows for one physical switch to accommodate multiple logical networks. Consider a 16-port switch. If no VLANs are used, the switch can only support *one network*. With VLANs, the switch can accommodate 16 logical networks. Each VLAN, now, is considered its own broadcast domain.

QoS

QoS allows you to prioritize traffic on a network. This can be useful for ensuring that critical applications receive the bandwidth they need. QoS is implemented on switches by configuring different queues for different types of traffic.

When it comes to critical applications and prioritization, the network architect must make considerations for the following:

- **Virtual desktop infrastructure** (**VDI**)
- Critical business applications
- **Voice over IP** (**VoIP**)
- Video conferencing and streaming
- Real-time audio
- Network management traffic and critical network signaling

> **Note**
>
> Specific priority traffic types can vary depending on the organization's needs and the nature of the network. QoS mechanisms can be configured to prioritize and allocate network resources based on the traffic types and their associated requirements.

Media access control security

Media access control security (**MACsec**) is a security standard used to provide data confidentiality and integrity for Ethernet networks. It is an industry-standard security protocol defined by the IEEE *802.1AE* standard.

MACsec protects Ethernet frames between two directly connected devices by encrypting the data payload, ensuring that only authorized devices can access the data. It operates transparently without affecting higher-layer protocols or network applications.

It's commonly used in environments where data security is critical, such as government networks, financial institutions, and data centers where an additional layer of security beyond network-level protocols, such as IPsec, ensures end-to-end security at the link layer, protecting data as it travels across the network.

> **Note**
>
> MACsec supports port-based authentication using IEEE *802.1X*, enabling devices to authenticate each other before establishing a secure connection.

Switches

Switches are multiple port networking devices that can connect multiple devices within the LAN, across **campus/metro area networks** (**CANs** or **MANs**), or across DCIs. Switches can vary from five ports (used for home networks) to hundreds of ports in large organizations.

More importantly, switches are used for connecting devices (applications and end users) to a core network to send and retrieve information:

Figure 6.14 – A five-port tp-link unmanaged switch for home use (left)
and Cisco Nexus 9000 series data center switches (right)

There are several types of switches available, designed to meet various networking requirements and deployment scenarios. Network architects must be familiar with the different types used through an enterprise network. Some commonly used types of switches are as follows:

- **Unmanaged switches**: Unmanaged switches are basic switches that operate out of the box without any configuration. These are plug-and-play devices that provide simple connectivity between devices with limited capabilities. Unmanaged switches are typically used in small home or office networks where basic network connectivity is required without advanced management features (see *Figure 6.14*).

- **Managed switches**: Managed switches offer advanced management capabilities, allowing network administrators to have control over the switch's configuration, monitoring, and security features. They provide features such as VLAN configuration, QoS settings, port mirroring, **access control lists** (**ACLs**), port security (that is, MACsec, *802.1X*), and more. Managed switches are commonly used in larger networks where centralized control and advanced network management are necessary.

- **Layer 2 switches**: Layer 2 switches operate at the data link layer (Layer 2) of the OSI model and make forwarding decisions based on MAC addresses. They are capable of creating and managing VLANs, implementing STP for network redundancy, and supporting features such as link aggregation. Layer 2 switches are commonly used in LAN environments for intra-network communication. An example is a Cisco Catalyst 2960X switch:

Figure 6.15 – Cisco Catalyst 2960X-48FPD-L

- **Layer 3 switches**: Layer 3 switches, known as multilayer switches, operate at both the data link layer (Layer 2) and the network layer (Layer 3) of the OSI model. In addition to Layer 2 functionality, Layer 3 switches have the ability to perform routing functions, such as IP packet forwarding, based on IP addresses.

They maintain a routing table and make forwarding decisions based on the destination IP address of incoming packets. This allows them to route traffic between different subnets or VLANs within a network. Layer 3 switches are used in medium to large networks where the need for inter-VLAN routing, improved network performance, and network segmentation are required by offloading some routing tasks from routers:

Figure 6.16 – Cisco 3850-48P Layer 3 switch

- **Power over Ethernet (PoE) switches**: PoE switches provide power to network devices over Ethernet cables, eliminating the need for separate power sources. They comply with the IEEE *802.3af* or IEEE *802.3at* standards, allowing devices such as IP phones, **wireless access points (WAPs)**, and security cameras to receive power and data connectivity through a single Ethernet cable. PoE switches simplify installation and reduce cable clutter in network deployments:

Figure 6.17 – Cisco Meraki MS120-8 PoE switch

- **Stackable switches**: Stackable switches are designed to be physically stacked or interconnected, creating a *single logical unit* with shared management and forwarding capabilities. By stacking switches, network administrators can manage multiple switches as a single entity, reducing management overhead and simplifying network expansion. Stackable switches provide **high availability (HA)**, simplified management, and scalability for growing networks. An example is the Aruba 2930M:

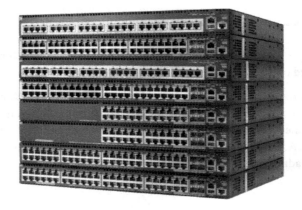

Figure 6.18 – Aruba 2930M stackable switch series

- **Data center switches**: Data center switches are specifically designed for high-performance and high-density environments, such as enterprise data centers or **cloud service providers (CSPs)**. They offer features such as high port densities, low latency, high throughput, advanced traffic management, and support for virtualization technologies. Data center switches enable efficient and reliable connectivity for demanding applications and workloads in data center environments. An example is Arista 7320X:

Figure 6.19 – Arista 7320X series cloud data center switches

- **Wireless switches/controllers**: Wireless switches or wireless LAN controllers are used in wireless networks to manage and control WAPs. They provide centralized management and configuration of APs, seamless roaming, and enhanced security features for wireless networks. Wireless switches enable efficient control and scalability in large-scale wireless deployments:

Figure 6.20 – Aruba 7010 mobility controller

Key switching functions

As mentioned, switches play a vital role in network infrastructure by facilitating connectivity and efficient communication between devices within a network. Some key functions switches fulfill in a network infrastructure are as follows:

- **Device connectivity**: Switches provide multiple Ethernet ports that allow devices such as computers, servers, printers, IP phones, network storage devices, and other networking equipment to connect to the network. Each device can be connected to a dedicated port on the switch, enabling communication and data sharing.

- **Packet switching**: Switches use packet-switching technology to forward data packets between connected devices. When a data packet arrives at a switch, it examines the destination MAC address of the packet and determines the appropriate outgoing port to forward the packet. This process ensures that data is efficiently and directly transmitted between devices, minimizing unnecessary data transmission and collisions.

> **Note**
>
> Packet switching is a method of data transmission in computer networks where data is divided into smaller units called *packets* before being sent across the network. Packet switching is *connectionless* and relies on upper-layer OSI protocols and routing to send information to and fro. This differs from circuit switching, which requires the source and destination to have a *dedicated connection* (that is, an analog telephone).

- **Segmentation and traffic isolation**: Switches segment the network into multiple collision domains, which help reduce network congestion and improve performance. By using MAC address tables, switches can forward packets only to the port where the destination device is located, preventing unnecessary packet transmission to all connected devices (as seen in a hub-based network). This segmentation also isolates traffic between different ports, improving security and network management.

- **Increased bandwidth**: Switches provide dedicated bandwidth to each port, allowing devices to transmit and receive data simultaneously. Unlike hubs, which share the available bandwidth among all connected devices, switches offer full-duplex communication, effectively doubling the available bandwidth for connected devices. This increased bandwidth capacity enables faster data transfer, reduces latency, and enhances overall network performance.

- **Broadcast control**: Switches control and manage broadcast traffic within the network. Broadcast packets, such as **Address Resolution Protocol** (**ARP**) requests, are typically forwarded to all devices connected to a network. However, switches intelligently forward broadcast packets only to the ports that require them, minimizing unnecessary network traffic and improving network efficiency.

- **QoS and traffic prioritization**: Switches support QoS features, allowing administrators to prioritize certain types of network traffic over others. This ensures that critical data, such as real-time voice or video traffic, receives higher priority and better performance. QoS capabilities in switches enable efficient utilization of network resources and ensure optimal performance for specific applications or services.

- **Network expansion and scalability**: Switches provide the flexibility to expand the network as the organization grows. Additional switches can be added to accommodate more devices, and switches can be interconnected or cascaded to create larger network architectures. Switches support network scalability and enable businesses to adapt to increasing connectivity demands and accommodate new devices and users.

- **Centralized network management**: Managed switches offer advanced management features that allow network administrators to centrally configure, monitor, and control the network. They provide a centralized interface for settings such as VLAN configuration, port security, and access control. Centralized management simplifies network administration, enhances security, and improves troubleshooting capabilities.

A network architect must be familiar with switches, the *family of switches*, switching technology, and their capabilities as they are fundamental building blocks of modern computer networks. As part of the network design, *traffic analysis and application patterns* must be taken into account when determining which switch is to be used and suited for the purpose.

> **Note**
>
> A network architect must design and "architect" the network with the intention of supporting current organizational needs and future growth – typically for 1-3 years. This implies the current switch(ing) design chosen should support this requirement without having to change from year to year.

In summary, network switches are essential components in network design principles as they provide connectivity, facilitate efficient packet forwarding, enable network segmentation, control, and prioritize network traffic, support scalability and redundancy, enhance network security, and assist in network monitoring and troubleshooting. They are crucial in creating robust, high-performing, and secure network infrastructures.

Routers and routing concepts

Network routers are essential networking devices that play a crucial role in IT infrastructure and networks. Routers operate at the network layer (Layer 3) of the OSI model and are responsible for forwarding data packets, based on the optimal path selected, between different networks or subnets.

Routers perform traffic directing by connecting dissimilar networks together via the routing process. For example, look at the following diagram – on the left of the router exists the 12.11.0.0/24 network, and on the right exists the 5.18.0.0/24 network (these IP addresses and networks are used for illustration purposes only):

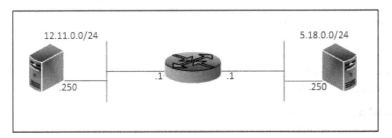

Figure 6.21 – Simple routed network

Under normal operational conditions, these end devices will not be able to communicate with one another as the devices are not on the same network segment. A network router is utilized to perform routing functions to allow these end devices to communicate with each other. Routers play a critical role in directing network traffic, enabling communication between devices and networks, and ensuring data is delivered efficiently and securely.

Let's go over a few routing concepts that are necessary for a network architect to know and, again, have a full understanding of.

Routing concepts

Routers have several capabilities and functions that are essential for the operation and management of computer networks. Here are some key capabilities and functions of routers:

- **Packet forwarding**: Routers receive data packets from one network and forward them to their intended destination network based on the destination IP address. They make routing decisions using a few factors:

    - The routing protocol used (that is, **Open Shortest Path First (OSPF)**, **Enhanced Interior Gateway Routing Protocol (EIGRP)**, **Border Gateway Protocol** (BGP), static routes, directly connected)

    - The trustworthiness of the routing protocol, known as the **administrative distance (AD)**

    - Other route protocol specifics metrics:

        • OSPF costs

        • EIGRP K1 to K5,

        • BGP **autonomous system** (AS) path, route origin, weight, local preference, **multi-exit discriminator** (MED)

By consulting their routing tables and choosing the optimal path for packet delivery, routers ensure the data (packets) are correctly sent to the proper destination.

- **Network interconnection**: Routers connect multiple networks or subnets together, allowing devices in different networks to communicate with each other. They serve as gateways between networks, facilitating data exchange and enabling inter-network communication.

- **Routing and path selection**: Routers employ routing protocols and techniques to exchange routing information with other routers, enabling the building of routing tables and the determination of optimal paths for packet forwarding. Routing protocols include OSPF, BGP, **Routing Information Protocol (RIP)**, **Intermediate System to Intermediate System (ISIS)**, and EIGRP.

Note

RIP is not commonly used anymore on enterprise networks but still needs to be mentioned as it's one of the first routing protocols used. ISIS is rarely seen on enterprise networks either – it gave way to OSPF. However, it's still used in **Service Providers' (SPs)** networks.

Routers determine the best path for data packets to travel based on factors such as hop count, link cost, bandwidth availability, and network congestion. All of this is determined by the routing (dynamic) protocol selected. The goal is to select the shortest, fastest, and most reliable path for efficient data transmission. *Table 6.4* shows the various metrics used to enable optimal route selection:

Rotuting protocol route selections metrics		
Protocol	**Metrics Used**	**Description/Usage**
RIP	Hop Count	The path with the fewest hops to a destination is considered the best. The maximum allowable hop count in RIP is 15, with 16 being considered unreachable.
ISIS	Cost	Similar to OSPF, IS-IS uses a cost metric to determine the best path. This cost can be based on various factors, including the bandwidth of the links, with lower cost paths being preferred. Other factors are delay, expense, and error.
OSPF	Cost	Typically based on the bandwidth of the links. The cost of a route is the cumulative cost of all the links in the path. A lower cost indicates a better path.
EIGRP	Composite Metrics	Factors are bandwidth, delay, load, and reliability, thought by default, it primarily uses bandwidth and delay. More complex than other protocols and provides a more granular way to determine the best path.
BGP	Path Attributes	Attributes such as AS_Path length, origin type, MED (Multi-Exit Discriminator), local preferences, and next-hop reachability determines the best path. BGP's decision process is more complex and include various criteria beyond simple metric values.

Table 6.4 – Routing protocol path selection metrics

Routers can adapt to changes in network topology or link states by dynamically updating their routing tables. They can reroute traffic in response to network changes, ensuring efficient packet delivery and network resilience.

> **Note**
> Though static routing is not a routing protocol, it's a method of configuring network routers where an individual has complete autonomy to define the paths that data packets should take to reach specific destinations.

- **Network address translation (NAT)**: Network routers support NAT, allowing multiple devices within a private network to share a single public IP address when accessing the internet. NAT conserves public IP addresses and provides an additional layer of security by hiding internal IP addresses.

- **Firewall and security**: Routers often incorporate firewall functionalities to enforce access control policies, filter network traffic, and protect against unauthorized access and malicious activities. They can implement ACLs, stateful packet inspection, and other security measures.

- **QoS**: Routers can prioritize certain types of network traffic over others to ensure that critical applications, such as voice or video, receive the necessary bandwidth and low latency. QoS mechanisms allow traffic prioritization and resource allocation based on predefined rules.

- **Network segmentation**: Routers enable network segmentation by dividing a large network into smaller subnets. Each port on a router is a network. Since routers do not pass along broadcast traffic, each port is its own broadcast domain.

- **Redundancy and HA**: Routers can be configured with redundancy protocols, such as **Virtual Router Redundancy Protocol (VRRP)** or **Hot Standby Router Protocol (HSRP)**, to ensure network availability and failover mechanisms. Both support link redundancy and load balancing for improved network reliability.

- **Network monitoring and management**: Routers provide management interfaces or protocols for network administrators to configure, monitor, and troubleshoot router settings. **Simple Network Management Protocol (SNMP)** is commonly used for network monitoring and management tasks.

- **Virtual private network (VPN)**: Many routers offer VPN capabilities, allowing secure remote access and encrypted communication between remote locations and the main network. Routers can establish VPN tunnels and provide encryption and authentication services for secure data transmission.

These capabilities and functions make routers vital components of computer networks, enabling inter- and intra-network communication, secure connectivity, efficient traffic routing, network segmentation, and management. Routers form the backbone of modern network infrastructures, facilitating reliable and secure data exchange across diverse networks and locations.

Router types

As with network switches, there are various router types. Each is designed for different purposes and network environments. Some common types of routers are as follows:

- **Home routers**: Home routers are typically used in residential settings to connect multiple devices to the internet. They often combine a router, a network switch, and a WAP into a single device. Home routers are designed for ease of use, providing basic routing functions and wireless connectivity for home networks:

Figure 6.22 – Verizon internet home router with four-port integrated switch

- **Enterprise routers**: Enterprise routers are used in large organizations or businesses to connect multiple networks and provide connectivity across a **wide area network (WAN)**. These routers offer advanced features, high performance, scalability, and robust security. Enterprise routers are capable of handling heavy network traffic and supporting a large number of devices:

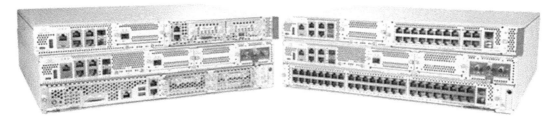

Figure 6.23 – Cisco Catalyst 8300 series enterprise routers

- **Core routers**: Core routers are high-end routers that form the backbone of a network infrastructure. They are designed to handle large amounts of network traffic and provide high-speed data forwarding between different networks or network segments. Core routers are typically found in **Internet Service Provider (ISP)** networks and large-scale enterprise networks. An example is Cisco's 8800 core router series:

Figure 6.24 – Cisco 8800 modular core router series

- **Edge routers**: Edge routers are positioned at the edge of a network, serving as the entry point for traffic coming from external networks, such as the internet, and routing it to the appropriate internal networks. They provide access control, security, and traffic management at the network perimeter. Inversely, they are the exit point from an organization's internal network.

Edge routers commonly connect other *edge networks*, such as the following:

- WAN Edge
- Cloud Edge
- Services Edge (third-party solution)
- Security Edge
- Metro Edge:

Figure 6.25 – Arista 7050X3 edge high-performance router

- **Branch routers**: Branch routers are used in remote office or branch office locations to connect those sites to the main corporate network. They are typically smaller and more affordable than enterprise routers, providing basic routing functions and connectivity to the main network. These routers perform local traffic offloading, meaning traffic destined for the internet leaves the branch office device to the internet versus going through the organization's internal network and then going out to the internet:

Figure 6.26 – Cisco ISR 4431 branch router

- **Wireless routers**: Wireless routers combine the functions of a router, a network switch, and a WAP into a single device. They provide routing functions for wired and wireless devices, allowing wireless connectivity to the internet or a local network.

Wireless routers are used often in small office/home office networks where connectivity to the corporate network is accomplished with VPN tunnels over the internet:

Figure 6.27 – Cisco ISR880 wireless branch/SOHO router

Note

Consumer-based wireless routers do offer some of the functionality of enterprise-grade devices. In some cases where cost is a factor (remote office with minimal staff), you will find a consumer-based wireless router providing wireless connectivity.

• **Service provider routers**: SP routers are designed for the specific requirements of telecommunications SPs and ISPs. They are highly scalable and capable of handling large-scale networks and high-speed connections. SP routers often incorporate features such as traffic shaping, traffic engineering, and support for multiple network protocols.

SP routers are often interchangeable with core routers' vernacular. However, SP routers have a different routing operating system designed specifically for SPs and ISPs. An example is the Nokia 7250IXR:

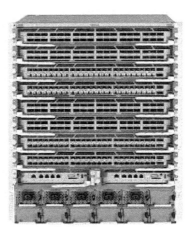

Figure 6.28 – Nokia's 7250 IXR SP router

> **Note**
>
> These router types are not mutually exclusive, and some routers may serve multiple functions. The choice of router type depends on the specific network requirements, scale, performance needs, and budget of the network deployment.

Network architects should have a comprehensive understanding of network routers and should be well versed in each type of router and usage, along with hardware design to meet the requirements to support the needs of the organization.

Supporting vendors

In the world of IT and networking, there are many companies/vendors to choose from. As a network architect, or any other IT architect for that matter, you must evaluate supporting vendors/suppliers to determine if their solutions and offerings are a proper fit for the organization's overall IT/networking initiatives.

The list presented next is not an exhaustive list of all vendors in the respected domain. However, it gives you an idea of the major players in IT networking.

> **Note**
>
> For a more comprehensive view of leaders, challengers, and niche market vendors, it's best to look at *Gartner Magic Quadrant* for domain-specific solutions.

Fiber optics

The following companies have a strong presence in the fiber optics market and are known for producing high-quality fiber and related products:

- **Corning**: A leading manufacturer of optical fiber and is known for its innovative and high-performance fiber products. They have a long-standing reputation for producing reliable and high-quality optical fiber solutions.

- **Prysmian Group**: Prysmian is a global company with a strong presence in the fiber optics market (underground and submarine). They offer a wide range of optical fiber products designed for various applications.

- **AFL Telecommunications**: AFL is a well-respected manufacturer of optical fiber and related products. They provide a diverse portfolio of optical fibers suitable for various network types and environments.

- **OFS (Furukawa Electric Group)**: OFS is a subsidiary of Furukawa Electric Group and is known for its fiber optic solutions for various industries, including telecommunications, data centers, and medical applications.

- **Sumitomo Electric Industries**: Sumitomo Electric is a major player in the fiber optics industry, providing a range of optical fibers and components for telecommunications and other applications.

Networking

The networking industry is highly competitive, and the landscape is constantly changing to meet the demands of customers and use cases. The following vendors are known for providing top-quality routers and switches:

- **Cisco Systems**: Cisco has long been a dominant player in the networking industry and is renowned for its extensive portfolio of routers and switches. They offer a wide range of products suitable for enterprises, SPs, and data centers.

- **Juniper Networks**: Juniper is known for its high-performance and scalable routers and switches, particularly in the data center and SP segments.

- **Arista Networks**: Arista is a significant competitor in the data center networking space, offering cloud networking solutions and high-performance switches.

- **Aruba – HPE company**: Provides a comprehensive portfolio of enterprise networking switches and routers for wired and wireless networking solutions.

- **Huawei Technologies**: Huawei is a major global networking equipment provider, offering a wide range of routers and switches suitable for various network sizes and types.

- **Nokia (Alcatel-Lucent)**: Nokia is a prominent vendor in the telecommunications industry, offering routers and switches for carrier-grade networks and SPs.

Security

There are several vendors providing top-quality firewall and security appliance solutions. However, the cybersecurity landscape is continually evolving, with new developments. The following are leaders in the security space:

- **Zscaler**: Zscaler specializes in cloud-based security solutions, including cloud firewalls and secure web gateways, providing security for users connecting from remote locations and mobile devices.

- **Cisco Systems**: Cisco is a leading vendor in the network security space, offering a range of firewall solutions, including **next-generation firewalls (NGFWs)**, **adaptive security appliances (ASAs)**, and cloud-based security products.

- **CrowdStrike**: A prominent and well-regarded cybersecurity company, specializing in endpoint security and **threat intelligence (TI)**. CrowdStrike is known for its cloud-based Falcon platform, which provides endpoint protection, threat detection, and response capabilities.

- **Carbon Black**: Carbon Black focuses on providing a comprehensive suite of endpoint security and threat detection solutions, with a particular emphasis on endpoint protection, detection, and response.

- **Palo Alto Networks**: Palo Alto Networks is a prominent player in the cybersecurity industry, specializing in NGFWs with advanced threat prevention capabilities, URL filtering, and application visibility and control.

- **Fortinet**: As with Palo Alto, Fortinet is a well-known vendor offering a wide range of cybersecurity solutions, including **unified threat management (UTM)** devices and NGFWs.

Virtualization

Virtualization (hardware) is prevalent in all modern (networking) infrastructure. It's the foundation for all software and application development. Virtualization allows for the efficient use of hardware platforms (that is, servers) to maximize their usage, IT agility, flexibility, and scalability while creating significant cost savings. The following is a list of leaders in this space:

- **VMware**: VMware is one of the leading and most well-established virtualization vendors. Their flagship product, VMware vSphere, is a widely used virtualization platform for server virtualization, enabling organizations to run multiple **virtual machines** (**VMs**) on a single physical server.

> **Note**
> As of this writing, Broadcom Inc. is in the process of acquiring VMware.

- **Microsoft's Hyper-V**: This is another popular virtualization platform that comes integrated with Windows Server. It provides robust virtualization capabilities and is commonly used in Microsoft-centric environments.

- **Oracle VirtualBox**: This is a powerful and free open source virtualization software that allows users to run multiple operating systems on a single machine.

- **Citrix**: Citrix Hypervisor, formerly known as XenServer, is a robust virtualization platform that provides features for server consolidation, **disaster recovery** (**DR**), and cloud management.

- **Red Hat Virtualization (RHV)**: This is an open source virtualization platform based on **kernel-based VM** (**KBVM**) technology. It offers features for virtual server and **virtual desktop infrastructure** (**VDI**) deployment.

- **Nutanix**: Nutanix is known for its **hyper-converged infrastructure** (**HCI**) solutions, which integrate virtualization and storage in a single appliance, making it easier to deploy and manage virtual environments.

- **Kernel-based Virtual Machine (KVM)**: KVM is an open source virtualization solution that is widely used in Linux environments, often as the basis for various commercial virtualization platforms.

Server

The server market is just as competitive as the others. Listed are some of the major vendors we see today:

- **Dell EMC**: Dell EMC is a major player in the server market, offering a wide range of servers suitable for various workloads and deployment scenarios, including data centers, edge computing, and cloud environments.

- **Hewlett Packard Enterprise (HPE)**: Another prolific leader, HPE offers a comprehensive portfolio of servers designed for different applications and industries. Their servers cater to enterprise workloads, **high-performance computing** (**HPC**), and edge computing.

- **Lenovo**: Lenovo is known for its robust server offerings, including tower, rack, and blade servers, suitable for data centers and enterprise environments.

- **IBM**: IBM's Power Systems and Z systems are known for their reliability and scalability, especially for critical workloads.

- **Cisco Systems**: Cisco provides servers that integrate well with their networking and data center solutions, catering to various enterprise needs.

- **Supermicro**: Supermicro specializes in building custom servers and offers a wide selection of server components for various server configurations.

- **Inspur**: Inspur is a major server vendor with a strong presence in the Chinese market and is increasingly gaining recognition on the global stage.

- **Huawei Technologies**: Huawei provides servers suitable for cloud computing, big data, and AI workloads, among others, with a focus on performance and efficiency.

With this, let's recap what we have learned.

Summary

In this chapter, we began to look at the foundational aspects of what network architects should and need to be aware of when designing and implementing robust and efficient network infrastructures.

The physical infrastructure and routing and switching concepts presented are fundamental to a network architect's career as they form the backbone of data communication in modern networks. A network architect's ability to design efficient, secure, and scalable networks depends on a strong grasp of these principles. It will enable them (and to adjust when necessary) to build robust and high-performing network infrastructures for organizations of all sizes.

While this book is not intended to go in-depth on switching and routing granular design and practices, a network architect *must* be fully aware of those design practices that best suit the overall solution outcome.

In the next chapter, we'll continue with *Part 2* of *Foundations of Network Architecture* and discuss network services such as load balancers, firewalls, DNS, and more.

Further reading

To learn more about the topics that were covered in this chapter, take a look at the following resources:

- *Packet-Switched Network vs. Circuit-Switched Network: Understanding the 15 Key Differences*: `https://www.spiceworks.com/tech/networking/articles/packet-switched-vs-circuit-switched-network/`

- *Security Features on Switches*: `https://www.ciscopress.com/articles/article.asp?p=1181682&seqNum=5#:~:text=Spanning%20Tree%20Protocol%20(STP)%20resolves,prevents%20loops%20from%20being%20formed`

- *Spanning Tree Protocol*: https://en.wikipedia.org/wiki/Spanning_Tree_Protocol#:~:text=The%20Spanning%20Tree%20Protocol%20(STP,radiation%20that%20results%20from%20them

- *STP*: https://www.ciscopress.com/articles/article.asp?p=2832407&seqNum=5

- *ANSI/TIA-568*: https://en.wikipedia.org/wiki/ANSI/TIA-568

- *T568a vs T568b: Which To Use*: https://www.truecable.com/blogs/cable-academy/t568a-vs-t568b

- *Shielded twisted pair (STP)*: https://www.techtarget.com/searchnetworking/definition/shielded-twisted-pair

- *What is Fiber Optic?*: https://telecom.samm.com/what-is-fiber-optic

- *RJ45 CONNECTOR: WHAT IS IT AND HOW DOES IT DIFFER FROM RJ11?*: https://www.linx-com.com/rj45-connector-what-is-it-and-how-does-it-differ-from-rj11/

- *Fiber Transceiver Solution*: https://www.fiber-optic-transceiver-module.com/introduction-to-10gbe25gbe40gbe100gbe-fiber-optic-cabling.html

- *How Data Moves Across a Network*: https://www.secplicity.org/2019/03/01/how-data-moves-across-a-network/

- *The 10 Largest Server Companies in the World, and What They Do*: https://history-computer.com/largest-server-companies-in-the-world-and-what-they-do/

- *Select BGP Best Path Algorithm*: https://www.cisco.com/c/en/us/support/docs/ip/border-gateway-protocol-bgp/13753-25.html

- *OSPF Areas Types, OSPF Router Types & OSPF Route Types*: https://blog.router-switch.com/2012/11/ospf-areas-types-ospf-router-types-ospf-route-types/

7

The Foundation of Network Architecture, Part Two – Network Services

In this second chapter on the foundation of network architecture, we'll discuss a bit more about the network services you'll find in an organization. Networking services are the essential building blocks that enable seamless communication, data sharing, and resource access within an organization's network infrastructure.

These services encompass a wide range of functionalities, from providing internet connectivity and email communication to facilitating secure remote access and centralized data storage. Additionally, network services play a crucial role in implementing robust security measures, safeguarding the organization's sensitive data and assets against cyber threats.

As a network architect, the knowledge of networking services allows you to make informed decisions when selecting the appropriate technologies, protocols, and configurations for different network components. Whether it's designing robust routing protocols to optimize data traffic, implementing secure access controls to safeguard sensitive data, or ensuring seamless collaboration through unified communication services, networking services form the bedrock upon which a successful network architecture is built.

In this second chapter dedicated to the foundation of network architecture, we'll explore the following topics:

- Understanding load balancing
- Exploring **domain name services (DNS)**
- **Dynamic Host Configuration Protocol (DHCP)**
- **Network address translation (NAT)**

- What are **access control lists (ACLs)**?

- Understanding firewall rules

- Miscellaneous network services

Let's get started!

Understanding load balancers

In the fast-paced world of modern computing, organizations face ever-increasing demands for high availability, scalability, and optimal performance of their online services and applications. Network load balancers are an integral component of modern network infrastructure, playing a crucial role in managing the distribution of network and application traffic across multiple servers. It's a solution designed to ensure efficient resource utilization and prevent any single server from being overwhelmed and being a single point of failure:

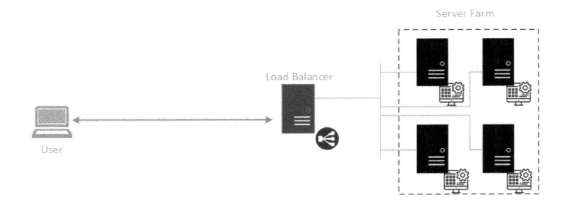

Figure 7.1 – Example of a network load balancer

Load balancers provide the following benefits:

- **Increased scalability**: They enhance the capacity and reliability of applications by ensuring no single server becomes a bottleneck

- **Improved performance**: They reduce response time by efficiently managing traffic and ensuring that no single server is overburdened

- **High availability**: They ensure continuous service availability by rerouting traffic in case of server failure

- **Session persistence**: They maintain user session data, which is crucial for applications where the user's session needs to be persistent

Next, we'll look at the different types of load balancers.

Types of load balancers

As a network architect, it's advantageous to have a comprehensive understanding of various types and kinds of load balancers available for use on a network. This knowledge is crucial for designing *resilient* and efficient network infrastructures tailored to specific organizational needs. Load balancers, differing in their methods of traffic distribution, features, and deployment models, play a pivotal role in optimizing network traffic, ensuring high availability, and maintaining application performance.

Concerning IT infrastructure, network load balancers are categorized based on *how* they handle traffic and *where* they operate in the OSI model. Here are the primary types:

- **Network load balancer (NLB)**
- HTTPS load balancer
- **Global server load balancer (GSLB)**

Let's look at them in detail.

Network load balancer (NLB)

As the name implies, an NLB (*Figure 7.1*) Operates at layer 3 of the OSI model by utilizing IP (source) as load balancing criteria to forward requests. In addition, these load balancers distribute traffic based on OSI Layer 4 (transport) protocols, such as TCP/UDP ports.

Some additional characteristics and features of NLBs are as follows:

- **High availability**: NLBs are designed for high availability and fault tolerance. They continuously monitor the health of the target servers and automatically route traffic away from unhealthy servers to healthy ones. This helps ensure that the application remains accessible even if some servers fail.

- **Scalability**: NLBs can handle a large volume of incoming traffic and can distribute it across a cluster of servers, making it easier to scale an application horizontally by adding more servers as needed.

- **Session persistence**: Some NLBs support session persistence, which means they can direct a client's requests to the *same* backend server for the duration of a session or connection. This is important for applications that require *stateful* communication.

- **IP address preservation**: NLBs can also preserve the client's IP address when forwarding traffic to backend servers, which can be useful for logging and auditing purposes.

> **Note**
>
> Some NLBs include DDoS protection mechanisms to help mitigate and absorb malicious traffic.

HTTPS load balancers

An HTTPS load balancer, also referred to as an **application load balancer** (**ALB**), is a type of load balancer that is specifically designed to handle and distribute HTTPS traffic. It operates at the application layer (Layer 7) of the OSI model and is responsible for load balancing incoming HTTPS requests across multiple backend servers or resources (*Figure 7.2*):

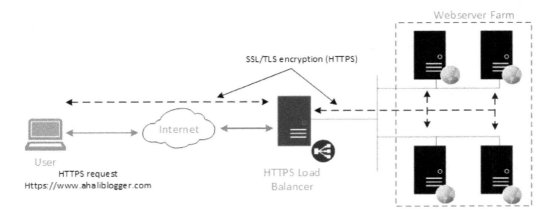

Figure 7.2 – HTTPS load balancer

Unlike NLBs, HTTPS load balancers understand and can perform content-based routing for HTTP and HTTPS traffic. They can inspect HTTP headers, URLs, and payloads, allowing for more advanced (granular and complex) load balancing strategies based on application-specific criteria. *Figure 7.3* shows a comparison of the two:

Attribute	Network Load Balancer	HTTPS Load Balancer
How it's used	Traffic is directed based on: IP/Port/Protocol	Direct requests from incoming web traffic based on Layer 7 request header data
OSI model layer it operates on	Layer 3/4 – Network/ Transport Layers	Layer 7 – Application Layer
Protocols supported	IP, TCP, UDP, TLS*	HTTP/S, TLS, SMTP
Algorithms supported	Round Robin, Least Connections, IP Hash, Weighted Round Robin, Weighted Least Connections	Round Robin, Least Connections, IP Hash, Least Response Time (Least Time), Weighted Round Robin, Weighted Least Connections, URL Hash (Content-Based Routing), Session Persistence (Sticky Sessions), Adaptive Load Balancing (various dynamic algorithms)
Benefits	Faster than ALBs – doesn't examine content of higher layer protocols. Optimized for low-latency, high-throughput, and high connection-per-second workloads	More granular inspect of traffic. Can route traffic based on content within HTTP requests, such as URL paths, headers, and query parameters. SSL/TLS encryption termination, offloading the decryption process from backend servers and improving their performance

*TLS passthrough

Figure 7.3 – Network and HTTPS load balancer comparison

Here are the key characteristics and features of HTTPS load balancers:

- **SSL/TLS termination**: HTTPS load balancers typically terminate the SSL/TLS encryption of incoming HTTPS traffic at the load balancer itself. This means that the load balancer decrypts the incoming requests, processes them, and then re-encrypts the responses before sending them back to the clients. This offloads the SSL/TLS encryption and decryption process from the backend servers, improving their performance.

> **Note**
> HTTPS can perform SSL/TLS passthrough. The backend servers will then be responsible for SSL/TLS termination.

- **Content-based routing**: HTTPS load balancers can perform content-based routing, also known as application-layer routing. They can inspect the content of HTTP requests, including the URL, headers, and even the payload, to make routing decisions. This allows for more advanced load balancing strategies based on application-specific criteria.

- **SSL certificate management**: HTTPS load balancers often provide features for managing SSL/TLS certificates, such as certificate termination and rotation. This makes it easier to maintain and update SSL certificates for the services behind the load balancer.

- **Session persistence**: HTTPS load balancers can provide session persistence or Sticky Sessions as a feature to ensure that client requests from the same session are consistently directed to the same backend server. This is important for applications that require stateful communication and need to maintain session information between the client and server. Session persistence helps maintain user sessions and can be crucial for applications such as e-commerce websites, online banking, and interactive web applications.

- **Health checks**: Like other load balancers, HTTPS load balancers use health checks to monitor the health and availability of the backend servers or target instances. Health checks are an essential component of load balancing because they allow the load balancer to automatically route traffic away from unhealthy servers, ensuring that clients are directed only to servers that can respond to requests.

- **Scalability**: HTTPS load balancers can distribute HTTPS traffic across a cluster of backend servers, allowing for horizontal scaling of applications to handle increased load.

> Note
>
> ALBs may incorporate or function in tandem with security features such as **Web Application Firewall** (**WAF**) capabilities to protect against common web application attacks, such as SQL injection and **cross-site scripting** (**XSS**).

Global server load balancer (GSLB)

A **GSLB** is a specific type of load balancer that focuses on DNS-based load balancing and traffic routing. Primarily used to enhance the availability, performance, and reliability of applications and services that have a global or distributed user base, these load balancers use DNS resolution to direct clients to the most suitable and available server or data center based on factors such as geographic proximity, server health, or application-specific criteria. GSLBs often make real-time DNS changes to steer traffic (*Figure 7.4*):

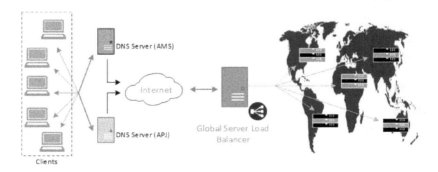

Figure 7.4 – Global Server Load Balancers

Here are some of the key benefits of GSLBs:

- **DNS-based load balancing**: GSLBs work by using DNS to resolve domain names to IP addresses. Unlike traditional load balancers, which operate at the network or application layers, GSLBs manipulate DNS responses to direct client traffic to the most suitable server or data center based on various criteria.

- **Geographic proximity**: One of the primary criteria used by GSLBs is geographic proximity. GSLBs can determine the geographic location of the client making the DNS query and route the request to a server or data center that is *physically* closer to the client. This minimizes latency and improves response times for users.

- **Health monitoring**: Like all load balancers, GSLBs continuously monitor the health and availability of the backend servers or data centers. If a server or location becomes unavailable or experiences performance issues, the GSLB can automatically remove it from the DNS responses to ensure that client traffic is not directed to problematic resources.

- **Failover and redundancy**: GSLBs support failover and redundancy by directing traffic away from failed or unreachable servers or locations. If a server or data center becomes unavailable, the GSLB can reroute traffic to healthy and available resources to maintain service continuity.

- **Load balancing algorithms**: GSLBs often support various load balancing algorithms, such as Round Robin, Least Connections, or Weighted Distribution, to ensure fair and efficient distribution of client requests among healthy resources.

- **Traffic steering**: GSLBs can implement sophisticated traffic steering policies based on criteria other than geographic proximity. These criteria may include server load, application-specific requirements, or business rules. This allows GSLBs to optimize traffic distribution based on application needs.

- **Global redundancy**: GSLBs themselves are often deployed in a redundant and geographically distributed manner to ensure their availability. They may have a global presence with DNS servers located in multiple regions to handle DNS resolution requests efficiently.

- **Traffic management**: In addition to load balancing, GSLBs can provide QoS features, such as traffic shaping, rate limiting, and traffic optimization, to further enhance the performance and reliability of global applications.

In summary, NLBs, HTTPS load balancers, and GSLBs are vital components in network architectures. Each has a design significance on how to distribute incoming traffic into an organization's IT infrastructure to the relevant backend server or application farms. A network architect must be well-versed in these load balancers to be able to do the following:

- Design resilient, highly performant, and globally available systems

- Ensure seamless user experiences

- Provide fault tolerance and scalability in the face of increasing network demands and distributed deployments

Next, let's look at the methods these load balancers use to distribute traffic.

Load balancing algorithms

Load balancing algorithms are the essential *logic* or strategy used to distribute network traffic across multiple servers or resources to achieve better performance, availability, and resource utilization. These algorithms (predefined rule sets) determine how incoming requests or connections are allocated among the available backend servers. Load balancing algorithms are used to prevent any single server from becoming overloaded while ensuring that all servers share the workload fairly.

A network architect must be familiar with the differences and benefits of each load balancing algorithm to support its intended use. Some of the most common algorithms are as follows:

- Round Robin
- **Weighted Round Robin (WRR)**
- Least Connections
- Least Time
- Source IP Affinity (Sticky Sessions)
- IP hash

We'll discuss each of these next.

Round Robin

Round Robin is a widely used load balancing algorithm that's employed by load balancers to distribute incoming requests or network traffic evenly across a group of backend servers or resources. It cyclically forwards client requests via a group of servers to handle client requests.

When a new request or connection arrives at the load balancer, the Round Robin algorithm selects the next server in the list of available backend servers. The selected server is the one that follows the previously selected server in the order of the list. If the list of servers is viewed as a circular queue, the algorithm loops back to the beginning of the list when it reaches the end (*Figure 7.5*):

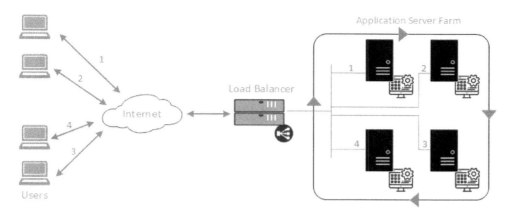

Figure 7.5 – Round Robin load balancing algorithm

Round Robin ensures that each server in the pool receives roughly an equal share of requests over time. As a result, it evenly distributes the workload across all available servers. Round Robin is a stateless algorithm, meaning it doesn't consider the current server's state, load, or responsiveness when making routing decisions. Each request is treated independently.

Here's why Round Robin is used:

- **Simplicity**: Round Robin is easy to implement and understand, making it a straightforward choice for load balancing in scenarios where simplicity is a priority. There are no intricate decision-making processes. The algorithm follows a cyclic order when distributing requests among servers (*Figure 7.5*).

- **Equal load distribution**: Round Robin is known for its ability to provide an equal distribution of requests or network traffic among a group of backend servers or resources, preventing any single server from becoming overloaded while ensuring that all servers are utilized.

    It does this by selecting backend servers sequentially, one after another, in the order they are listed or configured. When a new request or connection arrives at the load balancer, it is directed to the next server in the list. Each request is assigned to the next server in the sequence, ensuring that every server receives its fair share of traffic (*Figure 7.6*):

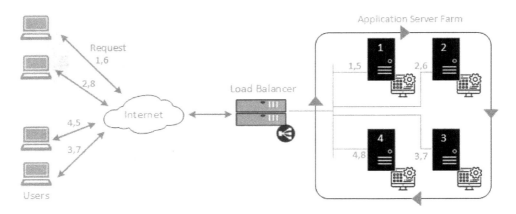

Figure 7.6 – Round Robin – equal load distribution

- **Predictable behavior**: Because of its cyclical and sequential manner of load distribution among backend servers, the algorithm's predictable behavior makes it suitable for basic load balancing needs, such as distributing incoming requests among a group of web servers or application instances.

- **Statelessness**: Round Robin is inherently stateless. It doesn't rely on the monitoring of server health or load. Incoming requests are forwarded to the next server in the sequence, regardless of which server handled the previous requests from the same client. This can be an advantage in situations where such monitoring is unnecessary or complex.

> **Note**
>
> While Round Robin's equal distribution of traffic is one of its strengths, it's important to note that this simplicity can also be a limitation in certain scenarios. For example, it doesn't consider the actual server load, capacity, or response times, which can result in uneven server loads if servers have different capabilities. In such cases, more advanced load balancing algorithms that take server health and performance into account may be preferred. A network architect must be able to determine when to use Round Robin or a more advanced technique in dealing with workload requests and responses.

Weighted Round Robin (WRR)

WRR is an advanced version of the basic Round Robin load balancing algorithm. It improves upon the standard Round Robin approach by considering the capacity of each server when distributing the network traffic (*Figure 7.7*).

In WRR, each server is assigned a *weight* based on its capacity, such as CPU, memory, or network bandwidth (or even the server's historical performance data). This weighting mechanism allows load balancers to allocate a proportionate share of traffic to each backend server based on predefined weights of traffic that each server will handle, making it essential to assign them accordingly.

Weights are relative, not an absolute figure. Each backend server in the pool is assigned a weight that represents its relative capacity or capability. Servers with higher weights receive a larger share of the traffic, while those with lower weights receive a smaller share. For example, if one server has a weight of 2 and another has a weight of 4, the latter is *expected* to handle twice as much traffic as the former. Like Round Robin, WRR operates by sequentially selecting backend servers in the order they are listed, but with consideration for the assigned weights:

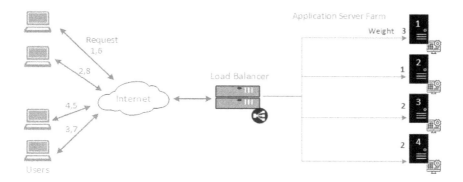

Figure 7.7 – Example WWR algorithm

When a new request or connection arrives at the load balancer, the algorithm directs it to the next server in the sequence, but the server's weight *influences* how many requests it receives. Servers with higher weights are selected more frequently than those with lower weights (*Figure 7.8*):

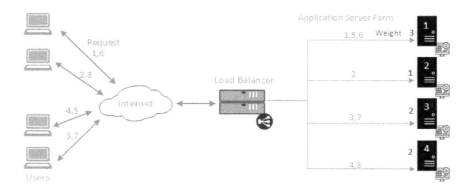

Figure 7.8 – Example WWR selection

Here's why WRR is used:

- **Capacity and capability**: WRR is used to reflect differences in the capacity or capability of backend servers. Understanding and effectively leveraging these aspects is essential for optimizing performance and reliability. Servers with higher capacities or better performance can be assigned higher weights to handle more traffic.

  The capability aspects involve the specific functions or applications a server is optimized to perform. For instance, some servers might be optimized for compute-intensive tasks, while others might be optimized for memory-intensive tasks. This capability can influence how weights are assigned based on the type of requests the server is expected to handle.

- **Resource optimization**: WWR prevents any single server from becoming overloaded as it distributes traffic according to the assigned weights. It optimizes resource utilization by directing traffic in a way that matches the capacity of each server. Conversely, WRR also prevents underutilization. Servers with lower weights may not be overwhelmed by traffic, ensuring that their resources are used efficiently.

- **Proportional distribution**: WRR ensures that each server receives a proportionate amount of traffic based on its weight. This is particularly useful when some servers are more powerful or have more resources than others.

- **Scalability**: WRR allows for easy scaling of the backend server pool by adjusting the weights of new servers. New servers can be added with appropriate weights to influence their share of traffic.

- **Customized load balancing**: WRR provides a degree of customization in load balancing that can accommodate diverse server capabilities and requirements.

- **Predictability**: Like Round Robin, WRR offers predictable behavior. Network architects can design to anticipate how traffic will be distributed among servers based on the assigned weights.

In summary, WRR is used to ensure that each backend server receives workloads and requests that align with its capacity or performance capabilities. It offers more flexibility and fine-grained control over traffic distribution compared to the traditional Round Robin algorithm, making it suitable for environments where servers have varying (heterogeneous) levels of capacity or where resource optimization is essential.

Least Connections

The Least Connections load balancing algorithm is a dynamic and intelligent method of distributing network traffic across a pool of servers. It is designed to distribute incoming requests or network connections to backend servers in a way that minimizes the number of active connections on each server. Unlike simpler algorithms, such as Round Robin, Least Connections considers the current state of each server before routing traffic to it (*Figure 7.9*).

A load balancer that uses the Least Connections algorithm continuously monitors the number of *active connections* to each server in the pool. When a new request arrives, the load balancer checks the current connection count for each server and routes the request to the one handling the least amount of connections at that moment. This approach helps in evenly spreading the load, especially in environments where request handling times are variable and unpredictable. By favoring servers with fewer active connections, it reduces the risk of overburdening any single server, thereby improving overall response times and server efficiency:

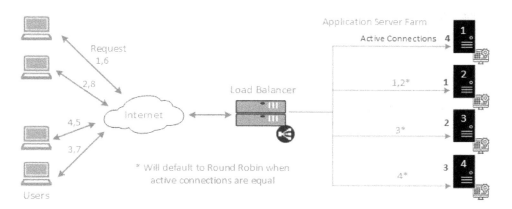

Figure 7.9 – Example of the Least Connections load balancing algorithm

> **Note**
>
> One thing to keep in mind is that this algorithm does not account for the differing capacities of servers; all servers are treated as equal in terms of their ability to handle new connections.

The Least Connections algorithm offers several benefits, particularly in dynamic and variable load environments. Some advantages of using this algorithm are as follows:

- **Improved load distribution**: Unlike static algorithms such as Round Robin, Least Connections takes into account the *current state* of the server pool. By directing new requests to the server with the *least* active connections, this algorithm helps distribute the load more evenly across servers, preventing any single server from becoming overwhelmed.

- **Dynamic responsiveness**: Least Connections is highly responsive to real-time changes in server load. As the number of connections on each server fluctuates, Least Connections dynamically adjusts the routing of incoming requests to ensure optimal distribution based on the current state.

- **Reduced server overload risk**: By avoiding servers that are already handling a high number of connections, Least Connections minimizes the risk of overloading servers. This is especially beneficial in scenarios where some requests are significantly more resource-intensive than others.

- **Better handling of variable session lengths**: In environments where session lengths are unpredictable or highly variable, Least Connections can manage the load more effectively than algorithms that don't consider the number of active connections. It's particularly adept at managing long-running connections.

- **Scalability**: The algorithm supports scalability in network infrastructure. As traffic volume grows, Least Connections can help ensure that new requests are balanced effectively across the server pool, including any newly added servers.

- **Flexibility**: It is suitable for a wide range of applications, especially those where traffic patterns are unpredictable and session duration varies, such as in web services, e-commerce platforms, and cloud-based applications.

The Least Connections algorithm is a more dynamic and responsive approach to load balancing that's especially suited to environments with uneven or unpredictable request patterns. By focusing on the current number of connections to each server, it aims to provide a more balanced distribution of traffic, improving overall network performance and reducing the risk of server overload.

> Note
> The Least Connections algorithm requires more real-time data analysis, which can add computational overhead and may not be as effective in environments where servers have significantly different processing capabilities.

Least Time

The Least Time algorithm is an advanced method that's designed to optimize network traffic distribution by assessing *both* the number of active connections and the response times of servers (**time to first byte (TTFB)**). This algorithm goes beyond the basic strategy of distributing requests based solely on the number of connections (as seen in the Least Connections algorithm) by also considering how quickly servers are responding to requests (the Fastest Response Time algorithm) to optimize network traffic distribution (*Figure 7.10*).

When a new request comes in, the load balancer evaluates each server, taking into account not only the current load (number of active connections) but also the average response time for each server. Then, it directs the request to the server that has the best combination of fewer active connections and lower response time. This dual-criteria approach ensures that the server that's selected to handle the request is positioned to do so efficiently, both in terms of existing load and performance capability:

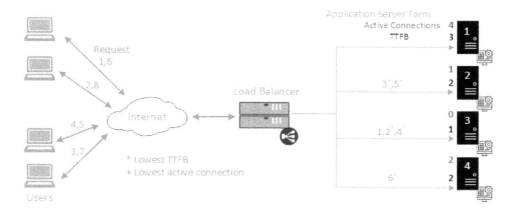

Figure 7.10 – Example of the Least Time load balancing algorithm

Least Time offers several significant benefits, making it an excellent choice for certain network environments. Here are some key advantages of using this algorithm:

- **Optimized load distribution**: By considering both the number of active connections and the response times, Least Time ensures a more balanced load distribution. It not only looks at how many requests a server is handling but also how quickly it is handling them, preventing servers that are fast but already handling many connections from becoming overloaded.

- **Enhanced performance and efficiency**: Servers with quicker response times typically have more available resources or are less busy. Routing requests to these servers can lead to faster processing and reduced latency, enhancing overall system performance.

- **Adaptive to server performance fluctuations**: The algorithm is responsive to real-time changes in server performance. If a server starts responding more slowly, perhaps due to a high load, the load balancer will start directing new requests to faster servers, ensuring consistent performance.

- **Improved user experience**: Faster server response times directly contribute to a better user experience. Websites and applications feel more responsive, which is crucial for customer satisfaction and retention, especially in services such as e-commerce, online gaming, or any interactive web application.

- **Dynamic and intelligent traffic management**: Least Time is particularly effective in environments where traffic patterns and server response times are highly variable. It dynamically adjusts to current conditions, making it suitable for complex, high-demand applications.

- **Prevents server overload**: By considering response times, the algorithm naturally avoids sending new requests to servers that are already slow, potentially due to high load, thus preventing them from becoming even more sluggish.

- **High availability and reliability**: Efficient and intelligent distribution of requests leads to higher overall availability and reliability of network services as no single server becomes a bottleneck.

- **Ideal for high-traffic environments**: For environments with a large volume of requests and where performance is a key concern, such as large-scale web services or cloud-based applications, Least Time provides an effective load balancing solution.

The Least Time algorithm stands out as an advanced method for managing network traffic, combining the principles of Least Connections and Fastest Response Time. It optimizes network efficiency by considering not only the number of active connections to each server but also their average response times. This dual-criterion approach ensures that the selected server is optimally ready to handle the request, both in terms of capacity and performance.

Source IP Affinity (Sticky Sessions)

Source IP Affinity, often referred to as Sticky Sessions or Session Persistence, is a load balancing technique that's used to ensure that all requests from a particular client or user are consistently routed to the *same* backend server throughout their session. This is achieved by assigning an identifying attribute to a user, such as a cookie, or tracking their IP details. The load balancer then uses the tracking ID to route all of the user's requests to a specific server. Once this association has been established, all subsequent requests from the same client with the same source IP address are directed to the same backend server for the duration of the session. This approach is particularly important for applications that require stateful communication or maintain session-specific data.

> **Note**
> Source IP Affinity distributes traffic using a two-tuple hash (source IP and destination IP) or a three-tuple hash (source IP, destination IP, and protocol).

Source IP Affinity is used for several important reasons:

- **Session continuity**: Sticky Sessions ensure that *all requests* from a particular client or user during a session are consistently routed to the same backend server. This is crucial for applications that maintain session-specific data or state, such as user authentication, shopping carts, or game sessions. Without Sticky Sessions, a user's session data could be lost or inconsistent if requests are sent to different servers.

- **Stateful applications**: Applications, such as eCommerce websites, online banking platforms, and online gaming services, are inherently stateful. They rely on maintaining session-specific information, such as login credentials, user preferences, and shopping cart contents. Sticky Sessions enable these applications to function as expected by keeping users' session data intact on a single server.

- **Personalization**: Sticky Sessions help provide a personalized and consistent user experience. When a user interacts with an application, the server can remember their preferences and activities, offering recommendations, personalized content, and an overall tailored experience.

- **Reduced overhead**: In stateful applications, initializing and managing sessions can be *resource-intensive*. Sticky Sessions reduce the overhead associated with constantly reinitializing sessions on different backend servers as the client's session remains on the same server throughout the session.

- **To prevent data loss**: Sticky Sessions prevent data loss that could occur if a client's session data is stored on one server and subsequent requests from the same client are directed to a different server that does not have access to the session data.

- **To ensure transaction integrity**: For applications involving financial transactions, database updates, or multi-step processes, Sticky Sessions help ensure transaction integrity by keeping all related requests on the same server. This prevents issues such as incomplete transactions or data inconsistencies.

In summary, Source IP Affinity is a crucial load balancing technique that's employed in web applications to maintain *session continuity* and preserve user-specific data. It's utilized to ensure that all requests from a particular client or user during a session are *consistently* directed to the same backend server. This is essential for applications that require stateful communication, such as eCommerce platforms, online banking systems, and gaming platforms. By associating a client's source IP address with a specific server, Source IP Affinity enables the server to maintain user session data, preferences, and transaction states, ensuring seamless and uninterrupted user experience, preventing data loss, and optimizing the performance of stateful applications.

IP hash

The IP hash algorithm is a method that's used to distribute network traffic among multiple servers based on the IP addresses of clients to convert it into a unique *hash* value. The resulting hash value is then used to allocate the request to one of the available servers. This is typically done by dividing the hash by the number of servers and using the remainder to select a server to handle user requests.

Since the same IP address always results in the same hash value, all requests from the *same client* will be directed to the *same server*. This ensures session persistence, meaning that a client's multiple requests will be handled by the same server during any given session.

> **Note**
> Although both Source IP Affinity and IP hash maintain a user's session and appear to be similar, they are different. Source IP Affinity typically employs a direct mapping approach as opposed to the IP hash approach for consistent user-server interaction.

Here's why IP hash is used:

- **Consistent server interaction**: Since the client's IP address determines the server to which requests are sent, all requests from the same IP address are handled by the same server. This consistency is of great importance for applications where the user's session needs to be persistent, such as in online shopping carts or personalized user interfaces.

- **No server-side affinity mechanisms**: With IP hash, the load balancer takes care of maintaining session persistence, thereby eliminating the need for more complex session affinity mechanisms on the server side, along with consuming unnecessary server resources.

- **Deterministic behavior**: The algorithm offers a predictable pattern of traffic distribution as a particular IP address *will always* be directed to the same server, so long as the server pool remains unchanged.

- **Equal distribution for diverse IPs**: In scenarios where the client base accessing a service is large and varied, with clients having a wide range of distinct IP addresses, the IP hash algorithm can achieve a more balanced and randomized load distribution, reducing any one server in the pool being overtaxed.

- **Minimal processing requirements**: This refers to IP hash's operational simplicity and low computational overhead compared to more complex load balancing methods. This aspect is a significant advantage in certain network environments. Unlike algorithms that assess server load, response time, or other changing metrics, IP hash does not require ongoing monitoring and analysis of server performance, which can be computationally intensive.

> **Note**
> Because of the simplicity of the IP hash algorithm, this means it requires fewer CPU cycles and less memory to operate. This efficiency is particularly beneficial in a high-traffic environment where the load balancer itself could become a bottleneck.

- **Straightforward implementation**: The logic behind IP hash is relatively simple compared to more complex algorithms, making it easier to implement and maintain.

In summary, IP hash is particularly advantageous for applications that require consistent interaction with the same server throughout a session. It provides a straightforward and efficient way to ensure session persistence without additional complexity on the server side. However, its effectiveness can vary depending on the distribution of client IP addresses and the uniformity of the server pool.

In environments where client IPs are concentrated or where servers have significantly different capabilities, IP hash might lead to uneven load distribution. Nonetheless, for many applications, particularly those where session persistence is a priority, the benefits of IP hash make it a valuable load balancing strategy.

Which load balancer should you choose?

When using and choosing a load balancer, network architects must consider several critical factors to ensure optimal performance, high availability, and seamless application delivery. This necessity stems from the critical role load balancers play in distributing network traffic efficiently across multiple servers. Some key considerations are as follows:

- **Traffic handling capacity**: A primary consideration when selecting a load balancer is its traffic handling capacity. The load balancer must be capable of managing the current and expected traffic demands, avoiding bottlenecks, and distributing requests efficiently across servers. It should support the required throughput and *concurrent connections* to handle peak loads without service degradation.

- **Load balancing algorithms**: As mentioned previously, load balancers employ various algorithms to distribute traffic, such as Round Robin, WRR, Least Connections, and Least Response Time. The key considerations for choosing an algorithm depend on the specific application requirements and workload characteristics. Network architects should assess the behavior of each algorithm to determine the best fit for their application owners, application, and traffic patterns.

- **High availability and redundancy**: Load balancers themselves must be highly available and redundant to avoid becoming single points of failure. As a best practice, network architects should deploy load balancers in an active-active or active-passive configuration to ensure continuous service availability. Additionally, they should consider GSLBs for geographic redundancy across multiple data centers.

- **Session persistence and affinity**: When designing the infrastructure to support customer and business applications, the network architect must be aware of applications requiring session persistence. The load balancer should support various methods of session persistence, such as Source IP Affinity or cookie-based persistence, based on the application's needs.

> **Note**
> Session persistence is a feature where the load balancer ensures that a user's subsequent requests are consistently directed to the same backend server during the duration of their session or connection to maintain the session state, as shown through the IP hash and Source IP Affinity load balancing algorithms.

- **Health monitoring and failover mechanisms**: Aside from the load balancer having to support session persistence, high availability in the event of a failure, or having to choose the most feasible load balancing algorithm, the load balancers must constantly monitor the health and availability of backend servers.

  If a server becomes unresponsive or experiences issues, application requests can be impacted and **user experience** (**UX**) will deteriorate. Since such events can occur, the load balancer must be able to automatically remove it from the pool and redirect traffic to healthy servers.

As such, network architects must define appropriate health checks and failover mechanisms for seamless *server* replacement.

- **SSL/TLS offloading**: Load balancers can offload SSL/TLS encryption and decryption, reducing the processing load on backend servers and improving overall performance. Network architects should be aware of the requirements for SSL/TLS offloading and determine if the load balancer supports SSL/TLS termination and re-encryption to maintain secure data transmission.

- **Application layer awareness**: In some cases, load balancers need to be aware of the specific application protocols and handle traffic accordingly. Application layer awareness allows load balancers to make more intelligent decisions based on application-specific requirements, such as Sticky Sessions or content-based routing.

- **Scalability and management**: The network architect must design the load balancer's infrastructure so that it can scale to accommodate future growth and evolving traffic patterns. In addition, they must facilitate monitoring, management, and troubleshooting by NOC or network support teams.

In conclusion, selecting an appropriate load balancer is crucial for maintaining highly performant, reliable, and scalable application delivery. Network architects must consider factors such as traffic handling capacity, load balancing algorithms, high availability, session persistence, health monitoring, SSL/TLS offloading, application layer awareness, and ease of management when choosing a load balancer that aligns with their organization's specific requirements and workload characteristics.

Exploring DNS

DNS is a fundamental component of the internet's architecture, playing a vital role in how users and systems interact online. For organizations, DNS is fundamental for establishing a robust online presence, facilitating seamless email communication and application reachability, and enabling efficient load balancing and service discovery.

DNS operates through a distributed and hierarchical network of servers, starting from root DNS servers down to authoritative servers for specific domains. This structure not only provides a scalable and resilient mechanism for domain name resolution but also plays a pivotal role in internet security, traffic management, and network performance.

Therefore, network architects must have a firm understanding of DNS to design, secure, and optimize network infrastructure, ensuring reliable and efficient inter/intra networking connectivity.

How DNS works

DNS operates by mapping a human-friendly domain name (for example, `www.ahaliblogger.tech`) into an IP address that computers use to identify each other on the network. If I issue a ping command to `www.ahaliblogger.tech`, the result would look something like this (*Figure 7.11*):

```
C:\Users\ahaliblogger>ping www.ahaliblogger.tech

Pinging ahaliblogger.tech [173.201.141.128] with 32 bytes of data:
Reply from 173.201.141.128: bytes=32 time=69ms TTL=54
Reply from 173.201.141.128: bytes=32 time=74ms TTL=54
Reply from 173.201.141.128: bytes=32 time=70ms TTL=54
Reply from 173.201.141.128: bytes=32 time=69ms TTL=54

Ping statistics for 173.201.141.128:
    Packets: Sent = 4, Received = 4, Lost = 0 (0% loss),
Approximate round trip times in milli-seconds:
    Minimum = 69ms, Maximum = 74ms, Average = 70ms

C:\Users\ahaliblogger>
```

Figure 7.11 – Example of a ping request/reply to www.ahaliblogger.tech

As you can see, the ping reply returned successfully. Did you notice the IP address? That's the IP assigned to this service. What occurred here was *DNS name resolution*. Let's look at a familiar diagram that was presented in *Chapter 1* (*Figure 7.12*):

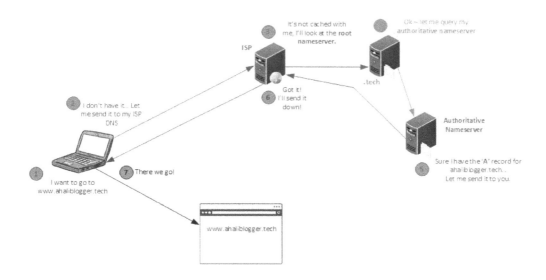

Figure 7.12 – Example of a DNS request workflow

This diagram highlights a client/server architecture, but it also shows a DNS request workflow. Let's explore this:

1. A user makes a request to `https://www.ahaliblogger.tech` via a web browser.

2. The user's computer checks if the IP address for the domain name is already in its local DNS cache. If it doesn't have www.ahaliblogger.tech cached locally, the request is sent to a recursive DNS server, typically provided by your **Internet Service Provider (ISP)**.

3. From there, the ISP will try to resolve www.ahaliblogger.tech. If the ISP does not have the domain name cached, it will send the request to the root nameserver. The root nameserver is at the top of the DNS hierarchy and guides the recursive server to a more specific DNS server for the **top-level domain (TLD)**. In our case, it will be the .tech TLD server.

4. The recursive server queries the TLD server for .tech., if the TLD nameserver doesn't have the exact IP address but knows the address of the authoritative nameserver for the domain.

5. Next, the recursive server queries the authoritative nameserver for the domain, which has the actual IP address for the domain (ahaliblogger.tech).

6. The response is sent back to the recursive server and cached.

7. Lastly, the recursive server sends the reply back to the user and displays the website for www.ahaliblogger.tech, at which point the user's computer caches the IP address for the website.

This entire process happens almost instantaneously, allowing for quick and efficient web and application activity.

Considerations for DNS design

When a network architect designs a DNS infrastructure, several key considerations must be addressed to ensure it is efficient, secure, and resilient. This section covers the primary aspects they should keep in mind.

Scalability and performance

Scalability and performance in DNS infrastructure design focuses on ensuring the system can efficiently handle growth and traffic fluctuations. Here are some things to consider:

- **Load balancing**: Beyond distributing DNS queries, load balancing can be used to manage the distribution of web traffic across multiple servers or data centers, enhancing the performance and reliability of web applications – especially if the organization experiences high traffic or has peak periods.

- **Geographical distribution and geo-based locations services**: Use geographically distributed DNS servers to reduce latency and improve response times for users in different locations. Implementing geo-DNS services can direct users to the nearest server location based on their geographical location, which can significantly improve load times for regional users.

- **Caching strategies**: Effective caching strategies are vital. Caching DNS responses at various levels – from the browser, operating system, and network to the recursive DNS servers – can significantly reduce the load on authoritative servers and speed up DNS resolution.

- **Anycast routing**: Anycast allows multiple, geographically dispersed DNS servers to share the same IP address. When a DNS query is made, it is routed to the nearest server location, which *reduces* latency and improves load time.

- **Traffic redirection**: Utilize DNS traffic management solutions that can *intelligently* redirect traffic based on server availability and performance metrics.

Redundancy and reliability

With a focus on both redundancy and reliability, network architects can design a DNS infrastructure that ensures ongoing service availability, even in the face of hardware failures, network issues, or other unforeseen problems. Here are some key points to consider:

- **Multiple DNS servers**: Deploy multiple DNS servers in different geographical locations to ensure that if one server fails, others can continue providing DNS resolution services.

- **Diverse network paths**: Connect these DNS servers through different network paths to minimize the risk of a single network failure impacting all DNS services.

- **Secondary DNS**: Implement a secondary DNS service, which acts as a backup to the primary DNS. If the primary DNS fails or experiences issues, the secondary DNS can continue to resolve domain names without interruption.

- **Anycast network configuration**: Utilize Anycast to allow multiple servers to share the *same* IP address and serve requests based on proximity, inherently providing redundancy.

- **Automated failover systems**: Network architects should design their DNS architecture with automated failover capabilities, where systems automatically detect a *failure* in the primary DNS server and switch to a backup server without manual intervention.

> Note
> Implement health checks to continuously monitor the status of primary DNS servers and trigger failover procedures when an anomaly or failure is detected.

Security considerations

When designing a DNS infrastructure, security is paramount to protect against a range of cyber threats and vulnerabilities. Let's explore some important security considerations:

- **Protection against attacks**: Like all systems and networks protecting against attacks, this is vital for organization sustainability. Key threats include **Distributed Denial of Service (DDoS)** attacks (attackers flood DNS servers with excessive traffic), DNS spoofing, and cache poisoning (attackers redirect users to fraudulent websites by corrupting DNS data), which can lead to service outages. To mitigate such attacks, initiate strategies such as rate limiting.

- **DNS Security Extensions (DNSSEC)**: DNSSEC adds a layer of authentication to DNS responses. It protects against unauthorized DNS tampering by ensuring the authenticity of the response(s) a client (or application) receives. This assurance is accomplished by DNSSEC providing a digital signature to DNS data sent to the nameservers.

- **Access control**: Restrict who can update DNS records and query servers to prevent unauthorized changes and reduce potential attack vectors. Utilize **role-based access control (RBAC)** to define and limit the levels of access based on user roles, ensuring that individuals can only access information and perform actions relevant to their job functions.

    Additionally, implement strong authentication methods for accessing DNS management systems, including **multi-factor authentication (MFA)** to add an extra layer of security.

- **Secure protocols**: Consider implementing **DNS over HTTPS (DoH)** or **DNS over TLS (DoT)** to encrypt DNS queries, enhancing privacy and security.

- **Network security**: Implement firewalls to protect DNS servers from unauthorized access and various network attacks. Add network segmentation to isolate DNS servers from other parts of the network, minimizing the risk of lateral movement in case of a breach.

- **Employ DNS filtering**: Also known as DNS-based web filtering, this is a technique that's used to block access to certain websites or web content based on their domain names. It's an effective way to enforce web access policies, enhance security, and reduce web-based threats.

Compliance and best practices

Compliance and best practices in the context of DNS infrastructure involve adhering to established standards and regulations, as well as following industry-recommended practices to ensure a secure, efficient, and legally compliant DNS setup. Network architects must be aware of this to meet the following requirements:

- **Adherence to standards**: Follow standards set by organizations such as the **Internet Engineering Task Force (IETF)** for DNS operations. This includes protocols and procedures for DNS management.

- **Privacy and data protection**: Ensure that your DNS practices comply with the relevant data protection laws, such as GDPR, HIPAA, or CCPA, especially when handling logs that might contain user data.

- **Industry-specific compliance**: For certain industries, there may be additional compliance requirements related to internet services and data security. A network architect must be aware of these and incorporate them into the DNS infrastructure.

- **Regular security audits**: Conduct periodic security audits of the DNS infrastructure to identify potential vulnerabilities or misconfigurations.

Monitoring and management

Monitoring and managing DNS infrastructure involves a set of practices and tools designed to ensure the system's health, performance, and security. Effective monitoring and proactive management are key to maintaining a robust DNS setup. Some key aspects are as follows:

- **Real-time monitoring**: Network architects and the NOC team must perform real-time monitoring of DNS traffic to ensure optimal availability and usage.

- **Traffic analysis**: Continuously monitor DNS traffic for volume, patterns, and anomalies. This can help in identifying potential DDoS attacks, configuration issues, or unexpected spikes in demand.

- **Performance metrics**: Track performance metrics such as query resolution time, server response time, and error rates. This helps in identifying performance bottlenecks and areas for optimization.

- **Health checks**: Implement regular health checks of DNS servers and services to ensure they are functioning correctly and are accessible.

- **Automated alerting systems**: Set up alerts for when certain thresholds are exceeded, such as traffic volume, query failure rates, or response times, to quickly identify potential issues.

  Utilize tools that employ anomaly detection algorithms to alert on deviations from normal operational patterns, indicating potential security breaches or system malfunctions.

- **Log management and analysis**: Use comprehensive logging mechanisms to ensure that all DNS transactions and administrative actions are logged. This includes queries, responses, system changes, and access logs. Use log analysis tools to process and analyze DNS logs for insights, trends, and anomaly detection.

- **Regular updates and maintenance**: Keep DNS server software and associated management tools updated with the latest patches and versions to address security vulnerabilities and improve functionality. Regularly scan DNS servers and systems for vulnerabilities and apply necessary security patches or configuration changes.

Documentation and policy development

Documentation and policy development involves creating, maintaining, and regularly updating detailed records and guidelines that govern the management and operation of the DNS system. Effective documentation and clear policy frameworks are crucial for ensuring consistency, security, and compliance in DNS management. Some documents and policy manufacturing enablement can come from a variety of sources, including leadership (for example, CTO, technical director, architect team, third-party OEMs or solution providers, and the industry). Some key elements are as follows:

- **Clear documentation**: Maintain comprehensive documentation of the DNS infrastructure, policies, and change management procedures. This is important for ongoing internal compliance purposes. Here are some examples of clear documentation:

  - **Configuration records**: Keep detailed records of all DNS server configurations, including zone files, server settings, and network configurations. This should also include documentation of any custom scripts or automation used in DNS management.

  - **Network diagrams**: Create and maintain up-to-date network diagrams that show how DNS servers are integrated into the larger network architecture, including connectivity with external DNS servers and services.

  - **Change logs**: Maintain logs of all changes made to the DNS infrastructure, including dates, details of the changes, and the individuals responsible for them.

  - **Disaster recovery plan**: Document a comprehensive disaster recovery plan specifically for DNS, outlining steps for backup, restoration, and failover in case of system failures or cyberattacks.

  - **Compliance documentation**: Maintain documentation that demonstrates compliance with relevant data protection and privacy laws, industry standards, and internal governance requirements.

- **Policy development and maintenance**: This involves developing a clear *policy framework* for DNS management that covers aspects such as access control, change management, security protocols, and compliance with legal and regulatory standards. Regularly reviewing and updating DNS policies helps ensure they remain relevant and effective, particularly in response to changes in technology, organizational needs (or changes), and the threat landscape.

- **Operational procedures**: This refers to the standardized, documented processes and guidelines that govern the day-to-day management and maintenance of the DNS environment. These procedures are designed to ensure consistency, efficiency, and reliability in DNS operations. Some of these items are as follows:

  - **Standard operating procedures (SOPs)**: Develop SOPs for routine DNS management tasks, such as updating DNS records, handling domain renewals, and responding to DNS queries

  - **Incident response procedures**: Document procedures for responding to DNS-related security incidents, including steps for identification, containment, eradication, and recovery

  - **Staff training documents**: Create training materials for staff involved in DNS management that cover operational procedures, security practices, and policy adherence

  - **User guides**: For organizations where DNS settings might be managed by non-technical staff (such as domain renewals), provide user-friendly guides and documentation

- **Monitoring policies**: Establish guidelines for the continuous monitoring of DNS infrastructure, including what metrics to monitor, alerting thresholds, and response protocols.

- **Reporting formats**: Define standard formats and intervals for DNS performance and security reporting, ensuring that stakeholders receive consistent and relevant information.

In summary, a network architect must design a DNS infrastructure that is not only capable of meeting current organizational needs but also adaptable to future requirements. It involves ensuring scalability, performance, redundancy, security, and compliance with best practices and legal standards – all of which form the backbone of a secure, efficient, and resilient DNS infrastructure, which is crucial for the organization's online presence and operational integrity.

Next, we'll explore DHCP and NAT.

DHCP

DHCP is a foundational network protocol that operates quietly behind the scenes yet plays a pivotal role in the functioning of modern computer networks. It's fundamental for both small and large-scale network environments, serving as a dynamic orchestrator of IP address assignments and network configurations. DHCP streamlines the process of connecting devices to a network by automating the allocation of vital network parameters.

Consider an enterprise network that has about 1,000 network devices, maybe 600 wireless APs, 1,500 servers, and 10,000 employees, each with two devices (laptop and cellphone) and 10 regional locations.

My questions are as follows:

- How would you go about assigning IP addresses to these devices and managing them?
- Would you assign an IP address to each employee and have them configure a corporate laptop?
- Would you statically assign an IP address to all your routers/switches, firewalls, servers, and SAN devices from the IP same range?
- Would you create an IP schema (IP pool) for the following?

  - Regional location
  - Device type
  - Department
  - Peripheral type (for example, printer, scanner, access point, and so on)
  - Client/employee

Ideally, DHCP is used to simplify the management of IP addresses in large networks. It reduces the risk of IP address conflicts and eliminates the need for network teams to manually configure these settings on *each* device.

How does DHCP work?

DHCP (operating at the application layer of the TCP/IP stack) is a network management protocol that automatically assigns IP addresses to devices on a network (*Figure 7.13*):

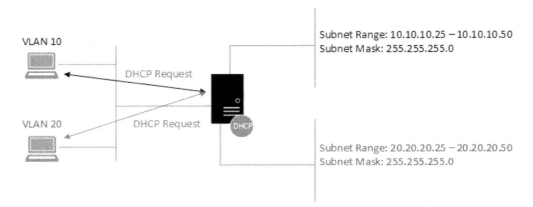

Figure 7.13 – Client DHCP request

DHCP also allocates other communication parameters (*Figure 7.14*):

- Subnet information

- Default gateway IP addresses

- Lease time

- DNS addresses

- **Network time server (NTS)**

```
subnet 172.16.5.0 netmask 255.255.255.0 {
range 172.16.5.100 172.16.5.110;
default-lease-time 600;
max-lease-time 7200;
option routers 172.16.1.1;
option broadcast-address 172.16.1.255;
option subnet-mask 255.255.255.0;
option ntp-servers 172.16.10;
option domain-name-servers 172.16.1.11, 8.8.8.8;
}
```

Figure 7.14 – Sample DHCP server configurations

DHCP works through a four-step process to assign IP addresses and other network configuration parameters to devices on a network (*Figure 7.15*):

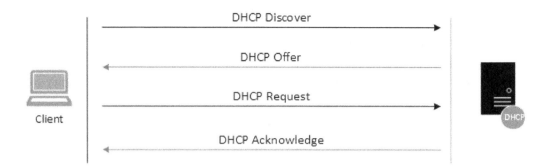

Figure 7.15 – DHCP phases of assigning an IP address to a client

Here's a breakdown of how it works:

- DHCPDISCOVER: When a client device connects to a network, it broadcasts a DHCPDISCOVER message to locate DHCP servers. This message is sent because the client does not know the address of any DHCP servers and needs to discover them.

- DHCPOFFER: DHCP servers on the network respond to the DHCPDISCOVER message with a DHCPOFFER message. This message contains an IP address *offer*, along with other configuration information, such as the subnet mask, default gateway, and DNS server addresses. If there are multiple DHCP servers, the client may receive more than one offer.

- DHCPREQUEST: After receiving one or more offers, the client selects an offer and responds with a DHCPREQUEST message. This message is broadcast to all DHCP servers, indicating acceptance of one offer and declining others. This broadcast ensures that only one DHCP server will allocate an IP address to the client, and any other offers are withdrawn.

- DHCPACK: The DHCP server that made the selected offer responds with a DHCPACK (acknowledgment) message. This message includes the IP address and other networking parameters for the client. Upon receiving this, the client configures its network interface with the provided settings and can now communicate on the network.

> **Note**
> These phases are often abbreviated as **DORA: Discover, Offer, Request, Acknowledge**.

Benefits of DHCP

The use of DHCP in a network offers several significant benefits:

- **Automated IP address management**: DHCP automates the assignment of IP addresses, subnet masks, and other network configuration parameters. This automation reduces the need for manual configuration, saving time and reducing the likelihood of errors.

- **Efficient utilization of IP addresses**: DHCP allows for efficient reuse and management of a limited pool of IP addresses. IP addresses can be assigned on a lease basis, meaning they are only reserved for a device while it is connected to the network.

- **Reduced network administration overhead**: By automating the IP assignment process, DHCP significantly reduces the workload on network teams. This allows them to focus on more complex tasks, rather than manually allocating and tracking IP addresses.

- **Simplified configuration of network settings**: Besides IP addresses, DHCP can automatically configure other important network settings, such as the default gateway, DNS servers, and other relevant configuration details.

- **Improved network stability and reliability**: DHCP helps in reducing IP conflicts and related network issues. This enhances the overall stability and reliability of the network.

- **Scalability**: DHCP makes it easier to scale up a network. As new devices are added, DHCP can seamlessly assign and manage IP addresses for them without the need to reconfigure the existing network setup.

- **Mobile and temporary devices**: DHCP is ideal for networks where devices frequently join or leave, such as laptops in a business environment or mobile devices in public Wi-Fi areas.

- **Centralized network management**: DHCP allows for centralized control and management of network resources, which is essential for maintaining the health and performance of a network.

Key considerations for using DHCP

When incorporating DHCP in IT network design, a network architect should consider several key factors to ensure the network is efficient, secure, and scalable. Here are some important considerations:

- **Network size and layout**: Understand the size and layout of the network. Large networks might require multiple DHCP servers or a distributed DHCP infrastructure to handle the load and provide redundancy.

- **Scalability, redundancy, and reliability**: Plan for future growth. Ensure that the DHCP design can accommodate an increasing number of devices without performance degradation.

  Also, implement DHCP redundancy to ensure high availability. This can involve setting up multiple DHCP servers or using failover configurations to prevent single points of failure.

- **Subnetting, IP address allocation, and lease duration**: Design an *efficient* subnetting strategy. This includes determining the range of IP addresses that will be dynamically allocated and ensuring that there are enough addresses for all potential network devices.

  Also, set appropriate DHCP lease times. Shorter lease times can provide more flexibility in reassigning IP addresses.

> **Note**
>
> Keep in mind that shorter lease times can potentially lead to an increase in network traffic due to more frequent renewals.

- **Integration with DNS**: Ensure smooth integration with the DNS, particularly for dynamic DNS updates, which can be critical for services that rely on name resolution.

- **Security, compliance, and policy alignment**: Implement security measures to prevent unauthorized DHCP servers (rogue DHCP) and DHCP spoofing attacks. This can include using DHCP snooping on switches and implementing **network access control** (**NAC**) policies.

  Ensure the DHCP setup aligns with organizational policies and compliance requirements, particularly regarding IP address management and data security.

- **Options and client considerations**: Utilize DHCP options for network customization. DHCP can be used to assign more than just IP addresses; it can also distribute information about network gateways, DNS servers, and other configuration parameters.

  Consider the types of clients that will be connecting to the network (for example, IoT devices, mobile devices, and laptops) and their specific configuration needs.

For a network architect, an in-depth understanding of DHCP is indispensable, allowing them to design and maintain efficient, scalable, and resilient networks by automating and managing the assignment of IP addresses, significantly reducing manual tasks and the potential for human error. It also plays a critical role in resource allocation and helps in optimizing the network's performance and reliability. Furthermore, familiarity with DHCP is vital for implementing network policies and addressing security concerns, such as preventing unauthorized access and DHCP spoofing attacks.

Network Address Translation (NAT)

NAT is another network service that's used in enterprise networks that allows multiple devices on a local network to access resources on the internet using a single *public* IP address. NAT acts like a *gatekeeper*, managing internal requests for access or communication to systems and applications external to the request being made. When data returns from the internet (external systems), NAT manages the reverse process, ensuring the information reaches the correct device.

> **Note**
> NAT operates at both Layer 3 and Layer 4 of the OSI model.

How does NAT work?

Imagine a large corporation with thousands of employees working in a headquarters office. The company has a private network with numerous internal servers, workstations, and other devices. The company also has a limited pool of public IP addresses that it obtained from its **Internet Service Provider (ISP)** (*Figure 7.16*):

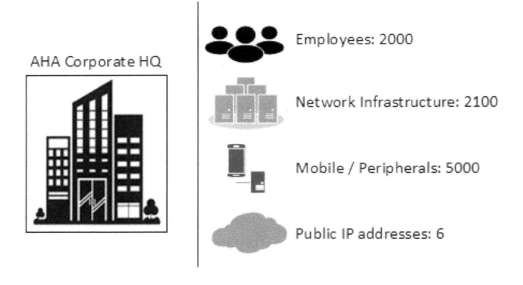

AHA Corporate HQ

Employees: 2000

Network Infrastructure: 2100

Mobile / Peripherals: 5000

Public IP addresses: 6

Figure 7.16 – NAT example

Within the company's headquarters, there are various departments, each with its own set of internal IP addresses designated by a network architect. For example, the finance department might use the 10.0.1.x range, while the marketing department might use 10.0.2.x.

The company has a few public IP addresses provided by the ISP. Let's say they have a range of public IPs – for example, 12.11.5.18 to 12.11.5.23.

When an employee in the finance department wants to access a financial database website on the internet, their internal device sends a request. Before the request leaves the company's network, the NAT device (usually a firewall, router, or edge appliance gateway) replaces the source IP address (for example, 10.0.1.134) with one of the available public IP addresses (for example, 12.11.5.18).

This way, the website sees the request as originating from the public IP address of the NAT device (*Figure 7.17*):

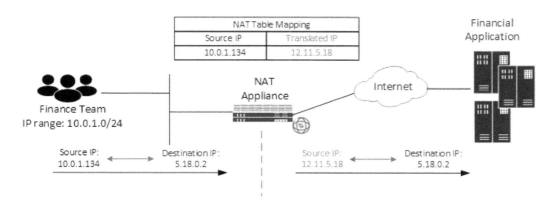

Figure 7.17 – Client IP translation to a financial application

If the website responds to the request, the NAT device remembers that it originally came from the internal device with an IP address of 10.0.1.134. When the response arrives, the NAT device uses this information (NAT mapping table) to route the response back to the correct internal device (*Figure 7.18*):

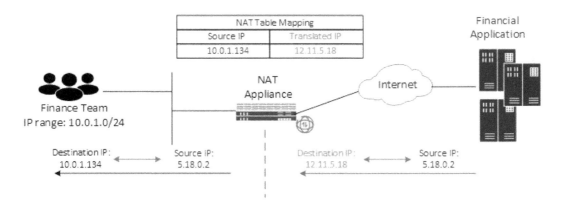

Figure 7.18 – Return traffic from the financial application to the client

> **Note**
>
> This is an oversimplified example of how NAT works. There are other services involved, such as firewalls, ACLs, and security appliances to make sure the information that's sent and received is from the intended recipients.
>
> NAT is not only used for translating internal corporate (internal) IP addresses to a public-facing IP address. NAT can be used to protect sensitive network resources. In general, NAT can be used from one private address to another private address.

Types of NAT

In enterprise networks, several types of NAT techniques are used, each serving a specific purpose and functioning uniquely. Let's take a closer look:

- **Static NAT (SNAT):** This type of NAT involves a one-to-one mapping between a private IP address and a public IP address. It's often used when a device inside the network needs to be *continuously* accessible from the internet, such as a web server. In SNAT, the IP address translation remains constant, allowing predictable and straightforward communication with specific internal devices (*Figure 7.19*):

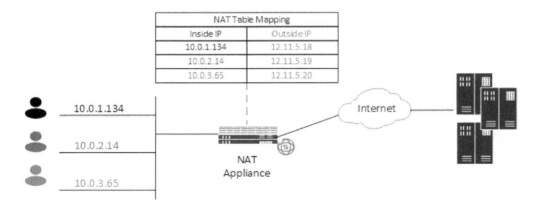

Figure 7.19 – SNAT

> **Note**
>
> SNAT can get expensive. At the time of writing, the average monthly price of a public address is about $65 to $70. If an organization has 10,000 employees and devices, all requiring public access, the cost would be around $650,000 to $700,000 per month!

- **Dynamic NAT (DNAT)**: Unlike SNAT, DNAT uses a *pool* of public IP addresses. When a device from the internal network requests access to the internet, it is assigned a public IP address from this pool, randomly. DNAT does establish a one-to-one mapping, like SNAT – however, the assignment is temporary and changes with each new connection. DNAT is efficient in managing a limited set of public IP addresses for a large group of devices:

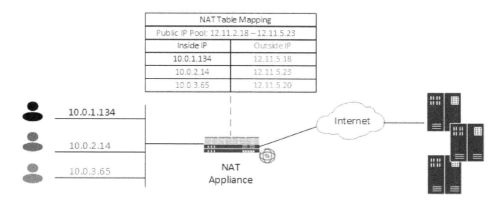

Figure 7.20 – DNAT

Note

DNAT follows the principle of "first come, first serve." However, more importantly, it *does not* guarantee the same public IP address for the same device across different sessions.

- **Port address translation (PAT)**: Also known as NAT overload, PAT is a variation of DNAT that allows multiple devices on a local network to be mapped to a single public IP address, but with *different* port numbers.

  When a request is sent out to the internet, PAT modifies not only the *source* IP address but also assigns a unique *source* port number to each session. This way, it keeps track of which response belongs to which internal device. PAT is extremely common in small to medium-sized networks because it allows the extensive use of a single IP address, maximizing efficiency:

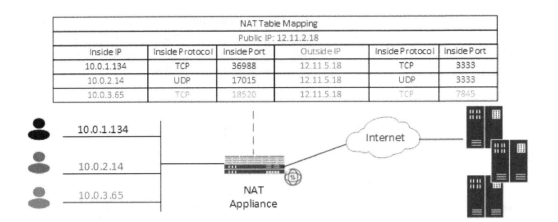

| NAT Table Mapping | | | | | |
| Public IP: 12.11.2.18 | | | | | |
Inside IP	Inside Protocol	Inside Port	Outside IP	Inside Protocol	Inside Port
10.0.1.134	TCP	36988	12.11.5.18	TCP	3333
10.0.2.14	UDP	17015	12.11.5.18	UDP	3333
10.0.3.65	TCP	18520	12.11.5.18	TCP	7845

Figure 7.21 – PAT (NAT overload)

> **Note**
>
> PAT divides the available ports per global IP address into three ranges: 0-511, 512-1023, and 1024-65535. PAT assigns a unique source port for each UDP or TCP session.

- **NAT64**: This is a special type of NAT that's used for translating IPv6 addresses into IPv4 addresses and vice versa. It's particularly useful in situations where newer IPv6 networks need to communicate with older IPv4 networks. NAT64 enables this communication by translating IPv6 addresses into IPv4 addresses, thus ensuring interoperability between these different network types.

- **Policy-based NAT (PB-NAT)**: PB-NAT is a more advanced and flexible form of NAT that allows network architects to define specific rules or policies that dictate *how* IP addresses are translated. Unlike traditional NAT, which typically operates on a more straightforward source or destination IP basis, policy-based NAT provides greater control over the translation process based on additional criteria. This approach is particularly useful in complex network environments where more granular control is needed.

NAT considerations

When designing NAT solutions, a network architect must consider several key factors to ensure the network is efficient, secure, and scalable. These considerations are as follows:

- **IP address allocation and management**: Determine the range of public and private IP addresses needed for the network. A network architect *must* plan for efficient use of IP addresses, considering future growth and the possibility of IPv4 address exhaustion. Assess whether SNAT, DNAT, or PAT is more suitable for the network's needs.

- **Network security**: NAT inherently provides a level of security by masking internal IP addresses, but it should be integrated with other security measures, such as firewalls and intrusion detection systems. Consider how NAT may impact the implementation of security policies and the monitoring of network traffic and infrastructure.

- **Application compatibility**: Some applications and protocols do not work well with NAT, particularly those that embed IP address information within the data payload.

> **Note**
>
> Some cases where NAT may not be acceptable include when protocols need to authenticate packet headers (IPSec) and use IP datagram types other than TCP/UDP and distributed applications.

- **Performance and scalability**: Network architects must evaluate the impact of NAT on network performance, including latency and throughput. Ensure that the NAT implementation can scale with the growth of the network in terms of the number of devices and the volume of traffic.

- **Port management and allocation**: For PAT configurations, network architects should plan how ports will be allocated and managed. Consider the limitations in the number of available ports and how this might impact large numbers of concurrent connections.

- **IPv6 transition strategy**: Considerations should be made regarding IPv6 and how, if any, NAT will play a role in the transition. NAT64 might be necessary for networks transitioning from IPv4 to IPv6, and dual-stack configurations may be needed during the transition phase.

- **Logging and troubleshooting**: NAT can complicate logging and troubleshooting since multiple devices share a single public IP, implementing robust logging mechanisms to track individual connections and aid in troubleshooting is important.

- **Network redundancy and high availability**: Design the NAT implementation so that it supports network redundancy and high availability. This may include using multiple NAT devices or configuring failover mechanisms to ensure continuous operation.

- **Compliance with standards and regulations**: As with all networking devices and services, network architects must ensure NAT configurations comply with relevant standards and regulations, particularly those related to data privacy and security.

- **Costs and resource allocation**: With all the considerations already proposed, costs associated with implementing and maintaining the NAT solution are paramount. Network architects must evaluate hardware, software, and operational expenses to determine which solutions best fit the organization's need to efficiently balance performance, security, and total cost of ownership.

By carefully addressing these considerations, a network architect can design a NAT solution that meets the organization's IT infrastructure needs while providing flexibility, security, and scalability for future growth.

In summary, DHCP and NAT are essential network services that significantly contribute to efficient and secure network design. DHCP automates IP address allocation, reducing manual configuration and the associated risk of errors, which is a crucial factor in dynamic network environments with frequent device turnover. This automation streamlines network management, making it easier for a network architect to maintain a large and evolving network infrastructure. NAT, on the other hand, is vital for conserving limited IPv4 addresses and enhancing network security. It allows multiple devices on a private network to share a single public IP address, addressing IPv4 scarcity while simultaneously shielding internal network devices from direct external access.

For a network architect, understanding and effectively deploying DHCP and NAT is key to designing networks that are not only scalable and efficient but also secure, ensuring optimal resource utilization and protection against external threats.

Next, we'll discuss ACLs and firewall rules.

What are ACLs?

ACLs are a set of *instructions* that are used to regulate access to network resources. Configured on network devices such as routers and switches, ACLs determine which traffic is allowed or denied in a network segment based on the following criteria:

- IP addresses
  - Source IP address, which identifies the originating address of the traffic
  - Destination IP address, which specifies the target address
- Protocol type
  - The type of protocol (for example, TCP, UDP, ICMP).
- Port numbers
  - The specific port numbers involved in the communication
- Traffic flow
  - Direction of traffic (ingress or egress)

Operating as a fundamental security tool, ACLs help protect the network from external threats and limit potential attack vectors.

> **Note**
> ACLs primarily operate at Layer 3 (the network layer) and Layer 4 (the transport layer) of the OSI model.

Let's look at an example:

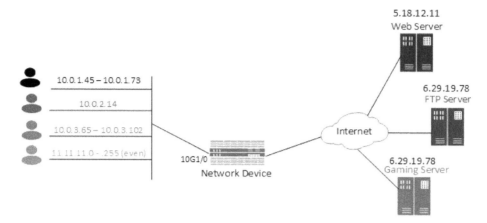

Figure 7.22 – ACL example

In this example, we have several subnet ranges that are connected to a network device on the TenGigabit 1/0 interface. An ACL needs to be configured on the network device so that it can do the following:

- Allow the IP range of 10.0.1.45 to 10.0.1.73
- Deny host 10.0.2.14
- Deny the IP range of 10.0.3.65 to 10.0.3.102
- Allow the IP subnet of 11.11.11.0 /24 but only the even host is permitted

Figure 7.23 illustrates the ACL entries that are necessary to accomplish the task, with the TenGigabit 1/0 interface applied inbound to the network device:

```
access-list 10 permit 10.0.1.45 0.0.0.28
access-list 10 deny host 10.0.2.14
access-list 10 deny 10.0.3.65 0.0.0.37
access-list 10 permit 11.11.11.0 0.0.0.254
access-list 10 deny any

interface TenGigabitEthernet1/0
  ip access-group 10 in
```

Figure 7.23 – Configuration of a standard ACL

Types of ACLs

There are two main types of ACLs, as well as one variant that's used on network devices. Let's take a closer look.

Standard ACLs

A standard ACL is a type of ACL that's used in computer networking to control and filter network traffic based solely on the source IP address. Standard ACLs are relatively simple and provide basic access control by permitting or denying traffic from specific source IP addresses or networks. They are typically identified by a numeric range, such as ACL numbers 1 to 99 or 1,300 to 1,999. Standard ACLs filter traffic based solely on the source IP address.

Their key characteristics are as follows:

- **Source IP address-based filtering**: Standard ACLs evaluate traffic based on the source IP address of incoming packets. They do not consider the destination IP address, port numbers, or specific protocols.

- **Simplicity**: Standard ACLs are straightforward to configure because they focus on source IP addresses only. They are suitable for simple access control requirements.

- **Permit and deny actions**: You can specify whether traffic from a particular source IP address or network should be permitted or denied. For example, you can allow traffic from specific source IP addresses while denying traffic from others.

- **Sequential processing**: Standard ACLs are processed sequentially, starting from the top of the list and moving down. The first match determines the action for the traffic – that is, the order of ACL entries matters.

Here are some use cases for standard ACLs:

- **Basic security**: Standard ACLs are often used for basic security purposes to control access to a network or specific resources

- **Traffic control**: In some cases, standard ACLs can be used to limit traffic to or from specific devices or subnets within a network

- **Traffic isolation**: They are used to isolate or segment parts of a network by permitting or denying communication between certain subnets or devices

Extended ACLs

An extended ACL is a type of ACL that's used in computer networking to control and filter network traffic based on a variety of criteria and have more granular control over network traffic compared to standard ACLs. These ACLs are identified by a numeric range, such as ACL numbers 100 to 199 and 2,000 to 2,699.

Let's look at the previous example once more:

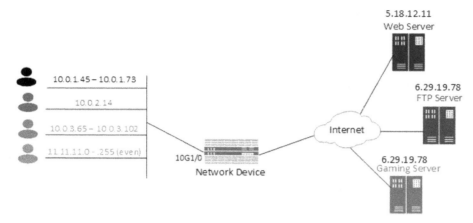

Figure 7.24 – Example of an extended ACL

This time, we want to accomplish the following:

- Allow the IP range of 10.0.1.45 to 10.0.1.73 to reach the FTP server with an IP address of 6.29.19.78

- Deny host 10.0.2.14 to web server 5.18.12.11

- Deny the IP range of 10.0.3.65 to 10.0.3.102 to UDP port 2020 but allow TCP 2020

- Allow the IP subnet of 11.11.11.0 /24 even hosts to reach the gaming server of 6.29.19.78 on ports 88, 3074, and 53 (TCP and UDP)

Figure 7.25 illustrates the extended ACL entries that are necessary to accomplish the task, as applied to the TenGigabit 1/0 interface inbound to the network device:

```
access-list 101 permit ip 10.0.1.45 0.0.0.28 host 6.29.19.78 eq ftp
access-list 101 deny ip host 10.0.2.14 host 5.18.12.11 eq www
access-list 101 deny ip 10.0.3.65 0.0.0.37 host 5.18.12.11 eq 2020
access-list 101 permit tcp 10.0.3.65 0.0.0.37 any eq 2020
access-list 101 deny udp 10.0.3.65 0.0.0.37 any eq 2020
access-list 101 permit ip 11.11.11.0 0.0.0.254 host 6.29.19.78 eq 88
access-list 101 permit ip 11.11.11.0 0.0.0.254 host 6.29.19.78 eq 3074
access-list 101 permit ip 11.11.11.0 0.0.0.254 host 6.29.19.78 eq 53
access-list 101 deny ip any any

interface TenGigabitEthernet1/0
 ip access-group 101 in
```

Figure 7.25 – Configuration of an extended ACL

Here are some of the key characteristics of extended ACLs:

- **Multiple criteria**: Extended ACLs allow you to filter traffic based on multiple criteria, including the following:

  - Source and destination IP addresses

  - Source and destination port numbers

  - Specific protocols

  This granularity enables more complex access control rules.

- **Source and destination-based filtering**: Extended ACLs consider both the source and destination IP addresses of incoming or outgoing packets, making them suitable for filtering traffic to or from specific hosts, subnets, or networks.

- **Port and protocol control**: You can specify port numbers (TCP/UDP) and IP protocols (for example, ICMP) to permit or deny traffic for specific applications or services. This is useful for allowing or blocking access to specific services running on well-known port numbers.

- **Sequential processing**: Like standard ACLs, extended ACLs are processed sequentially, starting from the top of the list and moving down. The first match determines the action for the traffic.

Here are some use cases for extended ACLs:

- **Fine-grained access control**: Extended ACLs are commonly used for fine-grained access control, allowing or denying traffic based on specific criteria (for example, permitting or denying access to web servers on port 80 from specific source IP addresses).

- **Security policies**: They can be used to implement security policies that dictate which hosts or networks are allowed to communicate with each other. This includes segmenting a network to isolate sensitive data or services or allowing only trusted devices to access critical resources.

- **Regulatory compliance**: Extended ACLs help in enforcing policies that comply with regulatory requirements, such as blocking unauthorized access to sensitive data.

- **Network optimization**: Extended ACLs can be used to optimize network performance by allowing or denying specific traffic flows. Here are some examples:

  - Prioritizing certain types of traffic, such as VoIP or video streaming

  - Blocking or throttling traffic that consumes excessive bandwidth

Named ACLs

Named ACLs are a type of ACL that's used just like standard and extended ACLs. However, they differ in their configuration syntax and are identified by *user-defined* names instead of numeric identifiers.

Looking back at the example shown in *Figure 7.25*, this time, named ACLs will be used. *Figure 7.26* shows what it looks like:

```
ip access-list extended MY_ACL
permit ip 10.0.1.45 0.0.0.28 host 6.29.19.78 eq ftp
deny ip host 10.0.2.14 host 5.18.12.11 eq www
deny ip 10.0.3.65 0.0.0.37 host 5.18.12.11 eq 2020
permit tcp 10.0.3.65 0.0.0.37 any eq 2020
deny udp 10.0.3.65 0.0.0.37 any eq 2020
permit ip 11.11.11.0 0.0.0.254 host 6.29.19.78 eq 88
permit ip 11.11.11.0 0.0.0.254 host 6.29.19.78 eq 3074
permit ip 11.11.11.0 0.0.0.254 host 6.29.19.78 eq 53
deny ip any any
```

Table 7.26 – Configuration of a named ACL

Here are some of the key characteristics of named ACLs:

- **User-defined names**: Instead of using numeric ACL identifiers (for example, 101, 102, and so on), named ACLs are identified by user-defined names that provide a more human-readable and meaningful representation of the ACL's purpose or function.

- **Enhanced readability**: Named ACLs make it easier to understand and document the purpose of each ACL in your network configuration. You can use descriptive names that convey the intended use of the ACL.

- **Flexibility**: Named ACLs can be used for *both* standard and extended ACLs. This means you can create named versions of standard and extended ACLs as needed.

- **Easier management**: Named ACLs are often easier to manage and update because you can modify them directly by their names without needing to remember or reference numeric ACL identifiers.

Here are some use cases for named ACLs:

- **Improved documentation**: Named ACLs enhance the documentation of your network configuration by providing clear and meaningful names for each ACL. This is particularly beneficial in larger and more complex network environments.

- **Configuration clarity**: Named ACLs make it easier for architects and network engineers to understand the purpose and function of each ACL. This clarity can help reduce errors in ACL configurations.

- **Complex ACL policies**: In networks with intricate access control policies, named ACLs can simplify the management of multiple ACLs with distinct functions by assigning descriptive names to each ACL.

- **Ease of troubleshooting**: When troubleshooting network issues or security incidents, having named ACLs can expedite the identification of the relevant ACLs and their associated rules.

- **Consistency and standardization**: Named ACLs can promote consistency and standardization across your network configuration as you can use standardized naming conventions for ACLs.

With that, we've explored the concept of both standard ACLs and extended ACLs. Standard ACLs focus on controlling access based solely on the source IP address and are useful for basic access control requirements. Extended ACLs, on the other hand, offer more granular control by considering multiple criteria, such as source and destination IP addresses, port numbers, and protocols, making them suitable for complex access control policies. Additionally, we delved into named ACLs, which provide user-defined names for ACLs, enhancing readability, documentation, and ease of management.

Now, let's explore firewall rules.

Understanding firewall rules

Firewall rules are another crucial component of network architecture, acting as the first line of defense (perimeter) in network security. Essentially, they are a set of guidelines that dictate how data packets are allowed to enter or leave a network. Network architects must be well-versed not only in understanding *how* firewall rules are applied on security devices but also in how they affect IT infrastructure, its distributed components, and end user's/application's capabilities to reach services.

Let's consider an example.

We want to create two rules: allow HTTP traffic (port 80) from the internal network (192.168.1.0/24) to the internet while denying all other traffic, and block all SSH traffic from external sources to a specific server (for example, 192.168.1.10) within the internal network.

Figure 7.27 shows the configuration, as configured on a Palo Alto firewall appliance:

```
set address internal-network ip-netmask 192.168.1.0/24
set address internal-server ip-netmask 192.168.1.10/32

set service HTTP protocol tcp port 80
set service SSH protocol tcp port 22

set rulebase security rules allow-http-from-internal name "Allow HTTP from Internal to External"
set rulebase security rules allow-http-from-internal source zone internal
set rulebase security rules allow-http-from-internal source address internal-network
set rulebase security rules allow-http-from-internal destination zone external
set rulebase security rules allow-http-from-internal application MY-Application
set rulebase security rules allow-http-from-internal service HTTP
set rulebase security rules allow-http-from-internal action allow

set rulebase security rules block-ssh-to-server name "Block SSH to Internal Server"
set rulebase security rules block-ssh-to-server source zone external
set rulebase security rules block-ssh-to-server destination zone internal
set rulebase security rules block-ssh-to-server destination address internal-server
set rulebase security rules block-ssh-to-server application MY-Application
set rulebase security rules block-ssh-to-server service SSH
set rulebase security rules block-ssh-to-server action deny
```

Figure 7.27 – Palo Alto firewall rules configuration

Firewall rules determine how the firewall filters incoming and outgoing network traffic to protect the network against unauthorized access, cyber threats, and unwanted traffic. Firewall rules act to protect networks in various ways:

- **Filter traffic based on IP addresses and ports**: Firewall rules can allow or block traffic based on source and destination IP addresses, as well as port numbers. An example rule can block all traffic coming from a known malicious IP address or permit traffic only through certain ports associated with specific services.

- **Protocol-based filtering**: Rules can be set to filter traffic based on protocols such as **Transmission Control Protocol** (**TCP**), **User Datagram Protocol** (**UDP**), **Internet Control Message Protocol** (**ICMP**), and so on. This helps in managing different types of data packets according to their intended use.

- **Directional control**: Firewall rules can be inbound (which govern the traffic coming into the network) and outbound rules (which manage the traffic leaving the network). These rules can differ, allowing fine-grained control over both types of traffic.

- **Application-level filtering**: Some advanced firewalls (WAFs) can create advanced rules to filter traffic based on application data. This means the rules that are applied allow for content inspection of the data packets to determine which application they are associated with and make decisions accordingly.

- **Blocking or allowing specific services**: Firewall rules can be configured to block or allow specific services (such as HTTP for web browsing, SMTP for email, and so on). This is crucial for organizations that want to restrict access to certain internet services.

- **Time-based rules**: Some firewall rules can be time-sensitive, allowing or blocking access during specific hours or days. This is useful in scenarios where access needs to be restricted during non-business hours.

- **Rate limiting and mitigation of DoS attacks**: Firewall rules can be set to limit the rate of traffic from specific sources, which is a crucial feature for mitigating DoS attacks.

- **User or group-based rules**: In more sophisticated setups, firewall rules can apply to specific users or groups, allowing for personalized access control based on user identity.

What does this mean for a network architect?

For a network architect, firewall rules represent a critical aspect of designing and maintaining a secure and efficient network infrastructure. Here are a few points of interest:

- **A core element of network security**: A network architect must understand how to effectively use firewall rules to protect the network from unauthorized access and various cyber threats.

- **Designing secure networks**: Knowledge of firewall rules enables network architects to design inherently secure networks, incorporating firewalls strategically to protect critical assets.

- **Tailoring security needs**: Different networks have different security requirements. A network architect needs to know how to customize firewall rules to match the specific security needs of their network, whether it's a small business, a large enterprise, or a specialized industry.

- **Performance and security balance**: Effective firewall rules help in balancing security with network performance. Overly restrictive rules can hamper legitimate network activities, while lax rules can leave the network vulnerable.

- **Regulatory compliance**: Many industries have specific regulatory requirements regarding data protection and network security. Knowledge of firewall rules is critical to ensure compliance with these regulations.

- **Identifying and mitigating risks**: By understanding firewall rules, network architects can identify potential security risks and take proactive measures to mitigate them.

- **Technological advancements**: As network technology evolves, so do firewall capabilities. Architects need to stay informed about the latest developments in firewall technology to make the best use of them.

In summary, ACLs and firewall rules are critical components in network security, serving as the first line of defense against unauthorized access and cyber threats. ACLs, configured on network devices such as routers and switches, determine which traffic is allowed or denied in a network segment based on criteria such as IP addresses, protocol type, and port numbers. Firewall rules, on the other hand, are security policies that permit or deny data packets based on predefined rules and more granular inspection.

Together, ACLs and firewall rules form an integral part of an organization's security posture, ensuring that only legitimate traffic flows through the network, while malicious or unnecessary traffic is effectively blocked.

Let's move on to the final topic – miscellaneous network services.

Miscellaneous network services

Miscellaneous network services refer to a variety of less commonly used services that support network functionality and management or provide additional features but are outside the scope of a network architect's responsibility, in my opinion.

Some of these services are as follows:

- **Network Time Protocol (NTP)**: This synchronizes the clocks of computers over a network, ensuring that the time is consistent across all devices.

- **Simple Network Management Protocol (SNMP)**: This is used for managing devices on IP networks. It helps in monitoring network-attached devices for conditions that warrant administrative attention.

- **Syslog**: A standard for message logging, this allows logs to be collected from various sources and stored in a central repository.

- **Virtual Private Network (VPN)**: This provides secure access to a private network over the public internet. It's often used for secure remote work access.

- **Lightweight Directory Access Protocol (LDAP)**: This provides a method for accessing and maintaining distributed directory information services, such as user information, over an IP network.

- **Simple Mail Transfer Protocol (SMTP)**: The standard protocol for sending emails across the internet.

- **Internet Message Access Protocol/Post Office Protocol (IMAP/POP)**: This is used for retrieving emails from a server. IMAP allows access to emails stored on a server, while POP downloads emails locally.

- **Remote Authentication Dial-In User Service (RADIUS)**: A networking protocol that provides centralized authentication, authorization, and accounting management for users who connect and use a network service.

- **Network monitoring tools**: Various tools, such as Nagios, Zabbix, and PRTG, are used for monitoring network traffic, server health, and performance.

- **Content Delivery Network (CDN)**: This is a system of distributed servers that deliver web content to a user based on the geographic locations of the user, the origin of the web page, and a content delivery server.

- **Intrusion Prevention System/Intrusion Detection System (IPS/IDS)**: This monitors network and/or system activities for malicious activities or policy violations. An IDS typically reports on an intrusion, while an IPS will actively block or prevent such threats.

Considerations for a network architect

A network architect must be familiar with various miscellaneous network services for several key reasons, each contributing to the effective design, implementation, and management of network infrastructure. This is crucial for several reasons:

- **Comprehensive network design**: Network architects are responsible for designing networks that are robust, scalable, and secure. Understanding various network services such as LDAP, SNMP, VPN, and others enables architects to create a network infrastructure that supports a wide range of business needs, ensuring both functionality and efficiency.

- **Security and compliance**: Security is a critical aspect of network design. Services such as VPNs and IPS/IDS are fundamental in protecting network resources from unauthorized access and attacks. Familiarity with these services allows architects to incorporate necessary security measures effectively, ensuring compliance with industry standards and regulations.

- **Performance optimization**: Services such as CDNs and **Quality of Service** (**QoS**) management play a significant role in optimizing network performance. Network architects must understand these services to ensure the network can handle high traffic volumes, provide low latency, and prioritize critical traffic efficiently.

- **Fault tolerance and reliability**: Knowledge of services such as NTP, SNMP, and network monitoring tools is vital for maintaining network reliability and uptime. These services help in synchronizing time across devices, monitoring network health, and proactively addressing issues, which are crucial for ensuring business continuity.

- **User and resource management**: Services such as LDAP and RADIUS are important for managing user access and authentication. Familiarity with these services allows network architects to design a network that provides secure and efficient access control to network resources.

- **Compliance with standards**: Networking standards ensure interoperability and reliability across different devices and systems. Familiarity with these standards, and the services that support them, is crucial for network architects to ensure that the infrastructure they design adheres to industry norms.

- **Troubleshooting and problem-solving**: An in-depth understanding of network services is essential for diagnosing and resolving network issues efficiently. This knowledge enables architects to identify the root causes of problems and implement effective solutions quickly.

In summary, a network architect's proficiency in various miscellaneous network services is essential for designing and maintaining a network that is secure, efficient, scalable, and aligned with the organization's objectives. This knowledge, which is accumulated over many years in IT, forms the backbone of effective network management, ensuring that the infrastructure can support the diverse and evolving needs of the organization.

Summary

This chapter delved into the complex realm of network services, highlighting their indispensable role in shaping the foundation of network architecture within an organization. We explored the critical functionalities and operational dynamics of load balancing and DNS, which ensure efficient traffic distribution and reliable domain name resolution, respectively. The significance of DHCP and NAT in managing IP address allocation and facilitating secure communication across networks was also examined. Furthermore, the discussion on ACLs and firewall rules underscored the paramount importance of network security, emphasizing how these tools effectively regulate access and protect the network from potential threats. Lastly, our overview of miscellaneous services, including essential protocols and systems such as IPS/IDS, VPNs, and content delivery networks, illuminated the diverse spectrum of services that contribute to a robust, secure, and highly functional network. This comprehensive exploration not only equipped you with the knowledge to design and implement effective network solutions but also underscored the importance of these services in maintaining the integrity and efficiency of an organization's network infrastructure.

In the next chapter, we'll take a look at the foundations of network automation.

Further reading

To learn more about the topics that were covered in this chapter, take a look at the following resources:

- *What is load balancing?* `https://www.nginx.com/resources/glossary/load-balancing/`

- *What Is Server And Application Load Balancing? Types, Configuration Methods, And Best Tools*:

  - `https://www.dnsstuff.com/what-is-server-load-balancing`

- `https://cloud.google.com/blog/products/infrastructure-modernization/design-reliable-infrastructure-for-workloads-in-google-cloud?utm_campaign=62ccbca99df1f00001742562&utm_content=63bf184092cee000010a1434&utm_medium=smarpshare&utm_source=linkedin`

- `https://developers.google.com/machine-learning/crash-course/ml-intro`

- `https://docs.google.com/forms/d/e/1FAIpQLServ0tNGkr-dYAfmez_Gdk74dmVypZjzUKrkVFtFcArzhmPow/viewform`

- `https://www.techtarget.com/searchnetworking/feature/12-common-network-protocols-and-their-functions-explained?utm_campaign=20230517_ERU-ACTIVE_WITHIN_90_DAYS&utm_medium=email&utm_source=SGERU&source_ad_id=252487950&src=15001528&asrc=EM_SGERU_267759856&Offer=abt_pubpro_AI-Insider`

- *Experimental Setup For Investigating The Efficient Load Balancing Algorithms On The Virtual Cloud*:

  - `https://www.mdpi.com/1424-8220/20/24/7342`

  - `https://www.businessinsider.com/i-tried-monk-mode-productivity-hack-worked-2023-1?utm_medium=referral&utm_source=yahoo.com`

- *DNS Best Practices for Security and Performance*: `https://phoenixnap.com/kb/dns-best-practices-security`

- *DHCP defined and how it works*: `https://www.networkworld.com/article/966242/dhcp-defined-and-how-it-works.html`

- *IPv4 Address Prices and Pricing*: `https://ipv4.global/blog/ipv4-address-prices/`

Foundations of Network Automation

In the dynamic landscape of modern technology, the need for efficient, scalable, and secure IT network infrastructure has never been more critical. As businesses continue to expand their digital footprint and embrace cloud-based solutions, data center consolidation, and better end user experience, the complexity of managing networks has grown exponentially. To keep pace with these demands, IT professionals (network architects especially) are turning to automation as a transformative solution.

Over the years, manual configuration and management of network devices have proven time-consuming and error-prone, leading to potential bottlenecks, project revisions and delays, increased lead times, and security vulnerabilities. By introducing automation into the equation of building and maintaining IT infrastructure, IT teams can unleash a *new era* of efficiency, empowering them to focus on strategic tasks rather than mundane, repetitive operational tasks.

In this chapter, we'll explore the following topics:

- Fundamental building blocks of network automation
- Understanding the role of SDN
- Exploring NFV
- Scripting languages and automation tools
- Understanding IaC

Let's get started!

Fundamental building blocks of network automation

In the ever-evolving landscape of information technology, the complexity and scale of network infrastructures continue to grow exponentially. To meet the demands of modern businesses and users, network automation has emerged as a powerful solution. By automating repetitive tasks, streamlining configurations, and optimizing network management, organizations can achieve higher efficiency, greater reliability, and enhanced agility in their network operations.

Consider the simple example shown in *Figure 8.1*:

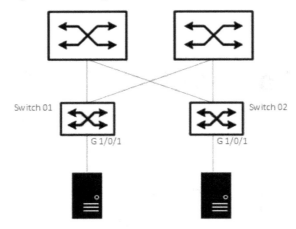

Figure 8.1 – Basic spine/leaf diagram

Let's assume that we have what's shown in the preceding diagram and we need data to be configured on the switches for downstream servers to run an application:

- Switch 01:

    - Loopback IP: `192.168.0.1`

    - Loopback mask: `/32`

    - Interface GigabitEthernet 1/0/1 IP: `192.168.10.1`

    - Interface GigabitEthernet 1/0/1 mask: `/24`

- Switch 02:

    - Loopback IP: `192.168.0.2`

    - Loopback mask: `/32`

    - Interface GigabitEthernet 1/0/1 IP: `10.0.0.1`

    - Interface GigabitEthernet 1/0/1 mask: `/24`

The steps would be as follows:

1.   Start an SSH session on your local laptop or workstation. In some cases, you may need to log into a bastion host (username and password) and then start an SSH session.

2. Ensure reachability to the switches' loopback IP addresses.

3. Have proper credentials (username and password) to log into each switch (via SSH) sequentially and run the following commands:

Switch #01: 192.168.0.1

```
enable
configure terminal
interface GigabitEthernet1/0/1
ip address 192.168.1.10 255.255.255.0
no shutdown
exit
exit
```

Switch #02: 192.168.0.2

```
enable
configure terminal
interface GigabitEthernet1/0/1
ip address 10.0.0.1 255.255.255.0
no shutdown
exit
exit
```

Figure 8.2 – Configurations on switches 01 and 02

4. Then, verify whether the configurations are correct.

5. Verify whether the interface and link status are up.

6. Verify connectivity/test to servers.

7. Save your configurations and verify them.

8. End the switch session and log out of each device accordingly.

9. If a bastion host is used, end the session.

In this scenario, there are nine steps to undertake (assuming change control and initial device setup has been completed and tested). If I were to configure these switches, which I oversimplified here, it would take me about 10 minutes (5 minutes on each device), maybe less once I've logged in. If I pre-write the configurations and then copy and paste, I would say perhaps 6 minutes total.

These operations may seem quite fast considering the steps outlined here. However, this design only called for one interface on each device. What if I have to configure 24 to 48 ports on each switch and then routing, VLANs, port channels, ACL list(s), or more? In this case, I'm probably spending my entire day on these two switches – which isn't bad at all.

Now, what if I have to configure 16 to 20 switches? In this case, it looks like I'll be sitting in front of a workstation for 3 weeks repeating task after task manually.

As an IT professional, I'd be more than happy to be a part of this project to get the job done! But at the same time, is my effort being utilized in the most *efficacious* manner? Probably not! To better utilize my time, it's worth using automation to get the desired results. Perhaps Python can help me achieve this goal! Let's take a look.

The script would look something like this (*Figure 8.3*):

Switch #01

```
switches_data = [
  {
     "switch_ip": "192.168.0.1",
     "interface": "GigabitEthernet1/0/1",
     "ip_address": "192.168.1.10",
     "subnet_mask": "255.255.255.0"
  },
  {
     "switch_ip": "192.168.0.2",
     "interface": "GigabitEthernet1/0/1",
     "ip_address": "10.0.0.1",
     "subnet_mask": "255.255.255.0"
  },
  # Add more switch/interface configurations as needed
]
```

Switch #02

```
import requests

def configure_interface(switch_ip, interface, ip_address, subnet_mask):
    url = f"http://{switch_ip}/api/interfaces/{interface}"
    data = {
      "ip_address": ip_address,
      "subnet_mask": subnet_mask
    }

    response = requests.put(url, json=data)

    if response.status_code == 200:
        print(f"IP address {ip_address} set successfully on {interface} of {switch_ip}.")
    else:
        print(f"Failed to set IP address on {interface} of {switch_ip}. Error:
{response.text}")

# Loop through each switch/interface configuration and make the API call
for switch_data in switches_data:
    configure_interface(
      switch_ip=switch_data["switch_ip"],
      interface=switch_data["interface"],
      ip_address=switch_data["ip_address"],
      subnet_mask=switch_data["subnet_mask"]
    )
```

Figure 8.3 – Python script for configuring switches 01 and 02

All of those manual steps have been completed within this script. I no longer have to manually log into each device to configure them. All I have to do is to initiate the run of the script!

The question to ask here is, "How long will it take to configure these two switches now?"

I would say 5 minutes total as the configurations are done in parallel versus sequentially. This outcome is expected.

However, let's say I have to complete routing, VLANS, ACLs, and more. How long will the script take now? I would say about 10 to 15 minutes. What about if there were 16 to 20 switches? I would say about 20 minutes. I'll give it 1 hour for simplicity.

What was the point of this example? Well, it showed a few things:

- Repetitive tasks can be done in parallel as configurations are pushed to devices simultaneously.

- The logic and knowledge are in the scripts and are centralized.

- Configuration can be *templatized*, which means it can be utilized (asset) in different IT environments.

- Configuration errors are mitigated as an individual is no longer manually provisioning the devices.

- Efficiencies can be achieved – for example, 1 hour for completion versus 3 weeks (120 hours). That's an efficiency rate of 99.16%.

- Cost savings at almost the same rate from an employee perspective.

- Time allocation (119 hours) has been recouped to work on other business-centric tasks.

> **Note**
>
> I've oversimplified the operations of configuring an infrastructure fabric here. However, by considering doing tasks in an automated fashion versus manually, you can achieve efficiencies in the range of 85% to 90%.

The power lies in network programmability.

Network programmability

Network programmability is the ability to transform traditional static networks into agile, adaptable, and intelligent infrastructures. By leveraging programming languages, APIs, and automation tools, network programmability empowers IT professionals to dynamically control and configure network devices, manage traffic flows, and respond in real time to changing requirements (*Figure 8.4*):

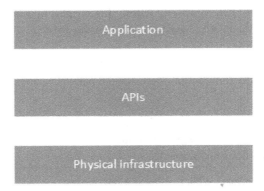

Figure 8.4 – The building blocks of network programmability

Network programmability is the core foundation upon which network automation is built. It enables network architects and others to interact with network devices programmatically, reducing the reliance on manual, CLI interactions.

With programmability, IT teams and professionals can dynamically configure network devices and perform repetitive tasks, such as configuration changes, device monitoring, and provisioning, more efficiently and consistently. This shift from a manual to a programmatic approach not only accelerates tasks but also enhances consistency, accuracy, and scalability in network design and management.

Next, we'll look at **application programming interfaces (APIs)**.

APIs

APIs act as the bridge that connects network devices with automation tools and scripts. It's a set of rules and protocols that allows different software applications to communicate and interact with each other. They provide a standardized set of commands and data structures that facilitate communication and data exchange between different components of the network infrastructure.

These APIs enable administrators to send and receive information from network devices, retrieve operational data, and issue commands for configuration changes in a programmatic manner.

> Note
> By exposing APIs on network devices, vendors enable IT professionals to interact with the underlying hardware and software programmatically, eliminating the need for manual and time-consuming CLIs or **graphical user interfaces (GUIs)**.

APIs can be based on different technologies and data formats, such as **Representational State Transfer (REST)**, **Simple Object Access Protocol (SOAP)**, **JavaScript Object Notation (JSON)**, **eXtensible Markup Language (XML)**, and **Remote Procedure Calls (gRPC)**, among others.

> **Note**
>
> An in-depth discussion of these API formats is outside the scope of this book. For more suggested reading material, go to *Chapter 12, Further Reading*.

Through APIs, IT professionals can retrieve real-time operational data, issue configuration commands, and monitor network devices efficiently and consistently. These interfaces empower automation tools and scripts to control and manage network elements swiftly, revolutionizing network operations and allowing IT teams to focus on strategic initiatives while significantly reducing the risk of human errors from manual operations.

The extensibility and versatility of APIs make them critical enablers of network programmability, paving the way for agile, scalable, and efficient network infrastructures that adapt dynamically to the evolving needs of modern businesses.

Some APIs that are commonly used for automating IT networking infrastructure are as follows:

- **RESTful APIs**: RESTful APIs are widely used in networking for their simplicity and ease of use. HTTP methods such as GET, POST, PUT, and DELETE are used to perform **Create, Read, Update, Delete** (**CRUD**) operations on network devices and resources. Many modern networking devices and management tools provide RESTful APIs for automation.

- **Network Configuration Protocol** (**NETCONF**): NETCONF is a standardized network management protocol defined by the **Internet Engineering Task Force** (**IETF**). It allows for remote configuration and management of network devices using XML-based data encoding.

- **Simple Network Management Protocol** (**SNMP**): This is an old, widely used protocol for network management. It allows monitoring and control of network devices by exchanging data with network agents. SNMP is extensively used for gathering network statistics, monitoring device health, and triggering actions based on specific events.

- **Python libraries**: Python is a widely used programming language for network automation. Many networking vendors provide Python libraries or **software development kits** (**SDKs**) that allow developers to interact with their devices and services programmatically.

> **Note**
>
> Some Python libraries that are commonly used by networking vendors include PyATS, developed by Cisco, pyEAPI, which is designed for Arista EOS devices, Junos PyEZ for Juniper devices, and **Network Automation and Programmability Abstraction Layer with Multivendor support** (**NAPALM**), which is designed to abstract the differences between different network device operating systems.

Keep in mind that the technology landscape evolves rapidly, and new APIs and tools may have emerged since my last update. It's best to keep informed with respective vendors' documentation and communities for the latest information on their APIs and automation capabilities.

Benefits of network programmability

Network programmability offers a wide range of benefits that revolutionize the way networks are managed, operated, and scaled. These advantages empower organizations to stay competitive, respond quickly to changing demands, and deliver enhanced user experiences. Here are some key benefits of network programmability:

- **Automation and efficiency**: One of the primary benefits of network programmability is automation. By utilizing APIs and automation tools, IT teams can automate repetitive and time-consuming network tasks, such as device provisioning, configuration changes, and troubleshooting. This automation reduces the manual effort required to manage networks, minimizes human errors, and allows IT professionals to focus on higher-value tasks, ultimately boosting overall efficiency and productivity.

> **Note**
> Consider the example I showed previously. If the fabric needs 20 switches to support new server deployments, it needs to be done in 5 days. You'll need two FTE employees to accomplish the task. With automation, you only need one FTE and 1 to 2 days to complete the task. Employee efficiency is increased by 100% and the completion rate is increased by 60%.

- **Rapid network deployment**: Programmable networks facilitate rapid network deployment and configuration changes. With the ability to automate the configuration of network devices, new services and applications can be provisioned swiftly, allowing businesses to respond quickly to customer (internal and external) needs and market demands. This agility is especially critical in modern dynamic environments where speed and flexibility are paramount.

- **Scalability and flexibility**: Network programmability enables the easy scaling of network infrastructure. IT teams can programmatically add or remove devices, adjust network settings, and allocate resources as needed, allowing networks to grow or shrink in response to changing requirements. This flexibility ensures that the network can keep pace with the organization's growth and evolving demands.

- **Consistency and standardization**: Programmable networks promote consistency and standardization across the entire network. Automation ensures that configurations and policies are *applied uniformly*, reducing configuration drift and potential inconsistencies that can lead to network disruptions. Standardization also simplifies troubleshooting and maintenance, making network management more efficient and reliable.

- **Enhanced network visibility and monitoring**: Network programmability enables extensive network monitoring and telemetry. By collecting real-time operational data from network devices, organizations can gain deeper insights into their network performance, traffic patterns, and problematic areas. This enhanced visibility allows proactive monitoring, rapid issue detection, and improved network optimization.

- **Security and compliance**: Programmable networks enhance security and compliance measures. With automation, security policies can be consistently enforced across the network, reducing the risk of misconfigurations or policy violations. Additionally, automation allows rapid response to security threats, enabling administrators to deploy security updates and patches promptly.

- **Support for software-defined networking (SDN) and network function virtualization (NFV)**: Network programmability is a critical enabler for SDN and NFV technologies. SDN allows centralized control and management of network resources, while NFV virtualizes network functions for increased flexibility. Programmability provides the essential means to interact with and orchestrate these dynamic networking technologies effectively.

In summary, network programmability is a paradigm shift in networking that empowers organizations to automate and orchestrate their network infrastructure using software-based solutions. By leveraging APIs, SDNs, and network automation tools, network programmability enables the creation of agile, scalable, and intelligent networks. This approach abstracts complex network tasks, facilitating rapid configuration changes, proactive monitoring, and consistent policy enforcement. By eliminating manual processes, network programmability enhances operational efficiency, reduces errors, and streamlines network management.

Now, let's explore SDN.

Understanding the role of SDN

SDN emerged as a transformative way of networking and networking infrastructure in the early 2010s. This paradigm-shifting approach to networking has revolutionized how IT networks are designed, managed, and operated. Up to this point in time (in some respects, it's continuing), traditional network architectures were rigid and complex, with control functions tightly integrated into network devices such as routers and switches. SDN, on the other hand, decouples the network's control plane from the data plane, centralizing the control in a software-based controller. This decoupling allows network professionals to dynamically manage and configure the network, making it more agile, flexible, and responsive to changing business needs and requirements.

To gain a better understanding of SDN, let's take a look at *Figure 8.5*:

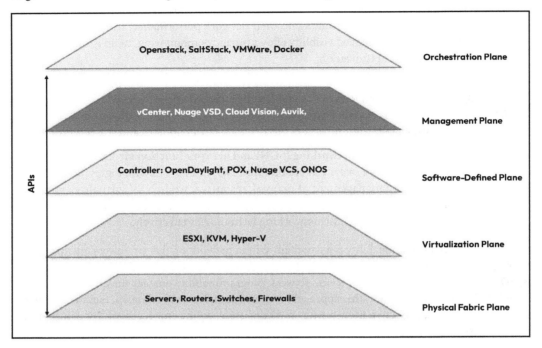

Figure 8.5 – The SDN plane

As we can see, several planes make up the overall SDN stack. Each plane has a defined function with communication flowing (APIs) in a north-south direction between each plane.

Though the SDN components are software in nature and are *technically* virtualized, which means they are *in* the virtualization plane, their **function** resides in their respective planes. This visualization shows how each component **interacts** with the others.

> **Note**
> Many other solutions/technologies exist that are supported in each plane of the SDN stack. The ones shown here are those I've used and worked with on past projects.

Core principles and components

The fundamental principles of SDN revolve around abstraction, virtualization, and programmability. SDN abstracts the underlying network infrastructure, presenting a simplified and logical view of the network to administrators and applications. It allows for network virtualization, enabling the creation of multiple virtual networks on a shared physical network, leading to better resource utilization and isolation.

The core components of SDN are as follows:

- **SDN controller**: The centralized software controller is the brain of the SDN network. It communicates with network devices using southbound APIs and translates high-level network policies into low-level configurations for network switches and routers.

- **Southbound APIs**: These interfaces connect the SDN controller to network devices, allowing the controller to manage and control the forwarding behavior of switches and routers.

- **Northbound APIs**: These interfaces connect the SDN controller to applications and management and orchestration systems, enabling applications to communicate with the SDN network and leverage its programmability for various use cases.

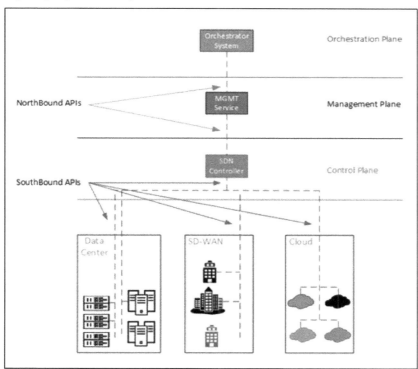

Figure 8.6 – Northbound and southbound APIs

Impact on organizations

SDN has a profound impact on organizations, offering transformative benefits that lead to improved operational efficiency, cost savings, and innovation. By simplifying network management and reducing manual efforts, SDN enables an organization's IT professionals to focus on strategic initiatives and accelerate the deployment of new services and applications. The agility and programmability of SDN also contribute to improved user experiences, increased network performance, and enhanced security measures.

SDN has a wide range of applications across different organization's networking environments, including data centers, campus networks, **wide area networks** (**WANs**), and telecommunications. Some important use cases to consider alongside the benefits of SDN are as follows:

- **Network virtualization**: This facilitates the creation of multiple virtual networks, each with distinct policies, on top of a shared physical infrastructure. Network virtualization enhances resource utilization and network isolation, enabling multi-tenancy. With network virtualization, SDN abstracts the complexities of the underlying hardware, presenting a simplified and logical view of the network to administrators and applications.

- **Centralized network management**: This is one of the key benefits of SDN and is made possible by the control plane being separated from the data plane. The centralization of control in the SDN controller simplifies network management tasks, providing network administrators with a single point of control for configuring, monitoring, and troubleshooting the entire network.

- **Dynamic traffic engineering**: The programmability offered by SDN allows dynamic traffic engineering, enabling the optimization of the network traffic flow to improve performance and minimize congestion throughout the network (overlay). This is a crucial capability that enables real-time optimization of the network traffic flow. IT professionals have a means to dynamically adjust traffic paths and distribution based on changing network conditions and application demands.

- **Network segmentation and security**: This provides *granular* network segmentation and policy enforcement, enhancing network security by isolating traffic and enforcing access control policies. By dividing the network into *isolated segments* with distinct security policies and access controls, each segment operates independently, preventing unauthorized access and limiting the impact of security breaches.

  Through centralized control (via an SDN controller), organizations can define and enforce security policies *consistently* across the entire network. Northbound APIs allow dynamic updates to security rules and adapt to evolving threat landscapes.

> **Note**
>
> SDN's programmability facilitates real-time threat detection and response, enabling the network to automatically react to security events and take appropriate actions, safeguarding sensitive data and ensuring the confidentiality, integrity, and availability of critical resources.

- **Automated network provisioning**: This revolutionizes the process of configuring and deploying network resources by leveraging programmability and orchestration. Through automated provisioning, IT teams can define network policies, configurations, and connectivity requirements using software-defined templates or scripts. These templates capture the desired state of the network, including virtual networks, routing rules, access controls, and quality of service settings. When triggered, the SDN controller or orchestration system translates these templates into actionable configurations for network devices, ensuring consistent and error-free deployment.

> **Note**
>
> This approach eliminates manual configuration steps, reduces human errors, and accelerates the provisioning process, allowing networks to adapt swiftly to changing demands. But now, IT professionals and teams can focus efforts on business continuum endeavors.

SDN has emerged as a game-changer in the networking industry, empowering organizations to build adaptive, scalable, and future-ready networks. The decoupling of control and data planes, along with the programmability of SDN, paves the way for efficient network management, innovative services, and better alignment of networking capabilities with the evolving demands of modern businesses.

Now, let's discuss NFV.

Exploring NFV

Like SDN, NFV is another paradigm in the networking industry that aims to **transform** traditional network architectures by decoupling network functions from proprietary hardware appliances and running them as *software-based virtualized instances* on standard (commodity) servers. NFV represents a shift from hardware-centric networking to a more agile, flexible, and cost-effective approach that leverages the power of virtualization and cloud computing technologies.

Traditionally, network functions such as firewalls, routers, load balancers, and intrusion detection systems were implemented as dedicated hardware appliances. Each appliance performed a specific function, and scaling or updating the network required adding or replacing physical devices. This hardware-centric approach often led to inefficiencies, high capital expenses, and operational complexities.

NFV addresses these challenges by virtualizing network functions, allowing them to run on general-purpose servers or cloud computing platforms. In this virtualized environment, network functions are implemented as software-based **virtual machines** (**VMs**) or containers:

Figure 8.7 – Hardware networking (left) versus software-based networking (right)

Decoupling functions from underlying hardware enables greater flexibility, scalability, and cost optimization in network deployments.

Key components of NFV

NFV comprises several key components that work together to enable the virtualization of network functions and their deployment on standard servers or cloud computing platforms. These components play different roles in the NFV architecture, facilitating the management, orchestration, and operation of virtualized network functions:

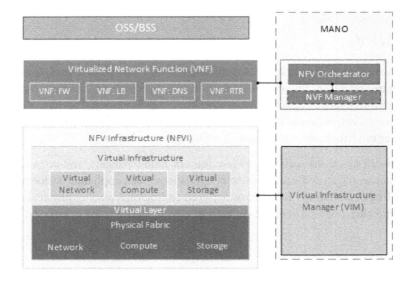

Figure 8.8 – NFV architecture components

The primary components of NFV are as follows:

- **Virtualized network functions (VNFs)**: VNFs are software representations of traditional network functions that run on virtualized infrastructure versus dedicated inflexible hardware appliances. They can be instantiated, scaled, and migrated dynamically based on network demands. Examples of VNFs include virtual routers, virtual firewalls, virtual load balancers, and virtual WAN accelerators.

- **NFV infrastructure (NFVI)**: NFVI constitutes the foundational layer of the NFV architecture. It comprises the underlying hardware and software resources for hosting VNFs resources, such as servers, storage, networking, and hypervisors or container runtimes.

- **NFV orchestrator (NFVO)**: The NVFO is a management and orchestration layer that's responsible for the life cycle management of VNFs and their associated resources. It handles tasks such as VNF instantiation, scaling, monitoring, healing, and decommissioning.

- **Virtualized infrastructure manager (VIM)**: The VIM is responsible for managing the virtualized resources within the NFVI. It interacts with the NFVO to provision and manage the compute, storage, and networking resources required for running VNFs.

> **Note**
> NFVI and VNF are closely related components within the context of NFV. They work together to enable the virtualization and deployment of network functions in a software-defined environment.

Benefits of NFV

The *cost benefits* of NFV are compelling drivers for its adoption in modern networking environments. These benefits can equip organizations with the resources necessary to maintain their stability and growth simultaneously, giving them the ability to pivot when changes in the market occur, when there's pressure from competitors, or when the need to introduce new products arises. A few additional points are as follows:

- **Cost savings**: NFV reduces capital and operational expenses by replacing dedicated hardware appliances with software-based VNFs running on cost-effective standard servers (commodity) or cloud platforms for hosting VNFs. It enables more efficient resource utilization and reduces the need for physical space, power, and cooling.

- **Agility and scalability**: NFV enables rapid deployment and scaling of network services. VNFs can be spun up or down quickly in response to changing network requirements, allowing operators to be more agile in delivering services, thereby enabling optimal resource utilization and minimizing operational expenses.

- **Service innovation**: NFV fosters innovation by allowing network services to be developed and deployed more rapidly. Service providers can experiment with new services, features, and configurations without the constraints of hardware limitations.

- **Network flexibility**: NFV abstracts network functions from the underlying hardware, making it easier to migrate services, implement redundancy, and adapt to dynamic traffic patterns.

> **Note**
> An easier way to remember NFV and VNF is that NFV represents the larger architectural approach, while VNFs are the individual elements that make up the virtualized network functions within that architecture.

NFV represents a significant advancement in the networking industry, offering flexibility, scalability, and cost savings. As organizations and enterprises continue to adopt NFV, its potential to revolutionize network architectures and foster innovation in networking services becomes increasingly evident. However, addressing performance, security, and interoperability challenges will be critical to unlocking the full potential of NFV and maximizing its benefits in modern network deployments.

Next, we'll explore scripting and automation languages.

Scripting and automation languages

In the dynamic landscape of technology and operations, where networks are expanding, systems are becoming increasingly complex, and efficiency is paramount, the role of scripting and automation languages has now become a focal point. Scripting and automation languages empower IT professionals to streamline tasks, enhance productivity, and enforce consistency by automating *routine processes* across various domains, including network management, system administration, and the software development life cycle. This section delves into the fundamental concepts, significance, and key languages that form the backbone of scripting and automation in modern IT environments.

The power of automation

Automation has revolutionized the way organizations manage and operate their IT infrastructures. It offers a systematic approach to executing tasks without manual intervention, resulting in reduced errors, accelerated processes, and enhanced scalability. Scripting and automation languages provide the means to create programs, scripts, and workflows that perform predefined actions, eliminating repetitive and time-consuming tasks. As networks grow in complexity and the demand for rapid provisioning and configuration increases, the use of these languages has become integral to achieving efficient and agile operations.

The power of automation lies not only in its ability to expedite processes but also in its potential to revolutionize workflows, increase operational agility, and drive innovation. By harnessing scripting and automation languages, IT professionals can unlock the capability to orchestrate intricate sequences of actions, ensuring seamless operations, efficient resource utilization, and the reallocation of human expertise towards strategic endeavors.

> **Note**
>
> As a network architect, you must understand the concepts, functions, and capabilities of automation within the IT infrastructure you're supporting and designing.

Figure 8.7 shows an example of a simple Ansible playbook script that *automates* the process of deploying a simple web server on remote servers:

```
---   [1]
- name: Deploy Web Server
  hosts: webservers  [2]
  become: yes

  tasks:
    - name: Install Apache web server [3a]
      apt:
        name: apache2 [3b]
        state: present

    - name: Start Apache service  [4]
      service:
        name: apache2
        state: started
                            [5]
    - name: Copy index.html file
      copy:
        src: /path/to/index.html
        dest: /var/www/html/index.html  [6]
```

Figure 8.9 – Ansible playbook to deploy web servers

Let's run through this example:

1. We begin the script with three hyphens (- - -), indicating that this is a YAML file [1].

2. The script will install a web server application [3a] called apache2 [3b] on hosts located in an *inventory* file with an anchor tag of webservers [2].

3. Next, the apache2 service will be started on those hosts [4].

4. Lastly, a file called `index.html` **[5]** will be copied from the source to the destination **[6]**.

> **Note**
>
> This simple script may look simple, but it's quite powerful. The power is in the script file(s), which allows for constant, efficient, scalable, and uninterrupted deployment of web servers. The inventory holds the server information. Regardless of whether 1, 10, or 1,000 servers are listed, they will all be configured the same without any errors or interruptions.

As network complexities grow, automation becomes a strategic ally, liberating IT professionals from mundane tasks and enabling them to focus on innovation, optimization, and strategic decision-making. Through automation, organizations unlock the potential to build agile, responsive, and robust network environments that not only meet today's demands but also lay the foundation for the dynamic digital future.

Scripting languages

Scripting languages are lightweight, interpreted programming languages that are designed for the quick development and execution of scripts – short programs that automate specific tasks in various computing environments. These languages prioritize ease of use, rapid prototyping, and interaction with system components. Scripting languages are particularly well-suited for automating tasks that involve system administration, data manipulation, and configuration management. They enable IT professionals to perform complex actions with minimal effort, making them essential tools for managing intricate IT environments.

As the name implies, scripting languages are used to create *scripts*, which are sets of instructions or commands written in a simplified programming language. These scripts are designed to automate specific tasks or processes, making them more efficient and less error-prone.

In the context of IT network infrastructure, scripting languages are used to automate and manage various tasks related to the configuration, monitoring, and maintenance of network devices and services. Here's how scripting languages are used in IT network infrastructure:

*   **Automation**: IT professionals can now automate repetitive and time-consuming tasks. These tasks can include device provisioning, configuration changes, backups, and software updates. By writing scripts, IT professionals can save time and reduce the risk of errors that might occur with manual interventions.

*   **Configuration management**: Scripting languages are used to define and manage the configurations of network devices. This includes setting up parameters, access control lists, routing configurations, and more. Configuration management scripts ensure consistency across devices and help maintain a *standardized* network environment.

- **Monitoring and reporting**: Scripting languages can create custom monitoring and reporting tools or facilitate sending data to other tools for SIEM activities. Scripts can retrieve data from network devices, analyze performance metrics, and generate reports. This helps administrators proactively identify issues and ensure network health.

- **Security tasks**: Scripting languages play a role in security-related tasks (whether passively or actively) such as automating security audits, managing firewall rules, and monitoring intrusion detection systems. This allows IT professionals to fortify network defenses and enhance data integrity.

  Scripting languages serve as versatile tools for automating security-related activities such as monitoring logs, managing firewall rules, conducting vulnerability assessments, and implementing access controls. They have the power to swiftly analyze security data, script-driven solutions detect anomalies, enforce security policies, and respond to threats in real time. Through scripting languages, security tasks are streamlined, enabling proactive measures to safeguard sensitive information and ensure regulatory compliance.

> **Note**
>
> Consider a task such as monthly data needing to be backed up and then archived for compliance and audit reasons but in a parallel search for archives greater than 18 months, which can be deleted. By using a scripting language, Ruby can streamline such activities.

- **Device interaction**: Scripting languages facilitate seamless communication between IT professionals and network devices. Scripting languages empower administrators to orchestrate intricate operations, such as configuring switches, routers, and servers, or retrieving vital data from network devices. Through protocols such as SSH, Telnet, web interface, and APIs, scripts act as intermediaries, issuing commands and capturing responses with precision.

> **Note**
>
> Telnet is still a viable way to access network devices – however, it's not as secure as SSH or secure web interfaces and secure APIs.

- **Orchestration**: Through the orchestration capabilities of scripting languages, IT professionals can seamlessly coordinate a symphony of tasks, applications, and resources across diverse systems. This encompasses automating multi-step operations, provisioning resources, configuring network devices, and scaling applications. By leveraging scripting languages for orchestration, organizations can achieve consistent and repeatable outcomes, optimize resource utilization, and create dynamic environments that respond to changing demands. This is particularly important in modern network environments where dynamic scaling and cloud resources are involved.

- **Custom tools**: Scripting languages empower IT professionals to craft tailored solutions that precisely address unique challenges. By leveraging the flexibility and automation capabilities of scripting languages, these custom tools transcend the limitations of off-the-shelf software. Engineers can design specialized utilities for specific tasks such as parsing intricate log files, orchestrating intricate network workflows, automating *proprietary processes*, and conducting custom analyses.

> **Note**
> For a network architect, you can think beyond the norm or status quo and begin to innovate.

Common scripting languages

The most common (popular) scripting languages that are used by IT professionals today for provisioning IT network infrastructure are as follows:

- **Python** (`https://www.python.org/`):
  - Widely regarded as one of the most versatile and popular scripting languages
  - Extensive libraries and frameworks for network automation, configuration management, and interaction with APIs
  - Used for tasks such as device configuration, monitoring, data parsing, and custom tool creation

- **Bash** (`https://www.gnu.org/software/bash/`):
  - Essential for Unix-like systems (Linux, macOS, and others)
  - Primarily used for system administration, file manipulation, and basic automation tasks
  - Often used in conjunction with other tools and languages for network automation

- **PowerShell** (`https://learn.microsoft.com/en-us/powershell/`):
  - Dominant in Windows environments
  - Specialized for Windows systems administration and management
  - Offers integration with Microsoft products and services

- **Ruby** (`https://www.ruby-lang.org/en/`):
  - Known for its elegant syntax and readability
  - Used for general scripting tasks, web development, and automation
  - Can also be used for network scripting and automation

- **Perl** (https://www.perl.org/):

    - Historical significance in network automation and system administration

    - Valuable for text processing, regular expressions, and automation tasks

    - Still used for legacy systems and specific tasks

- **Tool Command Language (TCL)** (https://www.tcl-lang.org/):

    - Often used for automating network device interactions

    - Utilized with the `Expect` library for scripting interactive tasks

    - Commonly associated with Cisco network devices

- **JavaScript (Node.js)** (https://nodejs.org/en):

    - Growing in popularity for web development and server-side scripting

    - Used for automating tasks that involve web-based interactions and APIs

Each scripting language has its strengths and is chosen based on the specific requirements of IT network infrastructure tasks, the target environment, and the familiarity that IT professionals have with the language. These languages provide the flexibility to interact with network devices, automate tasks, and customize solutions based on the organization's network architecture and requirements. Again, the use of scripting languages enhances operational efficiency, reduces human errors, and enables IT professionals to focus on higher-level tasks that require problem-solving and innovation.

Automation tools

Automation tools have become essential components of modern IT network infrastructure management. These tools empower organizations to streamline workflows, enhance operational efficiency, and ensure the reliability of network services. From provisioning and configuration to monitoring and security, automation tools play a pivotal role in maintaining a robust and agile network environment.

At the heart of network automation tools lies the ability to define configurations, policies, and workflows as code. This code can be written in specific scripting languages or expressed using *declarative languages* such as YAML. Automation tools interpret this code to orchestrate various network-related actions, ensuring that networks are set up, managed, and maintained according to established standards and best practices.

> **Note**
> A declarative language is a type of programming or scripting language that focuses on describing "what" should be done rather than "how" it should be done. In other words, instead of providing explicit step-by-step instructions for achieving a task, a declarative language allows you to define the desired outcome or state, and the underlying system or interpreter figures out the most efficient way to achieve that state.

Automation tools can be categorized into different types based on their focus:

- **Configuration management tools**: Configuration management tools (*Figure 8.8*) are essential components in modern IT infrastructure management, enabling organizations to efficiently control, maintain, and automate the configurations of software, hardware, and network devices. These tools facilitate the consistent setup and management of systems, ensuring that they adhere to predefined standards and policies. This not only streamlines the deployment process but also helps prevent *configuration drift* and ensures that systems remain in a secure and compliant state over time:

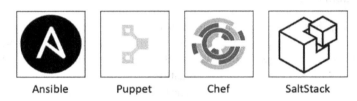

Ansible   Puppet   Chef   SaltStack

Figure 8.10 – Common configuration management tools

- **Orchestration tools**: Network orchestration tools (*Figure 8.10*) automate complex workflows involving multiple devices and systems. They provide a holistic view of network resources and enable the coordination of tasks, ensuring seamless interactions across the network infrastructure:

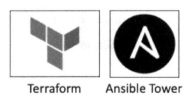

Terraform   Ansible Tower

Figure 8.11 – Common network orchestration tools

- **Network monitoring and management tools**: These tools (*Figure 8.11*) automate the collection of network performance and status data, providing IT professionals with essential insights into the health, availability, and utilization of network devices, servers, and applications. The real-time insights into network health trigger alerts based on predefined thresholds, ensuring prompt responses to network issues by IT teams:

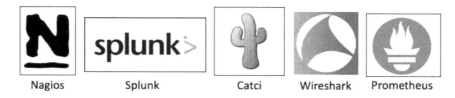

Figure 8.12 – Common network monitoring tools

- **Continuous integration/continuous deployment (CI/CD) tools**: Though not exclusive to networks, these tools (*Figure 8.12*) play a crucial role in network automation by facilitating CI/CD pipelines. These pipelines automate the testing, deployment, and monitoring of network changes, enhancing collaboration and software delivery speed:

Figure 8.13 – Popular CI/CD tools

> **Note**
> While CI/CD tools are more commonly associated with software development, they can also be adapted for network infrastructure automation.

Automation tools are a cornerstone of network infrastructure management, offering a transformative approach to managing complex IT landscapes. They are used to streamline operations, increase efficiency, and ensure consistent and error-free configurations across network devices. By harnessing these tools, IT professionals can create scripts, templates, and workflows that automate routine tasks such as device provisioning, configuration changes, and performance monitoring. This not only accelerates deployment and reduces human error but also enables teams to focus on strategic initiatives.

Automation tools bring agility to network infrastructure, enabling rapid response to changing business needs and scaling up as demands increase. With reduced manual intervention, these tools enhance network reliability, security, and compliance while promoting best practices and standardization. In an era where networks are expected to be both dynamic and dependable, automation tools stand as an indispensable asset, empowering IT teams to manage complexity, optimize resources, and drive innovation.

Now, let's discuss IaC.

Understanding IaC

As the landscape of IT infrastructure management continues to evolve, ways of moving from manual tasks and manual updates have taken center stage. Weekly maintenance jobs such as configuration sanity checks or daily change request meetings have proven to be just a "wash-rinse-repeat" for many IT professionals. Though you're gaining valuable experience to move your career forward (that is learning processes, understanding best practices and network requirements, and so on), at some point, these tasks become banal and less challenging. If these processes were placed in a framework of sorts or perhaps a methodology/approach that involves treating network infrastructure provisioning, configuration, and management as software development tasks, then it would be more enticing and engaging.

A paradigm shift known as IaC has emerged as a game-changer. As organizations strive to meet the demands of scalability, agility, and reliability, IaC offers a novel approach that blends the principles of software development with network provisioning, configuration, and management. By treating *network infrastructure* as code, IaC revolutionizes the way network components are provisioned, configured, and maintained.

> **Note**
> IaC does not prescribe a specific framework but instead provides a framework-agnostic methodology that can be implemented using various tools and technologies.

What is IaC?

As mentioned previously, IaC is a methodology that treats network infrastructure provisioning, configuration, and management as software development tasks. Instead of manually configuring and deploying infrastructure components such as servers, networks, and storage devices, it involves using code – often expressed in domain-specific languages or standard programming languages – to define, automate, and manage those network resources, components, and configurations. This code is version-controlled, documented, and maintained in the same way as software code, allowing for consistency, repeatability, and collaboration.

A simple example (*Figure 8.13*) is provisioning a VM in Google Cloud:

```
# Configure the Google Cloud provider
provider "google" {
 credentials = file("path/to/your/credentials.json")  [1]
 project   = "your-project-id"
 region    = "us-central1"          [2]
}

# Create a Google Cloud instance (VM)
resource "google_compute_instance" "my_instance" {  [3]
 name      = "my-instance"
 machine_type = "n1-standard-1"
 zone      = "us-central1-a"        [4]

 boot_disk {
  initialize_params {
    image = "debian-cloud/debian-9"  [5]
  }
 }

 network_interface {
  network = "default"  [6]
  access_config {}
 }
}
```

Figure 8.14 – Using IaC to provision a VM in Google Cloud

Let's walk through this example:

1. In the `provider` section, we identified the path to the service account (JSON file) that's used to provision the VM [**1**], along with the *project* used and the specific *region* [**2**].

2. Next, we identified the *resource type* and its name [**3**], along with the specification of that resource and the *zone* within the region to use for resource provisioning [**4**].

3. Then, we identified the boot disk image for the VM's operating system [**5**].

4. Lastly, we identified the network (VPC network) to which the VM's network interface will be connected [**6**].

Using an IaC tool such as Terraform, a VM can be instantiated and quickly deployed to meet the requirements of application developers.

Here are some key aspects of IaC:

-   **Automated provisioning**: IaC allows you to automate the provisioning of infrastructure resources. As shown in *Figure 8.12*, you can use code to describe the desired state of your infrastructure, after which tools will automate the process of creating and configuring those resources accordingly. With IaC's *declarative* nature, automated provisioning takes center stage, enabling infrastructure to be created, modified, or scaled rapidly and accurately.

> **Note**
>
> In this context, declarative refers to a style of programming or configuration in which you specify the desired outcome or end state, rather than providing explicit instructions on how to achieve that outcome. In this approach, you focus on describing what you want, and the system or tool takes care of determining how to achieve it.

- **Version control**: Just like version control of software code, IaC encourages version control of infrastructure code. IT professionals can track changes, collaborate seamlessly, and maintain a *historical record* of modifications made to their infrastructure code base. Version control not only safeguards against accidental changes or errors but also empowers teams to work collaboratively on infrastructure configurations, facilitating continuous improvement and enabling confident deployment of changes to production environments.

> **Note**
>
> This approach provides a structured and efficient way to review, compare, and revert changes, ensuring transparency and accountability in the management of infrastructure resources.

- **Consistency**: By articulating infrastructure configurations through code, IaC ensures that every environment, from development to production, adheres to the same standardized blueprint. This consistency eliminates configuration drift and minimizes the risk of errors that can arise from manual setups. IaC's code-based definitions guarantee that each resource is provisioned and configured identically, reducing the chances of discrepancies that might lead to security vulnerabilities or operational issues.

- **Repeatability**: By defining infrastructure configurations from scratch using code, IaC enables the *replication* of entire setups with precision, eliminating the variations and uncertainties that often arise from manual provisioning. This capability holds immense value in scenarios such as testing, development, and disaster recovery, where the ability to replicate environments accurately is paramount. Repeatability empowers teams to confidently recreate infrastructure landscapes, ensuring that the same resources, configurations, and relationships are established each time, irrespective of the deployment environment.

- **Scalability**: Scalability is central to IaC, empowering organizations to seamlessly adapt and grow their *digital infrastructure* in response to changing demands. By codifying infrastructure configurations, IaC allows teams to define resource provisioning and management in a repeatable and automated manner. This paves the way for effortless replication of resources across environments, enabling swift scaling of applications and services and making it possible to accommodate increased workloads or sudden spikes in demand.

> **Note**
>
> Whether it's for repeatable or scaling purposes, once an IaC process has been solutioned for a specific set of services or deployment schemes, that pipeline can be considered a "golden IaC pipeline" that can then be leveraged for other projects teams may have. This is similar to having golden images for deploying operating systems on VMs.

- **Documentation**: With IaC, infrastructure configurations are expressed through code, serving as living documentation that (inherently) encapsulates the intentions and logic behind resource provisioning and management. Their self-documenting nature ensures that the intricacies of infrastructure setups are captured transparently, reducing ambiguity and promoting clarity among teams. IaC's code artifacts provide a *single source of truth* that can be readily reviewed, shared, and updated, offering a comprehensive reference for understanding how infrastructure is defined, deployed, and maintained.

> **Note**
>
> The self-documenting nature of IaC is indeed a significant and highly valuable aspect of the approach. It addresses the challenge of documentation in traditional infrastructure management, where keeping documentation up to date and aligned with the actual infrastructure state can be a daunting task.

Benefits to a network architect

Aside from the key benefits IaC has holistically, it offers network architects additional benefits that can significantly enhance their roles and contributions in designing, implementing, and managing network infrastructures (*Figure 8.14*):

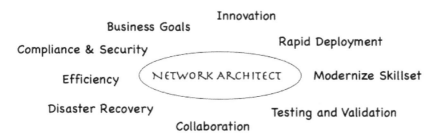

Figure 8.15 – Benefits of IaC to a network architect

Let's explore each in the context of a network architect:

*   **Efficiency**: IaC automates the provisioning and configuration of network resources, saving time and reducing manual efforts. Network architects can focus on high-level design and strategic decisions rather than repetitive tasks.

*   **Rapid deployment**: With IaC, network architects can deploy complex network setups quickly. This agility supports faster response to business demands and enables the rapid creation of development or testing environments.

*   **Collaboration**: IaC promotes version control and collaboration practices. Network architects can work together on code repositories, track changes, and review modifications, enhancing teamwork and knowledge sharing.

*   **Testing and validation**: IaC allows network architects to test and validate network configurations before deployment. Simulations in controlled environments identify potential issues, reducing risks associated with live deployments.

*   **Compliance and security**: Network architects can embed security and compliance policies directly into code, ensuring network configurations adhere to established standards and simplify audits.

*   **Innovation**: IaC encourages innovative network design approaches. Architects can experiment with new technologies and configurations, fostering creativity and continuous improvement.

*   **Modernize skillset**: IaC expertise is highly sought after in the industry. Network architects with IaC skills possess a modern and adaptable skillset that aligns with emerging technology trends.

*   **Career growth**: IaC proficiency opens opportunities for career advancement. Network architects who excel in IaC-related roles can move into senior positions and lead complex projects.

*   **Business alignment**: IaC aligns network architectures with business goals. Network architects can quickly adapt networks to changing business needs, supporting strategic initiatives.

Note

Incorporating IaC into your skillset as an aspiring network architect not only enhances your technical capabilities but also aligns you with the future of network infrastructure management. As networks become more complex and dynamic, architects with IaC expertise are well-positioned to excel and drive innovation in their field.

As organizations embrace IaC, they harness a powerful tool to achieve infrastructure agility, optimize resource utilization, and align technology with business objectives. This paradigm shift empowers organizations to automate and standardize infrastructure setups, enhancing efficiency, consistency, and scalability. Its self-documenting nature ensures transparent configurations, simplifying troubleshooting and knowledge sharing.

By automating provisioning, enhancing consistency, enabling rapid scaling, promoting collaboration, and providing testing and documentation capabilities, IaC transforms how network architects *approach* their roles. With IaC, network architects gain the ability to focus on strategic design decisions, drive innovation, and ensure operational efficiency, ultimately contributing to more agile, resilient, and adaptable network infrastructures that align seamlessly with modern business requirements.

Summary

In the ever-evolving landscape of IT, the foundations of network automation have emerged as a pivotal driver of innovation, efficiency, and scalability. By bridging the gap between human intervention and the dynamic demands of modern networks, network automation empowers organizations to streamline operations, reduce errors, and allocate resources more intelligently.

Through the mastery of programming languages (such as Python and Ruby), APIs, automation tools (such as Ansible and SaltStack), CI/CD tools (such as GitLab and GitHub), IaC methodology (such as Terraform) configuration management tools (such as Puppet and Chef), network architects can shape the future of their network infrastructures, enabling them to evolve in response to changing requirements.

Embracing network automation's building blocks – ranging from programmability and APIs to SDN and orchestrators – empowers professionals to orchestrate, configure, and manage networks with a *level of precision* and agility that was once incomprehensible. In this era of digital transformation, a strong foundation in network automation is no longer a luxury but a strategic necessity, unlocking the potential for organizations to thrive in a rapidly changing technological landscape.

In the next chapter, we will begin exploring the paradigm shift to the cloud and cloud computing.

Further reading

To learn more about the topics that were covered in this chapter, take a look at the following resources:

- *Software-Defined Networking Approaches for Link Failure Recovery: A Survey*: https://www.mdpi.com/2071-1050/12/10/4255

- *List of SDN controllers*: https://www.researchgate.net/figure/List-of-available-SDN-controllers_tbl1_338703576

- *Defining the elements of NFV architecture*: https://blog.equinix.com/blog/2019/10/17/networking-for-nerds-defining-the-elements-of-nfv-architectures/

- *NFV*: https://www.sciencedirect.com/topics/computer-science/network-function-virtualization#:~:text=The%20NFV%20concept%2C%20which%20was,ISG)%20for%20Network%20Functions%20Virtualization

9

Paradigm Shift to Cloud Computing

In the ever-evolving landscape of technology, only a few innovations have had such a transformative impact as cloud computing. The shift towards cloud-based services has brought about a new era of efficiency, scalability, and accessibility, revolutionizing the way individuals and organizations operate in the digital age, where the static constraints of physical machines yield to the dynamic elasticity of virtual resources.

In an era defined by the relentless pursuit of efficiency, scalability, opportunity, and *interconnectedness*, organizations and IT professionals are re-evaluating whether maintaining data centers (whether large or small, distributed or not) is a prudent investment. As applications are more SaaS-based, data center hardware is under-utilized for the cost paid, and their workforces are mobile and not necessarily tied to a specific geographical region.

Here's an example:

An organization has a data center (one of many) with over 100 data switches, at capacity, 250 servers, SAN networking, security devices/appliances with various capabilities, and other networking and application services. They have over 100 applications in production, which fluctuates throughout the year. The servers are averaging 50% utilization yearly. The TCO per year is $5.5M, not including staff and maintenance.

From a network architect's perspective, consider how you might answer the following questions:

- Does it make sense to keep such a large footprint where scalability and agility are limited?

- Should we be paying double for server usage? Are we actually getting the best value for what we purchased? Does it make sense to have staff focus on maintenance?

- In the next fiscal year, TCO is increasing by 15%, data center maintenance will increase by 15%, and hardware/software SLAs are up for renewal simultaneously; a refresh is on the horizon. How do we handle this?

This chapter should help you answer the preceding questions, and we will also explore the significance of cloud computing in a network architect role.

In this chapter, we'll explore the following topics:

- What is cloud computing?
- The need for cloud computing
- Cloud services
- Cloud design and architecting
- What does it mean for a network architect?

Let's get started!

What is cloud computing?

In the vast expanse of the digital realm, some 20 years ago, a new concept emerged, heralding a revolutionary paradigm shift in the world of computing: the cloud. It represents a departure from traditional computing models, where physical hardware and software were tightly bound to individual devices or data centers. The cloud, on the other hand, offers a flexible, scalable, and interconnected ecosystem that empowers users and organizations like never before.

Cloud computing is a computing paradigm that has transformed the way information technology is accessed, delivered, and utilized. Instead of relying on local servers and physical infrastructure, cloud computing enables users and organizations to access and utilize computing resources, such as servers, storage, databases, software applications, and more, remotely through the internet.

> **Note**
> When I refer to the internet, I'm referring to accessing services outside the boundaries of data centers and organizational networks, whether this is over the internet, leased lines, or dark fiber.

The essence of cloud computing lies in its agility and flexibility. In the past, organizations had to invest heavily in building and maintaining their *own* physical IT infrastructure, including servers, data centers, fabric infrastructure, security appliances, and complementary hardware and software. This approach was not only capital-intensive but also inflexible. Scaling up or down to meet changing demands required significant time, added complexity, and resources. Additionally, ensuring the security and reliability of these on-premises systems was a constant concern.

Instead, organizations can leverage **cloud service providers** (**CSPs**) that *own and maintain* the infrastructure, allowing their IT professionals to *scale* resources up or down based on demand or the needs of the business. This pay-as-you-go (consumption) model not only reduces capital expenses but also ensures optimal utilization of computing resources, making it a cost-effective solution for businesses of all sizes.

> **Note**
>
> This is important to understand. As the paradigm moves away from capital expenses (purchasing and owning hardware) to operational expenses (consuming a resource), you now have a bit more *control* over costs and investments; those that were once fixed are now more fluid.

The benefits of cloud computing extend far beyond cost savings and scalability. Cloud-based services foster collaboration and connectivity, enabling teams to work seamlessly across geographical boundaries. With data stored in the cloud, users can access information from any device with an internet connection, promoting productivity and mobility. Additionally, cloud computing enables faster deployment of applications and software updates, ensuring that users have access to the latest features and security enhancements.

Cloud computing is a comprehensive ecosystem comprising various components that work together to deliver computing services over the internet. These components collectively create a flexible, scalable, and interconnected framework that enables users and organizations to access and utilize computing resources remotely (*Figure 9.1*).

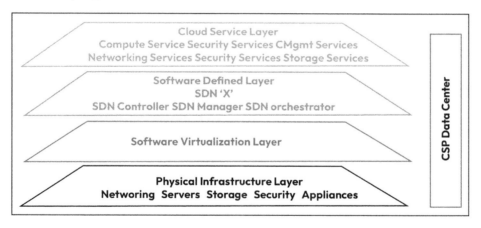

Figure 9.1 – Cloud computing infrastructure stack

The key elements that make up cloud computing are as follows:

- **Infrastructure**: At the heart of cloud computing lies the infrastructure, which consists of physical data centers and servers, networking equipment, and storage devices. These resources are owned and maintained by cloud service providers, which manage the underlying hardware and ensure its availability and reliability.

- **Virtualization**: Virtualization technology plays a pivotal role in cloud computing by abstracting physical hardware into virtual resources. This process allows multiple **virtual machines (VMs)** to run on a single physical server, enabling efficient resource allocation and maximizing hardware utilization. Virtualization is a key enabler of scalability and cost-effectiveness in the cloud.

- **Deployment models**: Cloud computing provides different deployment options to suit specific requirements and security considerations:

  - **Public cloud**: Services are available to the general public over the internet or via dedicated connectivity to cloud service providers.

  - **Private clouds**: These clouds are dedicated exclusively to a single organization, whether they are hosted on-premises within the organization's data center or by a third-party cloud provider. In a private cloud, the infrastructure and resources are not shared with other organizations, ensuring a higher degree of control, security, and customization compared to public cloud environments.

  - **Hybrid cloud**: This combines elements of both public and private clouds, allowing data and applications to be shared and integrated between them. The goal is to leverage the strengths of both public and private clouds while addressing specific business needs, such as scalability, security, and compliance.

- **Connectivity**: Robust networking is a critical component of cloud computing, ensuring seamless data transmission between users and cloud services. High-speed internet or dedicated connectivity and data centers equipped with redundant network connections facilitate reliable and low-latency access to cloud resources.

- **Security and compliance**: Cloud computing incorporates comprehensive security measures to protect data and applications. These measures include encryption, access controls, firewalls, and multi-factor authentication. Cloud providers also comply with industry standards and regulations to ensure data privacy and legal compliance.

- **Scalability and elasticity**: Cloud computing offers the ability to scale resources up or down based on demand. Scalability ensures that organizations can accommodate changing workloads, while elasticity allows resources to be automatically adjusted to match fluctuating requirements, optimizing cost efficiency.

- **Management and orchestration**: Cloud management platforms and tools allow users to provision, monitor, and manage cloud resources effectively. Cloud orchestration enables the automated deployment and coordination of complex applications and services, streamlining operations and enhancing efficiency.

Now that we know of the key elements, let's look at the various cloud models next.

Cloud computing models

Cloud computing offers various service models to cater to different needs. There are three *primary* service models (as outlined), which can be referred to as traditional service models, each catering to specific needs and requirements. These models provide users and organizations with different levels of control and responsibility over the underlying infrastructure and applications.

> **Note**
>
> These models serve as the foundation for subsequent "as a Service" solutions. Two that are becoming more common are **Container as a Service (CaaS)** and **Function as a Service (FaaS)**.

Figure 9.2 shows the typical responsibility matrix between the cloud service provider and an organization:

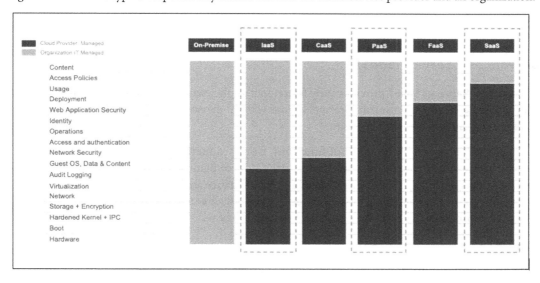

Figure 9.2 – Cloud provider service model

Let's discuss each one briefly.

Infrastructure as a Service (IaaS)

Infrastructure as a Service (**IaaS**) is the foundational layer of cloud computing. It provides virtualized computing resources over the internet, allowing users to rent virtual machines, storage, and networking capabilities on a pay-as-you-go basis. With IaaS, users have the flexibility to deploy and manage operating systems, applications, and development frameworks on the cloud provider's infrastructure.

This model liberates businesses from the burden of maintaining physical servers, fabric, and appliances, allowing them to focus on their *core objectives* and innovation. IaaS is particularly beneficial for organizations seeking a scalable and cost-effective solution, as resources can be easily scaled up or down based on demand.

Platform as a Service (PaaS)

Platform as a Service (**PaaS**) *abstracts* the underlying infrastructure and provides a complete development and deployment environment for developers to build, host, and manage applications. This model can offer a range of tools and services, such as programming languages, databases, middleware, and development frameworks.

PaaS eliminates the need for developers to manage the underlying hardware and operating systems, enabling them to focus solely on writing and deploying code. The results are faster development cycles and shorter time to market for applications, making it an ideal choice for developers and development teams looking to streamline their processes and drive innovation.

Software as a Service (SaaS)

Software as a Service (**SaaS**) provides fully functional applications over the internet. With SaaS, organizations can access and use software applications without the need to install, maintain, or manage the underlying infrastructure or software.

SaaS applications cover a wide range of functions, from productivity and collaboration tools to customer relationship management and enterprise resource planning systems. This model offers immense convenience to end users, as updates and maintenance are handled by the cloud provider. SaaS is particularly popular among businesses seeking cost-effective and accessible software solutions, as they can subscribe to SaaS applications on a subscription basis.

Container as a Service (CaaS)

Container as a Service (**CaaS**) is similar to IaaS. While not for deploying and managing VMs and operating systems, CaaS provides a platform for creating, deploying, and managing containers within a cloud environment. It abstracts infrastructure and simplifies container orchestration and management.

> **Note**
> CaaS can be thought of as an extension or variant of the IaaS service model.

Function as a Service (FaaS)

Function as a Service (**FaaS**) is a paradigm that instituted a *serverless* computing model where the cloud provider automatically manages the infrastructure and execution of code, scaling up or down in response to events or triggers. Developers write a piece of code (functions) and the cloud provider handles resource allocation and demand activities.

The need for cloud computing

Cloud computing solves several critical problems in the realm of IT and technology. Let's consider the following scenario regarding data analytics:

Data-intensive projects, such as a scientific research initiative, where massive amounts of data need to be ingested, analyzed, and stored.

From the perspective of a network architect, what would be required to build a data-centric architecture to support this initiative on-premises? We'll need the building blocks: network (fabric), compute, storage (DBs, SAN, NAS, etc.), software (OS, virtualization, middleware, patches, etc.), and data applications (processing, analytics, correlations, home-grown). Let's keep it at this for now and break down each:

- **Networking**: To support this from a (physical) network layer perspective, the architecture will need high-speed, non-blocking, low-latency switches and routers with possibly large queuing buffers and hardware-based encryption for crucial data transfers and communication between servers and storage endpoints.

  A minimum data speed of no less than 10 GB (maybe 25 GB at the time of writing) is required for the downstream servers, SAN, and NAS and to identify the optimal fiber optics specification between the following:

  - Server and **top of rack** (**ToR**)
  - ToR and ToR
  - ToR and backbone
  - ToR and SAN
  - SAN and SAN

  Along with the IP scheme for the various teams (i.e., analytics, data scrubbing, developers, data scientists, and others), MCEC, routing, switching, and ACLs between devices and end users.

- **Servers**: These should be powerful **high-performing compute** (**HPC**) servers with multiple processors (CPUs), significant RAM and cache buffers, and high-speed internal storage with **network interface cards** (**NICs**) for data speeds of 10 GB or higher. Essentially, these servers should be capable of handling the computational demands of data processing and analytics.

  Servers with **graphical processing units** (**GPUs**) may be needed for AI capabilities for home-grown applications. Clustering will be important for **high availability**, and virtualization can make better use of server hardware.

- **Storage systems**: A project of this magnitude would require significant storage capacity. This means high-capacity storage systems, such as **network-attached storage** (**NAS**) or **storage area network** (**SAN**) systems and database systems.

The storage system may require its own network (i.e., FCoE, FibreChannel, ISCS) and hardware to support big data frameworks, such as Hadoop, Spark, Storm, Druid, or TeraData.

Consider what the appropriate storage technology is based on your needs. This may include traditional **hard disk drives (HDDs)** for high-capacity storage, **solid-state drives (SSDs)** for high-speed access, or a combination of both (hybrid storage) for a balance of performance and capacity. Capacity should be in the realm of terabytes to petabytes.

Then, implement redundancy to ensure data availability and fault tolerance. Consider **redundant arrays of independent disk (RAID)** configurations, such as RAID 5 or RAID 6, for data redundancy and protection against disk failures.

- **Applications**: These will vary based on developer needs. Some of interest are as follows:

  - Data integration and **extract, transform, and load (ETL)**

    - Apache NiFi, Talend, Informatica

  - Data visualization and reporting

    - Grafana, Tableau, Power BI

  - Data catalog and metadata management

    - Apacha Atlas

  - Stream processing and **complex event processing (CEP)**

    - Apache Kafka/Storm/Samza

  - Data quality and governance

    - Collibra

  - Custom data applications

- **Software**: Various software and middleware will be required:

  - Servers

    - Linux variants
    - Windows variants

  - Network

    - Routing/switching NOS (Cisco, Arista, Cumulus)

- Storage
  - Oracle, Cassandra, MongoDB
- Backup/recovery
  - Veeam, Commvault

Considering everything I mentioned, consider how you would answer these questions:

- What will be the timeline to implement (design, test, build, deploy, verify) this architecture?
- What will be the **level of effort** (**LoE**) required?
- What will be the cost? In year 1, year 2, and year 3?
- What will be the TCO and ROI?
- If we need to pivot due to pressure (market, industry, competition), can we do so?
- What will be the cost to upskill current employees to support this build?

For the sake of simplicity, let's say the cost would be $2 million (capital expense) to deploy on-premises. This is quite significant given the fact I didn't include costs related to security, compliance, loss prevention, maintenance, leasing, HVAC, or anything of the like.

> **Note**
>
> Keep in mind that this would be the cost for a single data center location. What if there's a need to have another center in another place, city, or country? How would the cost be affected?

If we were to architect in the cloud, what would the cost (operational expense) be? Given the building blocks and what was defined, I would have to say about $10,000 – 25,000 per month, which equates to $120,000 – $300,000 per year.

Although I've oversimplified the example, I think you get the idea that cloud solutions offer tremendous value. The same $300K per year in the cloud also offers the ability to shift workloads to other locations for flexible accessibility for developers and other end users, whereas on-premises doesn't give you that kind of flexibility.

> **Note**
>
> Yes, you can connect to an on-premises from another location via VPN, dark fiber, internet, and lease lines. But you may experience delays for time-sensitive data, or result return times will increase due to the time of day and other factors. Not to mention the additional overhead for management and the costs of the connectivity options.

Architecting for another on-premises location will require the same cost ($2M) or more.

Let's look at the cost-value savings:

- One location:

$$\frac{(On - premise) - Cloud}{On - premise} = \frac{2M - 300K}{2M} = 0.85 \sim 85\%$$

Figure 9.3 – Costing for one location

- Two locations

$$\frac{(On - premise) - Cloud}{On - premise} = \frac{4M - 450K}{4M} = 0.88 \sim 88\%$$

Figure 9.4 – Costing for two locations

Cost savings will be roughly 85% and 88%, respectively, to develop and architect in the cloud.

Benefits of the cloud

As seen in the example in the previous section, cloud computing offers a wide range of benefits for businesses and organizations of all sizes. Key advantages include the following:

- **On-demand self-service**: Cloud computing enables users to provision and manage computing resources as needed without requiring human intervention from the service provider. Users can request resources such as VMs, containers, storage, security capabilities, and networking via web interface portals, APIs, or IaC.

- **Cost efficiency**: By leveraging cloud services, organizations can allocate their budgets more effectively, maximize resource utilization, and ultimately drive significant cost savings, making cloud computing a strategic choice for modern businesses seeking to streamline their IT expenditures. Two key impacts of cloud computing are as follows:

  - **Reduced capital expenditure**: Utilizing cloud computing eliminates the need for organizations to *invest in* and *maintain* expensive on-premises hardware and data centers.

  - **Pay-as-you-go pricing**: Cloud services often operate (operating model) on a subscription or pay-as-you-go model, offering organizations the flexibility to pay only for the resources and services they use. This model avoids upfront capital expenses and aligns their costs directly with their usage.

- **Scalability**: The elasticity of cloud environments provides dynamic and adaptable IT infrastructure that can effortlessly adjust to the ebbs and flows of business operations. Scalability ensures that an organization's computing resources – whether this is processing power, storage, or network capacity – can seamlessly *expand* or *contract* in real time based on demand.

  This *litheness* not only enhances performance and responsiveness but also drives significant cost savings by eliminating the need for overprovisioning (under-utilization), which allows organizations to optimize resource allocation, improve cost efficiency, and ensure performance and availability.

- **Flexibility and agility**: Though both may be considered the same concept, they're more complementary to each other relative to the cloud and cloud services:

  - **Flexibility**: In the context of the cloud, this refers to an organization's capability to choose from a wide range of services and configurations to tailor their IT environment to their specific needs. It also encompasses the ability to adjust configurations and services as business demands, requirements, or strategies change.

  - **Agility**: Agility focuses on the *speed* and *ease* with which changes can be made to the IT environment. An agile infrastructure allows organizations to quickly deploy, modify, or remove resources and services in response to changing conditions or business demands.

  It's about being *responsive* and *adaptive* in a fast-paced environment, enabling the rapid development of applications and services.

- **Reliability and high availability**: Redundancy and high availability ensure that critical applications and services remain accessible and resilient even in the face of hardware failures or unexpected disruptions. This redundancy is further enhanced through automated failover mechanisms (either by the cloud provider or client) that seamlessly shift workloads to healthy resources in the event of a failure, minimizing service interruptions.

  Additionally, cloud platforms offer a wide array of high-availability features, such as load balancing, auto-scaling, and data replication, backup, and recovery, enabling organizations to design fault-tolerant architectures that can withstand even the most challenging scenarios. As a result, businesses can deliver uninterrupted services to their customers, enhance user experiences, and maintain operational continuity, ultimately bolstering their reputation and reliability.

- **Security and compliance**: Security and compliance are of utmost importance in cloud computing. Cloud providers offer robust measures to address these concerns. Cloud security encompasses multi-layered defenses, including firewalls, encryption, identity and access management, and continuous monitoring, to safeguard data and resources. Compliance is achieved through adherence to various industry-specific regulations and standards, such as GDPR, HIPAA, and SOC 2.

The benefits of cloud security and compliance are profound. Organizations can offload the responsibility of managing physical security, regular audits, and compliance checks to their cloud provider. This not only reduces the burden on internal IT teams and third-party services but also ensures that data protection and regulatory compliance are handled professionally.

• Additionally, cloud providers offer a range of security tools and services, empowering businesses to add another layer of protection by proactively detecting and mitigating threats (**TDIR**) and monitoring actively, bolstering their overall security posture. Ultimately, cloud security and compliance not only protect sensitive data but also enhance an organization's reputation and trustworthiness among customers and partners.

> **Note**
> Cloud providers institute various capabilities to protect data within and through the confounds of their data centers. They implement robust security measures including encryption (at rest and in transit) and access controls, several layers of physical security, hardware security, and more, ensuring data integrity, confidentiality, and availability.

• **Automatic updates and maintenance**: Automatic updates and maintenance are additional key benefits of cloud computing that streamline and enhance the management of IT resources. All software patches, security updates, and maintenance tasks are often automated, reducing the need for manual intervention and minimizing the risk of human error. This automation ensures that systems remain up to date with the latest security patches and improvements, reducing vulnerabilities and enhancing overall system reliability.

The benefits of automatic updates and maintenance in the cloud are significant. They allow organizations to focus on innovation and business growth rather than the tedious and time-consuming tasks of system upkeep. Furthermore, automatic updates help prevent security breaches and downtime, ensuring that applications and services are consistently available to users. This not only improves operational efficiency but also enhances the overall user experience, ultimately contributing to the success and competitiveness of businesses.

• **Data backup and disaster recovery**: Data backup and disaster recovery are essential components for an organization to ensure the safety and availability of critical data and applications. In the cloud, organizations can leverage automated and scalable backup solutions to create regular data snapshots and maintain copies of their data in multiple redundant locations. This redundancy is coupled with disaster recovery plans that outline procedures for rapid data restoration and system recovery in case of unexpected events such as hardware failures, natural disasters, or cyberattacks.

The benefits of these cloud-based data backup and disaster recovery strategies include the following:

  • **Data resilience**: They ensure that critical data is resilient and protected against various threats, including hardware failures, data corruption, and cyberattacks

- **Minimized downtime**: In the event of a disaster or data loss, rapid restoration of services, minimizing downtime, and ensuring continuity of business operations

- **Cost efficiency**: They provide cost-effective storage and recovery options compared to on-premises infrastructure

- **Automated backup**: Simplified backup processes ensure that backups are performed regularly and consistently without the need for manual intervention

- **Redundancy**: They maintain redundant data copies in multiple geographically dispersed locations, reducing the risk of data loss due to localized disasters

- **Accessibility**: Data can be accessed from anywhere with an internet connection, enabling remote access to critical information during disaster recovery efforts

- **Simplified management**: User-friendly management interfaces make it easier to configure and monitor data protection measures.

- **Faster recovery times**: Cloud-based disaster recovery solutions typically offer faster recovery times compared to traditional, on-premises infrastructure

- **Testing and validation**: Cloud-based disaster recovery plans can be regularly tested and validated without disrupting production systems, ensuring their effectiveness

- **Business continuity**: Robust data backup and disaster recovery strategies in the cloud contribute to overall business continuity by reducing the impact of disruptions

- **Peace of mind**: Knowing that data is securely backed up and can be recovered in case of unforeseen events gives peace of mind and confidence to organizations and their stakeholders

These benefits collectively contribute to the reliability, resilience, and overall operational efficiency of organizations, enabling them to focus on their core business objectives. Ultimately, data backup and disaster recovery in the cloud ensure business continuity, safeguarding against the potentially devastating consequences of data loss and system outages.

- **Innovation and competitive advantage**: Innovation and competitive advantages go hand in hand with the realm of cloud computing. Cloud technology empowers organizations to innovate at a rapid pace by providing easy access to a wealth of scalable resources, advanced tools, and cutting-edge technologies. This allows organizations to advance the culture of experimentation (R&D) and to develop and deploy new applications and services more quickly.

By harnessing the cloud's flexibility and agility, organizations can ingest data and respond swiftly to market trends and customer demands, gaining a significant competitive edge.

At the disposal of organizations (and beyond the common workload building blocks) are services such as machine learning, data analytics, ingestion queues, and artificial intelligence capabilities. These enable data-driven insights and informed decision-making. The benefits are multifarious, from enhanced customer experiences and improved operational efficiencies to the ability to stay ahead of competitors and market pressures.

- **Environmental sustainability**: The environmental sustainability aspect of cloud computing is increasingly significant as organizations are seeking to reduce their carbon footprint and contribute to a *greener future*. Cloud providers invest heavily in energy-efficient data centers, optimized hardware utilization, and renewable energy sources, which collectively lower energy consumption and greenhouse gas emissions, making the environment safer.

> **Note**
>
> Google Cloud has made substantial strides in creating carbon-free environments in its cloud data centers.
>
> For more information, check out these links:
>
> `https://www.google.com/about/datacenters/cleanenergy/`
>
> `https://sustainability.google/operating-sustainably/`
>
> `https://www.google.com/about/datacenters/locations/`

In contrast, on-premises network infrastructures typically require organizations to build and manage their own data centers or server rooms, which can vary widely in terms of energy efficiency. Older facilities may lack modern cooling and power management systems, leading to higher energy consumption and operational costs. Typically, capacity planning for on-premises data centers often involves provisioning for peak workloads, which can result in underutilized hardware during periods of low demand, further increasing energy waste.

By consolidating workloads on *shared infrastructure*, cloud computing effectively minimizes the need for individually maintained data centers, further reducing energy consumption and electronic waste.

This eco-friendly approach not only aligns with corporate social responsibility initiatives but also brings tangible benefits, including reduced operational costs, compliance with environmental regulations, and improved corporate reputation.

- **Cost transparency and management**: Cost transparency and management are critical aspects where cloud computing offers distinct advantages over on-premises infrastructure, providing organizations with greater financial flexibility and control. Cost visibility is enhanced through detailed billing and usage reports that allow businesses to monitor expenditures at a granular level. This transparency enables organizations to understand precisely how resources are allocated and consumed (daily, weekly, monthly, yearly), facilitating informed decision-making.

With cloud service pricing models (i.e., pay-as-you-go, spot pricing, sustained use), organizations are able to align costs with actual usage. This elasticity ensures that organizations can optimize costs by adjusting their resource allocation as business needs change. For example, during periods of increased demand, additional capacity can be provisioned, and during quieter times, resources can be scaled back, preventing unnecessary provisioning.

Cost management tools and dashboards, budgeting features, and alerts help organizations track and control their expenses *proactively*, empowering them to set budget limits, establish cost controls, and receive notifications when expenditures approach predefined thresholds.

Ultimately, this leads to greater *financial predictability*, reduced waste, and improved cost-effectiveness. Organizations can optimize their IT budgets, redirect resources to strategic initiatives, and respond more efficiently to changing business conditions—all while benefiting from the transparency and flexibility inherent in cloud computing.

> **Note**
>
> In the case of on-premises, such real-time visibility and control features are lacking and the financial approaches are more reactionary.

- **Global reach**: The global reach serves as a prime differentiator aspect of cloud computing compared to on-premises infrastructure, offering organizations unprecedented accessibility and scalability on a global scale. Cloud providers maintain a vast network of data centers distributed across regions and continents, enabling businesses to deploy resources and services in multiple geographic locations without incurring substantial costs or complex logistics.

  In the context of an organization with an international presence and a global customer base, having such reachability provides a strategic advantage. It allows for the efficient expansion of operations into new markets, as services can be deployed closer to end users, reducing latency and improving the user experience.

> **Note**
>
> Consider that the proximity to end users is particularly critical for applications with real-time or low-latency requirements, such as online gaming, video streaming, and financial services.

  The cloud's global presence enhances disaster recovery and business continuity efforts. Organizations can replicate data and applications across geographically dispersed data centers, ensuring that critical services remain available even in the face of regional disruptions or natural disasters. This level of redundancy and resilience would be challenging and costly to achieve with on-premises infrastructure.

  This global accessibility without the need for substantial capital investments or complex logistical arrangements provides businesses with a competitive edge in today's interconnected and dynamic global economy.

In summary, cloud computing offers a transformative shift from traditional on-premises infrastructure, delivering a wealth of benefits. It eliminates the need for substantial upfront investments, reducing capital expenditure while offering pay-as-you-go pricing models that align costs with actual resource usage. Cloud services provide unparalleled scalability, enabling organizations to flexibly adapt to changing demands and improve resource utilization. The cloud's global accessibility facilitates market expansion and enhances disaster recovery, all without the complexities and costs associated with on-premises geographic expansion. Streamlined IT management, including automated maintenance and updates, frees up internal resources for strategic innovation, thereby providing a means for organizations to optimize costs, drive innovation, and respond effectively to the evolving demands of the digital era.

Cloud services

Every cloud provider offers a wide array of services to meet the potential needs of businesses. It also enables them to access cutting-edge technologies, and as we've seen in the previous section, without the burden of managing complex infrastructure, fostering agility and growth.

A network architect, whose primary focus is to design on-premises solutions, must begin to foster ideas that abstract the concepts that once resided within a physical capacity to those of a logical one. Bridging networking solutions with those of cloud services is progress towards a *cloud-focused mindset*.

> **Note**
>
> For the purposes of this section, the cloud providers will be the big three: AWS, Azure, and Google Cloud. The focus will be on the building blocks as opposed to the entire portfolio offered.
>
> The service list below is not an exhaustive list of what cloud providers may offer. The services listed are commonly used by organizations and what I've been privy to working with.

All cloud providers offer a similar over-arching set of core cloud services and functionalities. While there are differences in the specifics of how each provider implements these services, they share common categories of cloud offerings. Some of the core services are as follows.

Compute services

As the name implies, these services enable organizations to deploy applications, execute code, and process workloads without the need for physical hardware (servers) provisioning or management. Users can deploy, manage, and run VMs, containers, or serverless functions, depending on the specific service and use case (*Table 9.1*):

	AWS	**Azure**	**Google Cloud**
Virtual machines	Elastic Cloud Compute (EC2)	Azure Virtual Machine (Azure VM)	Google Compute Engine (GCE)

Containers	AWS Elastic Container Service (ECS), AWS Elastic Kubernetes Services (EKS)	Azure Kubernetes Services (AKS)	Google Kubernetes Engine (GKE)
Serverless (VM)	Elastic Beanstalk	App Services	App Engine
Serverless (Containers)	Fargate	Container Apps	Cloud Run
Serverless (Functions)	Lambda	Azure Functions	Cloud Functions

Table 9.1 – Cloud compute services

Compute services empower businesses to dynamically scale their computing resources, optimize performance, and efficiently manage costs, making them a cornerstone of modern cloud infrastructure and application development.

Storage services

Storage services offer an organization the ability to store, manage, and access data and digital assets in a scalable, secure, and cost-effective manner. These services provide a range of storage options, including object storage for large volumes of unstructured data, file storage for shared file systems, and block storage for attaching to virtual machines (*Table 9.2*):

	AWS	**Azure**	**Google Cloud**
Object Storage	Simple Storage Service (S3)	Azure Blob	Google Cloud Storage (GCS)
File Storage	Elastic File Storage (EFS)	Azure Files	Filestore

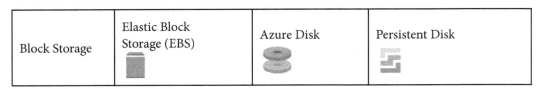

Block Storage	Elastic Block Storage (EBS)	Azure Disk	Persistent Disk

Table 9.2 – Cloud storage services

Cloud storage services are fundamental components of cloud computing ecosystems, enabling organizations to store, manage, and access their data reliably and efficiently. They're used for various applications, including data backup, content distribution, application data storage, auditing, lifecycle retention, and collaboration.

Database services

This is another type of integral cloud service for managing and organizing data efficiently, ensuring data integrity and enabling data-driven decision-making. They provide organizations with scalable, managed, and highly available database solutions that alleviate the operational burden of traditional database management.

These services offer solutions from traditional relational databases to NoSQL databases and data warehousing solutions. Databases provide organizations with structured data storage, enabling applications, websites, and systems to access and manipulate data reliably (*Table 9.3*):

	AWS	**Azure**	**Google Cloud**
Relational database	RDS, Aurora (Serverless)	SQL Managed Instance, Azure SQL DB (Serverless)	Cloud SQL, Cloud Spanner (Serverless)
Non-relational database	DynamoDB	Cosmos DB	BigTable
In-memory database	ElasticCache	Cache for Redis	Memorystore

Data warehouse	Athena 	Synapse	BigQuery

Table 9.3 – Cloud database services

Databases and database services are the backbone of modern data-driven organizations. Because of their ability to scale, many industries rely on them for modernizing initiatives such as gaming, agriculture, financial services, life sciences, retail and e-commerce, and media and entertainment.

Networking services

Networking services are a critical component of cloud computing, providing the infrastructure and offering a suite of solutions designed to optimize and enhance network connectivity within cloud environments and the tools necessary to manage resources efficiently.

These services encompass virtual networks, VPNs, direct connections, and SD-WAN solutions, enabling organizations to establish secure and high-performance connections between on-premises data centers and cloud environments (*Table 9.4*):

	AWS	**Azure**	**Google Cloud**
Virtual networks	Virtual private cloud (VPC)	Virtual network (VNet)	Virtual private cloud (VPC)
Connectivity	AWS Direct Connect, Hosted Connection, AWS VPN	Azure ExpressRoute, ExpressRoute Partner, Azure VPN	Dedicated Interconnects, Partner Interconnects, Cloud VPN
Routing	AWS Transit Gateway	Azure VNet Gateway	Cloud Router
Domain name service (DNS)	AWS Route 53	Azure DNS	Cloud DNS

Load balancing	Elastic Load Balancer (ELB)	Azure Load Balancer	Cloud Load Balancing
Firewall	AWS Network Firewall, AWS WAF, AWS Shield	Azure Firewall, Azure Web Application Firewall (WAF)	Cloud Firewall, Cloud Armor

Table 9.4 – Cloud networking services

Networking services empower businesses to design, optimize, and scale their network architecture in response to changing demands, supporting seamless cloud migrations, real-time data access, and reliable communication across distributed cloud resources.

Monitoring services

Monitoring services are essential tools for maintaining and providing a comprehensive view of the health, performance, and security of cloud-based applications and infrastructure, enabling real-time tracking and the analysis of performance metrics, system health, and security logs (*Table 9.5*):

	AWS	**Azure**	**Google Cloud**
Logging	CloudWatch Logs	Azure Monitor Logs	Cloud Logging
Monitoring	CloudWatch	Azure Monitor	Cloud Monitoring
Auditing	CloudTrail	Azure Audit Logs	Cloud Audit Logs
Tracing	X-Ray	Monitor App insights Distributed Tracing	Cloud Trace

Table 9.5 – Cloud monitoring services

By continuously collecting and analyzing data, monitoring tools offer invaluable insights into resource utilization, application behavior, and user experiences. This level of visibility is crucial for identifying and addressing performance bottlenecks, optimizing resource allocation, and preempting potential issues before they escalate into significant problems.

Security and compliance

Let's look at the security and compliance services provided by the leading CSPs:

	AWS	Azure	Google Cloud
Identity	AWS Cognito	Azure Active Directory	Cloud IAM
Key management	AWS KSM, AWS XKS, AWS CloudHSM	Azure Key Vault, Managed HSM	Cloud KMS, Cloud HSM, Cloud EKM
Organizational policy	AWS Organizations policies	Azure Policy	Organizational Policy
SIEM	Security Lake	Sentinel	Chronicle, Mandiant
Security and risk management	GuardDuty, Security Hub	MS Defender for Cloud	Security Command Center (SCC)

Table 9.6 – Security and compliance services

While similarities exist, it's important to note that each cloud provider has its own unique features, pricing models, and service-specific capabilities. As a result, network architects should embrace the cloud as complementary as opposed to adversarial. They should begin to take the concepts learned from traditional networking design and translate them to fabric architectures, taking into consideration their specific requirements, desired features, and end states.

Cloud designing and architecting

Cloud designing and architecting are disciplines in the realm of modern information technology, revolutionizing the way businesses manage and deploy their digital infrastructure. As organizations increasingly migrate their operations to cloud environments, understanding how to design, architect, and implement cloud services becomes indispensable. This intricate process involves careful planning, selecting the right cloud services, optimizing resource utilization, and ensuring security and compliance.

It refers to the strategic processes of planning, structuring, and creating cloud-based solutions to meet specific business or technical requirements of applications to maximize efficiency, scalability, and performance.

Designing in the cloud

Designing in the cloud primarily focuses on creating *detailed specifications* and configurations for individual components and services within a cloud-based solution. It involves making decisions about how each component will function, interact with others, and be configured to achieve specific goals. Designing in the cloud typically comes after the high-level architecture has been established. Some examples are as follows:

- **Designing a cloud database schema**: This involves defining the structure of a cloud database and specifying tables, fields, indexes, and access patterns. An example is designing a schema for an e-commerce platform's product catalog database in Amazon RDS.

- **Container configuration**: This involves specifying the configuration details for containers (e.g., Docker containers, sidecars, proxies) used in cloud deployments, including environment variables, dependencies, and startup commands.

Architecting in the cloud

Architecting in the cloud is a broader and more strategic process (that follows similar principles as discussed in *Chapter 4*). It involves designing the overall structure and *framework* of a cloud solution, considering how all the components and services fit together to achieve specific business or technical objectives. Cloud architecture decisions have a significant impact on the scalability, reliability, security, and cost-effectiveness of the solution. Examples are as follows:

- **Architecting a multi-tier web application**: This involves deciding on the architecture of a web application, including the use of load balancers (HTTP/S), application servers, databases, and **content delivery networks** (**CDNs**) to ensure high availability and performance

- **Architecting a cloud data lake:** Designing a data lake architecture using cloud storage solutions (e.g., Amazon S3, Google GCS) to store, process, and analyze large volumes of data from various sources in real time (i.e., Dataflow, Kinesis Data Streams)

Cloud architecture components

Cloud architecture comprises several essential components that collectively form the foundation for designing and implementing cloud-based solutions:

- Frontend
- Backend
- Cloud delivery model
- Network (fabric)

In the realm of cloud services, network architects must think about the process of an end user requesting something and obtaining that result from start to finish. An example is a person watching a video on a media platform. That user may want to watch a video, upload a video, or search for a video. The end results would be finding a video to watch, successfully uploading a video, or browsing search results, respectively.

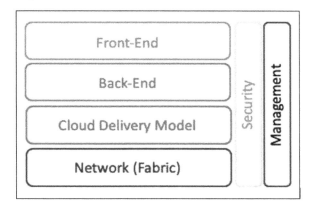

Figure 9.5 – Cloud architecture components

Let's discuss the architectural components.

Frontend

The frontend has two important inferences: the *client side* and the *cloud side*. The client side refers to the user interface of a cloud application, such as a desktop application, web browser, or mobile app. The cloud side refers to the demarcation where a user's request (query) is initially received before interfacing with the actual application. This frontend is usually a public IP hosted on services such as a load balancer (HTTP/S, TCP, SSL), NAT gateway, API gateway, or an appliance (i.e., firewall).

Backend

The backend is responsible for processing user requests, managing data, and performing various computations. These are applications, services, and storage.

Cloud delivery model

The cloud delivery model is how the architecture will be delivered. This is either IaaS, PaaS, or SaaS (see *Cloud computing models*).

Network (fabric)

The network, or fabric, as I like to call it, connects the frontend(s) to the backend, facilitating sending data back and forth. The fabric can be a combination of the internet, intranet, private lines, virtual paths, service points, and middleware.

Designing

Designing in the cloud shares some common principles with on-premises architecture, but there are also significant differences to consider. When designing for the cloud, it's essential to strike a balance between leveraging the advantages of cloud computing and addressing its unique challenges. Here's a comparison of designing in the cloud versus on-premises, along with key considerations:

Similarities:

- **Fundamental design principles**: Both on-premises and cloud architectures adhere to fundamental design principles such as scalability, reliability, security, and performance. These principles are essential for ensuring that applications and systems meet their objectives.

- **Application architecture**: The overall architecture of applications, including the separation of frontend and backend components, remains similar whether deployed on-premises or in the cloud. Functional requirements, user experience, and business logic drive the architecture.

Differences:

- **Resource provisioning**: In the cloud, resource provisioning is more dynamic and flexible. Cloud architects can provision virtual servers, databases, storage, and networking resources on demand, often through self-service portals or automation scripts. In contrast, on-premises environments require more manual and time-consuming resource provisioning and hardware procurement.

- **Scalability**: Cloud computing allows for *elastic scalability*, enabling resources to scale up or down automatically in response to demand. This scalability is often not as easily achievable in traditional on-premises data centers, where scaling may involve purchasing and configuring additional hardware.

- **Resource management**: Cloud environments require different resource management practices. Architects must manage cloud resources using cloud-specific tools and adhere to cloud provider best practices. In contrast, on-premises environments require management using traditional IT infrastructure management tools.

- **Network design**: Network design in the cloud involves virtual networks, subnets, and security groups, which differ from the physical network design typical of on-premises environments. Cloud architects must understand cloud networking concepts and services such as VPCs or **virtual networks** (**VNets**).

- **Security**: While the *fundamental* principles of security remain consistent between on-premises and cloud environments, there are notable differences and considerations that make cloud security unique. These include the shared fate model, IAM controls, and data encryption.

Considerations:

- **Cost optimization**: Cloud resources have associated costs, and architects must design for *cost optimization*. This includes selecting the right resource types, managing resource lifecycles, and implementing cost-control strategies.

- **Data management**: Designing for data storage, backup, and recovery in the cloud requires careful consideration of storage options, data transfer costs, and data integrity.

- **Proprietary solutions**: Some cloud services *may be* proprietary, making migration to another provider or on-premises challenging. Consider other strategies to mitigate associated risks (i.e., multi-cloud or hybrid cloud).

- **Monitoring and performance**: Implement robust monitoring and performance optimization practices to ensure your cloud architecture meets performance expectations while staying cost-efficient.

- **Compliance, governance, and data privacy**: Address regulatory and data privacy requirements specific to your industry and region when designing in the cloud. Cloud providers offer tools and services to help with compliance.

Let's look back at the example from the beginning of this section of designing and architecting a media platform, in which we must design and architect a media platform so that users can upload a video, watch a video, and search for a video.

First, let's look at the requirements:

- The ability to upload a video (write)

- The ability to view a video (read)

- The ability to search for a video

From a design standpoint, a user must have a way (from their endpoint or user interface) to initially upload a video to a storage location, after which it will be encoded into different file formats. From there, it is stored in another storage repository (a bucket).

When the video is uploaded, the information about the video must be stored in a searchable service.

The video must be formatted, aside from the resolution, to support efficiency when viewing. In other words, users shouldn't have to wait for the entire video to be downloaded to watch.

Also, the design and architecture should meet these **non-functional requirements (NFRs)**:

- Scalability
- High availability
- Security

Not much to ask for, right? Let's see what this architecture would look like.

> **Note**
> There are many videos on YouTube that relate to this kind of cloud (system) design for media platforms. I recommend watching them to get a better understanding of how it's done.

Let's try and architect this:

Video upload

First, a user uploads a video from their device to a storage location. How is that accomplished? A user has an application (client-side frontend) on their device that allows them to send a video (say, a .mp4 1080p format).

The design question is: what storage location should the video be uploaded to?

The answer is an object storage location, as it can store large amounts of data regardless of its structure. So, the video will be uploaded (write) to a storage bucket (raw video) via the cloud-side frontend, which will be an API GW (*Figure 9.6*). The video sent will also include the description and other information about the video.

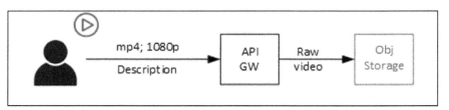

Figure 9.6 – User uploading a video to object storage

Once the video hits the storage bucket, a design question should be asked: "how should the video be encoded? It should support variable formats".

Also consider the following:

"The description and additional information should be captured for searching ability for users and respond fast.."

Considering these two design aspects, the architecture should include an encoding application, which will convert the raw video to the desired streaming options. So, after the video hits the initial object storage location, it is then sent to an encoder application where it's encoded to several resolution formats (720p, 960p, 1080p) so it can be viewed on different platforms.

Also, the description information (metadata) is stored in a searchable database service, such as Elasticsearch (*Figure 9.7*).

> **Note**
> Elasticsearch is a free, open source, real-time search and analytics engine. For more information, visit https://www.elastic.co/elasticsearch/.

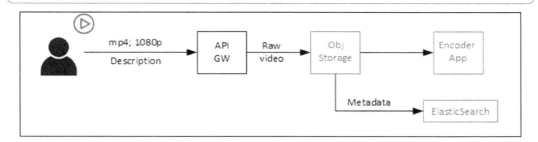

Figure 9.7 – Raw video sent for encoding and metadata sent to Elasticsearch

The next design question to ask is "Should these two actions run one after the other or in parallel?"

They should be run in parallel. Using a step function is one way to kick off these workflows once triggered by (raw) content delivered to the initial object storage (*Figure 9.8*).

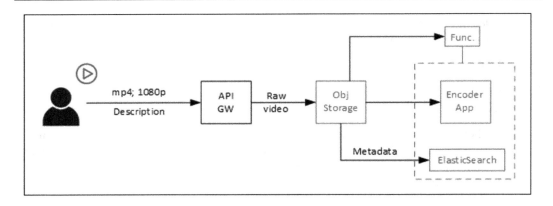

Figure 9.8 – Step function triggered to run the processes in parallel

Once the workflows are in progress, the encoder will process the raw video into the different formats and then store them in another object storage bucket:

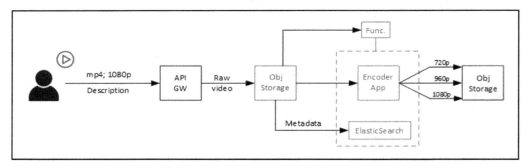

Figure 9.9 – Encoding application sends the formatted video to object storage

This takes care of the upload (write) of the video.

Now we'll go over searching for and viewing (read) the video.

Searching for a video

Once a user opens a web browser to reach the media platform, they are presented with a web page, which is pulled from a storage bucket behind the cloud-side frontend. In this case, it will be a load balancer.

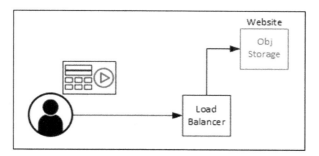

Figure 9.10 – User retrieves media platform web page

To search for a video, the user will make an API request based on input parameters, such as keywords, titles, names, and so on. The load balancer will forward the request to an API GW, which will then trigger another function to query the search database (Elasticsearch) and provide the results to the user:

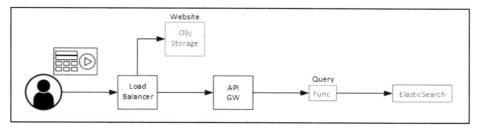

Figure 9.11 – User sends a query for a video

Once a user decides on the video they want to watch, another API request for that video will occur. Similar to the request for searching for a video, the request will make its way to the API GW, then a function to retrieve the video from its object storage location will be presented to the user for viewing.

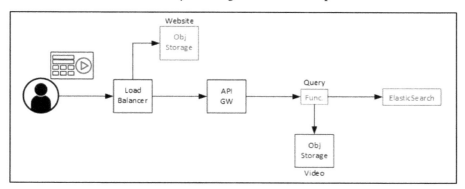

Figure 9.12 – User requests video after search

There's a design consideration to take into account: content should be stored closer to the end user to improve availability and performance.

If a video is stored in Europe and users in NYC want to view it, after the initial retrieval, must every user perform the same operation and incur latency as multiple requests are being made?

To alleviate performance and availability concerns, a CDN service is used (*Figure 9.17*):

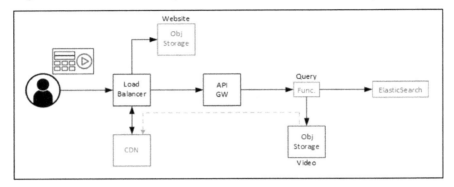

Figure 9.13 – Video is stored in CDN for performance and availability

So, the end-to-end architecture will look something like this:

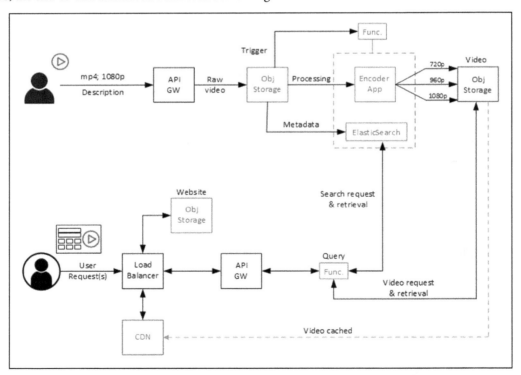

Figure 9.14 – End-to-end architecture for a video- viewing platform

Let's now address the NFR requirements:

- **Scalability**: Scalability is addressed by using the *auto-scaling* features of the services in use (i.e., encoding services, step functions, API GW, load balancers).

- **High availability**: High availability is achieved by deploying applications and storage buckets in different zones and regions for replication, backup, and DR purposes to the cloud provider specifications, and the deployment of CDNs for local caches in regions.

> **Note**
> Cloud providers offer continuous data replication. However, it's the user's responsibility to manage replication and availability across regions.

- **Security**: Security is achieved through various methods:

  - Users are authenticated using an identity service, such as Active Directory (Azure), Cognito (AWS), IAM (GCP), or Okta

  - Security of data in transit is accomplished through TLS, as well as API authentication (OAuth)

  - Security of data at rest is accomplished via encryption techniques such as KMS

  - Security in service communications is done through service accounts with permission to perform the required tasks

The complete end-to-end architecture looks like this:

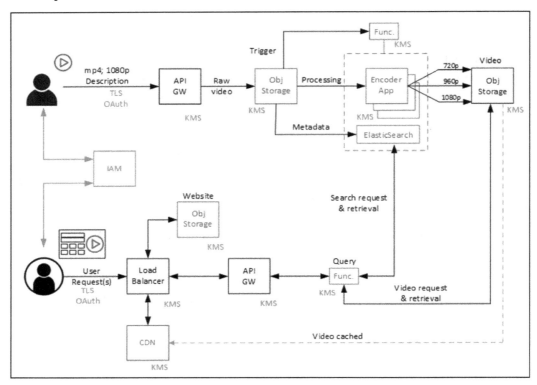

Figure 9.15 – Complete end-to-end architecture for a media platform

In the context of designing and architecting cloud solutions, these unique offerings of cloud computing greatly impact the way businesses approach technology. Designing in the cloud offers scalability, flexibility, and agility, which are not always achievable in traditional on-premises environments. Unlike on-premises setups, network architects can leverage a wealth of cloud-native services, including serverless computing, managed databases, and AI tools, which can simplify development and reduce operational overhead.

However, it requires architects (network) to adapt to cloud-specific technologies, consider cost implications, and leverage cloud-native services effectively to maximize the benefits of cloud computing while addressing its unique challenges.

What does it mean for a network architect?

The previous few sections discussed aspects of cloud computing, its services, design, architecting, and relative benefits. At this point, the following question must be answered:

What does it mean for a network architect?

As I mentioned before, it's adopting a cloud-focused mindset.

For a network architect, the paradigm shift from on-premises infrastructure to the cloud represents a profound transformation in their role and responsibilities. It means embracing virtualization, software-defined networking, and cloud-specific technologies to design, implement, and manage network architectures that are agile, scalable, and secure in the cloud environment.

The core principles of *networking*, such as routing, switching, security, and load balancing, still apply in the cloud, but their implementation and management take on new dimensions. Network architects must become adept at configuring virtual services (i.e., networks, security groups, and access controls) in cloud environments. They need to understand how to establish secure and efficient connections between on-premises data centers and the cloud, often using VPNs or dedicated network links.

Moreover, this transition means adopting shifts toward automation, agility, and scalability. **Infrastructure as Code (IaC)** becomes a key concept, as network configurations are defined and managed through code, allowing for automated provisioning and changes. The cloud's elasticity means that network architects must design for scalability, enabling networks to expand or contract on demand to meet fluctuating workloads.

Network architects must adapt to a world where physical hardware is *abstracted* and network configurations become code. It also involves a shift from a hardware-centric mindset to a more software-centric and automation-focused approach. This transition challenges network architects to not only master cloud networking concepts but also to collaborate closely with cross-functional teams, including cloud architects, security experts, DevOps teams, and application developers, to ensure that the network aligns seamlessly with the organization's cloud strategy and business objectives.

Preparing for the paradigm shift

Preparing for the paradigm shift from on-premises to cloud or hybrid environments as a network architect involves a combination of education (see *Chapter 11*), practical experience, and mindset adjustments. Here are essential steps to prepare effectively:

- **Cloud knowledge and training**: Invest in cloud-focused training and certifications from leading cloud providers (e.g., AWS, Azure, Google Cloud) to gain a solid understanding of cloud fundamentals, services, and networking offerings.
- **Understand your organization's goals**: Align your cloud networking strategy with the organization's broader goals, whether it's cost savings, scalability, global expansion, or digital transformation.

- **Master cloud networking concepts**: Learn about cloud-specific networking concepts such as VPCs, subnets, security groups, tags, labels, API GWs, load balancers, and CDNs.

- **Hybrid cloud expertise**: Understand how to connect on-premises data centers with cloud environments using technologies such as VPNs, direct/dedicated connections, and partner peering.

- **Security and compliance**: Gain expertise in cloud security practices, including **identity and access management (IAM)**, encryption, and compliance with industry-specific regulations.

- **Automation skills**: Develop scripting and IaC skills to automate network provisioning, configuration, and scaling.

- **Scalability design**: Learn how to design network architectures that can scale horizontally and vertically to accommodate varying workloads and application demands.

- **Cost optimization**: Familiarize yourself with cost management tools and practices to monitor and optimize cloud networking costs, including data transfer charges.

- **Collaboration and soft skills**: Enhance communication and collaboration skills to work effectively with cross-functional teams, including cloud architects, DevOps, and security experts.

- **Hands-on experience**: Set up personal cloud environments for practical experience and conduct pilot projects or proofs of concept to apply theoretical knowledge.

- **Stay updated**: Cloud technology evolves rapidly, so stay informed about the latest developments, services, and best practices by attending webinars, conferences, and industry forums.

- **Mentorship and peer networking**: Seek mentorship from experienced cloud architects or network architects who have made a similar transition. Connect with peers for insights and support.

- **Practice continuous learning**: Recognize that learning is an ongoing process. Cloud technology continually evolves, and staying up to date is essential for success.

Summary

The shift toward cloud-centric design and architecture presents both challenges and opportunities for network architects. Network architects must adapt to this changing paradigm by acquiring cloud-specific skills and knowledge. They need to transition from a *hardware-centric* approach to one that emphasizes virtualization, software-defined networking, and cloud-native services. Cloud architecture requires a deep understanding of cloud providers' offerings and services, as well as a keen focus on optimizing cost, security, and performance in dynamic, elastic environments.

The role of a network architect becomes more strategic as they design global, interconnected networks that leverage the cloud's capabilities for scalability and redundancy. It's a transformative journey, and network architects who embrace the cloud can play a vital role in driving innovation, enhancing flexibility, and ensuring the success of organizations in the cloud-first era.

In the next chapter, we'll explore how to prepare for certifications to take that next step in advancing to a role as a network architect, as well as how to crack those interview questions when they're presented to you.

Further reading

To learn more about the topics that were covered in this chapter, take a look at the following resources:

- *Why should network engineers leverage automation?:* https://www.nexuminc.com/nexum-at-red-hat-summit/

- *Advantages of cloud computing:* https://thevirtualassist.net/cloud-infrastructure-cloud-computing-advantages-types-examples/

- *Designing cloud computing:* https://www.linkedin.com/advice/0/how-can-you-design-cloud-skills-cloud-computing

- *Cloud architecture:* https://cloud.google.com/learn/what-is-cloud-architecture#section-3

- *CSP comparison:* https://cloud.google.com/docs/get-started/aws-azure-gcp-service-comparison

- *Developer cheat sheet:* https://googlecloudcheatsheet.withgoogle.com/log-in?referer=/architecture

Part 4 – Mastering the Craft: Advancing Your Journey as a Network Architect

The path to becoming a proficient network architect is as rewarding as it is challenging. It demands not only a solid foundation in technical knowledge but also a continuous effort to stay ahead in a rapidly evolving field. This section is dedicated to guiding you through the final stages of this journey, focusing on the preparation for certification exams, the cultivation of essential interpersonal skills, and the continuous learning process through recommended literature. As you delve into these chapters, you will gain insights into not only securing your position as a network architect but also excelling and continuously evolving in your role.

This section has the following chapters:

- *Chapter 10, Preparing for Certifications and Cracking the Job Interview*
- *Chapter 11, The Skills to Become a Better Network Architect and Overcome Daily Challenges*
- *Chapter 12, Additional Information and Recommended Books*

10

Preparing for Certifications and Cracking the Job Interview

So far, we've discussed many topics, from what is a network architect, to how a network is vital to an organization. This chapter will focus on preparing for certifications, and which ones are more favorable than others.

There are many IT certifications published by many IT solution providers and vendors. Picking the right one can be challenging at first. But once you formulate a plan that is applicable to your career advancement, current position responsibilities, industry outlook, and industry skill-set requirements, then it will be much easier to decide on the certification route you want to take.

I'd like for you to keep in mind that getting or becoming certified is only one aspect of becoming a network architect. I've come across many people in the industry with over 30 years of experience without any IT certification pursuant who are fine in their role. In today's world, it is a must-have if you want to advance.

In this chapter, we're going to cover the following main topics:

- Network architects' certification path
- Preparing for certifications
- How to crack interview questions
- Sample questions

Let's get started!

Network architects' certification path

Developing a path to becoming a network architect can be challenging on its own. It takes a tremendous amount of effort, time, and, above all else, discipline. Sometimes, experience alone may not be enough. But being certified can help establish credibility with employers (and future ones), clients, and the job market that you have the skills, (and a certain level of knowledge), necessary to perform duties above and beyond your current role. In addition, you're establishing yourself as a forward thinker and an individual willing to go that *extra mile* to pursue skills to maintain your relevancy and advance your career path.

> **Note**
>
> By being certified, you can potentially increase your salary by up to $13K: `https://www.dice.com/career-advice/how-much-will-certifications-skills-boost-your-pay`.

I'm sure there are many people reading this book who are either in the intermediate stage of their IT career or have substantial time thus far, meaning between 5 and 8 years' experience in IT. That doesn't mean those with fewer than 5 years won't benefit, as well. Those with 5-8 years' experience may or not have any certifications, and if they do, some may have active certifications or they may have expired.

In the next section, we'll be discussing IT networking certifications that, in my opinion, are critical for your advancement or your pursuit of becoming a network architect. So, we'll discuss the following:

- Foundational certifications
- Professional certifications
- Expert certifications
- Design expert certifications
- Miscellaneous certification and others
- Continued education

> **Note**
>
> If you already have foundational IT certifications, you may continue on to the *Professional certifications* section.

Foundational certifications

I believe, as with anything in life – such as building a home, designing a modern car, building a skyscraper, or even a business – it comes down to having a solid foundation and understanding the basics. It's the basics that provide you with that platform (support) to help you build and move forward.

Some foundational certifications worth pursuing, if not already achieved, are as follows:

- **CompTIA Network+**: This certification is great to pursue *if* you're looking to build confidence in your ability to become an IT networking certified professional. I personally took this certification, and it helped me gain confidence in taking the **Cisco Certified Network Associate (CCNA)** exam. More importantly, it provided me with the knowledge – 50% of what I needed to take the CCNA exam. In other words, CompTIA Network+ shortened the time needed to pursue the CCNA certification:

  `https://www.comptia.org/certifications/network`

- **CompTIA Security+**: Another certification by CompTIA to give you a baseline understanding of security with respect to enterprise networks. Once you're certified, you should be able to assess enterprise security, recommend solutions, monitor and secure cloud infrastructure, operate in compliance with policies and principles of governance, and respond to security incidents:

  `https://www.comptia.org/certifications/security`

- **CCNA**: The CCNA certification is a must-have for anyone pursuing a network architect's role. This certification will allow you to understand the fundamentals of networking, switching, routing, and wireless/mobility. Cisco is *the* global leader in networking since its inception, and it is the global leader in networking certifications. In my opinion, this is the flagship fundamental network certification.

> **Note**
>
> As of this writing, Cisco still holds the largest market share in IT networking infrastructure at 41%: `https://www.cisco.com/c/en/us/training-events/training-certifications/certifications/associate/ccna.html`

- **Linux Foundation Certified IT Associate (LFCA)**: Though this certification relates more to system administrators than network architects, keep in mind that all routing and switching platforms, and even the cloud, are built on some variant of Linux.

  Having knowledge and having a bit of expertise in Linux is not a bad thing:

  `https://training.linuxfoundation.org/certification/certified-it-associate/`

Professional certifications

Intermediate certification is a validation of your experience as you tackle daily activities and routines. At this point, you're a professional in your role, taking on more complex tasks and duties. Now, you need a professional-level certification to go along with it. Furthermore, it aligns with your future endeavors as you progress toward becoming a network architect and specializing in a specific technology.

With intermediate certifications, you begin to foster specializations in different areas of IT, as well as with networking. Some recommended certifications pursuant to becoming a network architect are as follows:

- **Cisco Certified Network Professional (CCNP)**: This certification validates a person's ability to plan, implement, verify, and troubleshoot local- and wide-area enterprise networks. It covers advanced routing and switching, security, wireless, and collaboration technologies.

  Just as with the CCNA, the CCNP certification is the flagship certification as you continue your networking journey. Many specializations fall under the CCNP umbrella, such as the following:

  - **Enterprise**
  - **Data Center**
  - **Security**
  - **Collaboration**
  - **Service Provider**

  The **CCNP Enterprise** certification is predominantly for infrastructure fabric design and solutions and is the standard route after passing the CCNA exam. After passing this certification, specializing in another CCNP track is often recommended:

  ```
  https://www.cisco.com/c/en/us/training-events/training-
  certifications/certifications/professional.html
  ```

> **Note**
>
> As of 2022, the CCNA certification is no longer considered a requirement for taking any CCNP certification track exam.

- **VMware Certified Professional - Data Center Network Virtualization (VCP-NV)**: For anyone pursuing to become a network architect, understanding virtualization is critical. Though organizations may have older (legacy) software and applications running on physical servers (called bare metal), the vast majority of their software and applications are running on **virtual machines (VMs)** in hypervisor environments.

  This hypervisor environment is the same as legacy ones, just in a software-defined aspect to better use the underlying hardware and resources. Even though the workloads are now virtualized, they still require networking to reach other workloads and systems outside their hypervisor environments. VMware is a global leader in this space. Having the VCP-NV certification will equip you with extending the physical network design to the virtualized network design to create an end-to-end network solution for an organization's critical software and applications.

  ```
  https://www.vmware.com/learning/certification/vcp-nv-nsxt.html
  ```

> **Note**
>
> Coupling VMware's VCP-NV with their VCP-DCV certification might be worth mentioning to bring the complete virtualization view together, though you won't necessarily be troubleshooting vSphere infrastructure:
>
> `https://www.vmware.com/content/vmware/vmware-published-sites/us/learning/certification/vcp-dcv.html.html`

- **Certified Information Systems Security Professional (CISSP)**: This certification is not specific to networking but covers a wide range of IT security topics, including network security, access control, and cryptography.

  Though it's not networking specific, having a CISSP certification will allow you to know how to design and solve problems to meet strict security requirements set forth by the organization. It will help in having conversations with security professionals who are required to provide the security measures to enforce compliance, **disaster recovery** (**DR**) and backup strategies, data prevention and loss, **confidentiality/integrity/availability** (**CIA**), and more:

  `https://www.isc2.org/Certifications/CISSP`

- **Kubernetes and Cloud Native Associate (KCNA)**: As you may know, over the last several years, there have been considerable developments in the open source community concerning the representation of workloads on the network fabric. Just as virtualization maximizes server hardware resources, containers maximize VM and hardware resources even further.

  Containers allow workloads and applications to have precisely what they need to operate – nothing more. In doing so, containers can scale (spun up or spun down) from one IT environment to another without losing integrity.

  KCNA is a professional certification offered by the **Cloud Native Computing Foundation** (**CNCF**). It validates the skills and knowledge in configuring and managing the network architecture for Kubernetes clusters.

  Although the KCNA certification is more focused on the cloud native ecosystem, open source community does reside in the data centers. Today's network architects should pursue the KCNA to increase their organizational value:

  `https://training.linuxfoundation.org/certification/kubernetes-cloud-native-associate/`

> **Note**
>
> As of this writing, I am pursuing the KCNA certification as well as the **Kubernetes Certified Administrator** (**CKA**) certification: `https://training.linuxfoundation.org/certification/certified-kubernetes-administrator-cka/`.

- **Cloud Solutions Architect Associate certifications**: As IT evolves rapidly, our perspective on networking architecture should also be. Organizations are evaluating cloud opportunities to reduce costs in different ways. It's a paradigm from traditional viewing of the network and its importance. As such, network architects should evaluate options to design networks in this new paradigm.

There are many cloud certifications out on the market. I'll list the Big Three that are most important in the direction you may want to take. Though some names include *Associate*, these certifications are more of an intermediary certificate, like the others mentioned:

- **AWS Certified Solution Architect – Associate**
  `https://aws.amazon.com/certification/certified-solutions-architect-associate/?ch=tile&tile=getstarted`

- **AWS Certified Advanced Networking – Specialty**
  `https://aws.amazon.com/certification/certified-advanced-networking-specialty/?ch=tile&tile=getstarted`

- **AWS Certified Solutions Architect – Professional**
  `https://aws.amazon.com/certification/certified-solutions-architect-professional/?ch=sec&sec=rmg&d=1`

- Google's **Professional Cloud Architect** certification
  `https://cloud.google.com/certification/cloud-architect`

- Google's **Professional Cloud Engineer** certification
  `https://cloud.google.com/certification/cloud-network-engineer`

- **Microsoft Certified: Azure Network Engineer Associate**
  `https://learn.microsoft.com/en-us/certifications/azure-network-engineer-associate/`

Note

There are other networking professional certifications, such as Arista's **Arista Cloud Engineering (ACE)**, **Juniper Networks Certified Professional** (JNCIP), and Huawei, HPE, and Aruba certifications. These are more specific to those networking platforms and more niche versus being universally recognized. For example, having a CCNP certification will get you a position designing an Arista network, while the reverse may not happen.

Expert certifications

As you progress as a network architect, you must continue to enhance the depth and breadth of your knowledge base and the ability to communicate effectively with your peers, subordinates, and upper management, along with making decisions for the organization's overall vision.

Expert-level certifications are essential for network architects because they demonstrate their in-depth knowledge and expertise in networking technologies, which is critical for designing and implementing complex network architectures.

There are several reasons to obtain an expert-level certification, including the following:

- Demonstrate advanced skills
- Enhance your credibility
- Increase earning potential

Some recommended expert-level certifications are as follows:

- **Cisco Certified Internetwork Expert (CCIE)**: This highly respected and challenging certification validates a person's expert-level skills in routing and switching. It covers various networking technologies, including routing and switching, security, wireless, data centers, and **service providers (SPs)**. The CCIE is considered the *gold standard* of all networking certifications.

  I have yet to encounter any other certification that is as intense, demanding, and challenging as the CCIE practical portion of the certificate. Once you've attained this credential, you'll be well-respected by your peers and colleagues. There are various CCIE tracks or specializations:

  - **Enterprise Infrastructure** (formerly **Routing and Switching**)
  - **Data Center**
  - **Collaboration**
  - **Wireless**
  - **Security**
  - **Service Provider**

  Each is designed for network architects who want to pursue that particular vertical in the IT industry or within an organization. For example, a **CCIE Service Provider** certification is designed for someone seeking a network architect role at a CSP/ISV/Telco. Each track requires you to pass a written exam and an 8-hour practical (hands-on) lab at a designated Cisco location:

  ```
  https://www.cisco.com/c/en/us/training-events/training-
  certifications/certifications/expert.html
  ```

Design expert certifications

Some vendors developed design expert certifications to take the expert certification a step further. From the name itself, you will have to go in front of a board or panel of other design experts and dissertate (defend) a particular network design you designed or take an 8-hour online/8-hour scenario-based exam. In some respect, these are considered, in my opinion, the PhD of IT certifications. (At one point, Cisco's CCIE was considered the PhD of IT.)

To date, only two design expert certifications have come to mind for network architects to pursue to develop further and enhance their credibility in the industry. However, these certifications require you to have substantial time in the industry (10+ years), design various architectures, have experience on the organization's business side, have pre-sales experience across multiple verticals, have depth in industry technologies and trends, and have a theoretical perspective.

These two are as follows:

- **Cisco Certified Design Expert (CCDE)**: The certification validates your expert-level skills in network design principles, including designing scalable, secure, and resilient networks, but also addresses business use cases and demands of an organization. It covers many topics, including routing and switching, security, network management, and network services, including cloud services.

  Ironically, there are no prerequisites besides taking its written exam, as with the CCIE:

  `https://learningnetwork.cisco.com/s/ccde-design-expert`

- **VMware Certified Design Expert - Network Virtualization (VCDX-NV)**: This certification validates a person's expert-level skills in designing, implementing, and troubleshooting VMware NSX-based network virtualization solutions. It covers advanced network virtualization concepts, design methodologies, and troubleshooting techniques.

  This certification requires you to have the VCP-NV certification, earn or have the VCIX-NV certification, review a blueprint, select and build a design based on that blueprint, submit an application, and pass the application and design review process:

  `https://www.vmware.com/learning/certification/vcdx-nv.html`

Both of these certifications are challenging. They require significant time, experience (theory and practical), dedication, patience, and preservation to achieve. To date, I have not encountered anyone who has achieved this on their first attempt.

Miscellaneous certifications and others

There are a few certifications that fall under the category of miscellaneous certifications. While not all will be relevant to every network architect, they're still worth mentioning. These are vendor-specific, which means it's worth obtaining if your organization has a substantial investment from these vendors.

Some that fall under this category and may be of importance are as follows:

- **Arista Cloud Engineer (ACE)**: Arista now offers a tiered cloud certification – from entry-level (L1) to expert (L6). These certifications validate the skills required to operate Arista's network operating system (**Extensible Operating System**, or **EOS**), automation, and cloud networking solutions.

- **Juniper Networks Certified Internet Expert (JNCIE)**: This certification validates expert-level knowledge in Juniper network technologies, including design, configuration, and troubleshooting.

- **Palo Alto Networks Certified Network Security Engineer (PCNSE)**: This certification validates expertise in designing, deploying, configuring, and managing Palo Alto Networks' security solutions.

- **F5 Certified Solution Expert (F5-CSE)**: Expert-level certification that validates the mastery of advanced concepts and skills required to design, deploy, and manage complex F5 solutions, including multi-domain and multi-cloud environments.

- **Certified Kubernetes Administrator (CKA)**: Demonstrates the ability to do basic installation as well as configuring and managing production-grade Kubernetes clusters.

Other vendors' certifications worth mentioning are as follows:

- Huawei
- **Certified Wireless Network Professional (CWNP)** (CWNE Wi-Fi Expert)
- Nutanix
- Aruba Networks
- Check Point
- F5

Here is a diagram depicting my view on networking certification related to its relevancy and difficulty in the industry:

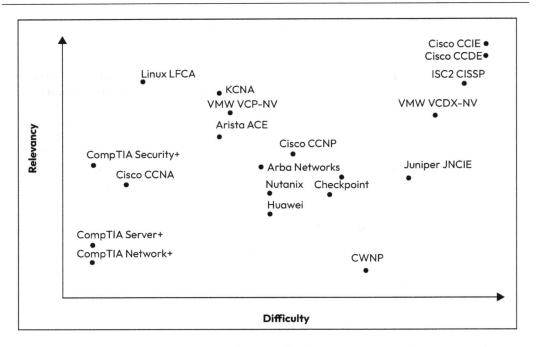

Figure 10.1 – Networking certification difficulty versus industry relevancy

Continued education

Almost all network certifications – generally, for that matter – have a lifespan of 3 years, which means you'll be required to recertify before their expiration. With other certifications, such as the Cisco CCIE, CCDE, and the ISC² CISSP, you may recertify by completing continuing education credits throughout your current certification time frame.

Part of the reason to recertify every 3 years is that technology/concepts change rapidly. Technology is constantly evolving, and new updates and features are released regularly as new ones are introduced – others will have to be deprecated or removed altogether.

The IT ecosystem is ever-changing, and as such, so are the certifications' requirements. As an IT professional, recertifying ensures that you stay current with the latest technological developments, maintain specific standards, continue developing your skills, and demonstrate your expertise in the industry.

In the next section, we'll discuss how to prepare for the certification exams.

Preparing for certifications

Throughout my IT career, I've taken over 100+ exams, from scantronic, bubble-in, computer-based, and of course, hands-on practical. A few questions that I'm often asked are these:

How do you prepare for your IT exams?

How do you study?... Any techniques used?...

Although these questions may be simple, they aren't easy to explain. It's a paradigm shift from what we were taught, or probably not taught directly, as children growing up. While we were in school, we were told, "Open your book to page...and read for 20 minutes quietly." When we got home, our parents would say, "Go to your room and study... your exam is tomorrow...", and we would go and read our book or notes. But is that studying?

Thus far, I have come up with several techniques worth mentioning for those looking for new or better ways of studying and preparing for your IT exam(s). As a matter of fact, for any studying, you may follow these.

Create an environment only used for studying

This may sound like a no-brainer, but only a few know what it means. Studying is similar to having a job or performing a task. For example: Would you wash dishes on the dining-room table? Would a doctor operate in a dusty closet? Well, the same holds true for studying.

Create an environment in your home designated for study-related activities. It must have all the items/tools/essentials required for you to accomplish your objective. This environment must be used and *only* used for this intended purpose. Things that should be in this environment include the following:

- A desk
- A reading lamp or lamps
- Pens, pencils, or highlighters
- Blank paper
- A computer or laptop
- Earplugs*
- Computer speakers*
- Noise-canceling headphones*
- A comfortable desk chair
- A timer*

In some respects, studying is a job in its own right. Having a suitable place designated for that will make you feel more comfortable and relaxed while focusing on your study-related endeavors.

Items that are recommended for studying, as discussed in the next sections

> **Note**
>
> Some places not considered good candidates for a study environment, although they may seem comfortable, are bedrooms and beds, floors, couches, and dining-room or kitchen tables.

Remove distractions

Again, this might sound like a no-brainer – but often, what we do subconsciously is put up with distractions as not being distractions, such as the television, music, other people talking, pets, pictures, external noises, and so on. We casually brush them off, but little do we know it has impeded our progress.

In this environment designated for studying, remove anything that might cause your mind to go off on a tangent. Items that should not be on your desk or in your immediate view are as follows:

- Pictures
- Trinkets and toys
- Phones and mobile phones
- Clocks
- Bills
- Drawings (not related to network architecture)
- Noise-related items
- Television/music
- Any items not related to what you are accomplishing
- Anything animated or moving

This is not an exhaustive list, but the intent is to eliminate as many distractions as possible to prevent your mind from wandering. Because an average person's attention span is about 30–45 minutes, *that* attention span time may be over 1 hour to 1 hour 15 minutes in total time if we begin to focus on other items versus our intended purpose.

Schedule your studying time

For anything we need to accomplish for ourselves daily – whether it's chores at home, meetings at work, DIY projects, or meeting someone – more often than not, we mark it in a daily calendar or build a schedule of activities for that day.

To ascertain your IT certification goals, you'll have to place them on your schedule or create a program for your studying activities. Creating a plan to study is vital for several reasons:

- **Helps with time management**: Allows you to organize your time effectively and prioritize your tasks and ensures that you are making the most of your available time and not wasting it on unproductive activities.

- **Increases productivity**: You're more likely to stay focused and motivated. As time progresses, you'll be able to get more done in less time and improve your overall productivity and efficient use of time.

- **Reduces stress**: Having a plan can help reduce the stress and anxiety that comes with trying to remember everything that needs to be done. A schedule provides a clear roadmap of what needs to be accomplished and when, thus reducing the feeling of being overwhelmed.

- **Improves learning outcomes**: By creating a schedule, you can break down large topics into smaller, more manageable pieces. This can help you better absorb and retain information, resulting in improved learning outcomes.

A key point with scheduling time to study is to allocate time consistently, not <u>randomly</u>. In other words – schedule the same *amount* of time, at the *same time* on the days you've designated for studying. For example, my current study schedule looks like this:

		Sunday	Monday	Tuesday	Wednesday	Thursday	Friday	Saturday
5pm	:00							
	:15							
	:30							
	:45							
6pm	:00							
	:15							
	:30							
	:45							
7pm	:00	Review						Review
	:15							
	:30							
	:45							
8pm	:00	Break	AWS SAP		AWS SAP		AWS SAP	Break
	:15							
	:30			GCP Net Eng		GCP Net Eng		
	:45							
9pm	:00		Break		Break		Break	
	:15		GCP Net Eng		GCP Net Eng		GCP Net Eng	
	:30			Break		Break		
	:45			AWS SAP		AWS SAP		
10pm	:00							
	:15		Break		Break		Break	
	:30							
	:45			Break		Break		
11pm	:00							
	:30							

Figure 10.2 – Example of study schedule

As you can see, my study schedule is clean, consistent, and concise. By doing this, you're training your mind to focus on studying at those designated times. From the plan, I can now dedicate and focus on the objectives I set for the times indicated.

Use earplugs, white/brown noise, or focus sounds

There are lots of distractions in our daily lives. Each one differs from person to person. To eliminate additional distractions, use earplugs.

Earplugs reduce external noise up to about 25 decibels. They aid in your concentration and create an isolated space where you are in your thoughts.

An aspect I've noticed when I use earplugs is a feeling of calmness.

If you're uncomfortable with earplugs, playing white/brown noise or focus sounds in the background through your PC/laptop speakers of your study area will not only reduce your mind from being distracted but will help you concentrate better.

> **Note**
> Music streaming services have playlists designed for studying. For example, Spotify's *Focus* genre is dedicated to this purpose.

Cone of Knowledge

The Cone of Knowledge is something I truly believe in. I came across this concept when I began in IT – to this day, I still use it. The Cone of Knowledge was developed by Edgar Dale in the 1940s, whereby his theory suggests that people retain information better when they encounter it multiple times and in different ways, as seen in his diagram here:

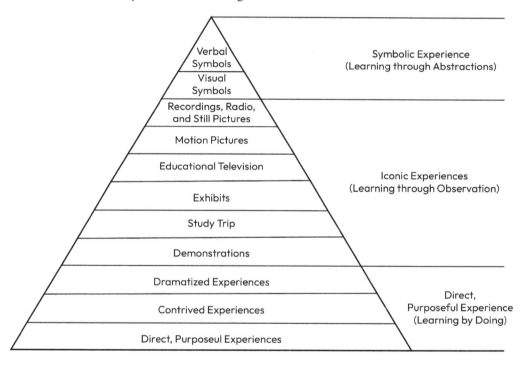

Figure 10.3 – Edgar Dale's diagram for the Cone of Knowledge (https://pressbooks. pub/lidtfoundations/chapter/edgar-dale-and-the-cone-of-experience/)

In other words – what we see, what we hear, and what we do (and a combination of them) affects a person's retention capabilities. A more familiar diagram would be this:

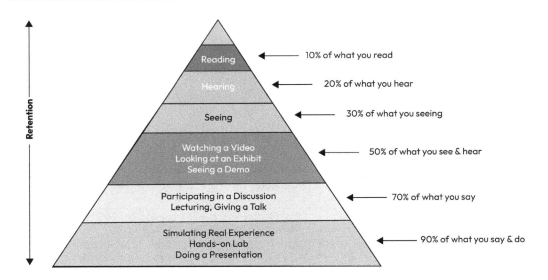

Figure 10.4 – More common view of the Cone of Knowledge

This concept is a great way to learn how to apply different aspects of the Cone of Knowledge to your studying aims. Good practice would be the following:

- **Highlight key concepts**: As you read, highlight important takeaways from the text (what you read and do).

- **Write in your own words**: After reading a paragraph or important topic, paraphrase that paragraph in your own words and say it aloud then put it on paper. By doing so, you're recalling from memory, which will aid your retention capabilities (what you say and do).

> **Note**
>
> As I was preparing for my CCIE certification, every study session, I would write out all of my configurations, while saying aloud on paper per device that I was going to configure that day. After that, I would throw the paper away. The next day, I would repeat the process. I incorporated all three aspects of the Cone of Knowledge – what I was seeing/reading, hearing, and doing. Going by the reference model, my retention was 210%!

Use a timer

You will not find this technique in any book. I came up with this technique one day while I was preparing for the CISSP exam in 2000. Time is something we cannot control; however, the *concept* of time we can! In essence, time is independent of time itself.

As I was studying one weekend afternoon, say 1 p.m., I would set an alarm for 2 p.m. No big deal, right? As the session progressed, I would glance at the time on the clock and get nervous or frustrated about how much I had covered in the time thus far, knowing 2 p.m. would be here soon. My mind would drift because 2 p.m. is midway through the afternoon, and I wanted to enjoy some semblance of the day—spending time outside, and so on. Anxiety has started to build, which is never good, especially for this exam.

The problem was the time moving from 1 p.m. to 2 p.m. Time was counting up and moving forward. The day continued, regardless of what I was doing. It became an emotional and psychological dilemma. I began to say the following:

> *Oh no! I only have 15 minutes left to complete...*

> *I can't cover that in 15 minutes...what am I going to do?*

When the next session began, I was already frustrated because of the previous session and didn't accomplish much. One day, while I was in my kitchen, I saw a food/cooking timer on the refrigerator. I stared at it, took it off the refrigerator, and began going through the functions. It was a *countdown* timer from 1 second to 24 hours. I said to myself the following:

> *I wonder if I can use this as opposed to an alarm?*

I tried it out and, well, the rest is history. I was able to feel more relaxed while studying. I wasn't concerned about *what time it was*. If the time was 1 p.m., 2 p.m., or 3:10 p.m, I was in a place where *my time* existed independently of *actual* time. There was no concept of a.m. or p.m. because the timer didn't care if it was a.m or p.m. If there were 15 mins left, 15 mins were left – end of discussion! Now, when I saw I had 15 mins left on the timer, my thoughts were the following:

> *I have 15 mins left. What more can I accomplish or do?*

> *I think I can finish in 15 mins. If not, I can cover it in the next session...*

The emotional and psychological dilemma was completely opposite – positive versus negative feelings, determined versus reluctant. Over (real) time, I became more efficient in utilizing this technique to get more accomplished in any given set period of time.

Note

For those starting out, I recommend starting at 30-minute intervals and then working your way up to 1-hour intervals.

Take breaks

This is quite simple but, simultaneously, recommended all the time. Taking breaks allows your mind to breathe again and decompress a little from the rigorous activity it just endured. However, it shouldn't be an opportunity to jump on social media, watch a movie, or begin a conversation with someone.

Taking a break is about immersing your mind in nothingness for a set time and collecting your thoughts. When taking a break, there are several things you can do:

- Close your eyes and recap what you just accomplished
- Stare at the room
- Look outside and at your surroundings
- Grab a beverage
- Anything else that is not over-stimulating

The idea is to refrain from engaging in anything detracting you from your thought collection.

Your study break should be between 8 and 15 minutes. No more or less. Too little will make you feel overwhelmed; too much will cause you to be unfocused and lose motivation to continue.

If you look at my example study schedule, I have a 15-min break after my first hour of studying on any given day. At that point, I leave my study area and sit somewhere else with my eyes closed and have my timer set for about 7 mins. After my timer goes off, I aimlessly look around until my break ends (setting my timer for the remaining time).

Training and study material

For whichever IT networking exam you're preparing for, there are lots of materials available, whether it's for training or studying. The determination of which material is the best is subjective. I would recommend several approaches:

- Do research on the study or training material specific to the IT exam you're preparing for
- Visit the company's certification website or portal to find recommended training and study material
- Speak to peers who've taken the certification and ask what they've used
- Visit online forums and discussion boards

Some resources to aid in your research are as follows:

- *Cisco*: `https://www.netacad.com/courses/networking`
- *VMware*: `https://www.vmware.com/learning.html`
- *Juniper*: `https://learningportal.juniper.net/juniper/default.aspx`
- *Arista*: `https://www.sdn-pros.com/training/`
- *Linux*: `https://training.linuxfoundation.org/full-catalog/`

- Online course vendors:

  - *Packt*: https://www.packtpub.com/search?query=networking

  - *Udemy*: https://www.udemy.com/courses/search/?src=ukw&q=IT+networking

  - *Coursera*: https://www.coursera.org/search?query=networking&

  - *LinkedIn Learning*: https://www.linkedin.com/learning

> **Note**
>
> Though most of the online training vendors require a subscription, from time to time they will offer free training courses. The same holds true for the individual vendors. See *Chapter 12* for more details.

Supplements and rest

Aside from choosing the certification path you want to take and the training/studying required in your undertaking, the next step in becoming a network architect – which is vitality necessary, in my opinion, above all else – is rest and having the correct supplements in your diet. If you're not sleeping well or getting enough rest, how can you concentrate or, better yet, stay awake to study? How can you generally function if you're not taking the correct supplements?

Adequate rest is essential for maintaining good physical and mental health, which can positively impact academic performance. When we sleep or take breaks (mentioned previously) from studying, our brain consolidates the information we've learned, making it easier to retrieve later.

Rest helps improve cognitive function, memory retention, and overall performance. Studying for IT networking exams and certifications can be mentally demanding; adequate rest can help prevent mental fatigue and improve focus and productivity.

Additionally, IT networks often require critical thinking and problem-solving skills; resting can help improve these skills.

> **Note**
>
> As a guiding rule, the average healthy adult needs about 7 hours of sleep per night. More information can be found at https://www.sleepfoundation.org/how-sleep-works/how-much-sleep-do-we-really-need.

There are several supplements that improve brain function and memory retention, as they claim to do, but it's important to note that the effectiveness of these supplements varies from person to person, and scientific evidence varies.

The most commonly used supplements I came across for brain function and memory include the following:

- **Omega-3 fatty acids**: Omega-3s are important for brain health and may help improve memory and cognitive function

- **B vitamins**: B vitamins, including vitamins B6, B9 (folic acid), and B12, play a crucial role in brain function and can help improve memory and cognitive function

- **Ginkgo biloba**: Ginkgo biloba is an herbal supplement that has been used for centuries to improve cognitive function and memory

- **Caffeine**: Caffeine is a stimulant that can improve alertness, attention, focus, and cognitive function, but it should be used in moderation

> **Note**
> I have used in some form a combination of the supplements listed. Just as with anything else, consult a doctor before trying anything new and use it in moderation or as prescribed on the label.

How to crack interview questions

Preparing for an IT networking technical interview can be challenging, but you can increase your chances of success with the right approach and preparation. Here are some tips to help you crack an IT networking technical interview:

- **Know the basics**: Make sure you have a solid understanding of networking fundamentals, such as the **Open Systems Interconnection (OSI)** model, the TCP/IP model, and standard networking protocols. Be prepared to explain these concepts in simple terms.

- **Understand the company's technology stack**: Research the company's technology stack, including the tools and technologies it uses. This element is often overlooked when interviewing with an organization. Researching the organization's needs will help you better understand what they are looking for and enable you to tailor your responses accordingly.

- **Review network architecture concepts**: Brush up on your knowledge of network architecture concepts, routing, switching, network security, and cloud computing—different technologies such as **Ethernet VPN (EVPN)**, **Virtual Extensible LAN (VXLAN)**, **Multi-Chassis Link Aggregation (MLAG)**, and other industry-neutral standards.

- **Practice common interview questions**: Review common interview questions for IT networking roles, and practice answering them. We'll review some in the next section.

- **Be prepared for technical challenges**: Some companies may include technical challenges as part of their interview process. Be prepared to demonstrate your technical skills, such as by troubleshooting network issues or configuring network devices, and the thought process involved.

- **Show off your problem-solving skills**: To complement technical skills, organizations are often looking for candidates who can solve problems and think creatively. You'll likely be asked to give examples of how you have solved complex problems in the past.

- **Demonstrate your communication skills**: Network architect roles often require strong communication skills. Prepare examples to discuss how you've communicated with colleagues and stakeholders in the past and how you've resolved conflicts or overcome communication challenges.

- **Stay up to date with industry trends and economic news**: Networking technology is constantly evolving, so make sure you stay up to date with the latest trends and developments. Follow industry news, blogs, whitepapers, and postings, and be prepared to discuss emerging technologies and how they may impact the company's network.

- **Confer with peers and colleagues who are either working or have worked with the organization**: Reach out to your peers, colleagues, or connections you may have at an organization to get a better understanding of what the organization is looking for. Gauge their perspective on what to do versus what not to do. Ask them the following:

  What is the company's culture?

  What's your impression of the organization thus far?

  Do you have any advice as I go through the interview process?

  Do you have or can you point me in the direction of resources I should be looking reviewing?

- **Know the audience**: Do some research on the person or persons you're interviewing with. Through the recruiter, you will be given the names of those interviewing you. Find out their role/position, get an understanding of what they do daily, and have questions prepared for them. When the interview concludes, you'll have the opportunity to ask your questions to these interviewers to show your interest in working for the company and with them.

> **Note**
>
> As you obtain the names of the interviewer(s), the recruiter will likely put in their LinkedIn profile for you to review. Take the time to look at their profile to gain a sense of who they are as well as their past experiences. It will aid in having engaging dialogue during the interview.

- **Ask questions**: At the end of the interview, ask the interviewer questions about the company, the team, and the role to show interest in the position and the company. Often overlooked are questions directed to the interviewer, such as the following:

  When did you start at the organization? What was it like for you coming in?

  What advice would you give someone new coming into the organization?

- **Interviewing practice**: When looking for real estate, the key is location, location, location. Interviewing is practice, practice, practice!

> **Note**
> Also, look at other job postings the organization may have to give you additional talking points during the interview process.

The next topic is sample questions you may come across during the interview process.

Sample questions

Interview questions can vary from interviewer to interviewer and company to company. Some organizations will prepare you for the interviews. Take Google Cloud, for example. Google will let you know from the first HR call you will have four interviews:

- A **Role-Related Knowledge (RRK)** interview
- A **General Cognitive Ability (GCA)** interview
- A Googleyness interview
- A panel interview

Others will have you speak to personnel as the interview process progresses.

Questions

Let's dive into some interview questions I've come across. I'll offer some suggestions on how to answer, but in all likelihood, you'll have to form your own answer/opinion:

1. *Can you explain how a packet moves across the network? In other words, how does a packet of data traverse the network from sender to receiver?*

    This question is a typical technical question at any level in your career. Most seasoned IT professionals, even I, would need help answering this question.

    It comes down to understanding how a data packet is broken down and the usage, ARP request, MAC tables, routing tables, and ARP flooding.

    Check out my *Walk like a Packet, Talk like a Packet* video: `https://www.youtube.com/watch?v=qIECIOj0chw&t=340s`

    It breaks down as follows:

    - **Packet creation**: The sender's device (such as a computer or a smartphone) breaks down the data it wants to send into smaller chunks called packets. Each packet contains a portion of the original data and additional information.

    - **Packet encapsulation**: Each packet is encapsulated with headers and trailers. The header includes the source and destination IP addresses, port numbers, and protocol information. The trailer contains error-checking codes for data integrity.

- **Routing**: The sender's device sends the packets into the local network, which could be a **local area network** (**LAN**) or a wireless network. The packets then start their journey toward the destination.

- **Switching**: Within the local network, packets are typically forwarded by network switches. These switches examine the destination MAC address in the packet's header and forward the packet to the appropriate port that leads closer to the destination.

- **Routing across networks**: If the destination is on a different network (such as sending data from your home network to a server on the internet), the packet is sent to a router. The router examines the destination IP address in the packet's header and determines the next hop toward the destination.

- **Internet backbone**: The packet travels through a series of routers, crossing various networks, until it reaches a router that is directly connected to the network where the destination device resides. This may involve passing through multiple **internet SPs** (**ISPs**) and their backbone networks.

- **Delivery to destination network**: Once the packet reaches the router connected to the destination network, the router forwards the packet to the appropriate switch within that network.

- **Delivery to destination device**: The switch delivers the packet to the destination device based on the MAC address in the packet's header. The destination device receives the packet and performs the necessary actions to reconstruct the original data.

It's important to note that the actual path taken by packets can vary due to network congestion, routing protocols, and network configurations. However, the general process remains consistent: packets are encapsulated, routed, switched, and delivered until they reach the intended destination.

2. *Can you tell me describe to me what happens when you go to a web address? In other words, what occurs as you make the web request, assuming you haven't visited the web URL before?*

   This question relates to what happens from a DNS resolution perspective. You'll have to explain what occurs after you hit *Enter/Return* on your keyboard. Explain what a URL is, what DNS is, and what the steps are in the DNS retrieval process.

   You can check out my blog related to DNS: `https://ahaliblogger.tech/my-name-is-dns-time-check-with-ntp-part-1/`.

3. *Can you tell me the difference between NAT, PAT, SNAT, and DNAT? And how are they used?*

   Can be easily answered. Speak on the definition and the devices they can be applied to.

4. *Can you describe the benefits of a Spine/Leaf architecture?*

   You'll have to go into detail about how a Spine/Leaf network design is better than the traditional 3-tier architecture Cisco made famous in the 1990s to 2005. Describe that on any given device they are no more than one hop away from their destination, with highly redundant backbone capacity.

5.   *When designing a network architecture, where is the best place to install an internet-facing firewall?*

Tricky question. The answer can be: *It depends...* But that is a good response for the interviewer. During an interview, the first thing is to ask clarifying questions. Good questions to ask are the following:

Is the firewall performing only handling inbound traffic?

Will NAT be performed on this firewall?

The idea is to defend your answer if you would do it that way.

6.   *Can you tell me a time when you disagreed with a colleague?*

This is an open-ended question. Here, no clarifying question is needed. But you can ask the following:

Does it matter about the topic?

Here, the interviewer wants to know how you would handle conflict. Have a few examples available to choose from.

7.   *Can you explain your experience in designing and implementing network architectures?*

Bring your experience from your current role. Explain what you have done and how it applies to the question. Give details on what you did, who you communicated with, why this design was effective, and how long it took to implement.

8.   *Can you walk me through the steps you would take to troubleshoot a network issue?*

All network-related issues are not necessarily the same, but the thought process may be. Don't assume it's between a server and the TOR. It may be application-related. Again, ask clarifying questions such as the following:

What kind of network issue was experienced?

Can you provide more details? What was the user trying to do?

What were the symptoms or what did the logs show?

Additional questions you may come across are as follows:

- *What is your experience with implementing and managing network virtualization technologies such as SDN and NFV?*

- *How do you ensure that network designs are compliant with industry standards and regulations?*

- *Can you give an example of a challenging network architecture project you worked on and how you overcame any obstacles?*

- *How do you stay up to date with emerging network technologies and trends?*

- *Can you explain your experience in cloud networking and how you have integrated a service or services?*

- *Can you describe a time when you had to communicate technical information to non-technical stakeholders?*

These questions are intended to assess your technical knowledge, experience, problem-solving skills, and communication abilities. It's important to be prepared to discuss specific technical concepts, tools, and methodologies that are relevant to the role and the organization's needs.

It's essential to prepare thoroughly for an interview by researching the organization, reviewing network architecture concepts, and practicing answers to these and other relevant questions.

Summary

In this chapter, we discussed certifications and their relevancy to anyone's pursuit of becoming a network architect. IT certifications are necessary because they demonstrate an individual's knowledge and expertise in specific technologies, tools, and methodologies essential to network architecture and design. Some important considerations are validation of one's skills, competitive advantage, professional growth, credibility, and additional opportunities.

We discussed how to prepare for certification exams based on what I've done throughout my IT career thus far.

We also looked at how to prepare for an interview by looking at what is needed for you to answer those interview questions you might be asked.

Last, we discussed how to crack interview questions you might encounter during the interview process.

What we discussed here is a partial list of certifications, methods of preparing for IT networking exams, or questions you'll be asked during the interview process. All are my recommendations, from my perspective, on the road to becoming a successful network architect.

In the next chapter, we'll discuss additional information, recommended reading, and more.

11

The Skills to Become a Better Network Architect and Overcome Daily Challenges

Becoming a proficient network architect is a dynamic journey that demands a diverse set of skills and a keen understanding of the ever-evolving landscape of networking technologies. In the digital age, where connectivity (that is, the cloud, data center, mobile, **Internet of Things (IoT)**, and edge) is the lifeblood of organizations and individuals alike, the role of a network architect is pivotal. These professionals are tasked with designing, implementing, and maintaining intricate network infrastructures that facilitate seamless communication and data transfer, coupled with a strategy to facilitate business longevity and sustainability. To excel in this role and overcome the daily challenges that arise in the world of networking, one must possess a blend of technical expertise, problem-solving acumen, and the ability to adapt to constant innovation.

At the heart of every skilled network architect's toolkit (which we covered in previous chapters) lies a profound understanding of networking fundamentals. This includes knowledge of networking protocols, such as TCP/IP, DNS, DHCP, and BGP, as well as an appreciation for network topologies, such as LANs, WANs, and VPNs. A firm grasp of these foundational concepts forms the bedrock upon which a network architect can build robust, efficient, and secure network solutions. Additionally, staying abreast of emerging technologies, such as **software-defined networking (SDN)** and IoT, is essential in an era where networks are becoming increasingly software-driven and interconnected.

While the technical expertise of a network architect is undeniably pivotal, its success often hinges on a suite of *intangible skills* that are beyond the realm of cables and hardware. At the heart of these is *empathetic communication*, the ability to articulate complex network designs in terms relatable to both tech-savvy and non-technical stakeholders. This is closely tied to *collaborative teamwork*, as architects often find themselves at the nexus of diverse teams, bridging gaps and fostering a unified vision. The road to implementing that vision is rarely without its roadblocks and challenges. Hence, *conflict resolution* becomes paramount, enabling architects to navigate disagreements with diplomacy and a focus on the greater organizational goal.

Beyond these, an intrinsic *growth mindset* and *adaptability* are crucial. As the technology landscape constantly evolves, successful architects proactively seek knowledge, embrace change, and instill the same ethos within their teams. In essence, while the blueprint of a network might be technical, the scaffold that holds it together is built on these intangible skills.

In this chapter, we'll dive into the following topics:

- Interpersonal skills – how to communicate effectively
- Engaging with your team or teams
- Conflict resolution
- Growing as a leader

Interpersonal skills – how to communicate effectively

In any professional arena, technical expertise often lays the foundation for success. However, it's the softer, intangible skills that truly elevate an individual's impact, and among these, interpersonal skills shine prominently. These skills, sometimes referred to as "people skills," are the conduits through which we connect, communicate, and collaborate with others. They dictate not only how we convey our thoughts and ideas but also how we listen, empathize, and respond to those around us.

While technical prowess can open doors, it's these interpersonal skills that enable individuals to navigate complex team dynamics, build rapport with colleagues and clients, and foster collaborative environments. The power of genuine understanding, reading non-verbal cues, and the finesse of navigating difficult conversations are all facets of these skills. In a world that's becoming increasingly interconnected, the ability to bridge cultural and personal differences through adept interpersonal interactions is not just a desirable trait but an essential one. It's these skills that often determine the success of projects, the cohesion of teams, and the strength of leadership.

> **Note**
> Interpersonal skills are an important facet of any professional's repertoire, regardless of their career status (that is, entry-level, mid-level, or senior).

Let's dive into a few crucial interpersonal skills.

Communication

At its core, communication is the process of transmitting information and understanding from one person or group to another. Whether it's a simple exchange of pleasantries or a complex discussion on global strategies, effective communication is essential to ensure that the intended message is conveyed accurately and understood clearly. I'll ask this question:

How would you go about asking for something from a friend, colleague, spouse/relationship partner, manager/boss, child/son/daughter?

How would you *speak* to them? Would you communicate in the same way with them all? Would there be a difference in tone, pitch, or approach? The answer should be yes.

Effective communication involves not only clear and articulate verbal expression but also the subtle nuances of non-verbal cues such as body language and tone of voice. Listening attentively and empathetically is equally important, as it fosters understanding and builds connections.

> **Note**
>
> Effective communication is vital for building and maintaining relationships, resolving conflicts, and achieving success in both personal and professional contexts.

There are several key aspects of communication.

Verbal communication

Verbal communication is spoken words, and it's what most people think of when they hear the term *communication*. It's the spoken component of human interaction, where words become the *vessel* for our thoughts and ideas. It is a powerful tool that enables us to express our intentions, share knowledge, and convey our emotions. Effective verbal communication requires not only clarity and precision in speech but also an awareness of the context and the audience.

Whether giving a speech, presenting an idea, asking a query, challenging a concept, or speaking to a friend/family member – choosing the *right words* and *tone* can make a significant difference in how our messages are received.

Here is an example of how the right and wrong tone/words can affect the outcome of a situation:

Situation: A person is sitting down, with their hands on their head, and seems to be in distress:

Figure 11.1 – Distressed person at a table

A friend comes over and says:

"*Why are you like that? What's wrong with you?*"

How would the distressed person react? The friend genuinely wants to know what's wrong with their friend and how they're feeling, but the verbal context is incorrect (and sounds antagonizing), which will lead to the friend closing or shutting down.

A change in words may lead to a better outcome:

"*Hey, is there something wrong? Would you like to talk about it? Perhaps I can help?*"

The verbal context this time is more *subtle* with thought in recognizing the situation. This time, the friend would be more inclined to speak.

> **Note**
>
> Take a moment to think about how you would approach this example and how you would verbally communicate as the person in distress or the friend.

The ability to articulate ideas clearly and effectively through spoken words is pivotal in achieving successful interactions and relationships. In the *business world*, it is often the key to presenting ideas persuasively, negotiating deals, and leading teams. In *personal relationships*, it fosters understanding, resolves conflicts, and strengthens emotional bonds. Verbal communication is not only about *what* we say but also *how* we say it, with tone, inflection, and context playing critical roles.

In essence, it's the cornerstone of effective human interaction, underpinning our ability to connect, collaborate, and navigate the complexities of our social and professional landscapes.

How to improve verbal communication skills

Improving your verbal communication skills is a challenging endeavor. Here are some approaches and steps to help you develop great verbal communication skills:

- **Practice active listening**: Active listening involves giving your full attention to the speaker, asking clarifying questions, and demonstrating empathy. Maintaining appropriate eye contact with the speaker shows that you are engaged and interested in what they are saying.

- **Remove distractions**: Remove distractions that will deter you from providing the undivided attention required to assimilate what is being said and how you'll respond. And resist the urge to interrupt or finish the speaker's sentences. Let them express their thoughts fully before responding. Interrupting can be perceived as disrespectful and can disrupt the flow of their communication.

> **Note**
>
> Listen to the *language* being used and the context of its usage. By understanding others better, you can respond more effectively and build stronger connections.

- **Expand your vocabulary**: A rich vocabulary is a useful way to improve your verbal skills. This allows you to express yourself more precisely, make your communication more engaging, and adapt your *language* (as previously mentioned) to various situations.

  An effective way to expose yourself to new words and concepts, as we all may know, is through *reading*. Diversify your reading materials, including books, magazines, newspapers, and online articles, to encounter a wide range of vocabulary.

> **Note**
>
> Periodicals such as *The New York Times*, *The Washington Post*, and *The Wall Street Journal* are great resources to help build a stronger vocabulary.

  Maintain a notebook or document where you jot down new words you come across during your reading or conversations. Include the word, its definition, and a sentence or context in which it was used.

  A thesaurus is a helpful tool for discovering synonyms and antonyms – when you encounter a word you want to replace or vary, consult a thesaurus to find alternatives.

  Try making a habit of learning and using one new word every day. Learning a new word every day not only improves your verbal skills but also removes monotony from *everyday* conversations.

> **Note**
>
> As a teenager, I wasn't much of a reader, or at least not interested in casual reading. But I did, and still do, enjoy learning new words... So, in lieu of novels or magazines, I would read the dictionary. I still pick up a dictionary to this day.

- **Speak clearly and slowly**: Enunciate your words clearly and avoid rushing through your speech. Speak at a moderate pace, organize your thoughts correctly, and accordingly improve comprehension.

  Pause to emphasize key points, allow for reflection, and give your audience time to absorb information. It's also important to pace your speech as it helps maintain a certain level of engagement and interest.

- **Pay attention to tone and pitch**: Your tone and pitch convey emotion and meaning. Pay attention to how your voice fluctuates and adapt it to match the context and message you want to convey.

  It's imperative to be aware of the tone utilized during conversations. Certain tones (and the same for pitch) have their place when needed and in situations where required. A negative tone may communicate frustration, anger, disappointment, or sadness, which can lead to misunderstandings or conflicts if not managed carefully. The same goes for sarcastic tones – while they can be humorous, they can often lead to confusion or offensive connotations if not used carefully.

> **Note**
> While there are positive, gentle, neutral, assertive, and empathic tones and pitches, ultimately it comes down to their usefulness and manageability.

- **Minimize filler words**: Avoid excessive use of filler words such as "um," "uh," "you know," or "like." This practice, which is used constantly and excessively in our everyday lives, doesn't bring value when trying to verbally communicate a thought or idea. Often, it shows discontinuity, loss of "train of thought," or lack of knowledge/perception on the subject matter. Among other things, it does the following:

  - Reduces clarity
  - Increases distraction
  - Shows a lack of confidence
  - Has an impact on professionalism
  - Could suggest time is wasted
  - Reduces the impact of an idea
  - Can make an implicit impression on others
  - Causes potential loss of credibility

- **Practice public speaking**: Join a public speaking club, take courses, or volunteer for opportunities to speak in front of groups. Over time, this can help you overcome nervousness, verbalize your ideas/thoughts with clarity, and become a more effective speaker.

- **Record yourself**: An effective way to work on verbal communication skills is to (audio) record yourself. Recording yourself while speaking is a great self-improvement tool. It allows you to gain invaluable insight into your communication style, identify areas for improvement, and track your progress over time.

  When you listen to the recordings of your speaking engagements, you can assess aspects such as tone, pacing, filler word usage, and clarity of expression.

Note

You'll be surprised to find out how many times you say "uh" or other filler words ("essentially," "to that effect," "so") and how you pronounce words, or even other *quirks* you may have.

- **Adapt to your audience**: Adapting to your audience is a fundamental principle of effective communication. Whether you're addressing a diverse group, a team of colleagues, or an individual, understanding your audience's background, knowledge level, and communication preferences is essential.

  Adapting to your audience fosters engagement and receptiveness, making it more likely that your message will be understood and well received. It demonstrates your respect for your listeners and your commitment to effective communication, ultimately enabling you to connect more meaningfully and achieve your communication objectives, whether they involve informing, persuading, inspiring, or collaborating.

- **Learn from communication role models**: Identify role models who exemplify effective communication and demonstrate the art of clear expression, active listening, empathy, and engagement. By observing and studying how skilled communicators navigate conversations, presentations, and interpersonal interactions, you can gain insights into their techniques, strategies, and nuances.

  Emulating the communication prowess of role models allows you to integrate their best practices into your own style, enriching your ability to connect with others, foster understanding, and influence positive outcomes in both personal and professional interactions.

Note

These role models can be anyone, whether they are public speakers, leaders, mentors, or even peers. Observe their techniques and incorporate them into your own style.

- **Obtain feedback**: Seeking and obtaining feedback from others is an essential element of personal growth and improvement in communication. Feedback acts as a *mirror*, offering valuable insights into your strengths and areas of development. Whether it's feedback from friends, colleagues, mentors, or audience members, it provides an external perspective on your communication style, effectiveness, and impact. Use their input to identify areas for improvement.

Constructive feedback can help you identify specific behaviors, habits, or patterns that may hinder your communication goals, allowing you to address them proactively.

> **Note**
>
> It's important to recognize that feedback – dare I say, criticism – given is not an indictment on what you've done wrong. It's more what can be improved to be a better and more engaging speaker.

Improving verbal communication skills takes time and effort, but the benefits are substantial. Effective communication enhances your ability to connect with others, convey your ideas, and achieve success in various aspects of life.

Non-verbal communication

While words convey the *explicit* content of a message, non-verbal cues, such as body language, facial expressions, gestures, and tone of voice, convey the underlying emotions, attitudes, and intentions behind those words. It often carries **more** weight than verbal communication, by virtue of providing context and emotional resonance to what is being said.

> **Note**
>
> In the example (*Figure 11.1*), what is the non-verbal communication illustrated by the person at the table?

Non-verbal communication plays a pivotal role in conveying sincerity, empathy, confidence, and trustworthiness. From a professional perspective, it influences perceptions, teamwork, and leadership. Understanding and enhancing non-verbal communication is essential for achieving effective and authentic communication, fostering positive relationships, and navigating the complex dynamics of human interaction while bringing clarity and impact to your messages.

How to improve non-verbal communication skills

Non-verbal communication skills are just as challenging as verbal communication skills. Developing strong non-verbal communication skills is essential for effective interpersonal interactions.

> **Note**
>
> In my opinion, verbal and non-verbal communication skills are two sides of the same coin.

Here are some approaches and steps to improve your non-verbal communication:

- **Self-awareness**: In this context, it's the ability to recognize and understand non-verbal cues and signals that you emit in your interactions with others. It involves being *conscious* of your body language, facial expressions, gestures, and other non-verbal elements that accompany your verbal communication. This alignment, ultimately, fosters trust, credibility, and authenticity in communication.

  Self-awareness enables you to align your non-verbal cues with your intentions, adapt to different situations, regulate your emotions, and build stronger connections with others as well as to identify areas for improvement.

- **Observe others**: Strategically speaking, keenly observe *how* individuals use body language, facial expressions, gestures, and tone of voice when viewing others communicating. We can gain useful insights into their emotions, intentions, and reactions. This observation allows us to better understand *unspoken* messages that often accompany verbal communication. By doing so, it enables us to adapt our own non-verbal cues to suit different contexts and audiences.

  Moreover, by paying attention to how others respond to various non-verbal signals, we become more skilled in assessing their feelings and needs, which can enhance our ability to connect, empathize, and build a stronger rapport.

> **Note**
> Aside from observing others on how to use non-verbal communication, equally as important are the non-verbal cues *we receive* and see from others as they *react* to what we say.

- **Maintain eye contact**: Another fundamental component of non-verbal communication is eye contact. When used effectively, it conveys engagement, attentiveness, and sincerity. Maintaining appropriate eye contact fosters trust and connection by demonstrating that you are *actively listening* and interested in the conversation.

  As the speaker, it conveys confidence (bravado) and truthfulness in what you're articulating. Conversely, avoiding eye contact can be interpreted as disinterest, lack of confidence, or even deception.

  As with other non-verbal cues, it plays a significant role in building a rapport, establishing authority, and, again, conveying empathy.

> **Note**
> Don't confuse eye contact with staring. Be mindful not to stare or make others uncomfortable.

- **Control facial expressions**: Our face is a powerful tool for conveying emotions and intentions. Practice controlling your facial expressions to ensure they match the message you want to convey. This alignment between what we say verbally and what our faces convey non-verbally fosters a reputable interaction.

- **Master gestures**: Gesturing is a valuable skill that can greatly enhance the effectiveness of your message. Gestures, whether subtle or pronounced, provide additional layers of meaning to your words, helping to clarify, emphasize, or reinforce your message. Used proficiently, gestures can make communicating more vivid and engaging to the audience on a deeper level.

> **Note**
> However, it's essential to use gestures purposefully and in alignment with your message – excessive or irrelevant gestures can distract from your communication.

- **Consider proximity**: Be aware of personal space and adjust your proximity to others accordingly. Standing too close can make people uncomfortable, while standing too far away may signal disinterest.

- **Use mirroring**: Mirroring is a technique of subtly mimicking or reflecting the body language, gestures, and expressions of the person you are interacting with. It can help establish trust and rapport by signaling to the other person that you are in tune with their feelings and perspectives.

> **Note**
> While mirroring is effective when relating to someone speaking, it's just as effective when you are presenting to have your audience relate to you.

- **Practice relaxation techniques**: Nervousness or anxiety can manifest in non-verbal cues such as fidgeting or tense body language. Practice relaxation techniques such as deep breathing or mindfulness to manage anxiety and appear more composed.

- **Video recordings**: A video recording is a great way to improve non-verbal communication by providing a *visual* of your interactions and presentation. It allows you to see yourself as others see you, providing insights into your body language, facial expressions, gestures, and tone of voice.

By reviewing these recordings, you can identify areas for improvement and better understand how your non-verbal cues may affect your message's *effectiveness* and the overall impact of your communication. Video recordings function as a self-assessment tool, enabling you to pinpoint specific non-verbal habits, such as nervous gestures or inconsistent facial expressions, which you can then work on modifying.

> **Note**
>
> As an instructor for CompTIA, I had to be recorded presenting to a class in order to be certified to teach their certification courses. The pre-recordings we did in the prep classes were a valuable experience. It showed me the nonchalant things I did that wouldn't make me an effective instructor, which, in turn, helped me hone my lecturing skills.

- **Seek feedback:** Soliciting feedback is an excellent way to improve your non-verbal interactions. Feedback from *trusted* friends, colleagues, or mentors provides valuable insights into how your non-verbal cues impact your interactions. Others can offer constructive criticism and identify specific areas where improvement is needed, whether it's controlling facial expressions, using gestures more effectively, or maintaining appropriate eye contact.

> **Note**
>
> A valuable point to make, as I mentioned in the *Verbal communication* section, is this: try to not take feedback too personally. The intention of obtaining feedback is to become better at your non-verbal cues.
>
> Every time I give a presentation or speech, I immediately ask for feedback on what I did well, what was not so good, where to improve, and more.

Improving your non-verbal communication skills takes practice and self-awareness, but the effort can significantly enhance your ability to convey your messages effectively, connect with others, and navigate professional (and social) situations with confidence.

Listening

Listening is often an underestimated aspect of effective communication. It involves not only hearing the words someone is saying but also *actively processing*, understanding, and responding to their message. Active listening is a crucial aspect of communication in general but is also a subset of both verbal and non-verbal communication.

Let's go back to the previous example (*Figure 11.1*).

Figure 11.1 – Distressed person at a table

Now that the friend has communicated in an effective manner, the person at the table has expressed themselves:

"There is so much going on... I don't know what to do."

"I'm behind on these tasks that are due in a few days – where do I start?"

"I think I took on too much! But I can't ask for help – I don't want to show I'm not a team player..."

After listening to the person express themselves (verbally with non-verbal attributes), the friend would be more inclined (potentially) to ask more questions, provide guidance, or find ways to help.

> **Note**
> How would you interpret these statements? What would you do? After listening, do you think you would offer help? How do you think the person at the table feels now, after they expressed their thoughts?

What makes listening an important asset for effective communication is the following:

- **Understanding**: Listening is the primary means (tool) by which we gain an understanding of others' thoughts, feelings, ideas, and perspectives. It helps us to grasp the full context of what is being communicated, enabling more meaningful and informed responses/dialogue.

- **Building trust**: Effective listening builds trust and rapport in relationships. When people feel heard and valued, they are more likely to "open up" and share honestly, leading to stronger and more authentic connections.

- **Conflict resolution**: Conflicts, misinterpretations, and misunderstandings can occur if we don't pay attention to the situation at hand. Listening is a key component that helps us identify underlying issues, acknowledge differing perspectives, resolve communication gaps, and work toward mutually agreeable solutions.

- **Effective problem-solving**: Along the same context of conflict resolution, by listening (attentively), you can identify core issues/concerns, root causes, and concerns surrounding a problem. It fosters a sense of trust and cooperation among stakeholders. As a result, the problem-solving process becomes more inclusive and informative, with all parties contributing their insights and ideas.

  It allows us to gather information, consider various viewpoints, and make informed decisions.

- **Leadership**: Having adept listening skills is a step toward becoming an effective leader. Bringing together all the concepts mentioned fosters trust, collaboration, and open communication within a team or organization.

  A good leader actively listens, demonstrates respect for their team members, values their input, and is receptive to their concerns and ideas. This not only encourages team members to speak up but also creates an environment where diverse perspectives are considered.

> **Note**
>
> Additionally, leadership can inspire trust, boost morale, and cultivate a motivated and engaged workforce, ultimately driving success and achieving shared goals.

How to improve active listening skills

Here are some practical steps to help you become a better active listener:

- **Give your full attention**: Minimize distractions and focus entirely on the speaker. Put away electronic devices, maintain eye contact, and show through your body language that you are engaged and attentive.

  By giving your undivided attention in this way, you convey respect and genuine interest in what your speaker is saying, which encourages them to *open up* and share their thoughts more openly.

- **Be patient**: Being patient is a vital component of active listening. Avoid interruptions, and let people express their thoughts and feelings fully before responding. For instance, during a team meeting, a team member might be discussing a complex project issue that requires careful explanation – resist the urge to interrupt or jump in with solutions. Instead, allow your colleague to finish explaining their perspective, even if it takes some time.

  By giving them space to express their thoughts completely, you gain a deeper understanding of the issue and can provide more relevant input or support. This patience not only shows respect for your colleague's viewpoint but also promotes a collaborative atmosphere where everyone can function constructively.

- **Ask open-ended questions**: Asking open-ended questions is a great technique that encourages whoever is speaking to provide more detailed and thoughtful responses. For instance, let's say you're in a performance review meeting with an employee. Instead of asking a closed-ended question, such as *"Did you meet your sales targets?"*, you can use an open-ended question such as, *"Can you tell me about your strategies for achieving your sales targets this quarter?"*.

  This open-ended approach invites the employee to share insights, experiences, and challenges, leading to a more comprehensive and productive discussion.

  Open-ended questions demonstrate a genuine interest in the employee's perspective and encourage them to express themselves in a way that fosters a deeper understanding of their achievements and areas for improvement.

> **Note**
>
> Encourage anyone speaking or your audience to elaborate on their thoughts and ideas by asking open-ended questions that cannot be answered with a simple "Yes" or "No."

- **Reflect and paraphrase**: This demonstrates your understanding of the speaker's message and encourages them to clarify or elaborate further. For instance, if a colleague is describing a complex project timeline during a team meeting, you can reflect and paraphrase by saying, "*So, if I understand correctly, the critical path for this project involves completing Task A and Task B before moving on to Task C. Is that accurate?*"

   This approach shows that you are actively processing their information and seeking confirmation, which can prevent misunderstandings and ensure that everyone is on the same page. It also reassures the speaker that you are fully engaged and interested in the details of their message.

> **Note**
> How often do you reflect and paraphrase during meetings or discussions you have in the workplace? Increase the usage of this technique and find out if it makes the dialogue beneficial for everyone. By paraphrasing, you're gaining not just clarity on the content and context but also comprehension for meaningful dialogue.

- **Avoid judgment**: Suspend judgment (judgmental thoughts) or criticism while listening, as it creates a *safe space* for open and honest communication. For instance, if a friend confides in you about a personal struggle they're facing, avoid making judgments or offering unsolicited advice such as, "*You should have done this differently...*".

   Instead, actively listen without criticism, saying something such as, "*I appreciate you sharing this with me. It sounds like you're going through a challenging time, and I'm here to support you if you need any...*".

   By refraining from judgment, you allow your friend, or anyone for that matter, to express their thoughts and feelings without fear of criticism, which can strengthen trust in your relationship and lead to more meaningful conversations where they feel heard and valued.

In summary, improving active listening skills involves giving your full attention to the speaker, being patient and allowing them to express themselves fully, using verbal and non-verbal cues to show engagement, asking open-ended questions to encourage detailed responses, reflecting and paraphrasing to demonstrate understanding, avoiding judgment to create a safe and non-critical environment, and practicing mindfulness to stay present during conversations.

Consistent practice of these techniques enhances communication, fosters empathy, and strengthens relationships, making active listening an invaluable skill for effective interpersonal interactions.

Empathy

A constant theme in this section on interpersonal skills is **empathy**. Empathy is the ability to understand and share the feelings and perspectives of others. It's about actively placing yourself in someone else's shoes to grasp *their* emotions and experiences. Understanding and acknowledging the emotions and feelings of others is a key element of effective communication. Empathy allows for more meaningful and compassionate interactions, as it shows that you care about the other person's experiences and perspectives.

> **Note**
>
> In gaining trust and resolving conflicts, empathy is *often more* effective than sympathy because it goes a step further to establish a deeper connection and understanding. However, the choice between empathy and sympathy may depend on the specific situation and the individual's preferences. Some people may appreciate sympathy, while others may respond more positively to genuine empathy. It's essential to gauge the emotional needs of the person you're interacting with and respond accordingly to foster trust and resolve conflicts effectively.

Adaptability

Adaptability in communication refers to the ability to adjust your communication style, approach, and message to effectively connect with different individuals and situations. It's a vital aspect of interpersonal skills because it allows you to navigate the complexities of various interpersonal interactions.

Being adaptable allows an individual to connect with people from various backgrounds, cultures, and communication preferences. It enables them to navigate complex interpersonal dynamics, resolve conflicts, and build trust in both personal and professional relationships.

Let's take an example as a reference of adaptability in communication in the context of balancing work and home life:

You're a working parent with a demanding job and a family to take care of. Your communication must adapt to the different circumstances and needs of both your professional and personal life.

- **Adaptability at work**:

  - **Meeting with your team**: At work, you have an important meeting with your team to discuss a new project. You adapt by preparing a well-structured presentation to communicate key project details, objectives, goals, and expectations. This aligns with the professional setting, where structured communication is often necessary for clarity and efficiency.

  - **Email communication**: Throughout the workday, you communicate with colleagues via email and **instant messaging** (**IM**) for quick updates and project coordination. You adapt by using concise, professional language to convey information efficiently and maintain productivity.

- **Adaptability at home**:

  - **Family dinner time**: At home, it's family dinner time. You adapt by putting away your work devices and giving your full attention to your spouse and children. You engage in open, relaxed conversations about their day and share stories of your own, fostering a warm and supportive family atmosphere.

- **Bedtime routine**: During the bedtime routine with your kids, you adapt your communication by using a soothing and reassuring tone. You read bedtime stories, listen to their concerns, and provide comfort, nurturing a sense of security and trust.

In this scenario, adaptability in communication allows you to effectively manage the demands of your professional life and maintain strong connections with your family at home. It involves switching between structured, task-oriented communication in the workplace and warm, supportive, and nurturing communication in the family setting. This adaptability ensures that you address the *unique needs* of each scenario, promoting both career success and a harmonious home life.

> **Note**
> It's important to recognize the situation and adapt accordingly. Think about experiences you have had thus far (professional or personal) and reflect on whether you had to adapt or get adapted. What was the outcome? Would the outcome have been the same if you hadn't adapted? And why?

In this section, we delved into the multifaceted world of interpersonal skills, exploring their importance, the various forms they take, and the profound influence they wield in fostering harmonious and productive work environments.

In both personal and professional settings, effective communication leads to better relationships, reduced misunderstandings, and more successful outcomes. It fosters trust, collaboration, and a positive atmosphere. Whether you are giving a presentation, having a one-on-one conversation, working within a team, or conversing personally, honing your communication skills is essential for achieving your goals and connecting with others on a deeper level.

In the next section, we'll discuss engaging with your team or teams.

Engaging with your team or teams

As a network architect, your role involves designing, implementing, and managing intricate network infrastructures. To excel in this role, you must engage with your teams as more than just colleagues; they are your collaborators in the pursuit of innovative solutions and the efficient operation of critical systems.

Effective engagement entails not only sharing technical insights but also fostering an environment where ideas flow freely, challenges are met with creativity, and everyone's expertise is valued.

Role of a network architect across teams

How a network architect interacts with teams depends on their role within the various teams they engage with. It will vary depending on the specific project, organization, and level of experience.

Figure 11.2 was introduced in *Chapter 4*, showing the relationship between a network architect and various **lines of business (LOBs)**:

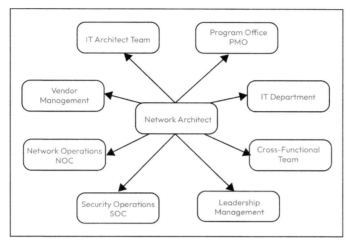

Figure 11.2 – A network architect's influence on other business units (BUs)

From an engagement perspective, *Figure 11.3* shows a more granular relationship:

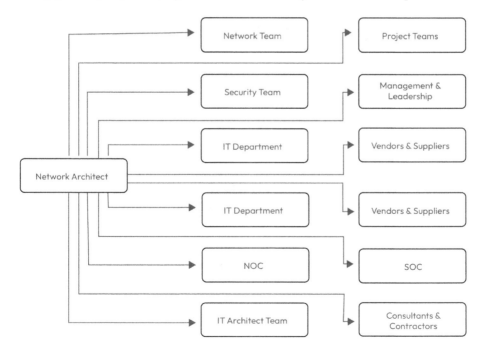

Figure 11.3 – A network architect's team engagements

These LOBs are, in fact, the teams a network architect will engage with daily. Here's a breakdown of how network architects may function within different teams:

- **Network team**

  - **Leader**: Network architects often provide leadership within the network team. They guide the team in making network-related decisions, setting standards, and ensuring that network designs align with the organization's goals.

  - **Subject-matter expert (SME)**: Network architects are SMEs who offer expertise in network design, configuration, and optimization. They provide guidance and mentorship to network engineers and technicians.

- **IT department**

  - **Collaborator**: Network architects collaborate with other IT professionals, such as system administrators and security experts, to ensure that the network supports overall IT infrastructure and security requirements.

  - **Consultant**: They may act as consultants, providing advice and recommendations on network-related matters to IT department members.

- **Project teams**

  - **Project lead**: In project teams, network architects often serve as project leads for network-related initiatives. They oversee project planning, execution, and completion, ensuring that network requirements are met.

  - **Technical expert**: Network architects contribute their technical expertise (SME/**subject-matter acquaintance**, or **SMA**) to project teams, offering insights on network architecture, infrastructure, and other fabric-related "architectures" needed to support business operations.

- **Security team**

  - **Security integrator**: Network architects work closely with the security team to integrate network security measures, such as firewalls and **intrusion detection systems (IDS)**, into the network architecture. They ensure that security considerations are embedded in network designs.

  - **Compliance expert**: In regulated industries, network architects work closely with compliance teams to ensure that network designs and operations align with legal and industry-specific standards.

- **Management and leadership**

  - **Strategic advisor**: Network architects advise executive and management teams on network strategies, technology investments, and alignment with business objectives. They provide valuable insights to support decision-making at higher levels.

  - **Stakeholder consultant**: Network architects communicate with a wide range of stakeholders, including executives, department heads, and non-technical staff. They translate technical details into business language to convey the value of network initiatives.

  - **Strategic planner**: Network architects participate in strategic planning discussions, helping shape the organization's long-term network architecture roadmap. They align network strategies with business goals and emerging technologies.

  - **Technical leadership**: Network architects set technical standards and best practices for the organization. They enforce network design and implementation standards, ensuring that network designs adhere to these standards and promoting consistency and reliability.

- **Project management office (PMO)**

  - **Project alignment**: Network architects work with the PMO to ensure that network-related projects align with the organization's strategic goals and initiatives. They provide technical input and expertise to help define project objectives and outcomes.

  - **Project planning**: During the project planning phase, network architects collaborate with the PMO to establish project timelines, budgets, resource requirements, and deliverables. They contribute insights into the technical aspects of the project plan.

  - **Resource allocation**: Network architects may assist the PMO in resource allocation, helping to identify the specific skills and expertise needed for network-related projects. They participate in discussions about staffing and resource availability.

  - **Risk assessment**: Network architects provide input on potential risks and challenges related to network projects. They work with the PMO to develop risk mitigation strategies and contingency plans.

  - **Project monitoring**: Network architects work closely with the PMO to monitor the progress of network projects. They provide regular updates on technical milestones, ensuring that the project stays on track and that technical objectives are met.

  - **Documentation and reporting**: Network architects assist in documenting project details, technical specifications, and performance metrics. They collaborate with the PMO to create reports and documentation for project stakeholders and leadership.

- **Vendors and suppliers**

  - **Evaluator**: Network architects evaluate networking products and services offered by vendors and suppliers. They assess these offerings to determine their suitability for the organization's network infrastructure.

- **Consultants and contractors**

  - **Collaborator**: Network architects collaborate with external consultants and contractors, sharing their expertise and ensuring that projects align with organizational goals and standards.

- **IT architect team**

  - **Collaborator**: Network architects collaborate with IT architects to align network designs with broader IT architecture strategies. They ensure that network solutions complement the overall technology infrastructure and meet architectural standards.

  - **Integrator**: They work closely with IT architects to integrate network components seamlessly into the organization's IT landscape, considering factors such as scalability, compatibility, and interoperability.

  - **Consultant**: Network architects may consult with IT architects when planning and implementing complex network projects, ensuring that the architecture supports the organization's goals.

- **Network operations center (NOC)**

  - **Advisor**: Network architects provide technical support and expertise to the NOC team. They assist in troubleshooting complex network issues and help develop protocols for efficient network monitoring and management.

  - **Documentation**: They contribute to the creation and maintenance of network documentation that aids NOC personnel in quickly identifying and resolving network problems.

- **Security operations center (SOC)**

  - **Security collaborator**: Network architects collaborate with the SOC to enhance network security. They help design and implement security measures, such as firewalls, IDS, and encryption protocols, to protect against cyber threats.

  - **Incident response (IR)**: In the event of security incidents, network architects work closely with the SOC to investigate breaches, analyze vulnerabilities, and implement corrective measures within the network infrastructure.

- **Cross-functional teams**

  - **Interdisciplinary projects lead**: Network architects participate in cross-functional teams that tackle interdisciplinary projects, such as cloud migrations, digital transformations, or infrastructure upgrades. They contribute their networking expertise to ensure that network requirements are met.

- **Communicator**: They serve as communication bridges between different functional teams, translating technical jargon into understandable terms and facilitating effective collaboration.

- **Problem solver**: In cross-functional teams, network architects often play a crucial role in problem-solving, particularly when technical challenges span multiple domains. They help identify solutions that consider networking aspects alongside other technology components.

In summary, network architects play versatile roles within the teams they engage with, ranging from leadership and technical expertise to advisory and collaboration. Their roles can adapt based on the specific requirements of projects and the organization's needs. Regardless of their roles, network architects are responsible for ensuring that network solutions are robust, secure, and aligned with the organization's strategic objectives.

Conflict resolution

Conflict resolution is often overlooked in the role, or even as a trait, of a network architect. As professionals responsible for designing, implementing, and managing network infrastructure, network architects often find themselves at the nexus of technology, business objectives, and diverse teams. Because of this multifaceted environment, conflicts can arise from various sources, including technical disagreements, resource allocation, project timelines, and differing priorities.

Technical disagreements

Firstly, network architects must navigate technical disagreements and decisions daily. They work with network engineers, system administrators, application owners, security experts, other IT architects, and product managers, each bringing their unique perspectives and expertise to the table. Conflicts may emerge when determining the best approach to network design, selecting technology solutions, or resolving performance issues and operational efficiencies. Effective conflict resolution ensures that technical disputes are addressed constructively, leading to well-informed decisions that benefit the organization.

Project alignment

Network architects often collaborate with cross-functional teams, including project managers, business analysts, and executives, on initiatives that impact the network, which will, in turn, impact revenue generation. Conflicts may arise when balancing technical requirements with project timelines, budgets, and business objectives. Network architects must skillfully mediate these conflicts to find mutually acceptable solutions that maintain network integrity while achieving project goals.

Procurement and relationship management

Network architects engage with external vendors, suppliers, and consultants to procure network equipment and services (professional, staff augmentation, contract), forming a critical link in the organization's technology supply chain. However, in the pursuit of aligning external offerings with internal network requirements, conflicts and disagreements can arise during various phases of this engagement. These conflicts may manifest during contract negotiations (pricing, terms, and conditions), product evaluations (seeking the most feasible solution), or service-level discussions (expected level of support and services desired).

In such scenarios, effective conflict resolution skills become indispensable. Network architects must adeptly navigate these negotiations, finding common ground, and forge agreements that not only satisfy the organization's technical prerequisites but also align with its financial objectives.

> **Note**
> Conflict resolution may play a critical role in addressing security incidents and breaches. A network architect will have to collaborate with security teams to investigate and mitigate security threats. In high-pressure situations, quick and effective conflict resolution is crucial for making rapid decisions that safeguard network integrity and data security.

Techniques to resolve conflicts

Conflict resolution techniques encompass a spectrum of interpersonal and communication skills that are crucial for addressing disputes and disagreements effectively, especially in the role of a network architect. These techniques, as discussed in previous sections of this chapter, involve active listening to understand underlying concerns in technical disagreements, empathy to acknowledge emotions when managing project conflicts, and clear communication to express one's own perspective in discussions with cross-functional teams.

In addition, several other techniques can help you in a role as a network architect to effectively manage and resolve conflicts as they arise:

* **Mediation**: As technical disputes and project complexities can arise frequently, network architects are often centered during these discussions. Mediation provides a structured and impartial approach to resolving conflicts. It allows network architects to act as neutral facilitators, guiding conflicting parties through productive discussions, helping them understand each other's perspectives, and ultimately reach mutually agreeable solutions. By leveraging mediation techniques, network architects can mitigate conflicts within their teams, with external vendors, and across cross-functional projects, fostering a collaborative atmosphere for achieving success in any project or implementation goal.

> **Note**
>
> By remaining impartial, a network architect can aid all parties in finding common ground and mutually acceptable solutions.

- **Problem-solving**: Since network architects are problem solvers (and this is a foundational skill), this skill is applicable when it comes to resolving conflicts. Network architects often find themselves at the intersection of complex technical challenges and diverse stakeholder interests. As conflicts arise, problem-solving skills enable them to assess the root causes of disputes, identify potential solutions, and navigate a path toward a practical solution or resolution.

  Whether it's addressing technical disagreements within their teams, negotiating contract terms with external vendors, or reconciling conflicting project priorities, network architects rely on their problem-solving abilities to find practical and innovative solutions. By approaching conflicts with a structured problem-solving mindset, they not only resolve immediate issues but also contribute to the organization's overall efficiency, productivity, and successful network initiatives.

> **Note**
>
> As a network architect, incorporate problem-solving capabilities such as brainstorming, **Stop, Slow down, Think and Act** (**SSTA**), and SWOT analysis, to explore options and make informed decisions.

- **Negotiation**: In efforts to resolve conflicts effectively, negotiation skills are a valuable tool for a network architect to reach compromises and agreements that satisfy the needs and interests of all parties. Again, conflicts can arise from differing technical viewpoints, resource allocation, or external vendors – being able to facilitate constructive dialogue, find common ground, and reach mutually acceptable agreements is monumental. Negotiation skills empower network architects to navigate conflicts while safeguarding network integrity and promoting collaboration.

  By adeptly negotiating resolutions, network architects not only address immediate conflicts but also contribute to the overall success of network initiatives and the organization's objectives.

As an example, I will share a conflict I once had with a manager on a project I was working on:

In a previous role as a network architect lead, I was collaborating with an ecosystem partner on a project to design a solution to support a private cloud offering within one of the major cloud providers. The **go-to-market** (**GTM**) forecast sales were northbound of $40M for the first quarter after successful implementation.

Because of the potential deal size (amount), my manager told me to include a software bundle as part of the purchase order and incorporate it into a design to provide network automation capabilities.

I was hesitant to do so, as the software stack wasn't fully vetted out in a PoC or pilot. To further complicate matters, I found out that my manager was directed to tell me to include the software from upper management. Though the directive came from upper management, I couldn't include untested software in a solution for customers to use without proper validation.

I began gathering some information on the software bundle and did some background research on its progression. I then asked to speak to my manager privately and began to show him evidence of why not to include the software bundle as part of this initial purchase order. After some time, my manager realized he had made a decision too hastily and agreed the software bundle wasn't ready.

As a compromise, I said:

"If the software is tested and validated, we can include it as part of our phase 2 rollout, which we're just about to kick off... and we can introduce the software bundle for existing customers as a no-cost upgrade... Is that an option upper management will be comfortable with?"

In the end, upper management agreed to the course of action.

This example shows how to effectively handle a situation in which there were conflicting viewpoints. Actively listening to my manager's request and having empathy for what the customer might experience and the need for a resolution by the GTM team, as well as the needs of upper management goals, coupled with a defined (negotiated) path forward, led to successful mediation between all parties involved.

> **Note**
>
> Whether it involves aligning technical requirements with project timelines, securing favorable terms with external vendors, project timelines, and resource allocation, or balancing technical specifications with budget constraints, network architects should be prepared to negotiate on technical and non-technical issues.
>
> If you want to learn about or are looking for a more structured approach to resolving conflicts, there are a few models, such as the **Thomas-Kilmann Conflict Mode Instrument** (**TKI**) or the *Harvard Negotiation Project*'s Principled Negotiation.

In conclusion, conflict resolution is integral to the role of a network architect. It enables them to navigate technical disagreements, collaborate effectively with diverse teams, make informed decisions, and maintain network integrity. By mastering conflict resolution skills, network architects not only enhance their technical expertise but also contribute to the overall success of their organizations.

Keep in mind that network architects serve as *technical leaders* within their organizations. They often mentor junior staff, guide team members, and communicate with stakeholders at various levels. Conflict resolution skills are instrumental in fostering a positive and collaborative work environment. By resolving interpersonal conflicts and promoting open communication, network architects can create a culture of teamwork and innovation.

In the next section, we'll see how a network architect can grow as a leader.

Growing as a leader

As a network architect, your role extends beyond technical expertise into leadership and mentorship. The evolving landscape of network technology demands that you not only design and manage intricate infrastructures but also inspire and guide teams toward common objectives.

This growth as a leader involves honing skills in effective communication, strategic thinking, and project management. Network architects are increasingly called upon to provide vision and direction, foster collaboration among cross-functional teams, and adapt to emerging technologies. The journey to becoming a leader is marked by a commitment to continuous learning, mentorship, and a passion for driving innovation in an ever-changing technical landscape.

> **Note**
>
> Another important aspect of growing into a leader is overcoming challenges/obstacles/impedance of progress from the likes of stakeholders, upper leadership teams, vendors, or the industry. Their view may not align with yours, currently, but that doesn't mean it's valid. It may not be an objective to undertake now or in the current roadmap. But the concept is that one must be patient, maintain focus, and not give up.

How do you become a leader?

Being a leader allows network architects to provide vision, guide teams, and align technical decisions with organizational objectives. Effective leadership fosters collaboration and innovation and contributes to the success of network initiatives. Leadership is not solely inborn; it can be developed and cultivated over time. While some individuals may naturally possess certain leadership qualities, effective leadership is largely a product of learning, experience, and personal growth.

Growing into a leadership role as a network architect is a deliberate and gradual process that involves the following steps:

- **Self-assessment**: Begin by assessing your current skills, strengths, and areas for improvement. Recognize your technical expertise as well as your leadership potential. Identify specific leadership qualities you'd like to develop.

- **Set clear goals**: Define your leadership goals and objectives. Determine the kind of leader you aspire to be and the impact you want to have on your team and organization. Having clear goals provides direction for your growth.

- **Seek mentorship**: Look for experienced leaders, both within and outside your organization, who can serve as mentors. Seek their guidance, ask for feedback, and learn from their leadership experiences. Mentorship can provide valuable insights and accelerate your growth.

- **Lead by example**: Exhibit leadership qualities in your daily work. Demonstrate qualities such as integrity, accountability, and professionalism. Leading by example can inspire others and build trust.

- **Embrace challenges**: Step out of your comfort zone and take on leadership responsibilities within your team or on projects. Embrace challenges and view them as opportunities for growth. Overcoming challenges can boost your confidence and leadership skills.

- **Build a collaborative culture**: Foster a culture of collaboration within your team. Encourage open communication, respect diverse viewpoints, and value contributions from all team members. A collaborative environment supports leadership growth.

- **Technical expertise**: Many network architects begin their careers as experts in network technology. Their deep knowledge and proficiency in designing, implementing, and managing complex network infrastructures position them as leaders in their field. Others naturally look to them for guidance and mentorship.

- **Experience**: Leadership often evolves from years of hands-on experience in network architecture. Network architects who have tackled diverse technical challenges and overcome complex issues tend to develop leadership qualities, as they gain a reputation for their problem-solving abilities and technical expertise.

- **Invest in training**: Consider enrolling in leadership development programs or courses that specifically address leadership skills and techniques. Such training can provide you with valuable tools and strategies.

Applying these steps will move you closer to becoming an effective leader.

Summary

For a network architect, success extends beyond technical prowess. It hinges on the mastery of interpersonal skills and leadership development, allowing network architects to thrive in their roles, foster teamwork, and drive innovation. This chapter delved into the essential aspects of interpersonal skills, communication, team engagement, conflict resolution, and leadership growth.

In this chapter, we explored the essential skills required to become a better network architect and effectively navigate daily challenges within this dynamic field. Effective interpersonal skills, underscored by mastery of communication, including active listening, vocabulary expansion, and tone control, form the cornerstone of success. Engaging with teams and fostering collaboration through leadership qualities such as adaptability and mentorship are pivotal in achieving shared goals. Moreover, conflict resolution abilities empower network architects to harmonize diverse interests and align technical solutions with organizational objectives.

The journey of growth as a leader is a continuous one, driven by self-assessment, mentorship, and a commitment to personal development. These skills collectively position network architects to excel in their technical roles, inspire their teams, and contribute significantly to the prosperous evolution of network technology.

In the next chapter, we'll dive in and discuss preparing for your IT certification exams, a network architect's career path, and getting a job by cracking interview questions.

Further reading

To learn more about the topics that were covered in this chapter, take a look at the following resources:

- *How do you transition from network engineering to network architecture or management roles?*: https://www.linkedin.com/advice/1/how-do-you-transition-from-network-engineering

- *How can you become a network architect?*: https://www.linkedin.com/advice/0/how-can-you-become-network-architect-skills-network-engineering

- *How to Become an Effective Leader*, by *Michael Brainard*: https://www.amazon.com/Become-Effective-Leader-Michael-Brainard/dp/1637351690/ref=tmm_pap_swatch_0?_encoding=UTF8&qid=&sr=

12
Additional Information and Recommended Books

Becoming a network architect is a multi-faceted journey that requires a blend of technical/business acumen, strategic thinking, and continuous learning. This role involves designing, implementing, and maintaining intricate communication systems that underpin our digital world. Network architects need a strong foundation in networking protocols, security practices, and infrastructure design.

However, as technology and IT philosophy evolve, so should a network architect. Subsequently, you should step outside of your comfort zone and begin to incorporate (maybe adapt to) other paradigms, such as embracing Dev(Sec)Ops, programming and scripting, AI/ML, IoT, SASE/SD-WAN, and others.

From *Chapters 1* to *11*, I provided insight into what it takes to become (or pursue a career as) a network architect. Whether it's career advancement, a pivotal point in your IT professional journey, or a new pursuit, this book has provided the foundations for you. Keep in mind that becoming a network architect doesn't happen overnight. It takes hard work, determination, drive, and focus (just to name a few), all of which can take years to ascertain. However, there is only so much I can provide or that can be fulfilled in the context and content of one book.

This chapter offers supplementary insights into the multi-faceted path of becoming a network architect. Again, the journey is one of perpetual learning. The intricacies of routing protocols, the artistry of scalability, the mastery of agility, the elegance of automation, and the architecture of security demand a commitment to ongoing education.

This chapter is dedicated to the following:

- Recommended books
- Other useful resources

While some of these books might be certification-focused or outside the primary scope of a network architect, all of them provide outstanding information for real-world concepts, design, understanding, and implementation.

> **Note**
>
> The list of resources identified in this chapter is an *opinionated viewpoint*. There is a tremendous amount of literature available for IT professionals to use. In fact, you might already have publications or other materials you're currently using. I'm only supplementing that.
>
> All of the resources mentioned in this chapter (whether it's a book, community, blog, website, support, and so on) are resources I've used to some extent in my career thus far, and will continue to use.

Let's get started!

Recommended books

In this collection of recommended books, I've chosen some titles that could be instrumental in your journey through IT networking, security, methodologies, cloud solutions, and automation. These books are not only informative but also transformative, offering insights into the intricacies of networking protocols, the boundless possibilities of cloud computing, and the incredible efficiency gains brought about by automation tools. Whether you are a seasoned IT professional or a newcomer eager to explore these domains, these recommended books are invaluable resources that can help you navigate, master, and excel in this ever-evolving technology realm.

Cisco Press

Being a double **Cisco Certified Internetwork Expert (CCIE)** – in Infrastructure and Data Center – I have a preference toward Cisco Press books as they were at one point (and probably still are) the holy grail of networking and infrastructure fabric.

The following books are by Narbik Kocharian – a three-times CCIE (in R/S, Security, and SP). He has written many books for Cisco Press.

Figure 12.1 – Recommended books by Cisco Press

Some of his books that I recommend are as follows:

- *CCIE Enterprise Infrastructure Foundation, 2nd Edition*: `https://rb.gy/bnatd`

- *CCIE Routing and Switching v5.0, Official Cert Guide, Volumes 1 and 2, 5th Edition*:

  - `https://rb.gy/2xcr7`

  - `https://rb.gy/yo97v`

- *CCIE Routing and Switching v5.1 Foundations, Bridging the Gap Between CCNP and CCIE, 1st Edition*: `https://rb.gy/f14m0`

A few other Cisco Press books include the following:

- *CCNP Enterprise, Core ENCOR 350-401 and Advanced Routing ENARSI 300-410, Official Cert Guide, 2nd Edition*, by Brad Edgeworth, Ramiro Garza Rios, David Hucaby, Jason Gooley, and Raymond Lacoste: `https://rb.gy/brjbe`

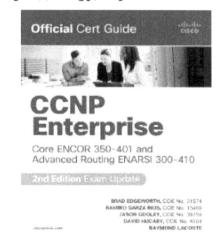

Figure 12.2 – CCNP Enterprise

- *Programming and Automating Cisco Networks, A Guide to Network Programmability and Automation in the Data Center, Campus, and WAN, (Networking Technology), 1st Edition*, by Ryan Tischer and Jason Gooley

Figure 12.3 – Programming and Automating Cisco Networks

- *BGP Design and Implementation, 1st Edition*, by Randy Zhang and Micah Bartell: `https://shorturl.at/vxyT8`

Figure 12.4 – BGP Design and Implementation, 1st Edition

Arista books

The following book is by Gary Donahue, who was an instructor of mine when I pursued Arista certifications:

- *Arista Warrior, A Real-World Guide to Understanding Arista Products with a Focus on EOS, 2nd Edition*, by Gary Donahue: `https://shorturl.at/mwxDP`

Figure 12.5 – Arista Warrior, 2nd Edition

Other networking books

These additional networking books are useful as not all IT infrastructure fabrics are homogeneous and dedicated to one specific solution provider:

- *Linux for Networking Professionals: Securely configure and operate Linux network services for the enterprise*, by Rob VandenBrink

Figure 12.6 – Linux for Networking Professionals

- *Understanding Linux Network Internals: Guided Tour to Networking on Linux, 1st Edition*, by Christian Benvenuti

Figure 12.7 – Understanding Linux Network Internals, 1st Edition

- *Mastering Palo Alto Networks: Build, configure, and deploy network solutions for your infrastructure using features of PAN-OS, 2nd Edition*, by Tom Piens, with a foreword by Kim Wens

Figure 12.8 – Mastering Palo Alto Networks, 2nd Edition

Automation and network programming

In today's modern IT world, the fusion of automation and networking programming plays a pivotal role in shaping the way our digital infrastructure functions. It's a landscape where software-defined networks and intelligent automation tools not only optimize operations but also open new frontiers of possibilities. In this collection of recommended books, the selection of titles serves as indispensable guides for both beginners and seasoned professionals. These books delve into the intricacies of network automation, scripting, and network programmability:

- *Network Programmability & Automation: Skills for the Next-Generation Network Engineer, 2nd Edition*, by Matt Oswalt, Christian Adell, Scott Lowe, and Jason Edelman:

  - `https://shorturl.at/pGPRS`

  - `https://shorturl.at/dJX03`

Figure 12.9 – Network Programmability & Automation, 2nd Edition

- *Mastering Python Networking: Utilize Python packages and frameworks for network automation, monitoring, cloud, and management, 4th Edition*, by Eric Chou: `https://shorturl.at/ctCKS`

Figure 12.10 – Mastering Python Networking, 4th Edition

- *Mastering Python Networking: Your one-stop solution to using Python for network automation, programmability, and DevOps, 3rd Edition*, by Eric Chou: `https://shorturl.at/cqGO4`

Figure 12.11 – Mastering Python Networking, 3rd Edition

- *Network Automation Cookbook: Proven and actionable recipes to automate and manage network devices using Ansible*, by Karim Okasha: https://shorturl.at/qAD59

Figure 12.12 – Network Automation Cookbook

- *Practical Network Automation: A beginner's guide to automating and optimizing networks using Python, Ansible, and more, 2nd Edition*, by Abhishek Ratan: https://shorturl.at/a0239

Figure 12.13 – Practical Network Automation, 2nd Edition

- *Mastering Ansible: Automate configuration management and overcome deployment challenges with Ansible, 4th Edition*, by James Freeman and Jesse Keating: `https://shorturl.at/nwK08`

Figure 12.14 – Mastering Ansible, 4th Edition

- *Practical Ansible: Learn how to automate infrastructure, manage configuration, and deploy applications, 2nd Edition*, by James Freeman, Fabio Alessandro Locati, and Daniel Oh: `https://shorturl.at/grCSW`

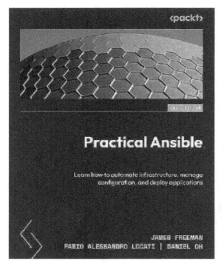

Figure 12.15 – Practical Ansible, 2nd Edition

- *Ansible Playbook Essentials: Design automation blueprints using Ansible's playbooks to orchestrate and manage your multitier infrastructure,* by Gourav Shah: `https://shorturl.at/1mAOV`

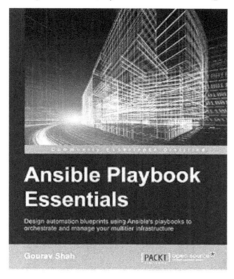

Figure 12.16 – Ansible Playbook Essentials

- *Terraform for Google Cloud Essential Guide: Learn how to provision infrastructure in Google Cloud securely and efficiently,* by Bernd Nordhausen: `https://shorturl.at/iqJ59`

Figure 12.17 – Terraform for Google Cloud Essential Guide

- *Terraform Cookbook: Provision, run, and scale cloud architecture with real-world examples using Terraform, 2nd Edition*, by Mikael Krief and Armon Dadgar: `https://shorturl.at/1wCDQ`

Figure 12.18 – Terraform Cookbook, 2nd Edition

- *Terraform Cookbook: Efficiently define, launch, and manage Infrastructure as Code across various cloud platforms*, by Mikael Krief and with a foreword by Mitchell Hashimoto: `https://shorturl.at/vQSVY`

Figure 12.19 – Terraform Cookbook

- *Infrastructure as Code for Beginners: Deploy and manage your cloud-based services with Terraform and Ansible*, by Russ McKendrick: `https://shorturl.at/gxJUV`

Figure 12.20 – Infrastructure as Code for Beginners

- *Mastering Linux Shell Scripting: A practical guide to Linux command-line, Bash scripting, and Shell programming, 2nd Edition*, by Mokhtar Ebrahim and Andrew Mallett

Figure 12.21 – Mastering Linux Shell Scripting, 2nd Edition

- *Puppet 5 Beginner's Guide: Go from newbie to pro with Puppet 5, 3rd Revised Edition*, by John Arundel

Figure 12.22 – Puppet 5 Beginner's Guide, 3rd Revised Edition

- *Learning Chef: A Guide to Configuration Management and Automation, 1st Edition*, by Mischa Taylor and Seth Vargo

Figure 12.23 – Learning Chef

- *Learning SaltStack, 2nd Edition*, by Colton Myers

Figure 12.24 – Learning SaltStack, 2nd Edition

Methodologies

Though not a primary skill set of a network architect, understanding different methodologies with their usage in developing IT fabrics is important from a cohesiveness perspective when working alongside project (management) leads and scrum masters. You'll be able to convey thoughts and ideas in a vernacular that is familiar to them. The following books will aid your understanding of methodologies used in IT fabric and system designs:

- *The Agile Developer's Handbook – Get more value from your software development: get the best out of the Agile methodology*, by Paul Flewelling

Figure 12.25 – The Agile Developer's Handbook

- *Fundamentals of Project Management, Sixth Edition*, paperback, by Joseph Heagney

Figure 12.26 – Fundamentals of Project Management, Sixth Edition

- *Articulating Design Decisions: Communicate with Stakeholders, Keep Your Sanity, and Deliver the Best User Experience*, by Tom Greever

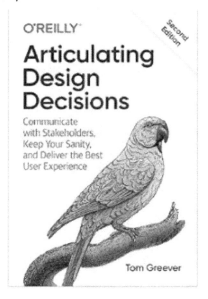

Figure 12.27 – Articulating Design Decisions

- *UX: 3 Books in 1: Beginner's Guide + Design Mastery, Tips and Tricks + Advanced Methods to Learn UX Design, UX Project, Lean Startups*, by Ryan Matthews

Figure 12.28 – UX: 3 Books in 1

Virtualization

Virtualization is a transformative technology that has revolutionized the way we manage and optimize IT resources. The following books offer a roadmap for harnessing the power of virtualization, enabling IT professionals to create efficient, scalable, and resilient infrastructures that drive innovation and cost savings in the modern digital landscape:

- *VMware NSX Cookbook: Over 70 recipes to master the network virtualization skills to implement, validate, operate, upgrade, and automate VMware NSX for vSphere*, by Bayu Wibowo and Tony Sangha

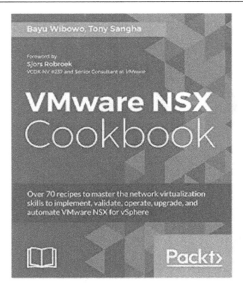

Figure 12.29 – VMware NSX Cookbook

- *Mastering KVM Virtualization: Design expert data center virtualization solutions with the power of Linux KVM, 2nd Edition*, paperback, by Vedran Dakic, Humble Devassy Chirammal, Prasad Mukhedkar, and Anil Vettathu

Figure 12.30 – Mastering KVM Virtualization, 2nd Edition, paperback

- *Mastering Kubernetes: Dive into Kubernetes and learn how to create and operate world-class cloud-native systems, 4th Edition*, by Gigi Sayfan, with a foreword by Bilgin Ibryam

Figure 12.31 – Mastering Kubernetes, 4th Edition

- *Learning Hyper-V: Learn how to design, deploy, configure, and manage virtualization infrastructure using Hyper-V*, by Vinicius R. Apolinario

Figure 12.32 – Learning Hyper-V

- *Mastering VMware vSphere 6.7: Effectively deploy, manage, and monitor your virtual datacenter with VMware vSphere 6.7, 2nd Edition*, by Martin Gavanda, Andrea Mauro, Paolo Valsecchi, and Karel Novak

Figure 12.33 – Mastering VMware vSphere 6.7, 2nd Edition

Security

Network security, compliance, and strategic planning are critical aspects of modern IT. To excel in these areas, it's essential to have the right knowledge and guidance. The following books serve as useful resources for IT professionals aiming to strengthen network security, meet compliance standards, and devise effective long-term strategies for their organizations:

- *CYBERSECURITY BASICS: CYBER ATTACKS, NETWORK SECURITY, AND THREAT PREVENTION*, hardcover, by Pete Michaels: `https://shorturl.at/qzJOW`

Figure 12.34 – CYBERSECURITY BASICS

- *Aligning Security Operations with the MITRE ATT&CK Framework: Level up your security operations center for better security,* by Rebecca Blair: `https://shorturl.at/pDH19`

Figure 12.35 – Aligning Security Operations with the MITRE ATT&CK Framework

- *Zero Trust Networks: Building Secure Systems in Untrusted Networks, 1st and 2nd Editions*, by Evan Gilman, Doug Barth, Razi Rais (2nd Ed.), and Christina Morillo (2nd Ed.):

  - `https://shorturl.at/inPY3`

  - `https://shorturl.at/fFHT6`

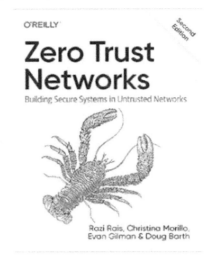

Figure 12.36 – Zero Trust Networks, 2nd Edition

- *Network Security Assessment: KNOW YOUR NETWORK, 3rd Edition*, by Chris McNab: `https://shorturl.at/aBFW6`

Figure 12.37 – Network Security Assessment, 3rd Edition

- *Network Security Strategies: Protect your network and enterprise against advanced cybersecurity attacks and threats*, by Aditya Mukherjee: `https://shorturl.at/hk1C3`

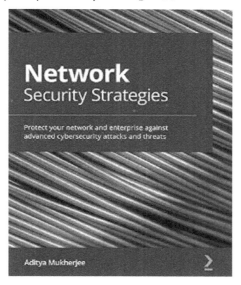

Figure 12.38 – Network Security Strategies

- *Diving into Secure Access Service Edge: A technical leadership guide to achieving success with SASE at market speed*, by Jeremiah Ginn, with a foreword by David H. Brown

Figure 12.39 – Diving into Secure Access Service Edge

Cloud computing

Cloud computing has become a cornerstone of modern IT infrastructure, where services are essential for an organization's growth, sustainability, and innovation. It's a paradigm shift for IT professionals who are most accustomed to the physical IT fabric. The paradigm is an inevitable one and must be embraced. These recommended books serve as a stepping stone for IT professionals looking to harness the full potential of cloud computing, enabling them to design, deploy, and secure scalable cloud-based solutions that drive innovation and efficiency in the digital era:

- *Azure Networking Cookbook: Practical recipes for secure network infrastructure, global application delivery, and accessible connectivity in Azure, 2nd Edition*, by Mustafa Toroman

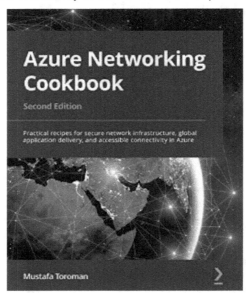

Figure 12.40 – Azure Networking Cookbook, 2nd Edition

- *Google Cloud Platform (GCP) Professional Cloud Network Engineer Certification Companion: Learn and Apply Network Design Concepts to Prepare for the Exam (Certification Study Companion Series), 1st Edition*, by Dario Cabianca

Figure 12.41 – Google Cloud Platform (GCP) Professional Cloud
Network Engineer Certification Companion, 1st Edition

- *Google Cloud Certified Professional Cloud Network Engineer Guide: Design, implement, manage, and secure a network architecture in Google Cloud,* by Maurizio Ipsale and Mirko Gilioli

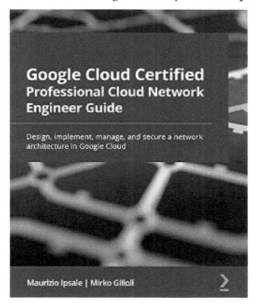

Figure 12.42 – Google Cloud Certified Professional Cloud Network Engineer Guide

- *Cloud Security Handbook: Find out how to effectively secure cloud environments using AWS, Azure, and GCP*, by Eyal Estrin

Figure 12.43 – Cloud Security Handbook

- *AWS for Solutions Architects: The definitive guide to AWS Solutions Architecture for migrating to, building, scaling, and succeeding in the cloud, 2nd Edition*, by Saurabh Shrivastava, Neelanjali Srivastav, Alberto Artasanchez, and Imtiaz Sayed, with a foreword by Dr. Siddhartha Choubey Ph.D.

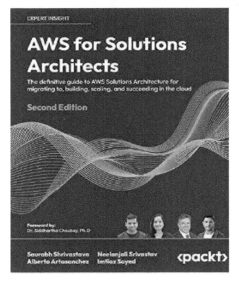

Figure 12.44 – AWS for Solutions Architects, 2nd Edition

- *Cloud Computing Demystified for Aspiring Professionals: Hone your skills in AWS, Azure, and Google cloud computing and boost your career as a cloud engineer*, by David Santana, with a foreword by Amit Malik

Figure 12.45 – Cloud Computing Demystified for Aspiring Professionals

- *AWS Cloud Computing Concepts and Tech Analogies: A guide to understand AWS services using easy-to-follow analogies from real life*, by Ashish Prajapati, Juan Carlos Ruiz, and Marco Tamassia

Figure 12.46 – AWS Cloud Computing Concepts and Tech Analogies

- *Designing and Implementing Microsoft Azure Networking Solutions: Exam Ref AZ-700 preparation guide*, by David Okeyode

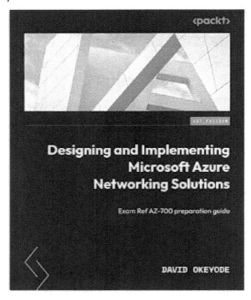

Figure 12.47 – Designing and Implementing Microsoft Azure Networking Solutions

Other useful resources

There are numerous other valuable resources available that can enhance your knowledge and provide fresh perspectives on a wide range of topics, including websites, blogs, whitepapers, and more.

Furthermore, libraries (both physical and digital) house an extensive collection of books, research papers, and journals that can serve as references for in-depth exploration. These additional resources complement traditional learning materials and can be instrumental for continued education.

Next is a collection of references that are just as valuable as the books I recommended. They range across design guides, vendor news press releases, training sites, and more.

Websites

When it comes to websites for IT networking professionals, these (recommended) websites provide a wealth of information, ranging from the latest industry news and trends to technical documentation, tutorials, and troubleshooting guides. As many of them are from direct networking OEM/vendors/ solutions providers, they act as go-to sources for staying informed about emerging technologies, security threats, and best practices in various IT domains, including networking, cloud computing, cybersecurity, and software development.

For IT professionals, these websites are more than just references; they are essential companions on the journey to staying current, honing skills, and solving complex challenges in the fast-paced and dynamic world of information technology. These recommended websites serve as hubs for learning, problem-solving, and staying informed in the rapidly evolving world of cloud technology:

- **Arista**:

  - `https://www.arista.com/en/solutions/design-guides`

  - `https://www.arista.com/en/company/news`

- **Cisco**:

  - `https://newsroom.cisco.com/c/r/newsroom/en/us/index.html`

  - `https://www.cisco.com/c/en/us/solutions/design-zone.html`

- **Cloud Native Computing Foundation (CNCF)**:

  - `https://www.cncf.io/`

- **Palo Alto**:

  - `https://www.paloaltonetworks.com/resources/datasheets/high-level-design-service`

- **Google Cloud**:

  - `https://cloud.google.com/architecture`

  - `https://cloud.google.com/?hl=en`

- **HashiCorp (Terraform)**:

  - `https://developer.hashicorp.com/terraform`

  - `https://developer.hashicorp.com/terraform/enterprise/reference-architecture`

- **ISC2**:

  - `https://www.isc2.org/`

- **AWS**:

  - `https://shorturl.at/qNR45` (AWS Architecture Center)

- **Microsoft**:

    - `https://learn.microsoft.com/en-us/azure/architecture/`

- **Red Hat**:

    - `https://www.redhat.com/architect/portfolio/`

- **Industry**:

    - `https://www.youtube.com/user/ahavts`

    - `https://www.cio.com/`

    - `https://www.techtarget.com/`

    - `https://www.idginc.com/`

    - `https://www.networkworld.com/`

    - `https://www.crn.com/`

    - `https://www.gartner.com/en`

    - `https://github.com/`

    - `https://www.sdxcentral.com/`

    - `https://seekingalpha.com/`

    - `https://stackoverflow.com/`

    - `https://techcrunch.com/`

    - `https://www.zdnet.com/`

- **VMware**:

    - `https://www.vmware.com/design.html`

    - `https://core.vmware.com/vmware-validated-solutions`

Blogs

Blogs have emerged as invaluable resources for IT professionals, serving as dynamic hubs of knowledge, insights, and expertise in the world of technology. These digital diaries penned by experienced practitioners and experts offer a wealth of information, real-world experiences, and cutting-edge trends that are often not readily available in traditional textbooks or documentation.

Blogs delve into the granular aspects of IT challenges, provide step-by-step tutorials, and share practical solutions, making them indispensable for troubleshooting and staying current in fields such as cloud computing, cybersecurity, programming, and network automation/administration. In the fast-paced realm of IT, blogs are not just resources; they are trusted companions on the journey. Next, you'll find recommendations on several blogs to aid in your journey to continuous learning and professional growth:

- **Ahaliblogger**: `https://ahaliblogger.tech`
- **Arista**: `https://blogs.arista.com/blog`
- **Aruba (HPE Company)**: `https://blogs.arubanetworks.com/`
- **AWS**: `https://shorturl.at/foDQ7` (AWS Blog)
- **Azure**: `https://azure.microsoft.com/en-us/blog/`
- **Cisco**: `https://blogs.cisco.com/`
- **Check Point**: `https://blog.checkpoint.com/`
- **Dell**: `https://www.dell.com/en-us/blog/`
- **Digital Ocean**: `https://www.digitalocean.com/blog`
- **Extreme Networks**: `https://www.extremenetworks.com/blog/`
- **F5 Networks**: `https://www.f5.com/company/blog`
- **Fortinet**: `https://www.fortinet.com/blog`
- **GitHub**: `https://github.blog/`
- **Google Cloud**: `https://cloud.google.com/blog`
- **HPE**: `https://blogs.hpe.com/`
- **Juniper Networks**: `https://blogs.juniper.net/`
- **Oracle**: `https://blogs.oracle.com/`
- **VMware**: `https://blogs.vmware.com/`
- **Palo Alto Networks**: `https://www.paloaltonetworks.com/blog/`

Periodicals

The tech section in the following periodicals will keep you up to date on what's going on in the industry:

- `https://www.wsj.com/`
- `https://www.nytimes.com/`

Communities and forums

- **Arista**: `https://arista.my.site.com/AristaCommunity/s/`

- **Azure**: `https://techcommunity.microsoft.com/t5/azure/ct-p/Azure`
- **AWS**: `https://shorturl.at/kuMP1`
- **AWS Cloud Builder**: `https://aws.amazon.com/developer/community/community-builders/`
- **Cisco**: `https://community.cisco.com/?profile.language=en`
- **GCP**: `https://cloud.google.com/communities`
- **GCP Innovators**: `https://cloud.google.com/innovators?hl=en`
- **GCP Innovators Plus**: `https://cloud.google.com/innovators/innovatorsplus?hl=en`
- **CNCF**: `https://community.cncf.io/`
- **VMware**: `https://communities.vmware.com/`
- **Linux**: `https://www.linux.org/forums/`
- **Linux Questions**: `http://www.linuxquestions.org/`
- **Stack Overflow**: `https://stackoverflow.com/`
- **SpiceWorks**: `https://www.spiceworks.com/`
- **Reddit**: `https://www.reddit.com/`
- **MS TechNet**: `https://social.technet.microsoft.com/`
- **Microsoft Developer Network (MSDN)**: `https://social.msdn.microsoft.com/`

Training

Training websites are additional resources for IT professionals, offering structured learning programs, courses, and certifications that empower individuals to acquire new skills and deepen their expertise toward career advancements. These platforms provide flexible and accessible ways to stay up to date with the latest technologies, tools, and best practices in the IT industry. Whether it's mastering a programming language, gaining proficiency in cloud computing, or enhancing cybersecurity knowledge, training websites offer a diverse array of courses to cater to specific career goals.

> **Note**
> It's worth following up within your organization to find out whether they have their own internal training platform or have a partnership with those listed here for a free subscription.

Listed next are several recommended platforms:

- **AWS**: `https://www.aws.training/`

- **Coursera**: https://www.coursera.org/
- **Cisco Digital Learning**: https://digital-learning.cisco.com/#/login
- **Cisco Learning Network**: https://learningnetwork.cisco.com/s/foryou
- **EDX**: https://www.edx.org/
- **GCP SkillsBoost**: https://www.cloudskillsboost.google/
- **ITProTV**: https://www.itpro.tv/
- **Pluralsight**: https://www.pluralsight.com/
- **VMware Education**: https://www.vmware.com/education-services/
- **Udemy**: https://www.udemy.com/
- **LinkedIn Learning**: https://learning.linkedin.com/

Summary

For individuals aspiring to become network architects or those already on the path, the recommended books, websites, and other resources are indispensable tools that can significantly accelerate their journey. These carefully selected materials offer a comprehensive education in IT networking – covering topics such as networking fundamentals, virtualization, network security, automation and programming, compliance, and strategic planning.

Practical experience, real-world problem-solving, and continuous learning through networking events and webinars further complement the knowledge gained from books and websites, enabling network architects to adapt to emerging technologies and evolving network requirements. The synergy between these resources, hands-on practice, and networking opportunities fosters the holistic development needed to excel as a network architect. This combination of resources equips network architects with the necessary skills and expertise to design, manage, and secure complex network infrastructures, ensuring they are well-prepared to excel in this dynamic and crucial role within the modern IT landscape.

Index

Packtpub.com

Subscribe to our online digital library for full access to over 7,000 books and videos, as well as industry leading tools to help you plan your personal development and advance your career. For more information, please visit our website.

Why subscribe?

- Spend less time learning and more time coding with practical eBooks and Videos from over 4,000 industry professionals

- Improve your learning with Skill Plans built especially for you

- Get a free eBook or video every month

- Fully searchable for easy access to vital information

- Copy and paste, print, and bookmark content

Did you know that Packt offers eBook versions of every book published, with PDF and ePub files available? You can upgrade to the eBook version at packtpub.com and as a print book customer, you are entitled to a discount on the eBook copy. Get in touch with us at customercare@packtpub.com for more details.

At www.packtpub.com, you can also read a collection of free technical articles, sign up for a range of free newsletters, and receive exclusive discounts and offers on Packt books and eBooks.

Other Books You May Enjoy

If you enjoyed this book, you may be interested in these other books by Packt:

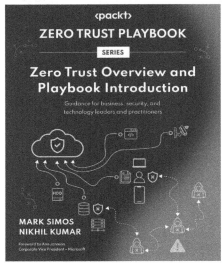

Zero Trust Overview and Playbook Introduction

Mark Simos, Nikhil Kumar

ISBN: 978-1-80056-866-2

- Find out what Zero Trust is and what it means to you
- Uncover how Zero Trust helps with ransomware, breaches, and other attacks
- Understand which business assets to secure first
- Use a standards-based approach for Zero Trust
- See how Zero Trust links business, security, risk, and technology
- Use the six-stage process to guide your Zero Trust journey
- Transform roles and secure operations with Zero Trust
- Discover how the playbook guides each role to success

Mastering Python Networking - Fourth Edition

Eric Chou

ISBN: 978-1-80323-461-8

- Use Python to interact with network devices
- Understand Docker as a tool that you can use for the development and deployment
- Use Python and various other tools to obtain information from the network
- Learn how to use ELK for network data analysis
- Utilize Flask and construct high-level API to interact with in-house applications
- Discover the new AsyncIO feature and its concepts in Python 3
- Explore test-driven development concepts and use PyTest to drive code test coverage
- Understand how GitLab can be used with DevOps practices in networking

Packt is searching for authors like you

If you're interested in becoming an author for Packt, please visit `authors.packtpub.com` and apply today. We have worked with thousands of developers and tech professionals, just like you, to help them share their insight with the global tech community. You can make a general application, apply for a specific hot topic that we are recruiting an author for, or submit your own idea.

Share Your Thoughts

Now you've finished *Network Architect's Handbook*, we'd love to hear your thoughts! Scan the QR code below to go straight to the Amazon review page for this book and share your feedback or leave a review on the site that you purchased it from.

`https://packt.link/r/1837637830`

Your review is important to us and the tech community and will help us make sure we're delivering excellent quality content.

Download a free PDF copy of this book

Thanks for purchasing this book!

Do you like to read on the go but are unable to carry your print books everywhere?

Is your eBook purchase not compatible with the device of your choice?

Don't worry, now with every Packt book you get a DRM-free PDF version of that book at no cost.

Read anywhere, any place, on any device. Search, copy, and paste code from your favorite technical books directly into your application.

The perks don't stop there, you can get exclusive access to discounts, newsletters, and great free content in your inbox daily

Follow these simple steps to get the benefits:

1. Scan the QR code or visit the link below

https://packt.link/free-ebook/9781837637836

2. Submit your proof of purchase
3. That's it! We'll send your free PDF and other benefits to your email directly

www.ingramcontent.com/pod-product-compliance
Lightning Source LLC
Chambersburg PA
CBHW060650060326

40690CB00020B/4582